W9-BWW-994

24.95

120976

Where Did I Go Right?

You're No One
in Hollywood
Unless Someone
Wants You Dead

Where Did I Go Right?

Bernie Brillstein

with David Rensin

Little, Brown and Company

Boston   New York   London

First Edition

The photographs following page 208 are courtesy of the author unless otherwise indicated.

Library of Congress Cataloging-in-Publication Data
Brillstein, Bernie.
      Where did I go right? : you're no one in Hollywood unless someone
wants you dead / by Bernie Brillstein with David Rensin. — 1st ed.
          p.   cm.
      ISBN 0-316-11885-0
    1. Brillstein, Bernie. 2. Motion picture producers and
directors — United States Biography. 3. Theatrical agents — United
States Biography. I. Rensin, David. II. Title.
    PN1998.3.B756A3   1999
    791.43'0232'092 — dc21
    [B]   99-21072

10 9 8 7 6 5 4 3 2 1

MV-NY

Printed in the United States of America

For my wife, Carrie, who has changed my life, and my children:
Leigh, David, Nicholas, Michael, and Kate.
This book is for you. I love you all very much.

"I do not choose to be a common man. It is my right to be uncommon — if I can. I seek opportunity, not security. I want to take the calculated risk; I want to dream and to build, to fail and to succeed, to refuse to barter incentive for the dole. I prefer the challenges of life to the guaranteed existence, the thrill of fulfillment to the stale calm of utopia."

PETER O'TOOLE

"A man's life is divided into four different times. Until you're twenty, you grow up and choose a life. From twenty to forty you lay the groundwork. From forty to sixty you make the money. After sixty you get to screw it up however you like."

MOE BRILLSTEIN

Contents

Where Did I Go Right?

A Few Words About One Word

Throughout this book, in my capacity as a personal manager, movie or TV producer, or studio head, I sometimes use the word "I" when writing about getting my clients a job. Take it from me, it is never one person who does anything in this business. Whenever I've helped put something together for a client, it's always been in concert with his agent and/or lawyer, and usually with input from the spouse, business manager, lover, personal trainer, cook, hairdresser, bodyguard, psychic, a couple fans, and anyone else who might be within earshot of the phone call. Sometimes the directors and writers help, too. So when I say "I," it's a *show-business "I"* that really means "*we*" or "*them*" or "*the entire cast of* Titanic." That is, unless everything falls apart. Then "I" means just me.

Remember: success has many parents, failure is an orphan.

Where Did I Go Right?

I'm not king anymore.

Talk about a strange feeling. The company I built is no longer mine. I never thought that giving up power could hurt so bad. It's really weird; it's like I'm watching this terrible thing happen to someone else, and that "someone else" has got one hell of a stomachache.

Yesterday, I was king. I was at the peak of a forty-plus-year career in show business during which I'd been an agent, a TV and movie producer, a studio head, and — mostly — the personal manager of people like John Belushi, Gilda Radner, Dan Aykroyd, Norm Crosby, Lorne Michaels, and Jim Henson. I even came up with the idea for the TV show Hee Haw, *for chrissakes. Today, I can walk into a store anywhere in the county, plunk down my credit card to pay, and more often than not the clerk will ask, "Are you the Bernie Brillstein?"*

In 1992 I co-founded Brillstein-Grey Entertainment, probably the most successful management-production company of the '90s, and, it seems, beyond. We have nearly 150 clients — actors, comedians, producers, writers — most of them household names. We make comedy shows for network and cable. We produce movies. We represent authors. In a town where power, or at least the illusion of power, belongs to the guy who controls the talent — you don't think the media once called agent Mike Ovitz "the most powerful man in Hollywood" because he was a wonderful human being, do you? — we're in great shape.

Only now it's no longer "we." This morning I sold my half of everything to my partner, Brad Grey. When he came to work for me in 1985, this place was still The Brillstein Company. Brad was twenty-six, bright, and ambitious. He had longer hair then, and baby fat on his cheeks, yet something about him — the look of resolve in his eyes, the way he cut through the chronic bull-

shit and got to the point — made me feel like he got it: the truth about show business and the way things really work. Even though we had different styles of doing business, from day one, and as the years went by, we were a great team. The press called me "Mr. Personality . . . larger-than-life . . . old showbiz . . . the last of a dying breed . . . the Godfather." Brad was "Mr. New Hollywood . . . The Genius . . . Michael Corleone." It's just my opinion, but I think they were right.

In 1989 I made Brad my partner.

Today I made him my boss.

I signed the papers a couple hours ago. Now I'm staring out my office window at the traffic on Wilshire Boulevard, watching a new generation of young Turks cruise by, cooing into their car phones, trying to seduce the next big deal, trading promises for power — while I feel like shit. I guess I'm just . . . adrift. It's been a very bizarre year, an emotionally draining time. I'm so tired. I don't feel like the old Bernie anymore.

A perceptive friend once said of me, "Bernie is either having the best day or the worst day of his life."

Today, both are true.

No wonder my stomach won't stop hurting.

• • • • •

Here's what happened:

For a couple years I'd told Brad I might be ready to slow down, work a little less, advise him, and let him do what he wanted to do. Enough already of the boring dinners, playing psychiatrist to insecure clients, and fighting network and studio executives who think they're more creative than the talent they hire. I know that old soldiers are supposed to die with their boots on, but more and more I no longer wanted to put on those boots or wage the wars.

The show business I got into in 1955 had totally changed, more than once, evolved as all things must, and I wasn't sure I wanted to keep changing with it. I started managing because I grew up with and around performers. I loved being near them. I was passionate and respectful of their talent even though I knew how their crazy and sometimes self-destructive minds worked — or didn't work. Some part of me even wanted to be them, but I didn't have their gifts or good looks; managing was a great way to join the club, to be-

long, to give that love and maybe get some back. These days it's ass-backwards. The talent has changed some — they have more leverage and bigger salaries — but mostly it's the business side that's mutated, that's full of MBAs, lawyers, and the not-so-smart-but-canny who love the smell of easy money and power and not much else. Most of them don't know what it's like to love the talent, or if they ever did — like some rock star they once couldn't get enough of — they've long forgotten.

I couldn't play that game if I wanted to. I got into show business for the thrill of it all, not the thrill of having it all.

From the William Morris mail room to a seat at the power tables, I've had a wild ride. That's not bad considering that I've always thought of myself as a man equipped to do nothing who did everything, someone who did more with less.

But every ride has to end.

One day I wrote a memo to everyone at Brillstein-Grey:

"It shocks me to know that my 65th year is approaching. As I've been doing this for forty-one years it's really time to take it a little easier. . . . I have always believed that every company should have one boss, one leader, and one person who has the freedom to choose the course. . . . I know that Brad is completely qualified to take all of you, and me, forward to the future we all want."

I meant every word. Of course, at the time I still had power. I'd only given Brad the reins, not the company. I could change my mind. Now I can't.

Maybe I should go home and "ice" myself; I'll just crawl under the covers and will my brain to become numb. That has to be better than feeling like no one appreciates me, understands me, or needs me — which is so unusual because my whole life has been about being needed: by my family, friends, clients. If I stick around the office I'm afraid the entire afternoon will be full of nothing but calls from "friends" nosing around about what happened. My real friends and my family already know. They were the first people I told.

I said, "Hey, I finally settled this thing and I'm thrilled. I cleared the decks. I made the deal. Here's what I'm going to walk away with. It's a lot of money. I'm really happy."

Not exactly true. I'm not quite ready to be happy. The people who love me could tell I was in shock and trying to convince myself that everything was okay. They were supportive. They think I'm wonderful, like I invented show business. Good: I expect them to feel that way. But I didn't get this far without being able to read a person's unspoken questions, so I made it very clear that the only thing that had taken me by surprise was the emptiness I felt.

"This didn't just happen," I said. "We've been talking about it for a while. Brad and I are okay." That much is true.

In a man's life, 50 percent is business and 50 percent is personal, and part of my problems was my private life. After twenty years my third marriage had failed. I needed money to settle things quickly. If not for Debbie and my splitting up . . . well, maybe I would have held on longer, but there's no percentage in thinking about what might have been. It's like in golf: you can't worry about the last shot, only the next. Besides, the moment would still have had to come. I couldn't expect Brad, who had worked so hard, to wait forever. It's his time. He's young. I'm old. I get it. I only wish understanding made me feel better.

I know Brad and I will be fine. I'm sure of that. That's very important to me. There aren't many business relationships these days that really mean anything, no matter how they look to the public, and I know that Brad and I have something real. I picked him. I've seen him grow. I'm godfather to his oldest son, Sam. Brad is the best and I'm really proud of what he's accomplished.

Everyone else can believe what they like. I know the town is already whispering, starting rumors, pitting me against Brad, trying to stir up trouble. This town is nothing if not opportunistic, and can so easily be evil. People here like to kill each other just for sport. And you know what? I understand that, too. People talk. In fact, most people in show business can't shut up. We all love to think that we know what's going on. The truth is that most don't have a clue — and never will.

• • • • •

So now what?

One reason I started The Brillstein Company in 1968 is that I never wanted to answer that question. My greatest fear has always been to be this age and have to go looking for a job. When I was a kid, I saw Death of a Salesman on Broadway and it scared the shit out of me: Willy Loman is loyal to the firm for thirty-odd years and then they just dump him. Every working man's nightmare must be that he's replaceable. That's why you go into business for your-

self. Better to be an owner than to depend on someone else to have your best interests at heart.

Now, my situation reminds me of the singer Frankie Laine, whom I represented when he was no longer a superstar, though at the time he was my biggest client, a guy who still made five or six hundred thousand a year. To sell him, I used to say, "He's Frankie Laine. He's played Command Performances. He was the biggest thing in the world in 1950 and 1951." Then I had to send him to Indianapolis for a weekend, in minus-eighteen-fucking-degree weather, for $12,500. This guy was once king, but he'd go. I've always wondered how he did it. I wonder if I can do it.

Brad says I'll never be out in the cold. He's asked me to stay here as long as I like. I'll stick around as long as I feel useful. Things have changed, but I can't believe my value is gone.

· · · · ·

A painting called Nebraska, by the late John Register, hangs on my office wall, above the couch. There are green and brown fields as far as the eye can see. Overhead, gray clouds butt up against a clear blue sky, but it's not certain which is disappearing and which is moving in. A two-lane blacktop from nowhere arrives quietly in the foreground at a weathered stop sign and a deserted intersection. The painting has always asked me this question: "What do you see: the stop sign or the open road?"

The answer was always a no-brainer.

Now I suppose I'll have to decide all over again.

Growing Up and Choosing a Life

Chapter 1

If You've Never Walked Through the Kitchen to Get Backstage at a Nightclub, You Don't Know Show Business

In 1955, when I was twenty-four years old, I got a job in the mail room at the William Morris Agency in New York. Like every young guy who worked alongside me, my first thought was, "How quickly can I get the hell out of here and become a *real* agent?" The first thing I did . . .

Wait. On second thought, let's forget the clichéd story that always kicks off a book about someone's life in show business. To tell you the absolute truth, getting ahead at William Morris was the least of my worries. After my first week on the job I took one good look around and knew I could handle it. Easily.

My real problem at the time was my ass. Literally. It was . . . leaking. I couldn't work that way, so I called the family doctor. He referred me to a guy whose name I'll never forget: Dr. Emil Granite. When I got to Granite's office the place was jammed with waiting patients overflowing into the hall. Even I know an ugly metaphor when I see one. Right away I was not thrilled.

Finally, it was my turn. Granite walked into the examination room and asked me to drop my pants, then helped me onto the big stainless steel table. "Knees to your chest," he said. I closed my eyes and began to sweat. An icy cold sweat. Then he put a big tube in my rectum, and there I was: lying on the table with my cheeks wide open, and a foreign object inside me. Then to make things worse, he blew into the tube a few times, moved it around a bit, made a couple thoughtful grunting sounds and said, "Mr. and Mrs. Brillstein, Mr. and Mrs. Pearl. He has a fissure."

Mr. and Mrs. *Brillstein?* Mr. and Mrs. *Pearl?* What the hell were my father, Moe, my mother, Tillie, my uncle Jack, and my aunt Winnie doing there? I couldn't believe it. I hadn't heard anyone come in. But I opened my eyes and there they were, peering at me with pursed, concerned lips.

And they were all *looking up my ass.*

I went berserk — but only in my mind, of course. It would have been disrespectful to say anything directly to my family, not to mention painful to make any sudden movements.

I'm not making this up. Who could? Who would?

It's all behind me now, but I probably shouldn't have been surprised. My family was what today we call "dysfunctional." That's a fancy name for screwed-up. Being raised in that environment cost me years of therapy and maybe more than one marriage. But you know what? I'm not angry. In fact, I'm grateful for their craziness. My uncle was a famous comic and radio personality who destroyed his career, my mother a bedridden depressive, my father a good Samaritan stuck in an unhappy marriage, and my older brother, Sam, unable to handle any of it. Growing up with them was the perfect career training for a life spent around people who put on makeup for a living and think every job is their last. That's why nothing in show business throws me. If I could survive my family, I could survive anything — and I pretty much have.

When the doctor was through, I got dressed and said good-bye to everyone. I still had to go back to work. Some guys would have snuck home, humiliated, and called in sick. That's not my style. Instead, I rushed to the office and immediately told everyone, in great detail, what had just happened.

Just like I'm telling you.

That's one of my big rules: when you have a great story, you tell it — no matter what.

• • • • •

My aunt Winnie and uncle Jack shared their nine-room apartment in the swanky Eldorado, at Ninetieth Street and Central Park West, with Jack's brother Benny, their dad, Grandpa Jake, my parents, my brother, and me. Jack Pearl was a comedian who'd made a fortune on NBC radio as the Baron Munchausen. (His signature line was, "Vas you dere, Sharlie?") Winifred Desborough Pearl was a Ziegfeld girl. I was born on April 26, 1931, and we lived with them until I was nine.

The building was a showplace. Art deco frescoes covered the lobby walls. A beautiful awning hung over the front door. It was Natalie Wood's home in the movie *Marjorie Morningstar,* and it's all still there, except for the awning. We lived in 26D, in the south tower. It was elegant as hell, with a butler and a maid, and a great view. You could look over Central Park and the reservoir, past Fifth Avenue to the East River, and out to Queens.

One evening, when I was eight, everyone gathered at the living room windows to watch as the lights of the 1939 World's Fair were turned on for the first time. Aunt Winnie hoisted me up by the armpits and held me high so I could also see. She pointed to a dark patch in the distance. Suddenly, there was a burst of light brighter than the flash of a thousand cameras at a movie premiere, and the fair was officially open. It was a keeper memory and, even more so, an important early lesson:

Life always looks better from the top.

If I'm not mistaken, that's also when I first knew I wanted to be in show business. And if it's not, it should have been.

•••••

The Brillsteins came from Mizerwicz, a little town on the Russia-Poland border. The family used to say it was really in Poland, until it got chic to be Russian. Then, of course, we were from the Mother Country.

My dad was born there in 1898, but when he was six months old the Cossacks invaded and that was it. My grandparents fled to America and moved to Harlem.

Years later, when I'd made some good money and the Communists were taking in tourists, I told my dad, "Let me send you to Russia." I thought maybe he'd like to see where he was born. I didn't know all that was left were twenty thousand graves.

"Nah, I don't want to go there," he said.

"How about London, or Japan, or Israel? I can afford it."

"Nah, I don't want to go there."

No matter how often I asked, all he ever said was, "Nah, I don't want to go there." I could never figure it out. Only after he died in 1990 did it occur to me that my old man was petrified to leave the country because he thought they wouldn't let him come back. I'm not even sure he had a passport. If he'd told me, I could have set him straight, but he was a typical Brillstein: he didn't want to bother anyone with his problems.

My mother was a different story. Her *mishegas* affected everyone. She rarely went anywhere because she seldom got out of bed. Occasionally, she'd show up at the dinner table for a meal, but it was like watching a ghost. No one knew it then, but she was clinically depressed. Her doctors treated her by handing out pills like they were candy. Lots of them. I'd get home and find her conked out on Tuinal or something stronger. She gradually became a basket case who required constant attention and service from everyone.

My brother never got over the family dysfunction, which might explain why he went into the finishing-and-dyeing business.

That left me. My problem was being fat.

For a long time, the husky department at Barney's was my second home. It was years before I'd go into a swimming pool without wearing a shirt. Until I managed the high school basketball team and had to take showers with the guys, I never knew that a man's shoulders are supposed to be wider than his hips. And tits . . . I didn't need girls, I had my own. Yet, big as I am, I have thin arms and thin legs. Juliette Prowse used to tell me, "You have the hands and legs of a ballet dancer." Unfortunately she didn't continue the analogy and say anything about an inner dancer waiting to get out.

No fat person is thrilled with their size. Imagine not being able to buckle the safety belt on an airplane. What's more embarrassing than saying, "May I have a belt extension, please?" Once, I flew to Rome, two days before a long Mediterranean cruise. At the airport, my baggage went missing. This is a fat man's worst fear. I have to buy at Rochester Big and Tall or have clothes made, and I didn't want to spend my vacation looking for a big and tall — or, as I say, fat and gross — store, especially in a country where everyone has a size-two ass. My wife Carrie searched the phone directory and found an extra-large-sizes clothing store in Rome. The proprietor was great. He made me two suits and a sports jacket. Shirts and underwear were in stock. There went a quick $3,000.

At first, I fought my weight. I wanted to be six foot two, with a thirty-inch waist. I fantasized about being a great athlete so I didn't have to work so goddamn hard to get women interested in me by being friends first and then, by laughing my way into bed. Can you believe it? some women actually don't like fat guys. It's amazing. It's even worse when you have a big waistline *and* a big ego. I think I'm charming. Some days I think I look great. Then I see pictures of myself and go, "Who the hell is that?"

I felt pretty bad about myself until one day, in a college management course, Professor DeFillippi (he was also a basketball referee at Madison Square Garden), wrote this on the blackboard: "You have to learn to live with who you are." For some reason it stuck. I knew in my gut that I would never be anyone but me. I decided to work really hard with what God gave me.

If I had to describe myself today, I'd say I'm the fat Kenny Rogers. Some people are more generous and say Santa Claus, but looks or the lack of them aside, if I walk into a room, I *walk* into a room. I don't need to attract a crowd, I am a crowd. I've always had this ability to get noticed, not by doing anything special, just by my bearing. Then, because I'm actually shy and not that good with large groups of people, I find someplace to sit with my back against the wall so that I can look around without feeling uncomfortable. That way, people come to me, even if they're just wandering by. I never wanted to be the putz who roams a party, glad-handing everyone.

It turns out that one's lot in life can be a lucky accident. In my case it has to be, because throughout my career my weight has always worked in my favor.

In business, no one is ever afraid of a fat man. People think a fat person is a lazy person. There's something vulnerable about an eighteen-wheeler-sized spare tire that everyone thinks they can handle. They don't stop to ponder how angry you might feel about your weight, or that you're holding it in. They figure you're jolly. So if you're smart you can use your size to your advantage. It's always been fine with me to be underestimated. I've always underplayed myself. It's a great way to get ahead.

Of course, if I'd had a thirty-two-inch waist, maybe by now I'd be president of the United States.

· · · · ·

My father was a small-timer in life, a big-timer at heart. I really loved and respected him. He sold millinery in the garment district, but his real calling was the Millinery Center Synagogue, between Thirty-eighth and Thirty-ninth on Sixth Avenue. He was the driving force behind a group who raised the money to build the temple. In return, they made him eternal president — at least until he died.

The temple was originally a convenience for the garment center guys who had to say Yiskor, a Jewish prayer for the dead, during the week and couldn't get to their own synagogues on Long Island or in Brooklyn, or wherever. Thanks to my father, they could pray locally. That was my old man. He birthed people, bar mitzvahed them, buried them. His natural inclination was to do nice things and favors. And you know what? He was right. You get a big return for that kind of behavior. You become more God-like. Any instinct I have for decency and doing the right thing I got from my father. I've tried to follow his example all my life.

My father also put together temple fund-raising shows twice a year at the Waldorf Astoria and the Plaza hotels that featured entertainers like Sammy Davis Jr., Nat "King" Cole, and Alan King. He got to know everyone in show business. I learned a lot of what I know today by watching him.

Sometimes my mother would come out of the house for these galas. My father, Aunt Winnie, and Uncle Jack would schlep her to the hotel in a cab and put her in a complimentary hotel suite. If a thousand people came to the show, four hundred would come upstairs to pay homage to my mother, who sat in bed in her bathrobe, like a queen.

She still had her charming moments and occasionally a sense of humor. In the early '60s, I started dating my second wife, Laura, when she was still married to a very rich guy in the advertising business. One weekend, Laura and her husband went to the Concord, a world-famous Jewish hotel and club on Lake Kiamesha, in the Borscht Belt. My mother and father were there, too. I waited at home, knowing that Laura would try to get close to my parents. Sure enough, my mother said, "Oh, that girl was there, with her husband."

"What did you think?" I asked.

"Well," my mother said, "he had gold cuff links, he had a gold tie pin, and a gold lighter. And when he kills you, he's going to do it with a golden gun."

Most of the time my parents didn't get along. I could always hear them arguing. Even as a kid I appointed myself referee, and I couldn't go to sleep until I made them make up. I'd fix them sandwiches hoping they'd stop battling and start eating. It worked for maybe a day. Sometimes, only an hour. As I got older it became obvious that my father found it impossible to live with an invalid whose disease he didn't quite understand. I guess that explains why he slept on the couch in the foyer for twenty years.

Three nights a week — Tuesday, Thursday, Saturday — my brother and I baby-sat my mother so that my old man could go out. Maybe he had a girlfriend. I don't know. He just wanted those evenings free to go downtown with the boys, drink scotch, and smoke cigars. He wanted some fun and some peace of mind. In that marriage it was the best he could hope for.

Now you see why my family was the perfect basic training for a life in show business. In one way or another, for more than forty years, I've continued to referee, to wait on the needy, to make sandwiches for peace, and to pull guard duty.

They call it being a personal manager.

Moe and Tillie's fighting drove *everyone* nuts. Eventually it chased away my aunt and uncle. For years they'd functioned as my nominal parents, and now the family was breaking up. I can still hear Winnie finally saying, "I've had enough of this shit, Jack. Let's get the hell out of this crazy house."

They moved to an apartment with two bedrooms and a den, overlooking Fifth Avenue: 875 Fifth. When the building went condo they told my uncle it would cost him $8,000 to buy his place. Like a typical comedian, even though he had plenty of money, he wouldn't pay. "Those thieves!" he said. Today the place is worth $3 million.

Why was my uncle so stubborn? Easy. Comedians are the strangest breed of all. They're definitely not like the rest of us. Anyone who can get up twice a night in front of a room full of strangers, have the first show work and the second show not isn't normal. They do it because they're terribly insecure, always need love, and will do anything to get it. I suppose lots of people are that way, but not many are willing to torture themselves on top of it by complaining to a million people about one little thing like their sex lives. Listen to the language of comedy: "I killed 'em. I knocked 'em dead. I bombed. I laid 'em in the aisles. I destroyed them." That describes perfectly the terrible angst a comedian experiences, and oftentimes what *I* experienced managing so many tormented funny men.

It's not hard to understand why they feel that way. Comedy is the least respected of all the arts. Rodney Dangerfield isn't kidding when he says he gets no respect, because he knows that the world is full of guys who think they can do what he does — in their sleep. It's not so easy. If a guy remembers a joke his boss told him at dinner, it's a miracle.

If you're alone with a comedian you can say something really funny and they'll accept it, but don't try it in a crowd. The comic always has to be the funniest guy around. Comedians are also conservative with their laughter and toughest on each other. If you were a garment salesman, how would you like it if, after you made a great sale, eight of your contemporaries said, "You didn't sell that right," or "That was *my* sales method," or "How dare you do that?" Comedians judge each other all the time, even if they're best friends. It's the nature of the beast. They never want you to be as funny as they are.

My uncle's insecurity put him out of business. He'd been in the Ziegfeld Follies and had made a movie in 1933 called *Meet The Baron*, with Ted Healy and his Stooges (Moe, Larry, and Curly). Then he quit comedy at the height of his popularity, saying, "I want to do drama." This was like Woody Allen in his Ingmar Bergman period, only Woody got the irony.

Since no one would pay my uncle to do drama, he didn't work. When World War II came, let's just say that his German-dialect comedy fell out of favor. He tried a few comebacks on Ed Sullivan's *Toast of the Town* and on Broadway, but they didn't work. He went from the top ten on NBC radio to nothing. Fortunately he had made and stashed enough money from the radio show to live quite well until he died in his late eighties. Recently, I listened to some tapes of his act, and you know what? I never knew he was so unfunny.

For most of my childhood I also didn't know that Uncle Jack paid for our apartment. I found out when he started giving me mysterious envelopes for my father. I looked inside and discovered cash. It destroyed me. Later, my father told me that he'd been my uncle's de facto manager — without getting a full manager's cut. My dad already had a job, so what he did for the family was expected and considered part-time. In exchange, my uncle paid some of the bills. My old man was never bitter, but later he told me he thought he'd been shortchanged. "He gave me a little money, but never ten percent." It was a lesson I didn't forget.

• • • • •

My family stayed in the Eldorado after my aunt Winnie and uncle Jack left, but we had to move to 3B, a smaller apartment on the third floor. We also inherited Uncle Benny, an alcoholic who left our uptown building every morning, with a sack lunch, for his job at the post office. Our new view was no longer of Central Park, but of Ninetieth Street, and my bedroom window overlooked the interior courtyard. A one-story brick terrace covered the lobby and divided the courtyard in half. To entertain ourselves, my best friend, Norman Kartiganer — who lived above me in 5B — and I skipped marbles across the rooftop, hoping to hear one break a window on the other side. We were often successful. We also had less destructive pastimes, like playing punch, stick and stoop ball on Ninetieth Street, hockey in the house, one-on-one football in the snow, and baseball in Central Park.

• • • • •

I was the poorest kid in a rich neighborhood, so I couldn't go to tony private schools like my friends. Instead I attended PS 166, Joan of Arc Junior High, and the all-boys Stuyvesant High School at Seventeenth Street and First Avenue. Stuyvesant was mainly for kids who wanted to be engineers and chemists. Sounds perfect for me, right? Hey, it was a free education. I also managed the basketball team.

Whenever I could, I went to the movies. The Stoddard, on Broadway between Eighty-ninth and Ninetieth. The Yorktown between Eighty-eighth and Eighty-ninth. The Thalia, an art house on Ninety-fifth Street, where I saw Marx Brothers movies. Double-bill features at the Beacon. One night my mother followed Norman and me to the pictures, sat eight rows behind us, and caught us smoking: Kools, Spuds, Old Golds.

The Loews on Eighty-third featured films from Paramount and MGM. The RKO at Eighty-first played movies from Twentieth Century Fox. I knew every star under contract to Paramount and MGM. I even knew the secondary players by heart. That's when movies meant something;

they were still about mystique and illusion. What mattered was what was on the screen, not what happened behind the scenes.

Today, everything has changed. The studios no longer have contract players or own theaters. Agents, managers, the talent, and conglomerates run the business. The Stoddard has been a supermarket for years. The RKO became a television studio/theater where I once saw Norman Jewison direct the *Hit Parade.* Last time I drove by, it was two retail spaces, one a Starbucks and one an empty store waiting for a tenant.

· · · · ·

My family may have been neurotic, but they gave me much more than simply an education in dealing with head cases. Thanks to my uncle and my father I experienced New York's two distinct show-business cultures, the East Side and the West Side. I learned to feel at home in the Stork Club and the Carnegie Deli, and could get a good table at both. By the time I went to college I knew the language of the swells and the streets. I could talk to anyone.

My uncle taught me the East Side: Fifth Avenue, Bergdorf-Goodman, the Stork Club (where you could see Ethel Merman and Walter Winchell), the Harwyn, Toots Shor's. Ordinarily I would never have gone to the East Side. It was Protestant Land. The girls were out of my league. Even the Jews east of Central Park were different. West Side Jews were garment center workers and roundabouts. The East Side had German Jews, not a good breed if you ask me. They're the ones who thought Hitler wouldn't come after them because they were a "better class" of Jew.

If I had my life to live again, I'd live it at Toots Shor's restaurant on Fifty-second Street. There I saw presidents, movie stars, ballplayers. Jackie Gleason. Joe DiMaggio. Mickey Mantle. Rodgers and Hammerstein. Jack Benny. George Burns. Even John F. Kennedy. All my heroes. Writers, too, like Damon Runyon, Mark Hellinger, Jimmy Cannon. Regular people went, too. Those with money sat up front; the farmers sat in back. I loved it. Everything I wanted, the essence of New York, in one place.

The late '40s and early '50s was a great time to be a celebrity in New York. My uncle and I could walk into any theater and see the shows for nothing. We'd stand in the back for the first act, then go to another theater for our "second act." My uncle liked to tell me showbiz lore, like the reason Ziegfeld insisted his Girls wear silk underwear. "Because it made them *feel* like Ziegfeld Girls." The lesson stayed with me. I like my clients to feel special. Sending a big gift is always nice. Even when they go on vacation, I send them something: not because they're not working, but because I'm thinking of them. I suppose, if there was anyone I wanted to be back then, it was Ziegfeld. Everything I heard about him, and his instinct for talent, said "show business."

At a club, my uncle and I would get backstage by going through a kitchen full of pungent odors to a tiny dressing room where we'd hang out with the performers. The place always smelled of flop sweat. Comedians who would in three minutes have to be hilarious might be red-faced and yelling at their girlfriends. A singer might be puking from the tension. It wasn't glamorous, just real. It's the reason I always say, "If you've never walked through a kitchen to get backstage at a nightclub, you don't know show business." You don't know the emotions or the sounds or the closeness of it all. You're behind the scenes, and the way it works is right there in front of you, and you are part of it. Not too many years later, I went to nightclubs for a living, but I would have gone for nothing. In fact, I would have paid. I loved being there with the customers and the stars.

What's lost today is that intimate connection to the process and the talent. Until the '80s, Harvard MBAs and Wharton grads went to Wall Street. Now they flock to Hollywood and Beverly Hills. They want to be in show business because it's chic and the money is intoxicating. It has to be when you can sell someone for $1 million and make $100,000 with one phone call. But that's not the thrill I'm talking about.

My contemporaries were streetwise people. Who knew from rich? Sure, you could make money — and we wanted to — but nowhere near the kind of money you can make in this business today. It wasn't about that. People were lured to entertainment largely by their dreams. It was wish fulfillment. They wanted to *be* the people on the stage and screen. Too many of today's show-business players just want to make the money their clients make. If power and notoriety are part of the bargain, all the better.

I believe the business, the art, and the public all suffer for it. If only today's hot shots could have sat five feet away from Dean Martin and Jerry Lewis, or Tony Bennett and a twenty-piece orchestra — or any act they love. There's nothing wrong with Mick Jagger prancing around in silk pajamas with his wiener poking out — it's great show business — but it's tough to get intimate in a baseball stadium, unless it's with your date or the person behind you who just threw up on your coat. Today, no one gets close because everything's too big. The closest thing to what I experienced is *MTV Unplugged.* It works because it has the timeless appeal of performers close up. In my day I didn't have to watch anyone on a huge screen. I could sit near enough to Frank Sinatra to see him perspire into my soup.

• • • • •

My father took me around the West Side: Madison Square Garden, Murray's Sturgeon Palace, Barney Greengrass, the Polo Grounds. I went with him to Fifty-second Street, where his friends from Harlem, the connected guys, owned the jazz clubs in which you could hear music like nowhere else in the city. My father, a respected temple elder, also showed me the world of strippers and hookers. My friends and I would meet him at Leo Bernstein and Henry Fink's Club Samoa, a bust-out joint on Fifty-second Street where guys could pick up broads. We'd eat club sandwiches and drink Cokes, and be treated like kings while the girls jerked off their other customers under the table. The girls would pretend they wanted to meet these losers later, but they never did. My father saw nothing wrong with me being in that environment, as long as I didn't have some gal's hand in my lap. That was fine with me. My reward was just being able to take my friends to these places. And the next night I'd be in the Stork Club or at Bill Bertolotti's, a fancy restaurant downtown, with Uncle Jack.

My favorite spot was the Copacabana.

The club was at 10 East Sixtieth. The phone number was Plaza 8-1060. It was technically on the East Side, but always West Side at heart. Today the entrance at that address is sealed, but in its day the blue awning floated above the doorway, and flowered paper covered the walls inside. It was known as a tough-guy hangout and the hottest club in New York.

The club's backstage entrance was in the far-right corner of the lobby of the Hotel Fourteen, next door. You'd walk down the stairs, through the kitchen, and into the action. The whole thing is immortalized in the motion picture *Goodfellas.* There was always a line around the block, so I used to sneak into the Copa the same way as Scorsese's camera. Once I got through the kitchen and into the club, I'd stand quietly against the back wall and see the shows for nothing. If the maître'd came up I'd give him five bucks to let me stay. After a while, he got to know me, and I could just mix in.

Every other week a new act opened at the Copa. Dates were not allowed on Sunday; you could only bring your wife and family. Friday was Wiseguy Night, a night on the town. Actually, every night was Wiseguy Night, but especially Friday. It all stopped when rock got popular and styles changed. Today, with the resurgence of Rat Pack nostalgia, the swinger's life may be back, but the old clubs are long gone.

My favorite Copa memory is seeing Dean Martin and Jerry Lewis play there when I was seventeen. I sat through every show for twenty-one days. I knew every line — every movement — of their act. I could recite it and work it — which, by the way, has come in handy because just to get a laugh, I've stolen a lot of their stuff over the years.

Like I said, the great thing about a club is that you can sit so close to the performers. On closing night I got lucky and sat almost against the stage. As the duo worked, Jerry Lewis saw me mouthing the words of the act. He grabbed the microphone, walked over to me, smiled at the audience and said, "Look at this kid. I'm getting all the money and he knows my act better than me. He's jumping on the punch lines."

I stared at his blue sapphire pinkie ring.

"You want to come up onstage with us?" he asked.

I just kept staring at that pinkie ring. I couldn't very well meet his eyes, could I?

One night my friend Larry Perse and I strolled into the lobby of the Hotel Fourteen after the second show. There, dead drunk and leaning against a column, was Frank Sinatra. This was before *From Here to Eternity*, when his career was cold, cold, cold. No matter, we idolized Frank. My brother had taken me to see him at the Paramount Theater. My father took me to his first nightclub engagement, at the Riobamba. Sinatra may have been stiffing, but he was still a hero. He was still The Guy. And at the moment he was blotto.

We'd read all the newspapers and knew that Sinatra stayed at the Waldorf. We also knew that in about five seconds he was going to fall on his ass. So we two schmucks called a cab, got in with him, took him to the Waldorf, and gave him to the doorman.

• • • • •

That was pretty much my life as the '40s gave way to the '50s. I was probably hipper than someone just going into college had a right to be — at least in my own mind. I'd lived through my Martin-and-Lewis stage. I'd watched Ray Charles, who was just coming up, at Carnegie Hall. I'd seen Lenny Bruce, and he blew my mind. After five minutes my friend Norm and I turned to each other and said the same thing: "He's talking about things we talk about every day — only onstage!" Gays, blacks, whites, Hitler. It was just so fresh and different. Can you imagine what it would have been like to have HBO back then? Everybody could have seen this stuff.

Those three events helped cement my emotional connection to the business, but I never quite understood why until recently, when I read a newspaper story about the singer-dancer Bebe Neuwirth. She was asked why she still did Broadway when she could easily do television. Her answer was a revelation: "On the nights when I'm perfect, the ensemble is perfect, the orchestra is perfect, and the audience is with us . . . I feel like I've been touched by God." That's what *I* felt watching Martin and Lewis, Ray Charles, Lenny Bruce, and others: touched by God. It's the same feeling I'd have years later when I helped Jim Henson, *Saturday Night Live*, the Blues Brothers, the people who made *Dangerous Liaisons*, my partner Brad Grey, and all the guys he represented get it right. When you ace something, knowing how tough it is, the feeling is unlike any other. That's why I do what I do, and why I've kept doing it.

After high school I went to NYU and got a BS in Advertising. But college seemed somehow tangential to everything else. In fact, one of the only lessons that stayed with me was learning about the "You Attitude."

In a nutshell: Talk about them, not you. Don't worry about what you want to sell, worry about what the customer wants to buy. What does he need? Get into his head. If what you have to sell is good, you'll eventually succeed, but there's a right time and a wrong time, and you've got to be sensitive to the other person. It's all about him, not you.

The "You Attitude" is at the heart of what it takes to be a good manager. In my business it's all about staying behind the scenes and making people feel good. My joke is, "I sublimate my ego for cash."

Once, I kiddingly called myself "the bowing Jew." (Jews aren't supposed to bow or kneel, which is why we always look awkward in a church.) Back when Mike Ovitz — the guy who from 1975 to 1995 built the Creative Artists Agency (CAA) into the most powerful talent agency

in Hollywood, and himself into one of the most feared men in town —
and I went to war, he'd always bitch to me about all the crap he had to do
for his clients. Half seriously I'd say, "Mike, you can be Mike Ovitz, and I
can be Bernie Brillstein; we're really wealthy, powerful guys. But we're
still slaves to the stars. You and I are nothing without our client lists. I will
say it until the day I die. All of us. If we don't have what they want, good-
bye and good luck."

• • • • •

After college I was drafted into the army — the only way I'd go. It
was 1953. I had never been far from New York, so I decided to make it a
test to see if I could get along in an environment over which I had no control. I was the Jew from New York in a world with few Jews, and not that
many people from New York, either. After basic training, I was posted to
England. I kept from doing any real work by doing what came naturally:
I produced shows. I'd seen a transvestite revue in college, in which people
from the audience were called onstage to dance in a number called
"Balling the Jack." So I stole it. Only I made sure officers were summoned
to dance with guys in drag. It wasn't hilarious, but at least it kept
me busy.

I was discharged on February 1, 1955. I moved back in with my
parents at the Eldorado and screwed around for a month. I'd been away
for two years and I knew the world was a bigger place than the garment
center and the Millinery Center Synagogue fund-raising shows. I was
restless and needed a job.

One day my uncle called and said he was good friends with a guy
who owned a television station, WGTH, in Hartford, Connecticut. If I
wanted a job, they had one. The pay was $125 a week — good money
then. I'd never learned to drive, so my brother took me to Hartford. I
smiled a lot during the interview and they made me a time salesman,
meaning I had to sell a fifteen-second spot after the *Lassie* show.

I lived at the Hublein Hotel. I met a willing girl at the TV station. We
necked under the broadcast tower. It helped pass the time. During the
day, when I was supposed to visit pet stores on Lassie's behalf, I'd go to the
movies instead. After a month I called Uncle Jack and said, "Look, I don't
want to do this. I'm coming back." Then I called my brother and said,
"Pick me up." I moved into the Eldorado with my parents once again.

In April, while playing softball in Central Park with my friend and NYU fraternity brother Billy Rubin, he said, "You know, Bernie, you'd make a helluva agent." Billy knew Lou Weiss at the William Morris Agency. He promised to set up a meeting.

It seemed like a good idea. Show business was in my blood. I knew the rhythms. The politics. The people. In fact, Billy's suggestion made so much sense, to this day I don't know why I didn't think of it first.

Laying the Groundwork

Chapter 2

A Show-Business
Education

Not long ago, Jackie Gleason's daughter and I talked about the old days in New York, when my uncle took me to Toots Shor's restaurant and I was overwhelmed by her dad and the other larger-than-life regulars who frequented the place. Shor knew everyone and everyone knew him, and by the time I got my first job in show business *I* knew that this was the life I also wanted. I told her how I'd dreamed of being accepted into that privileged world, for myself and not just as my uncle's guest, with all the respect and casually evoked power I imagined went with it. I didn't realize that my family had already shown me the best of it, that the most magical era was by then well into the history books. But even if I had known, it wouldn't have made a bit of difference. I'd peeked through the keyhole long enough and I couldn't wait to fling open the door and walk through on my own.

· · · · ·

Billy Rubin set me up with Lou Weiss, a cigar-smoking TV packager who handled NBC for William Morris. Now in his late seventies, Weiss is still at the agency. Whenever I see him, I remind him that he owes me a bonus.

In those days, the TV power base was all in New York. Advertisers and networks ran the show, with the talent caught in between. An agent would sell a show idea for his client to an ad agency for a specific sponsor, then together they'd go to the network and fight for a time spot. Every talent agency had a top man assigned to each network, and the networks would only deal with him.

In other words, it was a closed shop.

Today, an axe murderer can walk into a network or cable channel and, if they've got what someone there wants, sell a show. The competition is so intense that the outlets don't care who pitches, or who supplies them. They'll deal with the devil if they have to, as long as the devil (if an unknown) is willing to work with someone the networks have worked with before. To look at the many unseasoned writers and inexperienced producers today making outrageous sums of money for generally uninspired material, it's clear that the networks have probably been dealing with the devil longer than any of us realize.

Anyway, Weiss must have thought I was terrific because he sent me to Sid Feinberg, the office manager.

Feinberg was a civil servant type, with gray hair and glasses. His first question was, "Can you type?"

"Yes, I learned in the army."

His next was, "Do you know anyone in show business?"

"Yes, my uncle Jack Pearl." Everyone at the agency knew my uncle and probably assumed he'd arranged the interview.

Then Feinberg said, "You're terrific. There's only one problem. You're too old."

"I'm only twenty-four."

"That's too old to put up with the crap in the mail room."

I thought he was testing me, so I pressed him about how much I loved and understood show business. "I can put up with anything," I insisted. "I really want to work here." What I *didn't* say was that I didn't plan on hanging around the mail room long enough for the crap to get even ankle high.

He said he'd call.

Next, I had an interview with Larry Barnett at MCA, the agency run by the legendary Lew Wasserman. Like William Morris in that era of explosive TV growth, MCA made lots of money from packaging network shows. Packaging then meant putting together all the elements of a TV show — stars, advertiser, writers, producer, accounting, legal, production facilities, even health insurance — and selling it to a network. The agency took a packaging fee off the top, and because they more or less produced the shows for the producers, they deserved the money.

The cash flow got even better when Leonard S. Kramer, a savvy TV agent at William Morris, came up with the idea of forgoing the usual 10 percent commission from all the elements involved and taking instead as a packaging fee only *one-ninth* of the money the network paid to make the show — known as the "license fee." The clients thought it sounded like a deal. But think about it: one-ninth is really *11 percent*.

Today, it's no longer a ninth. Agencies get 6 percent: 3 up front and 3 deferred. Only William Morris does better. They get 5 up front and 5 deferred. The agencies also collect 10 percent of foreign and syndication sales. The big difference is that for all this money an agency now does little more than deliver the writer or the star. In other words, they make a few phone calls. Accounting, legal, health insurance — someone else's problem.

The MCA offices at 598 Madison were much more intimidating than the William Morris headquarters in the Mutual of New York building at 1740 Broadway. William Morris was full of scurrying elves whose jobs I thought I could easily do given time to observe. MCA was intense. Everyone wore black suits, white shirts, dark ties. They all looked about six foot eight. Every desk was an antique. The place was so well turned out that it made me nervous. I couldn't imagine fitting in, and I think Barnett knew it. He also said, "We'll get back to you."

I went home that night unsure of my next move. To my surprise I found a message from Sid Feinberg. "You got the job." I'd start on Monday, June 5, 1955. I still have my first pay stub. I made $38 a week — or $32.81 after taxes.

・・・・・

I started at William Morris with four goals in mind: Make some steady money. Have the one performer everyone wanted. Get the phone calls instead of having to make them. Know everyone when I walked into a restaurant and have them know me.

But first I had to get to the office. I'd never learned to drive, so I took the bus to work from Ninetieth Street and Central Park West straight down to Eighth Avenue and Fifty-seventh Street. I got off a block from William Morris.

My first day at work I wore a suit — my only suit — a tie, and a white shirt. Even a newcomer has to look as good as possible, which in my case, being so heavy, was never that good, or that possible. The suit was already wrinkled because I'd just come from my 6-to-8-A.M. typing and shorthand class at Sadie Brown's Collegiate Institute, where all Sadie wanted to do was fix me up with the rich yentas who went there. Even worse, William Morris wouldn't pay for my course, so I had to foot the bill. Nothing's changed.

The mail-room routine was simple, and after a couple days it was just like being in the army. I knew everyone, we were all pals, and I couldn't remember being any other place.

Our job was simple. Each employee had a mailbox; when the mail came we put it in the right slot. Three times a day, we'd deliver whatever was in the slots and collect outgoing mail, pushing our carts down the wood-paneled, carpeted hallways that muffled all unnecessary sound, though not always the more-than-occasional yelling that leaked from an agent's office. To train, I tagged along with a couple guys. Because I had a college degree I remember thinking, "Oh, how thrilling."

We had other exciting jobs, like collating papers and running mimeographs and dittos, which always stained your hands purple. We hauled kinescopes, scripts, and film cans around town to the networks, clients, and producers. We picked up stuff. And probably most important, we got the agents' lunch orders. It *really was* the army: the mail room was boot camp and our job was to learn and to survive any way we could.

The mail room is also the first place everyone learns that the guy who controls the talent is king. It was drummed into our heads: get next to them, have their ear, be in their good graces. Cozying up to the talent is the road to influence. Without it, you're just a worker bee.

On my first trip outside the office I delivered a $25,000 check to Red Buttons at 50 Sutton Place South. I knew what was in the envelope because, like any ambitious guy with a head on his shoulders, I opened all the interesting-looking letters and packages before handing them over. Everyone did it because information is king. We'd go into the men's room, run the water as hot as possible, and wait for the steam to do the rest. Then read and carefully reseal. I'd find client lists, contracts, personal correspondence, checks. I never worried about being caught because another guy from the mail room was often at the next sink doing the same thing.

Buttons's check was part of the hundred thousand a year he got from CBS to be exclusive. Go back to 1955: $25,000 was like, what? . . . three or four hundred grand now? If I could have made $25,000 a year somewhere — anywhere — I would have signed on for life.

Schlepping around New York carrying kinescopes and heavy film cans was no holiday for a heavy-set guy, and I would rather have stayed at the office. In order to steam envelopes, read memos, plot and plan, and learn the business, I had to be *in the building*. A trip involved a bus and lots of waiting. I'd be out of the loop for two hours. I might as well have worked in the garment center pushing dress racks along the sidewalk. To make friends, overhear something, be invited anywhere, or be in the right place at the right time to kiss a little ass, you had to be in the center of the action.

That's the big lesson: put yourself where the action is. It helps if you *love* the action. If not, you're in the wrong business.

Everyone in the mail room had a common agenda: to get the hell out as quickly as possible and become a real agent. We competed against each other like a school of baby sharks. Only a few would grow up to be, well . . . big sharks. I don't want to take anything away from the bright bunch of guys who worked alongside me, but I wasn't too worried. (Nor were they, I'm sure.) There was George Shapiro and his future partner Howard West, who now co-manage Jerry Seinfeld and also produced *Seinfeld;* Irwin Winkler, who directed *The Net* and *Guilty by Suspicion,* and produced forty movies, including *Rocky, Raging Bull,* and *The Right Stuff;* and Wally Amos, who later created Famous Amos Cookies. I didn't think they were any smarter about the business than I was, but even if they were, I still believed in myself and my instincts, which is not only a good thing, but the only thing.

In some ways I was different. Most of the mail-room guys came from Brooklyn or the Bronx. My roots were Manhattan. I grew up knowing the Stage Deli and the Stork Club and I was already comfortable around celebrities. And since I was still at the Eldorado, I lived much better than everyone but the bosses. I had no money, but everyone *believed* I was doing great and knew what was going on. (For some reason, it's still the same today, which is fine with me.) To some that made me a big shot. An arranger. Everyone asked me for advice: What should we do tonight? Where are we going to lunch? What are we doing this weekend? Who's the hot comedian or jazz musician?

Even the bosses knew it. Once, when Jimmy Durante was at the Copa, my family decided to go at the last minute. My father called Jules Podell, who ran the Copa. When we got there he put a table for us on the floor, in front of another table. I turned around and — holy smokes! — there were Nat and Harry Kalcheim. Nat Kalcheim was head of the William Morris personal appearance department. He handled all the big comedians and was the most respected man in the office. His brother Harry Kalcheim discovered Elvis Presley, Sid Caesar, Imogene Coca, and producer Max Liebman. He took care of what were, in those days, the unusual acts, the off-center types. I nodded at them: "Hello, Mr. Kalcheim. Hello, Mr. Kalcheim. How are ya?" Then I told my dad who they were and he whispered to me, "Fuck these guys, who do they know?" It was a great moment.

I tried to make my mail-room time bearable by having as much fun as I could at work. Once, when Esther Williams, the swimming movie superstar, walked out of her agent's office, saw me in the hall, and asked, "Do you know where I can find some water?" I fell on the floor laughing. It was perfect.

Another time, an agent named Arnold Sank and I were in the men's room on the twenty-first floor at William Morris. There were three or four urinals. We'd finished and were washing our hands when Nat Kalcheim walked in and noticed some urine still in a bowl. He turned to me and said, "Is that yours?"

"Yeah," I said, "but you can have it if you want."

Thank goodness he laughed.

Call me a character, a much nicer version of Sammy Glick bent on getting ahead, but not so narcissistic, selfish, or subhuman that I would willfully step on someone and hurt them in the process. In fact, here's what amazes me most about my career: I did it all the first ten years — most of them at William Morris — not knowing what the hell I was doing. I had no power, no access, nothing except the show-business instincts I was raised with — as well as the genetically inherited ability to stay alive by making the Cossacks laugh — and those were probably the purest years of my life. When I found out later how much having an edge — any edge — means, I looked back and said, "Holy shit, I must have been really good." Either that or so blissfully ignorant of how far I'd have to go to be anyone at all that I didn't get scared off.

Along the way I learned that ambition and instinct were part and parcel of becoming an agent and, later, a manager and producer. It turns out my "edge" (if any) was the narrow focus of believing I could do my boss's job. Also, when I got nervous and overthought a situation, I waited until I calmed down and came up with a plan before making a move. And, of course, I was damn lucky.

• • • • •

As long as I stayed in the mail room I couldn't earn anyone's respect. I'd be just another office boy who jumped when someone said, "Go get me lunch." Unfortunately, you can't just take a test, get an A, and be promoted out. You need to attract the attention of a higher-up who can help. That's why I've always believed that the people who *want* the jobs *get* the jobs. They're never content to sit and wait to be noticed. Any schmuck can do that, and lots of schmucks have.

I knew how to be discovered.

Kiss ass. But not the big executives'. I didn't want to reach too far, too soon.

Show up early for work. It sounds totally cliché, but it helped. Our office didn't open until 9 A.M., but I got in every day at eight o'clock because I knew that Nat Kalcheim walked in at 8:15 or 8:20. I made it my business to stroll through the halls so he'd see me. I never got pushy but he recognized my drive and responded well. (Watch *How to Succeed in Business Without Really Trying* to see how it's done.)

Another trick is to make friends with an agent's assistant. In my time they were mostly male, and we called them "secretaries." Since they'd also come from the mail room, they knew the procedure. Even better, they also wanted to move up the ladder, so if they could recommend you to take their place, all the better.

The all-time best way to score points with an agent is to do him favors. In other words, whatever he wants, within the law.

Some agents had clients on sitcoms, so I'd go to their shows and laugh. Seriously. I got $5 a show — nearly a day's pay — to sit under a microphone in the studio audience, and guffaw, chuckle, or titter my ass off. I knew how because I used to do it for my uncle. I can start any kind of laughter or applause you want. I still do it for clients today, only the pay is better.

I also monitored comedians for their agents in the nightclub department. This was important. A comedian performs on his own, so he can always pick up a night's work without using an agent, and save the commission. Our contracts entitled us to 10 percent whether we got them the date or not. Because I worked at William Morris, I could get into any nightclub in town, or the hotels — the Waldorf, the Plaza, the Pierre — just by flashing my agency card. If the place was sold out, I could stand in the back. (This was also great for dating. You could find something to do seven nights a week, if you had the energy.) I'd hang around the hotels to see who was performing; after the show, I'd make it a point to see the comedian and say, "Hi! I'm Bernie Brillstein from William Morris."

Any comic who'd thought of keeping our commission knew right away that he had to pay up.

• • • • •

William Morris had a great reputation for servicing. That means when you book an act at a nightclub or on a television show, someone from the agency goes to the date and lets the client know he's there to help. Generally the talent couldn't care less if anyone is around, but at William Morris, covering the client was covering our own ass. No one could complain that we weren't there. Not that the *responsible* agent, the guy the client might actually *want* to see, would service. Such an unenviable task was doled out to poor schmucks who wanted to score points and get out of the mail room. Thus more chances to perfect the greeting: "Hi! I'm Bernie Brillstein from William Morris."

My first servicing job was on Labor Day weekend 1955. Nat Kalcheim asked me to cover Billy Eckstine at the Brooklyn Paramount Theater. I was thrilled he chose me until I realized the show was on a Saturday, so I couldn't go out of town for the holiday. But I decided to be positive and think of the assignment as a chance to meet Eckstine and show off a bit.

I took two friends with me. After the show we went backstage. I called up to the dressing room for Mr. Eckstine. When he came down I said, "Hi, Mr. Eckstine. Bernie Brillstein from William Morris. I thought your show was terrific." He gave me one of these: "Thanks for droppin' by, baaaby," and walked out. And that was it. My whole weekend for a "Thanks for droppin' by, baaaby."

I liked to service only because I was ambitious, which is what the agency counted on. Otherwise, I thought it was bullshit, an old premise that served no function except to remind you of the good time you thought you'd have that didn't turn out that way. Like a hangover. I figured out quickly that when an actor performs or a singer sings, he has stuff to do. Responsibilities. As much as it may be a hassle for you to sit around doing nothing, it's a hassle for him to entertain some fresh-faced agent he hardly knows. Maybe he needs a little rest time. Maybe he wants to get laid. Maybe he wants to study the script. Or maybe he's just not in the mood for you to show up. "Oh, Bernie Brillstein's here. Shit, I've got to spend an hour and a half with him." They don't want to see anyone who isn't a true friend.

"Thanks for droppin' by, baaby."

Another servicing lesson: Thanks to Joey Bishop I learned when to talk and when to shut up around comedians — but not because he took me aside for some gentle mentoring.

Bishop was performing at some hotel in New York and I went to the show. I was a big fan. At the time, he had just landed his first film role in a war movie called *The Deep Six*. Afterwards, backstage, I introduced myself: "Mr. Bishop. Hi. I'm Bernie Brillstein from William Morris." Then I blurted out, "By the way, I'm so happy we got you the movie."

"What do you mean 'we' got?" he screamed at me. "I got it. I got it *myself!*"

"Okay," I said. "Okay, calm down." This seemed to work and he went back to ignoring me.

I've never again made the mistake of talking to a comedian when I have nothing to say. Do it and they'll bury you. They *listen* and they're just waiting for the chance to kill you because they don't want *you* to be funny or to take any credit for their success. They think their talent alone gets them every job. Plus, like all clients, they'd rather not pay commission and they don't like it when you remind them, even in the most indirect way, that they have to.

• • • • •

I got out of the mail room by finding a weak link in the company, someone whose personality and job performance created an opportunity. I could have tried to be an agent's secretary, but what for? When you're on a toll bridge you try and pick the line that moves the quickest. Some people wait for the best job. Some people wait for a middle job. I didn't care. I wanted *anything.* I thought, "Just get me outta here, because no one's gonna know I have any talent *until* I get out of here." In my heart I was always an agent, and just working to make it official.

Jerry Collins was head of publicity. He had dark hair and wore glasses and bad suits. He always looked rumpled; more like a press guy than someone in charge of dealing with them. A cigarette always dangled from his lips. He was probably fifteen years older than me, pushing forty.

I did Jerry favors until one day he said, "You seem bright. How would you like to work with me?" He acted like he was giving me the keys to the executives' bathroom. Here's what really happened: his assistant quit.

"Geez, Mr. Collins," I said, "that's great."

All my friends knew it was grunt work and said, "Don't take the job." But I knew three things: One, the publicity office was opposite Nat Kalcheim's office, and proximity is priceless. Two, in publicity you worked with *everyone* in the company. The job provided maximum exposure to agents, clients, and others who could help me take the next step up. And, three, I'd be *out of the mail room*!

This probably sounds terrible, but it's the truth: throughout my career I've always imagined the guy I worked for getting fired and me taking his job. I'm not talking about some hocus pocus, just visualization. I could always see myself moving up. It worked. When Jerry Collins got canned I took over.

Here's what I learned from him before he left: absolutely nothing. It seemed to me that Jerry Collins did as little as possible. But at forty, stuck in the firm's lowest-paying job, who wouldn't? My pay in publicity never topped $75 a week.

Running publicity in a theatrical agency was not a great job then, even worse than it is now. It's like being head dance instructor in a paraplegic ward. You'd send out eight-by-ten pictures of clients, with a bio that read something like: "One of the brightest stars on the show-business horizon is [fill in the blank], who opens at [fill in the blank]." I treated the job like a dating service, through which I could keep meeting new people. It worked. A young Mel Brooks used to hang out in my office to shoot the shit and use the phone. One day he showed me a screenplay called, "Springtime for Hitler." It was great; so great that I told him no one would make it because it was too bizarre. Thank God I was wrong. He made the film and called it "The Producers." It's my all-time favorite.

I just wanted to learn and help myself. For instance, I'd make flyers for our clients. I'd cut out newspaper headlines, put in a picture, and have them mimeographed. It was really just another way of kissing ass. I also had access to client lists, so I wrote some letters saying, "I'm Bernie Brillstein from William Morris. I saw your last show. It was great. I thought I'd let you know." No one told me to do this. Just instinct, I guess. Give some love, be hopeful I'd get some back.

· · · · ·

With a job, my ambition, and my crazy family, what more could I possibly want? A girlfriend, naturally. But I was still playing catch-up with the ladies.

When I grew up we were taught that nice girls didn't sleep around, and that sex should wait for marriage. Lots of guys ignored that, and I wanted to as well, but I couldn't bring myself to pressure a girl if she said no. I was too shy to even let it get as far as no. Perhaps if I acted with girls like I did on my job I would have been more successful, but that wasn't my nature. In college, I did a little better, though not much. In fact, my best memory is of a girl that a friend of my father's arranged for me when I was eighteen. She worked at the Club Samoa. I got to go to her room instead of getting jerked off under the table. When my father found out, he nearly killed his friend. Since my father hung out in these places, that seemed strange to me. I was old enough. I'd figured he wouldn't mind.

I fooled around a bit while stationed in England, but it was nothing to write home about. After my discharge, it was back to my pathetic ways. I remember one young woman — her name was Marilyn Boroy; she looked like Cyd Charisse — with whom I was really in love. Not that I ever told her. One night Marilyn called me out of the blue and said, "I'm coming to pick you up." She got me at 3 A.M. and we cruised up into Connecticut, past New Canaan, to Westport. A beautiful drive. We parked and saw the sunrise. I thought it was the most romantic thing in the world. I felt romantic, but with no clear sign that she felt romantic, I kept my hands to myself. After a while she drove me home.

Forty years later, while sitting in my shrink's office it finally dawned on me: Marilyn wanted to have sex of one sort or another. (At least I think she did; that's what's so crazy about this: I've never been sure.) At the time, I wanted a sign but I never stopped to think that maybe the whole trip was one huge, blinding neon sign. Marilyn Boroy . . . where are you now?

My friends knew I needed help, so Irwin Dubrow, whose family owned Dubrow Cafeterias in New York, Brooklyn, and Florida, introduced me to the world of high-class call girls.

Cindy Kay (I've changed her name to protect her innocence) was my first. She lived off Central Park West. Dubrow set me up and gave me the twenty bucks Cindy charged. I walked in and saw a girl in jeans and a T-shirt, no makeup. Early twenties. Gorgeous. She could have been a model or a college sophomore. We made love and it was terrific.

Even better, she let me go down on her. I say "let me" because it was my first time, and although I wanted to do it, I didn't want to take all the responsibility for what I'd been told was bad behavior, which made it all the more attractive. I must have been worried about the warnings, though, because right in the middle of it, I looked up at her and said, "You're not going to tell anyone, are you?"

"Bernie," she said, sweetly. "Who am I gonna tell?"

Me being me, Cindy and her friends became my friends. Sometimes we'd go to the movies. We were practically the same age, so it wasn't like hanging out with an older client. I didn't get anything for free, but I also didn't have to pay up front, like at some gas stations before they turn on the pump. Our time wasn't transactional, it was more like an easygoing date. I'd bring records from the office. We'd have a drink, kibitz. The big line was, "Do you want to go in the other room?" Then we would, and kiss, neck, the whole thing. And I could take my time.

The toughest part was coming up with the $20.

Well, maybe not. The hard part was dating and enjoying a regular girl. Compared to Cindy and her pals, regular girls seemed so fake and full of pretense. Sometimes I'd come home from a date and phone Cindy and she'd come over. We'd have fun. I could be myself. I didn't have to take her to dinner, unless we *really* wanted to go to dinner — which we occasionally did. I realize now that I was just needy and unsophisticated. It was so hassle free *because* I paid for it, but given the strictly moral times, what was a guy to do? Go without? Maybe I'm distorted but the whole business had nothing to do with love or emotions and I never felt there was anything wrong with it.

• • • • •

When opportunity knocks you'd better be ready to answer, whether or not you're supposed to.

One afternoon, Ed Bondy, an agent in the legit department, ran into publicity to see me. He said, "Molly Picon is leaving *Milk and Honey*" — a Broadway show about Israel — "and none of us knows any Yiddish actresses who can take her place. You do, because of your uncle Jack."

Molly was the preeminent actress of the Yiddish theater. Later she would appear in *Fiddler on the Roof* and *Come Blow Your Horn.* I thought for a moment. The only other Yiddish actress I knew of was Jenny Goldstein. I told Bondy.

"Great," he said, and left to call the producers. He came back a little later. "They're thrilled," he said, out of breath. "They'll buy Jenny Goldstein and give her five hundred a week."

"She was a star," I reminded him. "She wouldn't work for five hundred a week. Let's get her seven-fifty."

He called the producers again and got the $750. Then we called Jenny Goldstein with the great news and discovered she'd been dead for four years.

Now that's classic agenting. We got a dead person a $250 raise. I knew I was in the right business.

I also made my own opportunities.

John Aaron and Jesse Zousmer produced *Person to Person* with Edward R. Murrow. They were MCA clients, but booking guests on the show was open to anyone who could get across. William Morris didn't even pay attention because the celebrity subjects weren't paid for the interviews, so there was nothing to commission. That was shortsighted. It was a news show, but also one of the first promotional shows, and in prime time no less. I got the agency's permission to let me take a shot at *Person to Person* and I got on lots of our people. In fact, I was so relentless with ideas that Aaron and Zousmer fell in love with me.

Once, Aaron and Zousmer took me to Yonkers Raceway with Ed Murrow. You want to talk about feeling like you're in show business! It was Murrow! We had dinner and bet the horses. Murrow was, well . . . Murrow. Smoking. Half in the bag. Loaded. But charming, considering how little he said: maybe no more than "Who do you like in this race?" Not deep conversation. He really didn't give a shit about me. He was just there. But I didn't care. The whole evening made me feel like one of the boys.

I never saw Mr. Murrow again except on television. However, I've read everything about him, and what's really amazing is that in *his* book he never mentioned going to the track with *me*.

On the other hand, Aaron and Zousmer loved me so much that they said, "Bernie, we're thinking of leaving MCA. Sol Radim" — a big agent at William Morris — "has been after us, but we want *you* to go to your bosses and say you can sign us." They didn't mean they wanted me to be their responsible agent, and I didn't expect that. After all, I was still in publicity. But my ability to talk to people and make them feel comfortable had paid off. They wanted me to deliver the big news and get the credit.

When I did, people at William Morris took me a little more seriously.

· · · · ·

If it takes a character to know a character, then at William Morris, George Wood was probably my favorite. By the time I joined the agency, Wood had been there for almost fifteen years, booking nightclub acts like Berle, Durante, Sinatra, Joe E. Lewis, and Sophie Tucker, at the Copa, in Vegas, and at mob joints all over the country. Wood also handled the Scopatone project, the first jukebox with moving pictures. They had one in the William Morris conference room. The whole thing was a mob operation that eventually fell apart.

Wood could have easily stepped out of Damon Runyon. He was great and funny; he loved women, gambling, and a good time. Of course, Wood was handsome. I thought he looked like a shark. He also knew some sharks: guys like mobster Frank Costello. Occasionally a questionable guy came to see Wood in the office. When Jimmy "Blue Eyes" Alo decided to pay him a visit, my then-girlfriend, Carol, was the twentieth-floor receptionist. She'd recently blown in from Miami. Jimmy "Blue Eyes" walked up to her, and she said, "Can I help you, sir?"

In a deep, gravelly voice he said, "Georgey Wood."

She said, "Who should I tell him is calling?"

He said, "Jimmy 'Blue Eyes.'" Carol called George Wood's secretary and said, "Mr. Eyes is here to see Mr. Wood."

Not only was Wood rumored to be connected to the underworld, but he didn't mind if you knew it. On the morning of October 25, 1957, just after Albert Anastasia of Murder, Inc., was shot while getting a shave at the Park Sheraton barbershop downstairs, I ran into Wood in the office hallway.

I was almost too excited to speak. "Mr. Wood! Mr. Wood!" I gasped. "Albert Anastasia was just shot!"

First he looked at his watch, then he looked at me. "Ha, ten minutes late!" Did he know in advance? I've always wondered.

Sometimes, if he was in the mood, Wood let me listen in on his phone calls. I wish I'd been around for the one when Harry Cohn, head of Columbia Pictures, called to say he was going crazy over Sammy Davis Jr. dating Kim Novak. Cohn said, "He's ruining my business and my girl-friend. I want him out of her life." Wood made a few calls, then got Sammy on the phone. "If you don't get married tonight," he told him, "you're gonna be a fucking pretzel." Sammy tied the knot that evening in Vegas, with a woman of his own color.

It surprised me recently to find George Wood listed in a tribute to William Morris on their one-hundredth anniversary as someone they were proud of, but nothing shocked me more than the day he said, "Bernie, I hate to ask you, but . . . I need two thousand dollars until Mon-day." Like I said, he loved to gamble. He was tapped out. Because he was friends with my uncle — and because I wanted to be a hero — I decided to help. Some people think I gave him my Bar Mitzvah savings, but those bonds went to my college education. The only money I had was $2,000 in craps winnings I'd stashed. He took the money and placed bets, hoping to get even and pay me back. But his luck had already run out. That weekend Wood woke up feeling ill and checked himself into the hospital. Before the day was over, he died of a heart attack.

There's no lesson here, except perhaps never to loan money you can't afford to do without.

• • • • •

Listening in on a senior agent's phone calls was not only fun, it was educational. The right agents encouraged the practice. It gave you a feel for the rhythm of negotiation and the private side of a client's personal-ity. Nat Kalcheim often let me listen. He handled all the nightclub come-dians and commanded great respect. Once, I heard him call Jackie Gleason and tell him he had been "a bad boy."

"People have to live up to their agreements, Bernie," Kalcheim said, after we hung up. "We can't let them do otherwise." He was right. What an honorable man. But all I heard was the word "we."

Imagine that.

Kalcheim was also a strange guy. He was about five seven, tall for a William Morris man, with a full head of gray hair. Always wore a suit and tie. Always immaculate. Even his desk was immaculate; maybe too immaculate. On it he kept a yellow legal pad that never ran out of paper because he would write on the top sheet — a task, an idea — and when it was done, he erased it. He also wrote regularly to his mother. Not on the yellow pad, of course. He dictated the letters. While his secretary, Artie Moskowitz, scribbled, Kalcheim would look out his office window and say, "The Coca-Cola sign says it's seventy-three degrees here. I hope it's warm in Chicago." Then he'd sign the letter, "Your loving son, Nat Kalcheim." I know he signed his full name because Artie would show me the letters.

Nat's brother Harry Kalcheim had bushy gray hair and looked like a crazy professor. He was creative and eccentric and probably the agency's greatest talent finder. He had such good contacts all over the country that Colonel Parker called him when he found Presley.

One day in January 1956, Harry Kalcheim called me in and said, "Bernie," — he had a squeaky voice — "Saturday night Elvis Presley is doing *Stage Show*. Would you go and take care of him?"

Stage Show, featuring Tommy and Jimmy Dorsey, was a short-lived TV variety show produced by Jackie Gleason as a lead-in for *The Honeymooners*. I'd met Elvis earlier when he came in for his signing picture, but I still didn't know much about him. This was before the *Ed Sullivan* appearance, so he was still well below the pop-culture radar. In fact, *Stage Show* was his first TV appearance: Saturday, January 28, 1956.

I got to the rehearsal at CBS's Studio 50, between Fifty-third and Fifty-fourth Street, and found Elvis talking to a reporter from *Pageant* magazine. After a while I introduced myself.

"Hello, Elvis. Bernie Brillstein from William Morris."

"Hello, sir," he said. Sir? I was only a few years older, but the legend is true: Elvis was very polite.

It was cold backstage. As we talked I could see Elvis shivering. After a few minutes, I excused myself and ran across the street to a haberdashery and bought him a sweater. I gave it to Elvis and he loved it. The *Pageant* photographer took a few pictures of him holding the gift. I still have that photo on my office wall.

The more time I spent out of the publicity department, the more I learned. One night, Larry Auerbach, the William Morris agent who covered ABC, invited me along to see a new client, Jimmy Komack, open his stand-up act at the Club Elegante in Brooklyn. (Komack, who died in 1997, later became a writer, producer, director, and sometime actor.) It was an important date because Nat Kalcheim was also coming. Any push the variety department put behind Komack would have a lot to do with Kalcheim's reaction.

Kalcheim hated being too cold. The first thing he did when he went to a club was ask for the air conditioning to be adjusted. I took care of it. Kalcheim made himself comfortable, Komack did his bit, and then Kalcheim abruptly stood up and left. Everyone went nuts wondering why.

The next morning Kalcheim called us into his office.

"Well, Mr. Kalcheim," Larry Auerbach said, "what did you think?"

"He never should have worn that red watchband," said Kalcheim. "He looked like a nance."

Red watchband? Nance? Was the guy senile?

"I love his material, and he could be a star," Kalcheim explained. "But when you're a comedian, *do nothing* to distract the audience from what you're saying." It made sense. He was dead on. Komack wore a black suit, a white shirt, *and a red watchband.* Kalcheim figured if he'd noticed it, so would an audience. I can't count how many times I've repeated that story to the comedians I've managed. It always makes the point.

After a while I knew I'd done as much as I could in publicity, and it had done as much as it could for me. I couldn't be happy stuck in some dead-end service job. I wanted to make money for the company and myself. If I was going to be in show business, I wanted to be *in* it. It was time to move on.

I got out of publicity the same way I got out of the mail room: I looked for the weak link. I found it in the commercial department. Lee Karsian, who was married to the actress Pat Carroll, was my boss. But not for long. When he got fired — visualization again? — I took his place.

Putting clients in commercials wasn't the same as booking talent into nightclubs or on TV, but since it was a new department and outside of the mainstream, I felt like I had my own little business inside William Morris.

I decided to make the most of it.

Chapter 3

We Do Business
by Accident

When television boomed in the '50s, the business of TV commercials boomed right along with it. Little agencies already handled the scale actors and actresses, but Madison Avenue desperately wanted celebrities to hype their products. Every call I got from an ad agency started with the same line: "Get me Jack Lemmon." Why? He was the perfect white-bread guy. We represented Jack Lemmon, but you couldn't *get* Jack Lemmon because the snobs told stars, "You don't do commercials."

That seemed crazy and I wanted to change it, but I realized it would take time. Meanwhile, I convinced the ad people to use talent like Morty Gunty, a Jewish comedian; or Señor Wences; or Johnny Puleo, a midget and great harmonica player who fronted an act called Johnny Puleo and the Harmonica Rascals. Besides playing great music, part of his routine was biting people's legs. I consider it one of my greatest accomplishments to have gotten this extraordinary *visual* act a Dr Pepper *radio* commercial.

Middle-aged and older WASP women ran most of the ad agency talent departments. Nan Marquand at BBD&O was probably forty. Evelyn Pierce at J. Walter Thompson was pushing sixty. I was twenty-eight, and Jewish. At first I was concerned that my religion might hamper my prospects. I knew from a pre–William Morris job interview that the ad agencies didn't like doing business with Jews. My uncle had sent me to see Bill Warwick of Warwick & Legler, the agency that handled Chesterfield cigarettes. Warwick was the most gentile-looking guy I had ever seen in my life. Sandy-colored hair, suspenders, beautiful tie. We had a pleasant talk, and then he said, "Bernie, I love your uncle. You're a wonderful kid and you're going to be very successful. But — and if you tell your uncle this, I'll deny it — we can't hire Jews here." For a moment I didn't know how to feel, but I was glad he'd at least been honest with me — the rat bastard.

These *goyishe* women could have made my life difficult, but instead they liked me a lot. I'll guess they could tell I was serious about helping them, so they helped me in return. Sometimes we'd get together after work. I'd escort one or the other to the Copacabana and the Latin Quarter, to teach them a thing or two about nightclubbing. In return, they took me to the Museum of Modern Art, and taught me how to appreciate the great masters.

Eventually I convinced some celebrities to take a shot at commercials. I got Piper Laurie and Zsa-Zsa Gabor to do Lux commercials for J. Walter Thompson. I got Harpo Marx work. Then I landed a Pepsi-Cola commercial for the McGuire Sisters, for somewhere between $500,000 and $1 million, and other big clients finally started paying attention.

Though lots of minor agencies already repped scale people, I also opened a small department for scale and character actors, actresses, and models. I saw no reason why we shouldn't make piles of money from cigarette and soap companies.

I also had a selfish motive: Who doesn't like being around beautiful women? Of course, I had this silly rule about not taking advantage of my position, so I never tried to date clients. I had the power to get someone a job, so having sex with them — no matter how much I would have liked to — would have been sleazy and wrong. I still got some interesting offers, but I knew the score: I may have been charming and funny, but I never would have stood a chance with any of these women if I wasn't in show business.

Another reason I stayed away from the clients is that I wanted any woman I liked to like me *for me.* Call me insecure or a romantic, but when you have power it's hard to trust that the love you make will be the real thing — if the real thing is what interests you. For lots of people in this business it isn't; the exercise of power is all that matters. Should I have been so virtuous? Too late I realized that as a young man whatever might have happened because of my job might still have been plenty real enough at the moment, thank you. Instead, my reward is now being able to say, "I gave up the easy lay, but at least I have my integrity — and a big hard-on." It's like everything else in life: sometimes you're too moral and sometimes you're not moral enough.

Either way, after more than forty years I know this for sure: most men get into show business for the pussy.

Is that too honest? Okay: they get in for the power and the money, and figure out before lunch on their first day that there's also pussy. "You will get pussy" may not be written in the contract, but the thought that *maybe* you will is not lost on anyone! In the old days, when very few guys got filthy rich in this business, sex with gorgeous and semi-gorgeous women was the big perk. (Just plain sex was okay, too.) Look at Johnny Hyde, for chrissakes. A five foot four William Morris agent, he was no beauty contest winner. Yet he had Marilyn Monroe in her prime. MGM head Louis B. Mayer had a private "resting room" in his office, right on the lot, where he supposedly got blow jobs from aspiring and/or perspiring actresses. I know because I saw it years later when I ran Lorimar Pictures. My office was right next door to his old office. They say Twentieth Century Fox stopped every day at four o'clock for Darryl Zanuck to relieve himself in some manner. Harry Cohn was in love with every one of his stars. The old guys were swingers, gamblers, and drinkers. And it hasn't exactly stopped. What about directors who continue to audition pretty young things even after they've filled the ingenue role, just to meet the girls. It's not like these guys have to work hard for it, but the temptation is just too much. The examples are endless but they all add up to the same thing: for a long time there was a good chance that a woman had to do something sexual to get a job. I couldn't do it, it's degrading to both of us, but the old guys were pretty tough and back then sex was almost as good as money.

I don't think I'm telling you anything you didn't already know. Show business is a great way for a guy to get laid because most men in this line of work just aren't that attractive.

But the women are. Every year hundreds of beautiful girls with stars in their eyes come to Hollywood, where life is lived at a heightened level of unreality. They dream of being the next hot young thing on the cover of *Vanity Fair* or *People* or *Premiere.* They meet short, average-looking, overpaid men who can make those dreams come true. One's got the looks, the other's got the money, and it's a perfect fit in a town based on commerce in flesh and quid pro quo. Every day, men and women make deals in that gray area between taking the cash up front and taking it in clothes, cars, and an apartment in Beverly Hills–adjacent. Some women manage to score a wedding ring and a perimeter-protected compound in Malibu; others wind up charging you $1,500 an hour for the time of your life. A few even make it to the big or little screen and have real, satisfying careers — hoping never to read about their past in some tabloid headline. I'm not saying this happens to every young woman, but it happens. (To men as well, I suppose.) I *am* saying that any guy in show business knows the way to get the best pussy is by paying for it — one way or another.

I didn't get into show business for the women. But the thought that it might make that part of my life easier was not lost on me either.

• • • • •

I met my first wife at summer camp. Her name was Marilyn Gross. She went to Camp Allegro, for girls; I went to Camp Winadu, for boys. The two camps were about three miles apart in Pittsfield, Massachussets, and occasionally we had dances. My friend Larry Perse "went out" with Marilyn, as far as that sort of thing went in the '40s, and introduced us. It was a nonevent. I wasn't in her league.

Years later, when Marilyn was a minor actress using the last name Cole, she stopped by William Morris to audition for a legit theater agent. Just by chance, she saw me as she walked past the publicity department. Marilyn was even more gorgeous than I remembered, and, I believed, still unattainable. But she gave me a big hug, we talked, and one thing led to another.

We were married about six months later, in November 1957. I was twenty-six; she was twenty-three, a Jewish girl from West End Avenue. Beautiful, funny, crazy, and selfish — but then that describes at least my first three wives. Like my dad, her father also worked in the garment center. He was a lovely guy, but a gambler. I went to the track with him a few times. In fact, the night my daughter Leigh was born, he hit a parlay at Yonkers Raceway. He came to the maternity ward waiting room a little late, but flush with cash.

Meeting Marilyn finally got me out of the Eldorado and into the kind of apartment where real people lived. Too bad it was in Rego Park, in Queens. I had to commute an hour to work and I hated it. After nine months we moved to 55 East End Avenue, in Manhattan. Every penny went into rent. By then Leigh had arrived, so she got the single bedroom. Marilyn and I slept on a foldout in the living room. It was very intimate except that, like my mother, Marilyn stayed in bed a lot. I couldn't fix it, or stand it. After six more months, the marriage was over.

My divorce lawyer was Jerry Kushnick, late husband of the late Helen Kushnick, who once managed Jay Leno and produced his first year on *The Tonight Show* before she got too pushy for her own good and both NBC and Leno canned her. Thanks to Jerry's expert representation, I had to pay $125 alimony a week, the same as I made. There's nothing quite like pulling in minus money, so I lied on my expense account to break even. I also discovered — after innocently recommending some clients to an outside publicist — that I got a kickback equal to 15 percent of their fee. That helped. As for a place to live, Bernie Seligman, a William Morris guy who later sold cemetery plots, moved in with his girlfriend and gave me his one-bedroom apartment at the Park Vendome. It had a Murphy bed. Later, Señor Wences, a client and friend, also let me use his apartment when he and his wife were in Spain. He was a 's-aright guy.

Eventually, I found my own place at the Carnegie House.

When Leigh was six or seven, she and Marilyn moved to California. These days my ex-wife works in Beverly Hills, and Leigh, with whom I'm very close, is a hot agent at ICM. Everyone gets along great.

· · · · ·

Sometimes BBD&O or J. Walter Thompson would send me after a celebrity they wanted to hire, who had no agent. If I sealed the deal, I'd get the commission. When Nan Marquand wanted athletes for an Alka-Seltzer ad, I got her Yogi Berra, Ed Arcaro, Norm Van Brocklin, and Bob Cousy: that's baseball, racing, football, and basketball. The most they'd ever made was $1,000 for a commercial. I got them each $7,500.

One day Nan Marquand called and said, "Bernie, I got a good one for you. We're going to buy Herb Shriner for Dupont. We're going to pay him sixty-five grand," which in those days was a hell of a lot of money. "Here's his telephone number and how many commercials. I'll send you a copy of the offer by messenger."

Shriner was a comedian. He appeared occasionally on *Your Show of Shows*, hosted a game show called *Two for the Money*, and until 1956 had his own variety series on CBS. I immediately called him and said, "Mr.

Shriner, you don't know me. I'm at William Morris. I'm authorized on be-half of BBD&O to offer you $65,000 for this series of commercials." I laid it out and he said, "Please send me a wire, I accept."

BBD&O sent me a wire, I sent him a wire, and before I knew it, with a couple phone calls I'd made $6,500 for the company. That was more than half my annual salary, before bonus.

At the weekly Wednesday morning meeting, I expected to hear a few "Hey, hey's." I waited patiently while Nat Lefkowitz, a soft-spoken, conservative accountant who ran the New York office, went around the table, asking each agent for their status reports. Then they discussed old business and new, and brainstormed ideas. Finally, Lefkowitz turned to me and, in front of fifty people, said, "Bernie, did you get this commercial for Herb Shriner?"

"Yes." I felt like a hero.

"He's not a client, you know."

"I know." I waited for the compliment.

"You shouldn't have done it."

"What?" I said. "Excuse me?"

Suddenly the room got very quiet.

He said, "Herb Shriner's not a client. You should have gotten it for someone like Milton Berle. Milton is a client."

"Well, they didn't want Berle," I said. "They wanted Shriner and they were going to buy him one way or the other. Because of my relationship with BBD&O and Nan Marquand they called here and let us pick up the money. I just made us sixty-five hundred dollars. I'm happy about it."

He stared at me with one-way eyes and repeated, "You shouldn't have done it."

That got me crazy. I said, "You wanted me to tell her, 'No, I won't pick up the money'?"

"I'm telling you, you shouldn't have done it."

"Then you might as well take the sign 'Commercial Department' off the door," I said, "because I guess relationships don't mean anything to you. BBD&O, one of our biggest clients, would think I'm out of my mind."

No one said anything. Then Lefkowitz sighed and, using the tone you'd take with a slow child, said, "Let me ask you a question. If this af-ternoon they call you for a commercial and you can make the office fifty thousand dollars, and it isn't for a client, what are you going to do?"

The answer came automatically. "I'm gonna take it."

That did it. He got red and started yelling like a lunatic. "That's it," he said. "Meeting's over."

On the way out, Lou Weiss motioned for me to come into his office and close the door.

"You were right, you know," he said. "You were right."

"Well, thank God someone thinks so," I said.

"Yeah. But you still shouldn't have done it," he said.

I just shook my head. If William Morris was the kind of place where I could be right and *still* be wrong, I knew my days were numbered.

Did I do the right thing? Today an agency would probably take the easy commission, and then try to sign the talent. I wasn't interested in representing Shriner, and he didn't seem to care either. But since Nan Marquand wanted him, who was I to argue and try to shove a William Morris act down her throat? I took the money. It was the reward for developing a good relationship with my buyers. Lefkowitz hated that because he was an accountant who lived by rows and columns and numbers, profit and loss, not an agent who had to think creatively on his feet. He was afraid of our clients like Berle. I wasn't. He was my boss, but his attitude still drives me crazy, as I'm sure it would drive anyone in the same situation crazy. Who wants to be judged by a guy who doesn't get what you do, or how you have to do it, because he's never really done it himself? Right now I'm thinking about studio executives who try to tell writers and directors what works in film, and TV suits who can't stop fiddling with a show because they're uncomfortable with anything mildly creative. Things never change, do they? Lefkowitz is probably one of the few people I've met in the last forty years who didn't understand me. Why? I was show. He was business. I thought he had no business running the show. That as much as anything explains who I am.

$\bullet\ \bullet\ \bullet\ \bullet\ \bullet$

Fortunately my job had many rewards.

One day in 1960, Burr Tillstrom, the puppeteer and creator of the TV show *Kukla, Fran and Ollie*, called. I'd just gotten his three hand-operated stars a TV commercial, so he asked me to do him a favor and meet with a friend. Tillstrom said the guy needed an agent.

"Christ, Burr," I said. "Maybe I can get him a commercial, but beyond that, what do I know about puppets?"

"You'll like him," said Tillstrom. "He's funny. See him."

I didn't want to, but I said okay.

When the friend showed up, I couldn't believe my eyes. In walked this guy who looked like a cross between Abe Lincoln and Jesus: six three, hippie arts-and-crafts leather suit. He wore a beard, which I later discovered was to cover his acne scars. He was so gentle and unpretentious that he never spoke above a whisper. He'd brought a big box of puppets. When he put them on his hands, it was magic.

His name was Jim Henson.

I had no idea then that he'd become world renowned. I didn't think, "This is my lucky day, the beginning of my career." But for some mysterious reason, although I'd never met anyone like him before, when Jim performed I *understood* it. I got it. Instinct told me what to do.

After Jim left, my boss called and said, "Bernie, have you ever heard of Jim Henson and the Muppets? Someone wants to book him into Radio City Music Hall."

"Heard of him?" I said. "I just signed him!"

We were together thirty years, until he died.

I did it on instinct. There was nothing logical about it. I'd never been to a puppet show in my life. I wasn't even crazy about the enormously popular Charlie McCarthy; I liked him but didn't think Edgar Bergen was some genius because I could see his mouth move. Then out of nowhere I discovered a strong affinity for a towering, Mississippi-born hippie who liked to play with creatures made out of felt. We used to walk into restaurants together and people would laugh.

I don't know what I saw in him, but I saw something. I realize that at first, before we became close friends, Jim appealed to my perverse sense of humor. *Sesame Street*, which was still a few years off, was for kids, but Henson was not a kids' act. He was hip and slightly dark. He had cute little creations — and he liked to blow them up. Remember Glow Worm? "Glow little glow worm, glimmer, glimmer," and at the end, the cannon comes out of the monster's mouth and blows the glow worm away.

Now that's funny.

When we met, Jim lived in Washington, D.C., and was already doing TV there. He'd started in 1954 with *The Junior Good Morning Show*. Then, when he was a college freshman, he and Jane Nebel, his future wife and first performing partner, did the five-minute, twice-daily *Sam and Friends*. It aired on the local NBC affiliate, WRC-TV, just before

Steve Allen's *Tonight Show* and *The Huntley-Brinkley Report.* It won a local Emmy.

The show introduced the world to Kermit, though he wasn't yet a frog. Jim showed me clips of that as well as of some commercials he'd made that I thought were terrific. The one for Wilkins Coffee described his humor perfectly. A happy character asks a grouchy character what he thinks of the coffee. The grouch says he never tried it. Happy pulls out a cannon and blasts Grouchy. Then he points the cannon at the audience and asks: "What do you think of Wilkins coffee?" The other commercial was a dog food ad that featured a deep-voiced, brown Muppet dog named Rowlf.

A few years later I heard in a TV meeting that we'd just sold a program called *The Jimmy Dean Show.* It had a front porch set. That gave me an idea: Wouldn't it be logical to have a dog on the porch? I called the producers, Frank Peppiatt and John Aylesworth. I told them about Jim Henson and pitched the dog. "His name is Rowlf," I said. "He's brown, wisecracks, plays the piano, and sings."

They said, "Geez, that's interesting." I got everyone together and sold them Rowlf for $3,500 a week. The show was on ABC from 1963 to 1966, and right away — taking nothing away from the star — the dog got more mail than Jimmy Dean himself. The big secret is that Rowlf helped keep the show on the air. Jimmy loved the dog. Jimmy also seemed to like me, tough Southern guy that he was. We were both big Yankee fans. After I left William Morris, he offered me a job managing him for $750 a week (or $39,000 a year). But he didn't want me to manage anyone else, so I had to pass. The temptation of that kind of money aside, my instinct told me that depending on one client wasn't smart. They could always fire you, or, like my uncle the comedian, decide to do drama. And there goes your whole world.

My only frustration with Rowlf was that when I tried to get the dog billed not solely as Rowlf, but as the human beings behind him, meaning a credit for Henson and Frank Oz or Jerry Nelson, whoever worked Rowlf's other paw at the time, Dean turned me down flat. He said, "It would hurt the character's effectiveness." But let's cut through the bullshit. In plain English that meant Dean didn't want to screw with the viewers who thought the dog *could really talk*! So I settled for getting Rowlf raises, and in the end, Henson (I mean, Rowlf) made $7,500 a week.

• • • • •

Making out once is luck. Twice is coincidence. Do it three times or more and maybe you know something. Follow up enough of your hunches and one day people may call you a genius. To me, it's the continuity of luck that's interesting. Instinct is not something you can learn. There's no secret I can wow you with unless you're willing to be impressed that I figured it out in the first place. It's a gift. Having and using instinct separates the people who should be in this business from those who often are.

But what do I mean? Instinct for what?

First, for whether you can spot talent that people will respond to. Do you know something special when you see or hear it? When my instinct acts up I usually perspire and get little chills. It's like God is saying, "Pay attention." I feel the same way when I see a woman I know I'm going to like, or meet someone I want to be in business with. I experience security and safety. When my mother took me to see Dean Martin and Jerry Lewis at the Capital Theater when I was sixteen, I felt my whole body react. I knew I was seeing something special. I was right.

Some people think instinct means understanding why an act is a hit today. Wrong. It means you can see someone who's not yet hot and feel the potential for greatness.

About eight years ago my son David brought this sixteen-year-old kid to my office. He had a vision: he wanted to be in the record business. I liked him instantly, so I said, "Okay, I'll give you twenty-five thousand. Do what you want to do. If you make the money, give it back to me. If you don't, I made an investment." I didn't ask him for a partnership or anything. But the kid said, "I don't want your money. I want your help."

It was the right answer. Very impressive. Today, the kid is Guy Oseary, co-owner with Madonna of Maverick Records. He found Alanis Morrissette, who sold twenty million copies of her debut album. Guy commands incredible respect in the music business *for his instincts.* And he always gives me credit. Helping him — believing in him — was for me also a gut call. That's what it's all about.

Sometimes instinct can misfire.

A couple years ago I saw a young comic named Mike Morgan on *The Tonight Show* and at our next Brillstein-Grey staff meeting I said, "You mean no one has called him yet?" Turned out no one had seen him, either, except one of our managers, Ray Reo, but he didn't have an opinion. But I said, "Let's go after him. Not since Steve Martin have I felt so positive about someone's talent. I feel it in my bones." I got on the phone, found out where to reach him, and called Morgan in San Francisco. When he answered, I said, "Hello, this is Bernie Brillstein."

"Oh, my God! Yes?"

"Come down here. We want to represent you!"

I paid his way to Los Angeles, got him a hotel room, and set up a show at Igby's comedy club. I invited the whole office: Brad, Sandy Wernick, Cynthia Pett-Dante, Gerry Harrington, and Marc Gurvitz. Cynthia brought Ari Emanuel, head of the Endeavor Agency. I'd seen Dana Carvey for the first time at Igby's and I thought it was really lucky. I played the role of the boss who was showing the kids how management works in the business of comedy.

The poor kid comes out onstage, and that night his act just died. We've never seen a worse bomb — and that in itself became hysterical. We all sat on the right side of the room. Brad kept looking at me and I kept looking at Brad. Then I looked at Gerry. Then everyone started moving away from me like I had just farted. I had to break the bad news to Morgan, and he went back to San Francisco. I felt terrible. And no one has let me forget it. To this day, it's a big joke around the office. Every time I say someone is great, I hear, "Yeah, like Mike Morgan." I was so embarrassed.

By the way, that's why I love this company. Nowhere else does anyone pick on a boss like that — and get away with it. But bosses are human, too.

Following instinct is scary (not as scary as having to do the job once you make the deal), but I never second-guess. That's just stupid. I just do what I do and see what happens.

Instinct also means that you know the difference between hot and good, between style and substance. They're *not* the same. These days we have too much hot; performers who are flavors of the week, for maybe a day and a half, and then they're gone. I think the public resents the over-hyping.

The problem is that it's much easier to sell a hype than it is the reality. Myths can still become self-fulfilling prophecies because they haven't failed yet. They're untarnished. This town is full of myths that people keep buying because everyone wants to be known as a discoverer. Everyone wants to say, "I found. . . ."

Of course, if you're hot, it's great to be hot. You get three jobs from it. Guys who have never seen you say, "Hey, I've got to have him." Isn't that wonderful? You're not judged by your talent and your long-term prospects. You're just the thing that will make someone money *now*. Anyone can get hot: agents, managers, lawyers, writers, a model who'll swim topless at a horny director's house. I've been hot. It burns bright, but lasts only a moment.

But turn hot into good (or just *be* good) and that's a career. Robert Redford has a career. Matthau and Lemmon have careers. Bill Murray and Dan Aykroyd have careers. Brad Pitt, Nick Cage . . . hell, most of the people we represent have careers, which is why we represent them. But anyone can get lucky and trip over talent. Anyone. That doesn't mean they'll stay with the talent, guide the talent in the right direction, or keep them successful. But if your client has a career, you're a successful manager.

There's no formula for instinct. Either you have it or you don't. Some people can be exposed to talent all their lives and never understand what they've seen. Others can watch complicated deals being made and never have the touch to finesse one themselves — no matter how much they wish they could. You can't teach instinct any more than you could have taught Joe DiMaggio how to hit a baseball or could show Tiger Woods how to swing a golf club.

Maybe you just don't know yet what you have an instinct for. Could be horse breeding, but we're talking about show business now. If you're *really* blessed, your instinct won't be limited to a style, trend, fashion, or fad; it will span generations and not leave you stuck in an outdated niche. I've always cast my net over the edge, without even thinking about it. From Jim Henson to the idea of young people doing live TV comedy on Saturday nights to picking Brad Grey as my partner and successor, I just had a feeling. It's scary to trust that feeling, but that's all anyone has.

When I talk at colleges I tell the kids, "Every place you go, look around: on your level, the next level, at the bosses. If you say, 'I can't do that,' then I don't know if you should stick around too long." I always knew who I wanted to become next. Can you see yourself moving up the ladder? Can you imagine yourself doing what your boss does? Brad Grey certainly did. See? It even happened to me.

Test yourself. Allow three to five years, tops. It really takes that long if you're serious. Force yourself to make choices based on your gut, not on the promise of quick money or the beauty of the package deal. If you realize you're a plodder, get out or be happy being a worker bee. But I would say that for any business. Can you look in the mirror every day and still see your passion for what you do? Believe me, if you can you'll know. But remember: the lifestyle and the power are so seductive that the temptation to bullshit yourself can be irresistible. So don't; otherwise I promise your career will be a disaster.

By the way, you don't have to be perfect. No one has ever written a book called *How to Pick Hits and Avoid Misses.* William Goldman is right: no one knows anything.

Here's my corollary: everyone is full of shit. There is no right answer. *Forrest Gump* was around nine years before it got made. *One Flew Over the Cuckoo's Nest*, fifteen. It took *Seinfeld* three years to be a hit, and now it's our latest sitcom classic. My client Ed O'Neill, the star of *Married . . . with Children,* didn't get hot until he'd been in the business twenty years. I think our company is the best and yet we turned down *Dumb and Dumber* for every one of our comedians. Jim Carrey ended up doing it, and it was a hit. I'll say it again: no one knows anything. You only get to see how well your instincts stack up against real life *after the fact.*

If someone could predict hits, they would sit home like Reginald Van Gleason (today: Frasier Crane and his brother, Niles), in a penthouse, smoking French cigarettes, wearing a silk dressing gown and an ascot, saying, "Hello. Yes? Send me your ideas and I'll let you know."

I won't lie to you: that's the job I really want, the genius who gets scripts, records, and TV shows sent to his home, and says, "Hit, failure, hit, failure." I could save the industry billions of dollars.

Instead, as much as I've been right, I've also been wrong many times. I have personally wasted a lot of people's money on bad movies and bad TV shows. I didn't set out to make a failure — who does, really? — but it happens. So what do I know? Only that we do the best we can and sometimes you get lucky. I've gotten lucky more than most, enough that people have stopped calling it luck. Otherwise you wouldn't be reading this.

· · · · ·

After my divorce, life got strange, but in a good way. For some reason I was suddenly more handsome than I'd ever had any right to expect. I call it my good-looking period. Everything came together. I was Mr. New York. I was single. I had no money, but I was everywhere. Women became quite easy for me. I had the bachelor apartment, the sexy records (Frank, Dean, Gilberto), and red lights by the bed. Women would call me; they'd bring over steaks, oil and vinegar, and we'd fuck. I couldn't exactly explain my luck with the opposite sex, but as any gambler will tell you, you take your luck where you find it.

Dating wasn't *always* a breeze. As soon as I was officially single, my friend Billy Rubin said, "Come with me to the Concord Hotel. You're single."

At the bar I saw this blonde staring at me. She was quite pretty. Billy said, "Go over to her." Now, no matter how lucky I've ever been with women, I've *never* been good just picking up someone. I have to know them first, see if there's anything there. But Billy wouldn't let up. "She's staring at you, go over there."

So I did. We talked. Then she said, "Let's go to my room." I thought, "Oh, my God, this is the single life? This is great."

We went upstairs, got into bed, started making love, and suddenly she moans, "Do it to me, Gene."

I said, "Excuse me?"

She said, "Ohhh, I'm sorry."

I said, "My name's Bernie." My ego's deflating by the second, right?

After a few more minutes of sweating and pawing, she said, "Ohhh, do it to me, Gene."

It turned out that Gene was her former boyfriend and she couldn't get over him. And there I was, with the first woman after my divorce, and she's a complete lunatic. What a reentry into single life.

The toughest women were Copa girls: the tap dancers and show girls. Forget that to me they were the unattainable shiksa; forget that I'd fantasized about them since I was a teenager. It's just not easy to court a dancer. You need incredible stamina. You have to stay up until four o'-clock in the morning. Then you have to feed them. Then, if you still have the energy, you might get to sleep with them. By then it was time to go to work. It's no bargain.

Most of the regular action happened at Chuck's Composite at Fifty-second and Second, the first singles bar in New York. Three straight male models — Ray McHugh, Chuck Lester, and Chuck Bruce — owned the place. They knew the most beautiful female models in town, and most would show up. No wonder it got to be the hottest place in New York. Build it and they will come.

Chuck's owners were also members of the Englewood Country Club, in New Jersey. I belonged, too — not that I could afford the fee; I supplied comedians on Saturday night and got comped.

Another coincidence: Jim Henson's first Muppet office was in the same building as Chuck's, on the second floor right over the club. He used to meet me there a lot. When the club got slow, we'd go across the street to Rocky Lee's Choo-Choo Bianca. That used to be my life. Cheap pizza and Chuck's, where, even though I had no money, I could run a tab.

For some reason, probably because I was a good faker, I developed a semi-reputation as a ladies' man. It was mostly harmless, but once in a while someone at the office thought I would know how to get "a friend" laid. As head of publicity, I'd learned the town. If you needed a reservation at a nightclub or a restaurant, you called me. If you needed a place to stay, I'd tell you where. I was like my father; I helped in any way I could. But I wasn't a pimp.

One day Sammy Weisbord, a big shot agent in William Morris's Los Angeles office, called me. My first thought was, "They know I'm hot! They know I'm good! How great!"

He said, "Bernie, how are you?"

"I'm terrific, Mr. Weisbord. How are you?"

"Great. Listen, Bernie, I'm going to Sweden. Do you know any girls there?"

Sweden? I said, "Well, uh . . . no, I'm sorry."

"Oh, they told me Bernie would know girls in Sweden."

I wished I did.

· · · · ·

Quite unexpectedly, I also fell in love. Boy, was it love, that timeless '50s love. Passionate, but not exactly sexual. She was a client, beautiful, religious. I was a punchball player from Ninetieth Street with a little daughter and no money. The relationship broke my rule about dating people I represented, but I was helpless. We were crazy for each other, went everywhere together. It was wonderful — and, of course, doomed. The catch? Not only was she married but she'd been Miss America. It couldn't work out, and yet we continued for ten years, on and off, seeing each other, not seeing each other. Friends in love. The more I think about it now the crazier it makes me. It was the most powerful of connections.

• • • • •

Thanks to my assistant, Tony Fantozzi, the commercial department ran so well on its own that I almost didn't have to be there. So without giving up that job, I scuffled for more attention. Somehow I schnorred my way into working as an assistant to Wally Jordan, head of the New York television department. I'm not certain it was an official position, but I became his utility infielder. I gathered material, did reports, favors, anything.

At the Wednesday morning meetings, after Nat Lefkowitz did his business, Jordan would sit at the head of the table and go over every client who was in trouble or who needed something, plus we'd ask questions about television stuff, the variety shows, and guests. The pecking order was big agents in the front of the room, little agents in back. At first I sat in the back with the other young guys and played a game. We'd decided that most agents were full of shit, and these meetings confirmed it. All the agents lied. We kept a chart: Fake Outs, Cop Outs, Direct Lies. Every time an agent spoke, we'd note his name and mark his sin appropriately. It was hysterical. We were full of piss and not much else, but it was something to do to keep from getting nervous that we might get called on to speak. The exercise came in handy. Later, when I sat behind Jordan, to his right, he'd often lean over to me and whisper, "Bernie, what's the truth?"

And I could tell him.

Jordan taught me the basics of the TV business. We had a rapport. For once, I didn't imagine my boss getting canned. He was a smooth operator, the best television packager around. The way he sold a show was brilliant. He'd take the heads of ABC, CBS, and NBC, and their wives, to see an act at the Plaza. These were the top guys, not some self-important heads of development who couldn't really say yes to anything. Next morning he'd call around. If a boss's wife had said, "I like that act," he usually sold the show.

Not only was Jordan good, but, unlike most of his department, he wasn't Jewish. That was no accident. The network heads didn't like dealing with Jews any more than did the advertising agency people.

It seemed to me that Wally Jordan knew everything. He had information, and information, as I've said, is king. But he didn't get his information by running around like a scared rabbit. Instead, at 6:30 every night, he poured a glass of scotch on the rocks and called his agents into his office. There, they'd all drink and tell their stories of the day. Jordan assimilated the information, then called the three network heads and traded it among them.

"Hi, how are ya? I'm here having a drink. How was your day?" He shared his knowledge, and picked up theirs. He taught me that if you put it all together, patterns will form so you can plot and plan.

These days, most players prefer to keep things close to the vest. There are good reasons. Information is a very valuable and powerful commodity. Knowledge in the wrong hands can endanger a deal or a career. Yet, I'm convinced it really helps on all but the most delicate levels, to be more open — at least with the people you work with. Look at what happened at CAA after Ovitz took over. CAA was a well-oiled team with a common purpose. They worked in unison and captured the town. But things went south after Ovitz anointed himself king and started controlling the information both inside and outside the company. Only after he left did things there change for the better.

Working for Wally Jordan had a few unanticipated benefits, both professional and personal.

The guys in the William Morris television department seemed to think I was good company, so if there was an empty seat at a roast or some other function, Wally Jordan would invite me. He had to since I wasn't a member and couldn't afford it on my own.

Also, a model who'd done a popular cigar commercial called me. I'd represented her and now that I'd been promoted, she wanted to take me to lunch. I agreed — she was gorgeous — and we went to Alfredo's.

Over the fettuccine she kept saying, "I'm so proud of you," and other nice things. She was so major league–looking, with her yellow dress and her blonde hair spilling everywhere, that it was all I could do to keep from spilling my lunch on myself. When she got the check she said, "Do you *have* to go back to work?"

"No," I said, "I don't *have* to go back."

We went to her apartment. I thought I was sophisticated, but I was *not* sophisticated. We got inside, got undressed, and the next thing I knew she popped two amyl nitrates in front of me. I hit the ceiling. I felt nuts. Great nuts. Then we got down to business and it was certainly the best business I'd ever done.

Later, after she'd spread her legs, she jumped out of bed and spread her portfolio of eleven-by-fourteen pictures on the floor. It was like a cold shower, but I began to understand how the game really worked.

• • • • •

One big problem with William Morris was that most agents couldn't get a decent salary. To compensate, they gave us an annual bonus based on our performance. Unfortunately, the reward never matched anyone's idea of how hard they'd worked. Even worse, we sometimes had to borrow against that bonus to get by.

Each year we'd line up outside Nat Lefkowitz's office to hear the "good" news. For many it was their only personal contact with the boss. The door would open and some guy would walk out looking glazed and unhappy. Then the next victim would go in. Lefkowitz sat at his desk and you'd sit opposite. He always spoke so softly that you had to lean in to hear him. While he gathered his thoughts, you just waited there with flop sweat because you knew no matter what, you weren't going to like it.

It was the most degrading thing I ever put up with. Lefkowitz sat nearly motionless, holding his gold Cross pen between his middle and first fingers, curled under against his thumb, holding it backwards over a sheet of paper. Finally, he'd say, "You've had a very good year. Your raise is twenty-five dollars per week." I felt like puking. What was I supposed to do, beg for $50 or $75 from a guy I couldn't stand, and who couldn't stand me? Egotistical (or proud) schmuck that I am, I never asked for more just *because* it was never enough.

Then he'd say, "And you get profit sharing." That was money they stashed away in some account and you couldn't touch it while you worked there. You only got it when you left the company or retired.

"And, oh yes," he'd add, as if in afterthought, "I see your bonus is . . ."

One year my bonus was $1,500. Sounds like a lot, but wait, Lefkowitz is talking ". . . fifteen hundred. After what you've borrowed, you owe us eighteen dollars and seventy-five cents."

I couldn't believe he wanted the $18.75.

"Do you want cash or a war bond?" I asked.

He never cracked a smile. That's when I knew for sure he hated me. He took the $18.75 out of my next paycheck.

• • • • •

Phil Ford and Mimi Hines were a husband-and-wife comedy duo. After their 1963 appearances on *Jack Paar, Ed Sullivan,* and in Vegas, they got hot as a pistol. Too bad they weren't our clients. Marty Kummer at MCA, who handled the *Ed Sullivan* and *Jack Paar* shows, was their agent. But my friend Billy Rubin was their business manager, and he introduced us. We went for a few dinners, I tagged along when they did some dates at resort hotels in the mountains, and soon they started asking me what I thought about things.

Remember what I said about grabbing opportunities? Whatever knowledge I had, I used to make MCA look bad. When the agency wouldn't send Ford and Hines their cross-country-tour tickets by messenger — they insisted the duo go to the office and pick them up themselves — I said, "That's disgusting! They don't treat you like stars." Which, by the way, was the truth. My meaning was clear: at William Morris we'd take care of them. They understood and decided to sign with me. I'd be the responsible agent, but since I was still half-running commercials, agents more familiar with nightclubs and television would actually book the duo. Still, it was an improvement over signing Aaron and Zousmer, who just gave me the credit. At least now I had a little power.

I also had big plans. I talked them into doing a situation comedy. Wally Jordan took Tom Moore, the head of ABC, to see Ford and Hines at the Plaza. Moore loved them and wanted to buy the show. The wheels began to turn, but too slowly, I thought. I asked about the holdup. Finally, Lou Weiss took me aside and said, "First we have to get a producer. We're taking them to Four Star Productions."

Ford and Hines signed with Four Star, but according to the deal memo I read, the producers gave them no advance, plus they only made ten or fifteen grand per show between them, and 15 percent of the net, which was meaningless. It was the first time I'd seen one of these deals on paper and I was amazed. Ford and Hines were the show, yet they owned only a tiny, tiny piece of it.

Why had William Morris made such a bad deal for them? Easy. The agency also represented Four Star, and they were bigger clients, with four or five shows on the air. I complained, but was told to shut up. In the early '60s the big pitch to acts was, "Get a hit television show and you can make a fortune in nightclubs." No one got rich from television. No one knew from syndication then. The idea was to be on television every week and you'd make a fortune on the road.

True enough, but I still felt there was something wrong with the system and that Ford and Hines had gotten screwed.

The show, as put together by Four Star, never sold. Ford and Hines walked away with nothing, but I got something that money couldn't buy. I learned a fundamental truth about myself: I was not "the William Morris guy." My first instinct was to protect the talent. My passion came from my connection to the performer. I realized that most talent needed all the help they could get, because between wanting the public's approval and their own varying degrees of (necessary) ego and narcissism, they'd be picked clean.

• • • • •

Signing Ford and Hines did me a world of good *outside* William Morris. I'd stolen two of MCA's money-making client teams, so Marty Kummer made it his business to get to know me. He wanted to understand why, but he was nice about it. I discovered that he was also really smart, a lovely guy, married with a couple of kids. A character. A real New Yorker. He was about six feet tall, a tiny bit on the heavy side and balding. His eyes always seemed to pop out of his head. Even after he left MCA he always wore the regulation black suit and black tie.

Marty and I got along great. For one thing, we were both gamblers who loved the risk and the action. Before long he asked me to play poker on Monday nights with him and his pals, who turned out to be a group of leading MCA and General Artists Corporation (GAC) agents.

Being in that company each week made me realize how isolated I'd been at William Morris. No one from my agency played poker. They just weren't the hang-around type. Kummer and his friends reminded me of what I'd known most of my life: that showbiz was a club in which men often drank and gambled together. I had a sense again of belonging.

If only it was that much fun these days, but where can you go at 2:30 in the morning and see thirty people you know? Maybe 2:30 in the afternoon at the Friar's Club, but I don't feel *that* old. Now I settle for seeing ten people for lunch or dinner, when they walk by my table at Morton's, Nate & Al's, The Palm, or The Grill.

Kummer pulled me back into the real show business world, but it wasn't just his idea. I *wanted* in. I pursued it. Not in a pushy way, but in the same way I usually got laid: I laughed my way in, I calmed it in, I niced it in, I talked it in. I helped it in, I "got it coffee" in. I did everything to ingratiate myself. If you're not a threatening personality you can get away with murder. Besides, I was fun to be around. I had a famous uncle, knew sports, could talk show-business history, and go on about women, even though I had to fake most of that stuff — not that they suspected. I could get laughs about my crazy family or my marriage. I'd do jokes about Nat Kalcheim or Nat Lefkowitz. I even came up with a new William Morris slogan. The original is "William Morris. Established 1898. A show business tradition." I came up with "William Morris. We do business by accident."

The interaction gave me confidence. I felt like a guy waiting to happen instead of a guy who never would. The more I thought about the humiliation Lefkowitz put me through, the more I realized that at William Morris I was pretty much a fat peg in an uptight hole.

I didn't hide these feelings, either. There's a way in conversation to let people know you're not particularly happy and maybe, if a job comes up, you'd take it. Eventually, a manager named Ray Katz offered me a shot at $18,500 a year, but no split of the profits. I liked Ray — still do — but I said no.

One day, Marty Kummer called and asked me to meet him for lunch at Ruben's. "Pal," he said, "you know MCA's gonna break up." Marty always said "pal" or "kid." He picked it up from Gleason and I got it from Marty and do it to this day. "I'm gonna become a manager," he continued. "I'm gonna have Jack Paar." Then he offered me a deal: twenty-five grand a year, guaranteed; he'd keep Paar all to himself, and we'd go fifty-fifty on everyone else after I made back my guarantee.

His offer meant three things to me: Thousands of dollars more than I was making. The magic number I'd always lusted after. And a chance to be partner.

I took it.

When I told Lefkowitz I was leaving he said the following words, which I will remember as long as I live: "Why didn't you tell me you were unhappy?"

I didn't miss a beat. "Why didn't you know?" I asked.

That was it. As a boss, he should have known. But that was the William Morris way. Look at just a few of the people and the potential billions they've lost. David Geffen, Barry Diller, George Shapiro, Ted Ashley, Irwin Winkler, Howard West, Mike Ovitz, and his four original CAA partners. William Morris had gold for talent, but was slow to promote them, stingy paying them, deaf to good ideas, and too inflexible to respond quickly to changes in the business. Take just one example: if Ovitz had stayed, he could have reinvented the company.

To be fair, working for a company is not always a good place to satisfy grand personal ambition. Some people function better making *all* the decisions because they have a vision of where they want to go. Maybe the guys I've mentioned could never have been happy as part of a group instead of leading one. But any chance for creative self-fulfillment is still bound to be squashed when the people in charge of show-business companies are lawyers and accountants who think they know it all. Those guys usually don't know from love and perspiration unless they're playing tennis. They don't really connect with the talent — onstage or in the office — beyond its relationship to the bottom line, and they don't know how to grant creative freedom to those who do. George Steinbrenner may interfere with the Yankees, but he knows he needs a good team manager. The late Frank Wells was the perfect second in command to Michael Eisner at Disney. In fact, he was offered Eisner's job first but declined. Wells was a genius with people, numbers and vision, yet he knew he was basically a business-affairs guy who needed Eisner's creativity and personality to complete the team. He was willing to sublimate his ego for the ultimate good. The late Steve Ross, chairman of Warner Communications who merged it with Time Inc., loved show business. He knew enough to choose top division leaders and then support them — "You need the plane? What can I do for you?" — and leave them alone. Ted Turner is the same.

A good boss knows how to do all the jobs in his company. Iacocca could not only run Chrysler, he also knew how to build a car from the ground up because *he loved cars.*

I've heard people complain that Brad Grey is at heart only a political animal, a self-interested show-business player. Bullshit. Brad never makes a fuss about who he is. Brad just stands up for what he believes in. There are many examples, but I learned it very early on when he asked a

Fox network press guy to not announce the additions of *It's Garry Shandling's Show* and *Charlie's Angels '88* to the Fox schedule *at the same press conference.* Perhaps that's minor to some, but Brad wanted to preserve the distinction between the shows. The flack assured him, but Brad thought he was lying. To protect his client, Brad asked me to come with him to the event at the Century Plaza Hotel. He made sure we got there an hour early. (That's a real manager.) Not only were Brad's instincts perfect and his suspicions justified, but when he declared that we were walking out — and that Shandling wouldn't appear — he refused to be intimidated when then–Fox president Barry Diller tried to stop him at the sidewalk in front of the hotel. It got ugly. There was some shoving. And yet it's to Brad's credit that he and Diller are now fast friends. Diller *also* admires anyone who doesn't back down.

Nor did Brad give in when I didn't want to do business with CAA because I so detested Mike Ovitz. I had money, I didn't care if we were shut out. There were other agencies. But Brad said, "Why shouldn't we do business with CAA? It's right to have them working for us on some things." Most guys wouldn't have had the balls to say that to me, given the personal circumstance, but he did. He was smarter and I listened.

Brad is also one of the last young guys with a foot in both showbusiness cultures. He comes from passion; he started as — and still is — a manager who works with talent. Having passion doesn't mean he can't like power or money; it just means he has a connection to what he's doing even if that something is building a company. Believe me, there are days when he says loud and clear, "This business sucks." That's why, when it comes to crucial decisions that could significantly affect your clients and/or employees, the original feel for the talent gives you a human perspective that a ledger book never will.

There are two words in "show business." I find it ironic that so many people like to say, as if it's the gospel revealed, that one of the words is "business." Of course, that's true.

But the *first word* has always been "show."

· · · · ·

The day I walked out of William Morris was traumatic, but after almost nine years, what else could I expect? I'd never worked anywhere else. They were like my family — my real family — both nurturing and nuts.

The same thing might not have happened to me today. William Morris is past its hundredth anniversary, and a lot has changed. My friend Jim Wiatt, until recently co-chairman of rival agency ICM, now runs the show. He's a bright, creative guy who inspires intense loyalty. I'm sure he'll carry on in the spirit of former president Arnold Rifkin, who resigned to become a manager. Rifkin was a different kind of leader for William Morris. He sought out input and ideas. I have lunch with him once a month, and we always end up teaching each other a thing or two. I've even been to his house, which in this town says a lot. I think he did a great job, and I know that Jim Wiatt will do the same.

Then, frankly, I was depressed about leaving. Even though I had a job waiting, I thought that I had somehow failed and out of self-defense was quitting to keep from getting fired. On the other hand, I didn't want to walk in one day and wonder why I no longer got mail. Often, that's how they used to fire you at William Morris. No one said anything; your name was just taken off the mail distribution list. You'd sit there for three weeks and wonder what was going on until you finally got the hint.

Paranoid guy that I am, I still hadn't told my parents about my new job. When I called, my mother answered the phone. I said, "Mom, I have bad news for you: I'm leaving William Morris."

"Why?"

"Because I have a good opportunity to go into business with a gentleman."

"What's his name?"

"Marty Kummer." I was sure she hadn't heard of him.

"Is he Jewish?"

I laughed out loud. But for a change, my family's predictability made me feel less anxious. I knew that however uncertain my future, there were at least some things I could always depend on.

Chapter 4

What? And Get Out of Show Business?

Management is like making love. There's heat from both sides. You have an instinct to get together. You have no idea what you're really in for, but you do it anyway.

Management is like marriage. In fact, it's less predictable, if such a thing is possible, because you can't just live together first to see if it's going to work out. You have to plunge right in, knowing nothing is certain. The whole relationship is a leap of faith. Success with one client doesn't guarantee success with another. All you can do is work at it and wait and see. But you're in it together, and, at least at the beginning, it feels great.

Management is like parenthood. A magazine writer once said about me, "Bernie was onto something. He knew there was money to be made treating the talent like helpless children." I wouldn't go quite that far, but in some important ways it's true. You see your clients at their best and at their worst and you're expected to accept it all. Your job is to be supportive when they hate the director, when their price isn't met, when their dressing room is too small, when their wife leaves, when they can't get work, when they drink or do drugs, when they can't get it up, and when they're such self-involved pains-in-the-ass that everyone hates them — including you.

Of course, when they have a hit, it's *their* hit, not yours. If you're lucky, you may get a thank-you. If you're *really* lucky, they might thank you publicly. Sometimes I dream about a Manager of the Year Award show at which my peers and clients give me a standing ovation as I walk to the podium to accept a statuette — in the shape of a dollar sign, naturally — for my years of selfless service. But I'm no idiot. If there's one thing I understand about being a manager it's this: you have to endure all of the bad times but never take too much credit during the good times.

My clients have won so many Emmys I've lost count. Most of them have thanked me, some even from the podium. That's nice. We were both successful in our own ways; they did the work and I was a conduit for their genius. But you'll never hear me say, "We won." It's never "we."

That's the way it should be.

From the client's point of view I'm already well compensated. I get lots of their money for doing what most of them consider less than hard labor — in other words, everything possible to keep the good times rolling so that they can enjoy the success they hope to become accustomed to. That's why I'm up to my ass in the business end, suggesting this, finessing that, fixing another, protecting it all — and repeating nothing, as if their secrets were crucial to national security.

Even when a client says, "My manager blew that," I have to keep quiet even though I know he's full of shit. No manager or agent ever blew a deal. It's always the client. The clients hide behind their lawyer's back, they hide behind the manager's back, they hide behind the agent's back, they hide behind their wife's back, they hide behind their doctor's back. They don't ever want to be the bad guy.

That's why I'm a part-time shrink, coddling fragile egos and calming chronic fears of never working again. When things go wrong (and even if they don't), I may *also* feel inadequate and possibly get fired, but that's nothing compared to the painful *public* scrutiny and indignity my clients may suffer when a TV series is canceled, a movie doesn't open, a club appearance bombs, or, God forbid, someone forgets their name from the stage on Emmy or Oscar night. I recently read an interview with Jim Carrey in which he confirmed what I've long understood: "The worst part of show business is the terrible fear of being publicly humiliated."

Fortunately, I knew none of this the first time I thought about being a manager. It was 1956 and I was still a kid at William Morris reading booking slips. I discovered that Pearl Bailey had been offered $17,500 a week in Las Vegas, for eight weeks a year. That was a hundred and forty grand! I thought, "And her manager gets fifteen percent of that — more than twenty-five hundred a week — for doing nothing!" I know now that he wasn't doing "nothing," but at the time I was working my ass off for $50 a week, $2,500 a *year.* For eight weeks of representing Pearl Bailey, her manager made eight *years'* worth of my salary.

Management seemed like a great business.

• • • • •

Nine years later I *was* a manager, working at the new Kummer and Associates offices at 136 East 55th Street and Lexington Avenue. We had a pleasant fourth-floor apartment. The secretary sat in a small foyer. My desk was in a moderately sized living room. Marty Kummer's office was a small converted bedroom. Soon after I arrived he brought in another associate, an agent from APA named Shelly Brodsky, and we shared the living room.

Eventually I'd have to sign talent, but first, as I did with Brad Grey when he joined my company in 1985, Marty took me everywhere. (The only difference is that Brad already had clients and all I had when I joined Marty was my balls.) I tagged along in Marty's shadow, watching how he talked to people, how he did the job. Like my father and my uncle Jack, he introduced me around and taught me the big time. We went to *The Jack Paar Show, The Ed Sullivan Show,* and the Friar's Club for lunch, where he shared a table with his MCA pals. We'd walk into Danny's Hideaway and he'd know everyone in the joint. We still played poker on Monday nights. We had dinners. Socialized.

I got to meet people on a different level. I noticed that I could be friendly with the competition, with talent I didn't represent, because we were all part of the show-business fraternity. I loved feeling like I was part of the "in crowd." In the old days — about a month earlier — I'd see a comedian backstage at a nightclub and say, "Hi. I'm Bernie Brillstein from William Morris," and I hoped he'd acknowledge me. Now I'd sit with that same comedian at dinner and maybe trade a few wisecracks. I took that step up from being a schmucky kid agent to being a manager, able to do anything I wanted, if I could.

Unfortunately, I couldn't. All too soon reality set in. I had no master plan. I had no big clients to commission. Suddenly I wasn't the young hotshot from William Morris anymore, just a thirty-three-year-old man with no acts, trying to get something, anything, off the ground, and wondering how I could call myself a manager with no one to manage.

If you've ever been insecure you know how heavy and inescapable it feels. I was scared.

I couldn't spend *all* my time with Marty, but when he was busy I usually had nothing to do. I sat around. I talked to Shelly. I walked the streets. I waited for inspiration and lunch. I gambled. I had the good luck to meet a girl who lived on the fifth floor, and sometimes I slipped away and fooled around with her in the afternoons. Otherwise I was a lost soul. I couldn't wait until four o'clock, when I'd make believe I was going somewhere important. I'd go to my apartment at the Carnegie House instead, and fall asleep.

My situation then reminds me of an old joke: A guy goes to the circus. After the Big Top he strolls around the grounds and sees a man cleaning up the elephant shit. "That's disgusting," he says. "Can't you get a better job?" "What?" says the worker. "And get out of show business?"

• • • • •

What frightened me the most about my new career was the same thing that got me excited when I'd read Pearl Bailey's booking slips: *getting the money.* I'd have to find some performer willing to pay me an extra 15 percent *over and above* the 10 percent he already paid his agent — the guy who was *supposed* to get him work. But no one wants to spend more without a damn good reason, so I'd have to say the words that all talent both hates and loves to hear: "You're not doing so well. You could be doing better." Then I'd have to come up with some reasonable solutions, not pie in the sky. Imagining that sales pitch was tough.

Manager, agent, manager, agent. What's the big difference?

Five percent.

I'm not joking. Well, just a little.

The technical distinction is that only agents are legally licensed to get their clients jobs. For that they get 10 percent. For an extra 5 percent — or whatever managers can get away with; Colonel Parker took 50 percent from Elvis — we are supposed to "advise and consult" but not solicit work. It's in the contract — which to me is not worth the paper it's printed on: "We do not get you employment." The agent is supposed to find the jobs and negotiate, and the manager is supposed to say nothing more than, "That's a good offer/Let's pass/We want a million more/Forget those putzes," then discuss with his client the pros and cons and make a decision.

If I stuck to that rule I'd be out of business.

Smart managers, working *with* their clients' agents and lawyers, are part of the negotiating process. (Belushi, Gilda, Aykroyd, and others didn't have agents until I found them one. However, I always consulted with their lawyers. In Belushi's case it was Mark Lipsky, who later represented Eddie Murphy.) But let me be blunt, even if it's sacrilegious: if you don't help your clients find work and make them money, and that means the *right* work so they can build a career, you'll have no clients. To this day, I've rarely met talent that's truly unhappy when they're working; those who were, we no longer represent. The idea is to keep them working at quality stuff. You'll know you're in good shape when you no longer have to make the job calls, but the calls come to you. Once you create the marketplace for your clients, your life becomes much easier. Then it's just a matter of good problems: Should I take this TV show? Should I take that movie?

When I started as a manager I realized that if I wanted to get clients, I'd have to find them on my own. I couldn't count on an agent's help. No agent wants to recommend a manager because that's like admitting he can't do his job. It makes the agent vulnerable. Today, talent managers are much more common than when only big stars had them — often on a one-to-one basis — but it still takes a lot for an agent to tell his client to think about adding additional representation. However, if the agent is smart enough and secure, he'll do it because he knows it's better to add a manager than to subtract an agent — namely, himself. If the client does well, the agent will try and take the credit. If things get worse, having recommended the manager gives the agent at least a year until he gets fired because the manager has an unspoken obligation to the guy who brought him aboard. It's all very neat.

It also explains why, if an agent does suggest a manager, he does so with these considerations in mind, in the following order:

Which manager last gave us an act?

What other act do we have that the manager might want?

What manager do we want to do business with?

(And finally) Who can do a good job for the client?

That's why I love show business. We always have our priorities straight.

• • • • •

At Kummer and Associates, I was going nowhere. I'd generated no word of mouth. I had no track record and no one to recommend me. Marty, at least, was really well known in town. He had Jack Paar, the thousand-pound gorilla, the David Letterman of his day. Paar had hosted *The Tonight Show* from 1957 to 1962 before going on to his own variety series. As an MCA agent, Marty had also booked *The Ed Sullivan Show* and he was still very close to that operation. He had juice. He could get almost anyone on the phone. The truth is that all I *really* had going for me were Marty's connections and the possibility that he could make something happen for any clients I could entice.

Marty knew the score and was a tolerant boss. I was grateful he had faith in me, and that his clients and his friends liked me. I guess he figured I'd eventually get into the ball game. He knew I knew the basic show-business rule: "If you can't get the clients you can't get the money." I knew he wasn't paying me my dream salary of $25,000 a year just to hang out.

• • • • •

One afternoon I went to lunch at Al & Dick's Restaurant with Larry Auerbach, my friend from William Morris. I was halfway through a pastrami sandwich piled sky-high with coleslaw and self-pity, when the phone rang at the maître'd's desk. It was for me. My first thought was, "Oh God, someone's dead." I couldn't have been more wrong.

Jim Henson was on the line. He said, "I now know what you did for me when you were at William Morris. I can't do it without you." He didn't explain what, if anything, had happened to prompt his call. It just seemed like he missed working with me. I could understand why: we trusted each other and he knew he could depend on me. He finished by saying, "I want to come with you."

I was ecstatic. I hadn't tried to take clients from William Morris, but I'd always hoped that Henson would eventually come along. He was the only one really worth anything. He didn't have *Sesame Street* or *The Muppet Show* yet, but between the commercials and *The Jimmy Dean Show* he worked steadily, and the magic he made with those puppets really got to me. Now I'd have a chance to prove myself as a manager *and* make some money on top of my guaranteed salary. I quickly did the figures in my head: Fifteen percent of the $7500 a week he got for Rowlf, for twenty-six shows, times 50 percent on repeats. Plus a percentage of his commercial fees. I was in profit already.

I told Auerbach the news, and as I attacked my lunch with renewed gusto I began to feel as if my existence as a manager was a tiny bit more justified.

It had taken a while, and many years later, when I hired Brad Grey at The Brillstein Company, I knew from experience that his adjustment to a new work environment might also be tough, even though he was already a manager and had brought clients with him like Bob Saget, Garry Shandling, and Dave Coulier. I said, "Just get comfortable. Don't worry about signing anyone for a year." But Brad, being Brad, couldn't just wait around. He'd seen the Rob Reiner movie *The Sure Thing,* and he decided he had to represent its young star, Daphne Zuniga. I asked him why and he said, "She's adorable and wonderful and I think there's something great to do here."

Brad met with Daphne and her agents several times. He tried hard to convince her to sign with him. Unfortunately, she passed and Brad was crushed. It was a big jolt, and he felt very insecure about it. He said, "Oh my God, how am I going to build this place? What am I going to do when I can't even sign an actress?"

I tried to put it in perspective. "Forget it," I told him. "Years from now, we'll laugh at this." I knew we would; clearly we have. It just takes a while to get your rhythm and feel safe.

> Brad Grey:
> Actually, Bernie said, "Come on, kid. Don't worry. Who gives a shit?" It was typical Bernie, in that gravelly New York voice: "Come on, who cares? What's the difference?" Over the years that's been part of our role with each other: we make sure in trying circumstances that the other isn't too upset. I still wasn't thrilled about not signing Daphne, but what he said and the way he said it really helped."

Having Henson again helped jerk me out of the doldrums. I felt so confident that I decided to try and sign Norm Crosby. It was a ballsy move, me against the world. At the time Norm was the hot comedian, performing at the Latin Quarter nightclub, and everyone was chasing him. Even my old mail-room pal Irwin Winkler, with his partner, Bob Chartoff, wanted a piece. They handled Jackie Mason and Jackie Vernon and were trying to build a stable of comics. The only problem was that Norm already had a manager, the late Bobby Bernard. But we all knew he was inefficient and, most important, so did Norm.

In those days, when you wanted to score a client, you'd go to the nightclub for the show, and then, using a connection or just your own nerve, arrange to meet backstage. Maybe you'd have dinner. If the talent liked what you had to say, you'd bring him to the office and try to close the deal. I had a way to get close to Norm. My "in" was a guy always on the lookout for an angle to work, my business-manager friend Billy Rubin.

Billy handled a grocery chain. Norm played at their Christmas party. After the set, Billy asked Norm if he had a manager.

"I have someone taking care of me, but he's really an insignificant guy doing nothing," Norm said. "The guy isn't hungry. He doesn't push me to do anything. He's satisfied if I work a club date on Saturday night. That's not what I'm looking for. I want to be *in* the business."

Billy said, "Well, I have a very close friend, Bernie Brillstein, who's a big manager" — ha! — "with Marty Kummer and Associates, and I'd love you to meet him."

I saw Norm's show at the Latin Quarter and afterwards I went backstage to wait for him. But when he came out of the dressing room, he asked me to wait while he called his fiancée, Joanie. "Sweet," I thought.

Norm got Joanie on the line and then he did something odd: Whenever he spoke, it was like anyone using a pay phone. But when she talked, Norm put the earpiece end of the handset to his chest. It was the funniest sight I'd ever seen. I didn't know if it was some sort of trick, and whether or not to laugh, but I couldn't help myself.

"Norm," I said. "I've never seen that. What the hell are you doing?" He explained that his ears had been injured in the war when his ship was bombed, so he wore a military hearing aid. The speaker and microphone hung on a sling around his neck, and were concealed under his shirt. What a hassle! I was amazed the guy could even perform with such a handicap.

That exchange broke the ice. Dinner went great. A couple days later I brought Norm to the office to meet Marty. They hit it off and I'm certain that because of what Norm thought Marty could do for him — which

was our plan all along — we signed him. As part of the deal we let Bobby
Bernard down easy by giving him all of Norm's commissions for a year.

I worked hard for Norm. First he got a raise at the Latin Quarter
from $750 a week to $1,000. Next, he did the Sullivan show. His trade-
mark comedy style of speaking with malapropisms caught on and he did
a twenty-six-week tour with Robert Goulet. Then he did seventy cities
with Tom Jones, became a fixture in Las Vegas, and was *always* on TV.
Norm's traveled the world, met politicians and superstars, and has the
pictures in his hallway at home to prove it.

• • • • •

One day, Marty Kummer got a call from Bernie Sahlins, the owner of
Chicago's Second City improv troupe. He said they were booked at the
Square East club in Greenwich Village and Marty should come down. He
took me along.

The Second City players did blackouts and character-driven comedy
sketches that were fresh, funny, irreverent, political, satirical, and satu-
rated in social comment — all at a manic pace. It was like nothing I'd
ever seen. I laughed my ass off, especially when Jack Burns and Avery
Schreiber did their now-famous "Cab Driver" routine. Jack was the pas-
senger and Avery the cabbie.

After the show, while people streamed out into the brisk Manhattan
night, I told Marty, "I want Burns and Schreiber."

"Go after them," he said.

I ran backstage.

When I found Burns and Schreiber I said, "I've never seen anything
quite like what you guys are doing." I meant it and they responded.
Everyone wants to be thought of as unique. Then I asked them to lunch.
The next day, I told them I thought I could help them get on a network
television show in three months and even have their own series in a couple years. They'd heard other pitches before, but they signed with me because they liked me for, of all reasons, my laugh.

The whole Second City concept blew me away. Bernie Sahlins had a
genius idea: take talented young kids who weren't necessarily stand-ups
and have them hone their work every night doing improv using suggestions from the audience. When you consider that Second City has trained
talents like Alan Arkin, Dan Aykroyd, John Belushi, John Candy, Chris

Farley, Robert Klein, Elaine May, Bill Murray, Mike Myers, Mike Nichols, Gilda Radner, Marty Short, George Wendt, and many others, you realize how well it worked.

I'd been brought up on Borscht Belt shtick and old-time show business comedy, like the Marx Brothers, the Ritz Brothers, and Durante, which segued into Alan King, Buddy Hackett, Jack Carter, Pat Cooper, Jackie Gayle, Shecky Green, Myron Cohen, Jackie Mason, Lenny Bruce, Henny Youngman, Mort Sahl, and the rest of the '50s and early '60s stand-ups. It was setup–punch line, quick and funny. Second City redefined comedy in a way that reinvigorated the blackout and the sketch.

They opened my eyes to something new.

I'd love to say that I *immediately* recognized the leading edge of a comedy wave that would soon include Monty Python, the Groundlings, Kentucky Fried Theater, the National Lampoon in all its incarnations, *SCTV, Saturday Night Live* and its imitators — but honestly I can't. I only knew that Second City was different and that I wanted to be part of it. Burns and Schreiber were my way in, and thus began an education that in 1974 would be crucial in helping me help Lorne Michaels with *Saturday Night Live.*

· · · · ·

Once I got Henson, Norm Crosby, and Burns and Schreiber, I was at least in the ball game. I had someone to talk to, agents to see, and meetings to attend. I felt like a human being again, but now I worried about something else: When would I actually feel like a manager?

Stupid me. I was *already* a manager. That's what I did for Ford and Hines at William Morris. It's why Henson wanted me back in his life. Caretaking just came naturally. My job as a child was to be the parent to my parents. I would do anything to make my mother and father talk to each other, to have them sleep in the same bed, to make them happier.

It was just the life I was trained to lead.

I also love people. The best managers do. I know it sounds touchy-feely, but it's true. Anyone can get lucky and discover talent. Likewise, talent can get hot without a manager or agent. But nothing lasts long in a vacuum. You need the right people around you. As a manager I instinctively developed *real* relationships and did whatever was necessary to earn my clients' trust. A manager can only function if his clients believe in him.

Management, at heart, is people-wrangling. I got inside my clients' heads. I knew what they were capable of, which people they could work with, and whom they shouldn't work with. I knew their habits. I understood their hopes and dreams and limitations. I knew their wives and kids and their lifestyles. I knew the business manager and how much money was in the bank. I knew what they needed to survive. I knew if someone was an alcoholic, a druggie, a gambler, or just promiscuous. If so, I could be counted on to tell them the truth — no matter what the consequences — and say, "Cool it. You're embarrassing yourself." Over the years, with few exceptions, they listened.

A good manager also believes in his client's talent, whether it's taking the town by storm or down for a short nap. I'm sure I'll repeat this a few times: talent never goes anywhere, it just rests for a little while. A manager has to demonstrate empathy. He has to cover the shit with flowers. Some managers are content to create the *illusion* of interest. Not me. Sorry, I can't fake it. I care because that's who I am. When a client shows the same concern for me, I feel wanted. I've had many great career moments, but that hasn't diminished my need for acceptance. It's always been that way. That's why I understand comedians and actors so well; we share some of the same psychology. The need for love drives me. Most of my friends and business associates believe that about me — though we don't talk about it — and I want them to know I know it, too. I admit it: I do this job for the emotional exchange. In good times and in bad it has sustained me.

• • • • •

Marty and I were together for about a year when I met Jerry Weintraub, another hot manager around town. His client, the singer Jane Morgan — her hit record was "Fascination" — brought him probably $60,000 or $70,000 a year in commissions. Weintraub also lived with Jane, so I suppose he also shared in the other 85 percent. (They've been happily married now for years.) Marty and I liked him and when Shelly Brodsky left, we decided to bring in Weintraub and change the company name to Management Three.

The new deal was the same as my old one. Kummer kept the Paar money and we threw all the other clients' commissions, including Jane Morgan's, in the pot to be divided three ways.

Weintraub could seem like a regular guy when he wanted to, but he was in fact a larger-than-life rogue with great flair. His career proves it: he's been a top manager, a studio head, an entrepreneur, and, for a time, he put Elvis on tour. It's not surprising. As a young man, Jerry had balls of iron. He could pick up the phone and cold-call anyone. I was always better in person, working the room. Take me to a party and let me sit with my back against the wall, so that people have to come to me, and I will eventually attract the people (or the woman) I want to attract. Have me call cold, on the phone, and I'm dead meat. I could hang out all night in a bar and not pick up anyone, even the bartender. I have to know it's safe to perform. I have to prepare to perform. Not Weintraub.

Weintraub was a powerful influence on his two more passive partners. He transformed us. For instance, he decided he wanted a Rolls-Royce Silver Cloud, with a driver, and that the company should pay. His reasoning: it was good for our image. Then Jerry needed a larger office with drapes that opened and closed when you pushed a button. We bought the drapes and broke through to the apartment next door. It cost a lot of dough, but again, he said it was good for our image.

Marty didn't object. After all, he lived the good life with a beautiful home in Great Neck, a couple kids, a yacht, and a Cadillac. He made good money. On the other hand, I lived without much furniture in the Carnegie House, and still couldn't drive. But, schmucky me, I went along with the changes because I was too insecure to object, or to fight for my own perks. Even though I had some good clients, most the time I still felt like the biggest loser in the world. A fake.

My personal life was to blame. I had two big problems and each made the other worse.

• • • • •

My first problem was women.

After my divorce, Marilyn and Leigh moved to Florida (before California). I hung out at Chuck's Composite with Henson and dated now and then. But mostly I was sort of in love with a woman I'd met just before I left William Morris. Laura was six years younger than me. She was funny, tough, and the prettiest girl at the Englewood Country Club. The place, frankly, was crawling with married ladies who fooled around. Laura didn't, which made her unattainable — so of course I had to attain her. As if that wasn't enough of a challenge, she also had two kids, and her husband, Seymour, was rich.

I prevailed in my usual make-'em-laugh, creep-in-slowly manner. Seymour was in the advertising business and played golf at the club. I played earlier than he did so I could finish first and head for the swimming pool, where Laura would be with her children. We'd talk. I found out we both loved João Gilberto and Morgana King. Once, before we were an item, I even double-dated with Laura and Seymour and took them to see Ms. King sing. It was our little secret. But pretty soon our affair was the scandal of the country club. Years later, at a book signing party for Alan King, Buddy Hackett told me that one day Laura's husband had walked up to him and said, "How do you like this sonofabitch Brillstein? I found the key to his apartment in my wife's purse." He was ready to kill me.

"I told him, 'Maybe she's a burglar,'" Hackett said.

What Seymour didn't tell Hackett is that he'd also found the number of my private phone line at William Morris in his wife's purse. I'll never forget when that extension rang and I picked it up and said, "Hello, sweetheart," thinking it was Laura. That's when a male voice — Seymour's — said, "No. This is Mr. Sweetheart, you sonofabitch." I hung up.

Laura and I had the kind of wild romance that I always figured would quickly burn itself out. It didn't, but just to stay honest while she was still married, I dated other women. Laura didn't like it. One night I brought a beautiful girl to a club dance. Laura was there with her husband. After one number, she walked by me on the dance floor and kicked me in the balls. Not nice at all.

Eventually Laura left her husband — not that I'd actually asked — and then we were together. It wasn't exactly a winning combination. We weren't your typical fun couple. Now alone, she had no money. I had no money. She had two kids. I couldn't see my kid. I knew I was in way over my head, but I didn't know how to get out. I still don't know how I got through that time. I've blanked out most of it. Everything was wrong; everything was out of kilter. I probably needed a psychiatrist, but who could afford one? Like a typical Brillstein, I tried to keep my depression hidden with a sense of humor. I guess I was a good actor. No one ever asked me if anything was wrong. Still, in my own head I was a loser, just hanging on for dear life.

• • • • •

My second problem was gambling.

Kummer, Weintraub, and I were all players, and we all knew it. Despite our respectable income, we were on the same roller-coaster ride. We never had much money left over because we bet it away. Kummer used to spend more time covering his debts than on show business. I remember one night I was in the office, on the phone with William Morris, when the line went dead and the lights went out. I looked out the window above Lexington Avenue and the whole city was dark. We'd had a blackout. Kummer, who had been on the phone with his bookmaker, walked out of his office and said, "What's going on?"

"The whole city is dark," I said. "Maybe it's the Russians."

"I wish, pal," he said, "but I'm not *that* lucky."

Sometimes we'd go to Las Vegas. A couple weeks after the Bonanza opened, Jane Morgan headlined and Burns and Schreiber opened for her. The gambling fools from Management Three went along. I had the least money, and went bust first. Then Jerry limped back from the casino, tapped out and white as a ghost in his white suit. Kummer walked in a little later, also dry. And this was the first night.

Later that week we ate in the Bonanza's special dining room for the gamblers and show-business people. A white-glove place. We had a table for twelve. While everyone ordered champagne I put on a big smile and said, "Hey, I'll sign it to the room." The check came and I saw the total: $1,400. I nearly passed out. Then I noticed the word "complimentary" at the bottom. I took a deep breath, but choked on it almost immediately when I realized I'd still have to come up with a couple hundred bucks for a cash tip. I didn't have it. We had to go around the table, scrounging. You can't imagine the embarrassment or the lunacy.

Another time, I was gambling in Vegas with a friend and had to make a plane back to New York. He told me I'd better get going, but I said that first I had to cash in my losings.

Unless we were in Vegas, the partners rarely gambled together. I mostly bet with Billy Rubin. We'd started in college. I'd work after school and bet what little I made, sometimes at the fraternity house, sometimes at the track. When I was desperate, I'd clip $20 from my father's pocket, trying to scare up $16 to bet $2 a race, and have enough left over for a bite to eat. Of course, I'd lose.

When I was at Management Three, Billy and I would lay down as much as $1,000 on a baseball game, and bet twenty games each weekend. Once, we hit on twenty out of twenty-one contests, and I think we made $28,000. I was usually in for 25 percent to a third of the stake. When we won, Billy was generous and gave me my share. When we lost I don't know how he dealt with wondering how I'd come up with the cash — but I always did.

The worst bet I ever placed was on the New York Giants–Green Bay Packers championship game of 1962. This was before the Superbowl, when there was only one championship game between the NFL East and West teams. The AFC was still the AFL.

It was New Year's Eve and we were at the Concord Hotel. The weather was miserable — about minus-twenty degrees with the wind chill — but Billy, Laura, and I drove to New York to see the game because we had season seats. I had the Giants and seven points. It seemed like a sure thing. At the last minute, Lou Michaels kicked a field goal and the Packers won 16–7, two more points than the allowable spread. I was out $7,500 plus 10 percent vigorish I had to pay the bookie because I lost. The damage came to $8,250, and I didn't have a clue how to pay it. Can you imagine the drive back to the mountains? Frozen and broke. Nineteen sixty-three around the corner. I can't even describe the depths of my despair.

I had a week to come up with the money, so I took a loan from a shylock. Nice guy. Easygoing. The deal was so much per week for about three years. I wanted to get out of hock sooner, so I went to Vegas, where I *really* lost a lot of money. Now I had to ask my friends to bail me out. Norman Kartiganer sent me $6,000 and a telegram that read, "Good luck, Riverboat." Irwin Dubrow, who's now dead, sent $10,000. A couple other people chipped in, and when all was said and done I owed another thirty grand, $70,000 altogether.

All these debts were too much to think about. I was under so much stress that I fantasized about going to Yankee Stadium and collecting a dollar from everyone at a sold-out game. Then I'd be even. Back in New York I swallowed my pride and went to see my father's sister's husband, Uncle Max, at Brookhaven Textiles. I said, "You've got to help me." Good old Uncle Max, he cosigned a loan. I paid off the shylock and everyone else, and then I only had to pay back my uncle. I could just about afford the monthlies, and that left me back where I'd started — with no money.

My uncle Max died a year later. When I heard, I felt terrible. I really loved him, and owed him. Then it struck me that his insurance would kick in and I'd be off the hook for the loan. Not a chance. He had no insurance. I kept paying every month until I was clear.

I guess it could have been worse. At least no one ever threatened my life or suggested cutting off body parts.

• • • • •

At first I gambled as a way to supplement my income. I wanted to have some extra cash, buy a few suits, take a vacation, show a girl a good time on a proper date. But as I got older, and even before I made more than enough money to take care of all my desires — not to mention cover my ass when I had a run of bad luck — I realized that my love of gaming went deeper.

I loved the action.

Maybe it's strange, but also how I define *show business:* the action.

In Las Vegas, my game is craps. You win fast and you lose fast. One night I dropped $100,000. Thirty-six hours later I won it back — and more. Craps is pure. It clears my head. I have a mathematical mind and I love to see it all laid out in front of me — all the bets, all the odds. I love to smell the table and the room. It's great to watch the people. Guys who away from a casino are the nicest people in the world change when they play. They get giddy, they get mean, they get greedy, they get stupid. Again, just like show business.

If you think about it, you can figure out someone's personality by how he bets his money. Brad, who rarely gambles, likes blackjack. It means he's a little more conservative and in control. With craps, you're never in control. You make a decision to hit or not hit, but the dice have no brain. When I'm at the table my true nature emerges. I never bet "Don't Pass," which means going against the shooter, and I always bet two and twelve, because it's thirty-to-one and you can make $3,000 for a $100 bet.

Gambling is in my blood. In fact, my betting experiences have made me a much better manager and negotiator. If you bust big at a craps table — not a penny left, no credit, no friends to call — your mind flips faster than when you have to figure the angles on some Hollywood deal. When you have to leave town with only a complimentary pack of cigarettes and the change from the five bucks someone loaned you for a cab, all you think about on the plane ride home is, "Where will I get the money? How can I do it without getting hurt?" If you owe a shylock $70,000 when you only make $25,000 a year — and all of that goes to rent and alimony — show-business anxiety is a piece of cake. You enter the negotiating arena with a unique frame of mind.

Let me put it in plain English: you're not scared. In a town that runs largely on fear, nothing is more valuable. So what if a deal falls through? If you're willing to walk away from a lot of money, the person you're negotiating with will usually back down. If someone I negotiate with goes back on a deal point, I just leave the table. When Brad and I did deals, if the other party said a particular word or advocated a position we couldn't tolerate we'd walk.

"Bye, gentlemen. The meeting's over."

I don't yell. In fact, I usually don't say anything. Most of the time they run after me. I've had network presidents chase me through parking lots. As long as your clients trust you and know you're acting in their best interests — and you'd better be — you're in the clear. If the deal dies, it was probably meant to. So you blew the commission. Trust me, you'll get it all back and maybe more some other time, when the deal is right.

There's a life span to every deal. If a negotiation goes for more than four days before someone says, "Okay, we're in the same ballpark," I don't believe it's ever going to happen. You can tell by the first phone call what's going on. If the other guy says, "I'm coming over now and I'm not leaving until I have the deal," you're in good shape. If he says, "What's the soonest you can meet?" you're in good shape. If he says, "Oh, I'm very glad to see your client is available and interested. I'll get back to you," then ninety-nine times out of a hundred it's never going to happen. In this business, timing is everything.

Does this mean that the art of the deal is like buying a car? More or less, except that you don't have to see the car salesman the next week at a movie premiere or sitcom taping. In show business, people you treat badly, or who treat you badly, have a habit of turning up when you least want to see them. So, if you're going to walk away from a deal, it's best to really believe in the principles you're standing on and not just play at them as a negotiating ploy. It's not always easy, particularly in a business dominated by short-term instead of long-term thinking. It's tough to see money slip away. The fear that your client will be pissed is chilling. But it's the best way. If you're moral and honest, people will gossip about that as much as anything else, and your reputation will precede you.

•••••

Laura hated my gambling. I don't blame her, because she hung in with me when I was broke and in the hole. Eventually she made me swear off, which I did until we got married in June 1967. I began to sneak around again. I guess in an unhappy marriage it was my way of proving to her that I could do what I wanted to, even if it meant walking away a loser.

That's pretty much how I felt in the mid-'60s. I was almost thirty-five. I didn't understand women, I owed money, and I'd begun to believe that I might not make it in life. Me being me, I tried to keep up a good front. I acted confident, well connected, hip, and in the know, a guy who got the joke — and I did. I played my "role" as a character and a good audience. But mostly things kept going wrong.

Once, to cheer me up, Jerry Weintraub and Jane Morgan took me to San Juan, Puerto Rico, where Jane was working. Right away I felt terrible that they insisted on paying for everything. At the hotel, they had a big suite and I had a tiny room. Walking through the hallway I ran into a girl I'd gone out with. She was a couple doors down — with another guy. I was so embarrassed that I just smiled and kept moving. When I got back to my room and used the toilet, it overflowed. My luck was so bad that even I had to laugh at how pathetic I was. Of course, I was also upset, but when you can't do anything about a situation the best thing you can do is move on. That's part of what makes me a survivor.

•••••

There was only one bright spot in my life: Management Three. We were growing. Weintraub signed Frankie Valli and the Four Seasons. Kummer brought in Julia Meade, and a choreographer named Hugh Lambert, who eventually married Nancy Sinatra. We had Paar, Jane Morgan, Henson, Norm Crosby, Burns and Schreiber, and a few others.

Then we became one-third owners, with Ward Ellis and George Wilkins, of a Los Angeles–based act called the Doodletown Pipers, a twenty-person young singing group (ten boys, ten girls), which I handled. With that, and our clients always in Las Vegas, and a desire to move into television, we realized that Management Three needed a West Coast presence.

One day, in early 1967, Ed Sullivan's son-in-law (and producer), Bob Precht, told us CBS wanted to do a summer show called *Our Place*, and they'd decided the Doodletown Pipers, Burns and Schreiber, and Rowlf the dog should host. Sounds boring now, maybe even then — particularly to the baby boomers in the Summer of Love — but I didn't care about that. Plenty of viewers from my generation, suckled on Mitch Miller sing-alongs, would be happy for an hour of lively entertainment to take their minds off their long-haired sons and incense-burning daughters. Besides, our fee would be $500 a week. In fact, forget the money; here was a network show with three of my acts on it. What a miracle! That did it. The show was in New York, but to take advantage of our first package on the air we knew we had to open up on the Coast.

Now the only question was who would go.

Of course, they picked me. I was still the only single guy and it made sense — at least according to my partners. I suppose so, but deep down I've always believed that they chose me because it left them in New York and in charge. We were all legally equal but because of Jerry's extroverted personality and Marty being Marty, I was really the junior member of the team.

In any case, they didn't need to convince me. It seemed like a great way to get out of my life and start over. Plus it was February in New York. Marty and I flew to Los Angeles and found an office at 144 South Beverly Drive, in Beverly Hills. It wasn't much, just one room on the fourth floor, but I thought it would be fine.

I told Laura and she wasn't thrilled. But she was still waiting for her divorce to become final, and I was glad to be away from her pressure, too.

I told my clients. Henson wasn't crazy about the move, but he understood. We figured Jerry or Marty could easily take care of him. Norm trusted me. He knew I wanted to get him on TV and that Los Angeles was the place. Burns and Schreiber agreed for the same reason. Jack was a great writer and Avery could do situation comedy.

I worried about what my parents would say, but my instincts said to seize the opportunity. Then my mother got sick. She checked into

Doctor's Hospital and had some tests. We all waited, on edge, until they decided she wouldn't die anytime soon. The day before I was scheduled to board a plane for Los Angeles, I visited her at the hospital. All the relatives were there, carrying on in my face: "How can you go to California? You've got to stay. How dare you?" That wasn't unusual. What Jewish family doesn't try to suck the kids into devoting their lives to them? It makes me think of a line Alan Zweibel once wrote: "My mother was never happy when I got married. She wanted me to marry one of my sisters."

My father listened to this for a while and then he took me aside and said, "Let's go for a walk." We meandered quietly, shoulder to shoulder through the antiseptic halls. Finally, he stopped, turned, looked me in the eyes, and said, "You want to end up a loser like me?"

My father was far from a loser, but I knew what he meant. "Not particularly," I answered.

"Then get the fuck out of here," he said, biting down hard on the sentence. "Get away from the lunacy. Get on that plane."

He literally pushed me out the door.

I was released.

Laura drove me to the airport. I had a B-24 bag — the kind pilots used during the war — with tape around it and all my worldly goods inside. As usual I had very little money. But so what? I was about to start a new life. In fact, I was excited and hopeful, except for the one thing that really scared me.

I was moving to a city where the car was king, and I'd never learned to drive.

Chapter 5

My Wink Is Binding

I arrived in Los Angeles on a Sunday afternoon. George Shapiro, my old friend from the William Morris mail room, met me at the airport. He'd become an agent in the West Coast office. Only a few years earlier I'd told him, "You're from New York. You're smart. Go to California. They're not real bright out there. You should do very well." George drove me to the Sunset Marquis, my hotel just off the Sunset Strip. Afterwards, we had dinner at Lawry's steak house on La Cienega and caught up on old times.

At six o'clock the next morning I had my first driving lesson. I went every day that week, at the same time, for two hours of intense instruction. On Friday, I took the test and got my license. Saturday morning I pulled out of the hotel garage in a brand-new blue Chevy Impala and smashed the fender into a concrete post. Good thing it was a rental. A week later, on my way to Beverly Hills, the rearview mirror fell apart and hung by a screw. I held it with one hand, the steering wheel with the other, and limped along at four miles an hour until I pulled into the Union 76 station at Crescent and Santa Monica. I rolled down the window and yelled: "New driver in trouble! New driver in trouble!" They were so nice to me that I still go there to get my gas.

My first day in the office started well. I walked in and heard the phone ringing off the hook. Right away I thought, "Hey, everyone knows I'm in California!" Then I discovered that my business number had once belonged to the casting office at Twentieth Century Fox. Want to know a manager's idea of hell? All day long people call you, desperate for jobs you can't get them.

I was lonely. Only the William Morris office a block away made me feel the least bit on familiar ground. Whenever I could, I prevailed upon old friends for lunch at the Hamburger Hamlet or Wil Wright's ice cream and sandwich shop. At night I had insomnia. On weekends, when the Sunset Strip was overrun with hippies and so packed with cars that you could only inch along, I'd get something to eat at Ben Franks's coffee shop and then get caught in traffic on purpose just to pass the time. Later, back at the Sunset Marquis, I'd call Laura.

Sometimes, I'd drive through Beverly Hills and Bel Air and look at the houses — mansions, to me. I figured the only way I could ever afford one would be to be like my friend Alan Bernard, who managed Andy Williams. Alan had just scored Williams a record deal with a $3 million advance, meaning his commission was at least $450,000. Add to that his percentage of Williams's TV and personal appearances, and Alan could support a home at each *end* of Bel Air.

Not that I had anything to complain about. Only ten years ago I'd made $32 a week at William Morris and for a $25,000-a-year contract I'd have sold out and signed up for life, saying, "Give me that security." Now I made that $25,000 and took Sunday drives in neighborhoods where you couldn't tell the movie stars' homes without a special map. I had a new idea of what success and security truly meant, and it made me want what I'd always wanted — only more so: to feel like a vital part of the show-business community, to walk into a restaurant and have everyone know my name. All I had to do was get the calls, not make the calls; have the client everyone had to have; come up with the hot idea that got me respect, and then execute it. Then, the money would come, and with it security and freedom. I knew money didn't buy happiness; I could be happy sitting in bed, eating a tuna fish sandwich, watching a ball game. You don't need much money for that.

I still awoke each day afraid that whatever I'd accomplished would go away, but somehow my anxiety had less edge. I suppose that driving every morning past the luxurious pink-stuccoed and palm tree–studded Beverly Hills Hotel — where one day I'd have a table permanently reserved for me in the world-famous Polo Lounge — made it easy to believe that good things were just around the corner. How could I not feel more confident than fearful in a place where the sun probably shined even when it rained? I knew people trusted me and that I could talk to anyone. I'd worked hard and survived some rough times. I believed I had a future. The only question was how that future would reveal itself. I didn't expect things to be easy, but I was willing to bet on myself. That wasn't some grand inspiration. I was on my own and had no alternative.

In the same building, on the third floor — I was on the fourth — was a hot management company called BNB. That stood for Sherwood Bash, Mace Neufeld (still a big movie producer), and Alan Bernard. They handled everyone from astronauts Neil Armstrong and Scott Carpenter to Andy Williams, Sergio Mendez, Herb Alpert, and Don Knotts. Meanwhile, I sat in my little office with the Doodletown Pipers and my dreams. I used to hang around BNB Management, and for some reason they were nice to me. I'd get their leftovers and good advice. (Too bad that spirit has disappeared from show business.) When they packaged *The Don Knotts Show*, they even hired Peppiatt and Aylesworth to produce. It was also the first time I'd seen managers package a show, and that gave me some good ideas of my own for the future.

After a few months, Jim Henson came to visit. I can still picture us in our bathing suits at the Sunset Marquis pool: one guy who looked like Santa's son, the other like a string bean in a Jesus wig; both of them staring at girls in bikinis and hoping the girls would stare back. I was glad Jim had come. I wanted to get back in his life, not leave him to Jerry and Marty. We talked and reestablished our personal connection. It also helped that I introduced him to some film people and landed him a few TV jobs.

A year later, when I booked Norm Crosby as a regular on *The Beautiful Phyllis Diller Show,* he and his wife, Joanie, moved west as Burns and Schreiber had earlier after finishing work in New York on *Our Place,* the CBS summer variety series. Soon, I signed the comedian Shelley Berman, and the singer Frankie Laine, a wonderful guy who still generated eighty grand a year in commissions. Life wasn't so bad.

I'd also returned briefly to New York in June 1967 to marry Laura. Eight of my friends took me out before the wedding and told me not to do it. What can I say? She was a tough, opinionated hustler with great legs, they didn't particularly like her, and they knew I had my own doubts. I didn't listen to them or myself. We got married at the Englewood Country Club, then Laura and her kids, Scott and Stacy, whom I've always loved, moved west. We rented a house and were finally one big . . . family.

• • • • •

Marty and Jerry told me to sign stars. That was easy for them to want, but hard for me to do. What was I going to say to a star? What did Steve Lawrence and Eydie Gormé need with me? But my partners insisted, so I arranged a lunch with Jack Palance, through his press agent. We ate at the Brown Derby and had a great time. When it was over Palance said, "Bernie, I love you, but what can you do for me?"

"Absolutely nothing," I said. "I'm too new at this. I don't get scripts. I can't do anything yet."

"Okay," Palance said, smiling that sly sideways smile, "then let's be friends."

That was fine with me. When you have nothing to offer, you can still offer your friendship.

Trying to do what Marty and Jerry wanted seemed to me like pursuing rejection. For nearly a year I came up dry. Then I wised up. I asked myself, "Since I can't get stars, who can I get? Where is no one else going?"

The answer hit me more out of desperation than inspiration: creative and below-the-line people. Writers, producers, art directors, wardrobe designers, choreographers, musicians. I was right. They were thrilled that someone even wanted to talk to them. Few had agents; most made their own deals.

My roster of nonperformers quickly became a great source of steady revenue. A comedian had to be booked every night or week. For the same sit-down negotiation, for the same phone calls, I could book a band leader on a show where *he'd stay for seven years*. I'd get commission every week. So what if the money wasn't the same? It was money. And it added up.

Another happy discovery: unlike actors and comedians, most of whom are terribly insecure, creative people recommend each other for jobs and will even tell their friends that they have a good manager. Based on referrals, I signed music directors Jack Elliot and Alan Ferguson, as well as a couple of producers from Canada, Frank Peppiatt and John Aylesworth, who'd run *The Jimmy Dean Show*. I also signed a young director named John Moffitt, who had worked on *Our Place*, and whom I had known since he was an assistant director on *The Ed Sullivan Show*.

I didn't realize it then, but going after writer-producers gave me a jump on the changes happening in TV production. For years, nonwriting producers and big-name stars had the most clout, but soon the men and women who could create a series and run it would become the medium's new royalty. Today the networks and studios, desperate to hang on to a shrinking audience, hand out multimillion-dollar deals like candy to writers and producers, hoping they'll come up with new hits.

It was just good luck. I had no grand plan, but timing is everything.

But Jerry and Marty weren't interested in my below-the-line clients. They kept yelling, "Stars! Stars! Stars!" That pissed me off, and Laura, too. After all, they weren't on the front line, and I was doing the best I could under the circumstances. Laura thought they still treated me like a junior member of the team.

The more Jerry and Marty pushed me, the more Laura pressured me to quit. The end came in 1968 after I'd pulled off a difficult booking and got Jane Morgan on *The Hollywood Palace*, because I'd made friends with the producer, Nick Vanoff. Nick liked me. I'd go to his office before the new season and take out my client list, half of whom he'd hire. He didn't mind making me a hero because he knew that if I ever had someone he wanted, he'd get the first shot.

I went to the dress rehearsal with Jane, but being a one-man company I couldn't stay for the show. I had to go back to the office. When Jerry found out, he was furious. That did it.

The actual breakup was surprisingly hassle-free. I left without trying to take any of my clients, but when it was done, eighteen stayed with me, including Norm Crosby, Jim Henson, Burns and Schreiber, Frankie Laine, Peppiatt and Aylesworth, John Moffitt, and the Doodletown Pipers. I was flattered and amazed. That I'd still have to share commissions on those acts for a year was besides the point.

All Marty, Jerry, and I had left to do was split about $100,000 we'd made after Marty had put together and sent on tour a South African variety show called *Wait a Minim*. We'd each wanted to grab our piece when we banked it but decided instead to set it aside in a special fund to do other shows. I thought I'd walk away with $33,000. But guess what? The money was gone. Marty had used it to cover a gambling debt. Jerry and I said, "What are we going to do, put him in jail? We probably would have done the same thing."

Like the company itself, or a bad roll of the dice, we just let it go. Typical gambler's mentality to the end.

• • • • •

I renamed my business The Brillstein Company and kept the office at 144 South Beverly Drive. Laura, who had never wanted me to be partners with Jerry and Marty in the first place, said, "I'll come in and help out, you don't need to hire anyone." She learned accounting over the phone from her mother, did my books and some of my clients' books, and shared secretarial duties. My job was to keep it all together and I wasn't doing half bad. So what if I didn't have any major stars? My clients were solid, the list was growing, and at least I no longer had to introduce myself as "Bernie Brillstein comma Management Three."

• • • • •

To be a manager you need a management philosophy, a mission statement. Mine was quite simple: have lots of clients. The reasons are both economic and primal.

Most managers in those days had only one or two clients. Their sales pitch was, "I can devote the time to *you*." I couldn't afford that. Without the guaranteed salary from Management Three, none of my acts generated enough in commissions to support me. I *needed* more, and as is often the case, budget dictated style.

Sometimes a comedian and I would talk about representation and he'd ask why he should come to me when I already had so many comedians. (He's really asking how he'll get the love and attention he wants.) It's a valid question, and I say, "First, I wouldn't represent you if I didn't believe in you. Second, since I have so many comedians, I know every job for every comedian. With me, you're in the mix."

I also figured that if I represented five comedians, what the first one couldn't do, maybe number four could. No reason not to hedge your bets as long as you believe in everyone you sign. I did. I wasn't about to sacrifice quality for quantity.

But on the most basic level, my reason for having multiple clients is that I simply don't trust show business. I'd learned from watching my uncle Jack not to depend on one person because at any moment he can decide to get out of the business and you'll starve to death. When only one or a couple people are responsible for your income, you're a slave rather than a friend or advisor. And believe me, talent can smell when you're vulnerable. I have never forgotten how, when I was just starting out, *in one day*, managers Al Bruno and Tom Shields lost Mike Douglas, Johnny Carson, and Jimmy Dean. Each thought the other was getting too much attention. Can you imagine the emotional and financial wreckage? That was enough to make anyone forever paranoid.

I approach management like the stock market. If I own only Disney shares, it's great when the company's doing well and the stock splits three for one. But what if Michael Eisner croaks and the company tanks? I'd rather be in mutual funds and spread the risk. That's pretty much what we do today at Brillstein-Grey. In a strong market we clean up; in a weak market we're diversified enough to survive.

I have clients I love so much — and vice versa — and I believe they will never leave me. But that doesn't mean I'll close my eyes and ears to the possibility, however slight. It happens.

From a personal falling out to not wanting to pay commission to the client discovering his house is smaller than yours, there are, to paraphrase Paul Simon, many ways to leave your manager. One of my favorites: When a client says "How come?" a good manager knows he's already dead meat. When a woman says it, same thing.

Some stars are simply self-destructive. You can believe in yourself as a manager all you want and it won't bring them back from the edge unless they want to come back. I saw my uncle Jack put himself out of business. I was there when John Belushi and Chris Farley died. Christian Slater saved himself. Phil Hartman didn't have a say. Garry Shandling . . . well, who can explain him? People who put on makeup for a living exist on mood, whim, impulse, and who knows what else? That's their great gift, and their great weakness.

Some guys who handle only one client think they have wonderful lives. Maybe they do. They book their act in Las Vegas for a month and then tag along. The hotel gives them a suite and complimentary food. It's a paid vacation. But I believe that the more the star sees his manager hanging around, the more pissed off he gets. Stars crave the attention, but somewhere in their brain they're thinking, "What the fuck is he doing here? I have to do two shows a night. What's he doing?"

Bottom line: you can be with someone for twenty years, have coproduction deals, vacation together, and be best friends, but it can still end in a minute. You can never tell which way the wind blows in this screwed-up business. If you're not careful it will knock you on your ass. People think show business is so wonderful — and it can be — but in other ways it's not so different from selling car batteries at Goodyear. If some guy walks in and breaks your balls, the dissatisfied customer is always right and you get the hook.

By the way, *always get the check.* I'm not talking about paying for your client's dinner. I mean make sure his checks come to you, or the agent, so commissions can come immediately off the top.

No matter how well a manager does for his talent, some still hate to pay their commissions. It's not because clients are criminals who want to stiff their representatives — even if it *is* true in some dark corner of their narcissistic little hearts — the real problem is psychological. Once a big check is in the client's hands he doesn't want to let it go. The bigger the check, the more it sticks — like superglue. In my experience, $10,000 is usually the cutoff point; never let anyone owe you that much or you'll never get paid because when the client sees a number that large or larger, he thinks three things:

"Why am I paying this much?"

"But I can't spare [fill in commission here] now, to write this check."

"What is he *doing* for that kind of money?"

You could be the smartest guy in the world and never have the right answers. Get the checks.

I have one other management rule: no contracts.

A handshake is good enough. My wink is binding.

If you have no contract there's nothing to break. You have to trust each other. It's me and the client against the world. When you no longer want to work together, good-bye and nice knowing you. No piece of paper will make someone stick around who wants to go. It won't guarantee getting paid, either. A contract to ensure that is like saying in advance that you don't trust the guy who's putting his life in your hands. Why set up that dynamic? If I'm as good as I think I am, and I make my clients happy, why in the world would they leave? Yes, I listed a few reasons above, but those guys I want gone anyway. Life is too short.

This approach hasn't hurt me; if it was bad business, then Brad wouldn't do the same thing today. We set up our management relationships as an honorable undertaking. People who understand this make the best clients.

For instance, Danny Aykroyd went his own way when I became head of Lorimar Pictures in 1987. He said, "I can't understand the head of a management company also running a studio. There's something wrong about it." I told Danny it could only work in his favor, but he laughed. He's such a straight citizen. Maybe he was right. With no paper to haggle over, the parting was friendly. And he's such a good guy that although I haven't represented him in years, every month he sends the Blues Brothers records' royalties I'm due, or a commission on an old acting job. Sometimes the check is for $17. Doesn't matter. I love that continuity and caring and respect, and I love giving it back.

• • • • •

While I slowly established my business, Norm Crosby began to get noticed in Las Vegas. He worked at the Sahara, consistently did well, and had a great relationship with the hotel. One day the entertainment director took him aside and said, "We're thinking about moving Don Rickles into the main room and putting you into the lounge as our headliner." The lounge was a great job, an intimate room that always filled up, and in those days they featured the stars: Shecky Greene, Count Basie, Duke Ellington, Don Rickles, Rowan and Martin. Big acts with marquee names. The headliner did two shows, one at 10:30 P.M., the other at 2:30 A.M.

Norm called to tell me about the offer. At the time, he was making probably $1,000 a week. I flew in and went up to his room. I said, "I'll go talk with them, figure out what they want. You stay here. I'll be right back."

This is what they offered: twenty weeks a year for three years; $5,000 a week the first year; $7,500 a week the second year; $10,000 a week the third year. It came to $450,000 for three years. My cut would be $67,000. It was a lot of money and we both needed it. I'm sure that while I took the meeting, Norm was already spending his newfound wealth — in his head: a house for his mother, cars for his dad and brother.

I came back and told Norm the offer. He stopped me in the middle and said there were so many numbers that he could use them to dial the telephone. Then I said, "That's funny, but I turned it down." Norm, who's hard of hearing, somehow heard perfectly. And he wanted to kill me. I told him to cool off and explained that while the numbers were seductive, they were also deceiving.

"First of all, they're not going to move Don Rickles out for another year," I said. "That means you'll be working the lounge at the in-between times for a year. You'll go on at four P.M. and seven P.M. There'll be six people in the audience: two drunks and two hookers with johns they're looking to promote. Maybe there'll be a couple cocktail waitresses waiting to go to work. If you sang and played guitar, you could do it to the wall. But to do comedy you need people. Lots of people. If you take this job it will break your heart.

"Also, even though the hotel wants you now, you're still not well enough known outside Las Vegas. You need more marquee value. Instead of jumping at what seems like a great offer, we should do some more TV and nightclubs and get exposure. Things are only improving for you, and I really believe we should wait until you can bring in people on your name alone."

"And then what?" Norm asked.

"And then I'll start you off at ten thousand a week, go to fifteen, then twenty thousand — and we'll do the same deal."

It took balls to pass, and for Norm to agree, but saying no made more sense than taking the easy money. Having a career means sticking around for a long time. If the talent is good and the manager isn't greedy, if he can think about the client's best interests and not his own percentage, the rest is easy. I always bet on my clients' long-term potential.

However, if Norm had said, "I've never seen so much money. I have two kids, I'm buying a house, I need it. I want it," then I would have gone back and said, "Deal."

As I'd hoped, Norm continued to make his name. Two years later the Sahara still wanted him, and I did exactly what I'd promised: I made the same deal, but for double the money. He went on at the right times and the place was always full. And here's the capper: when Tom Jones saw Norm perform, he asked him to open a seventy-city tour. His offer: $4,000 a show, a hotel suite, and first-class everything. Norm had a great time.

• • • • •

Jim Henson had always been one of my most popular and productive clients. He'd done the *Today* show, *The Tonight Show*, guest spots with Ed Sullivan, Steve Allen, Jack Paar, and most anyone else you could think

of. And Rowlf had starred on *The Jimmy Dean Show.* Jim still made commercials — remember the La Choy Dragon? — and in 1968 he made a
TV special about puppetry.

In the late '60s, Joan Ganz Cooney, a producer at the Children's
Television Workshop, met Jim at a conference and asked him to create a
cast of Muppet characters to populate a new educational TV show for
children. The show was based on the premise that kids were complex beings who should be treated with respect. She also asked him to help develop the program. That was *Sesame Street.* Jim asked me what I thought.

It seemed perfect for him. He always did odd and unusual projects
and this seemed to fit the mold. Most people don't know this, but between
1965 and 1969, Jim also did three award-winning experimental films —
Time Piece, Youth '68, and *The Cube* — without the Muppets. IBM's film
and video guy, David Lazer, who would one day become president of The
Henson Company, thought Jim was brilliant and approached him with
funding. Jim also made little "coffee break" films for IBM. It was as if the
guy had two careers: one public and successful, the other personal and
noncommercial. They fed each other.

Jim loved children, believed in educational TV, and found great joy
in designing and building his characters. For *Sesame Street* these included, at first, Bert and Ernie, Oscar the Grouch, Grover, Cookie Monster, and Big Bird. Even though these characters are as much a part of
our culture today as, say, baseball, Jim never thought of himself as just a
kids' act. In fact, the popularity of *Sesame Street* made him want to hang
on to his older audience even more.

In 1969 we decided to try and sell an adult-oriented *Muppet Show* to
TV. The presentation was a beautiful "book" depicting Kermit as a talk-
show host. (I still keep it in my desk drawer.) The concept was based on
Rowan and Martin's Laugh-In, which was a hit at the time. We figured that
puppets could get away with saying things that people couldn't, and I
thought, based on what Jim had already done, that selling the show to a
network would be a slam dunk.

I was wrong. Every network said, "A frog can't host a show," and
"Puppets don't work at night." Even Michael Eisner, when he was at ABC,
turned us down. That pissed me off. I knew instinctively — and I'll be
glad to raise my hand and take the credit on this one — that the Muppets
would work after dark.

My frustration gave me a bad case of insomnia. One night, I was so wide awake at 3 A.M. that I probably should have dressed and gone to the office. My restlessness must have been contagious because Laura also woke up.

"What are you doing?" she asked, half awake and annoyed.

"If I can't sell the Muppets, then I'm going to sell something else," I answered. I'd found a list of the week's top ten shows on my desk and I'd been staring at it, waiting for inspiration to strike. *Green Acres, The Andy Griffith Show, The Beverly Hillbillies, Laugh-In.* . . . Suddenly it hit me: How about a country *Laugh-In?* I turned to Laura and said, "What does a donkey say when he makes that fucking sound?"

"Hee-haw," she said.

"That's it!"

And that's how, at 3 A.M. a New York Jew named Bernie Brillstein created *Hee Haw.*

• • • • •

I couldn't sell *Hee Haw* if I went to a network by myself. Not because it was a crazy idea, but because nobody knew me. I wasn't on anyone's list of approved writers. I wasn't a producer or some wheeler-dealer. I knew very little about packaging a show. I was just a little manager with a few nice clients. Fortunately, I managed the guys I thought could take it all the way.

Frank Peppiatt and John Aylesworth were a couple of white-bread Canadian producers I knew from New York. They'd done *Sinatra: The Man and His Music.* They'd worked with my client Jack Burns on the teen dance show *Hullabaloo.* I'd sold them the Muppet dog Rowlf when they did *The Jimmy Dean Show.* They had an offbeat sense of humor. We all loved hockey and got along well. After I moved to Los Angeles, they came out in 1968 to produce *The Jonathan Winters Show.* When we got together they asked me to represent them even though they already had a manager named Jerry Katz. I had to split the commission, but I needed clients and I figured that handling *working* producers couldn't be bad. I took 5 percent. Katz wasn't thrilled at my participation, but eventually he welcomed the help because Peppiatt and Aylesworth were such crazy guys.

After coming up with the idea for *Hee Haw* I made some notes and got a couple hours sleep. Later that morning I called Peppiatt and Aylesworth and asked them to drop by the office. They made themselves comfortable and I came right to the point: "How about a country *Laugh-In*? We'll have a cornfield instead of a joke wall." Obviously, I'd liberally helped myself to everything I could from *Rowan and Martin's Laugh-In* — except the hyphen — and then changed it all around. What can I say? *Laugh-In* was a classic adaptable to many formats, from Muppets to moonshine.

Peppiatt and Aylesworth loved the idea and wrote it up that day. The next morning we had breakfast at the Polo Lounge in the Beverly Hills Hotel so I could go over the material and decide what to do next. While waiting for the check, I looked around the room and saw Perry Lafferty and Mike Dann at another table. Lafferty headed production and Dann ran programming at CBS. Lafferty loved Peppiatt and Aylesworth, so we took our balls in our hands, and walked over. On the spot I talked him into buying *Hee Haw* as a summer replacement series.

It was the first show I ever sold.

• • • • •

The best time spent with any project is when you put it together: having the idea is great, making the deal is fantastic, announcing it is wonderful. The whole thing is so seductive and romantic — then it's "Oh shit, now we have to do the work!"

When you sell a TV show, the network pays for it by giving the financially responsible producers — in this case, Peppiatt and Aylesworth — a weekly license fee. The money is supposed to cover what it costs to make the show. The network makes their money by selling commercial time during the program.

That's still how it works, except that when we did *Hee Haw*, an efficient producer could make the show for less than the license fee and actually walk away with a profit. Today, it's ass-backwards. Everything's too expensive. Unions, big writer-producer deals, and star salaries have driven up costs. With an average sitcom license fee of $600,000 to $700,000, there is no profit to the producers, and usually you run a deficit.

For thirteen summer shows, CBS gave us $85,000 for each hour. I got $1,000 per episode for having the idea. To save money, we shot an entire season in about five or six weeks at the CBS affiliate in Nashville. We did block shooting — all the music at once, all the comedy at once —

and then cut it together later. We paid the cast members only a couple thousand per show, but they didn't seem to mind. When we wrapped they went on tour and, because of our nationwide exposure, made a fortune. This wasn't the *Grand Ole Opry*. *Hee Haw* was seen on hundreds of stations.

Peppiatt, Aylesworth, and I had never been to Nashville. It was a world unto itself. The people at the Holiday Inn called me "Mr. Brill-en-stein" and gave me what I've always called "the Jew suite," at the back of the hotel, by the railroad tracks. Nashville was an unusual place for a Jew to be, and it caused a few problems. First, the station manager wanted to send our Jewish producer back to Los Angeles because he didn't "understand how things were done." Then, when we booked Ray Charles, who had a hot country album at the time, the cast walked out. It's a shame, but you can imagine why — and not because Ray was Jewish. We eventually coaxed them back and Ray did his song, but it taught me a lesson. From then on I had Jack McFadden — Buck Owens's manager — front for Mr. Brill-en-stein and take care of things. Of course, it's 1999, and I'm sure things have long since changed in Nashville.

Hee Haw debuted on CBS in the summer of 1969 and we did an incredible 41 share. A share measures what percentage of people watching TV at any one time are watching a given show. Share is different from rating. Today, a ratings point represents about 980,000 homes; it's about 1 percent of homes with TV sets. Ratings only measure how many people are watching. You need share to determine how big that group is compared to the total number of people in front of their sets at the time. These days what's most important to advertisers is demographics. The idea is to target products to specific audience age groups, eighteen to forty-nine being the desired range. A ratings point in the eighteen-to-forty-nine age group equals about 1.23 million people. A show watched by these consumers — even if low-rated — often has a better chance of being left on the air to find its audience. These days, the eighteen-to-thirty-four group is even more sought-after.

Hee Haw had a great summer, then got a big break. After three successful seasons, and being renewed for a fourth, *The Smothers Brothers Comedy Hour* was suddenly canceled.

I was sitting in my father's little office on Thirty-eighth Street, in the millinery district, when the phone rang. He answered it and said, "There's a guy named Mike Dann on the phone." (When they want you they find you wherever you are!) Dann told me he was giving *Hee Haw* a spot on the schedule, in prime time. I renegotiated our deal to up the license fee. Jerry Rubin, who had worked with me at William Morris and was then the head of business affairs at CBS, said he would give me the highest price they'd given anyone: $155,000 an hour for above- and below-the-line costs. When I just stared at him, Jerry realized that I had no idea what above and below the line meant. He told me it was the total cost of production, talent being above the line, crew and sets, etc., being below. Then he helped me through the deal like a good friend.

Using our block-shooting approach we were able to keep the budget at about $100,000. Peppiatt and Aylesworth split the rest. Now I got $2,000 a show. We were a big hit and stayed on for two highly rated seasons, until Fred Silverman — the programming legend who would soon make ABC number one and then run NBC until the early '80s — threw everything off CBS that was country.

That would have been it for most shows, but Peppiatt and Aylesworth didn't want to abandon such a popular series on a programmer's whim. Nick Vanoff, who owned *The Hollywood Palace,* had an idea: if the big networks didn't want *Hee Haw* they could still produce it and syndicate it to stations that did. At the time, first-run syndication was a relatively new concept. Today it's commonplace, and there's big money in shows like the *Star Trek* franchise, *Baywatch, Hercules, Xena, Oprah, Wheel of Fortune, Jeopardy,* and *The New Hollywood Squares.* Peppiatt and Aylesworth weren't ready to give up on the show and they decided to go for it.

In first-run syndication there is no license fee. The production company has to pay for everything. For *Hee Haw* they had to make new shows because the residual to cast members for reusing the original CBS hours would have put them out of business before they began. To raise the initial production capital, Peppiatt, Aylesworth, and Vanoff had to mortgage their houses. I didn't think that was smart. I fought with the guys. Sure, I'd make money if they were successful, but to risk their homes? As their manager I thought that was wrong. They didn't listen, so I helped set up a partnership between them and Vanoff called Yonge Street Productions. Vanoff owned 50 percent, and Peppiatt and Aylesworth split 50. Then we renegotiated all the players' contracts to get some breathing room.

At first everyone took scale salaries and made no money, but Vanoff sold the show relentlessly, bartering it in exchange for a percentage of revenue from advertising time sold during the time slot. A couple years later everyone made millions.

Everyone but me.

I was in for the same money as before, plus 10 percent of Peppiatt and Aylesworth's share of potential profits. Maybe I should have insisted on being a partner because the show was my idea, but managers were rarely producers or participants. I thought of myself as creative, but only in the sense that I had seven comedians in Las Vegas making $20,000 to $30,000 a week, so I was doing okay. I didn't know from being an owner. It wasn't something I ever thought about. Telling Peppiatt and Aylesworth not to mortgage their homes was the best advice I could give at the time, but it started to drive me crazy. It didn't seem fair that I got so little for my own creation. I realized I should have had a third of the show from the beginning, on CBS. I'd made a costly mistake.

Laura didn't let me forget. She kept nudging me. You know how a wife can nudge? "You're not getting enough. You're not getting enough."

I went to Nick Vanoff, panicked. I said, "Nick, I don't think I'm making what I should from the show."

He said, "Well, what do you want?"

I said, "Seventy-five thousand a year."

He said, "You've got it."

I said, "Why didn't you just give it to me?"

He said, "Why didn't you ask?"

The money made Laura happy, but I had grown increasingly unhappy with her. Laura had helped me build the company. She was ambitious and sharp, but she was not a manager. I know that sounds politically incorrect, but she behaved in ways that I considered detrimental to the business. She would insist I work with certain people and not with others. Sometimes she was right, but the way she put it was too rough. She came from the School of Fuck You! I had enough aggravation without her always turning incident into drama. Laura never got the big picture. She was always at war, not only with me but with some of the clients. A lot of people didn't like her.

In private, she could come home from the office, purse over her arm, and cook an incredible dinner for eight people. But she was also jealous and hard on the kids. She treated my daughter Leigh abominably.

I wanted peace and was ready to ask her not to come into the office anymore.

My relationship with Peppiatt and Aylesworth had also become ac-
rimonious because they stopped paying my commission. It was a strange
time, with yelling and screaming and recriminations between former
friends about who owed what to whom. Forget any extra money for my
having thought up *Hee Haw*, I'd made these guys millionaires and all I
wanted was to get what was rightfully mine. But I didn't see any money
again until Peppiatt's wife, Valerie, threatened to leave him if he didn't do
the right thing. When he did, so did Aylesworth. I understand why they
acted like pricks: no one likes to write the big check, and since the money
didn't go through an agency, it ended up sticking to their fingers. Later,
Yonge Street Productions sold the show to Gaylord Entertainment and I
got a chunk of money, but it was more of a fee than fair compensation. I
was pissed but there wasn't much I could do about it. The only way to
keep from dwelling on my mistake was to be philosophical. That's life.
Everyone in Hollywood has at least one of these stories, and more likely
ten. It's easier said than done, but I knew it was time to move on and remember the lesson: Never give away an idea. If you create it, be part of it.
Own your own stuff.

· · · · ·

If nothing else, the *Hee Haw* experience gave me a small reputation
as a junior packager. This helped me get more clients.

For me, having clients come in by referral was always preferable to
making the cold call. But now and then there were exceptions. One Sunday in 1970 I dozed off while watching a football game on CBS. When I
opened my eyes I saw something that made me wonder if I was still
dreaming: bums modeling clothes on TV. I couldn't stop laughing. The
show was called *The William Tell Oversight*, and the writers were two guys
named Tom Patchett and Jay Tarses. I'd never heard of either but I
wanted to meet them right away. I checked around the next day and
learned that Patchett and Tarses were represented by a guy named Dick
Howard. They had a stand-up act and played mostly at Playboy Clubs and
little lounges. In other words, they were going nowhere, slowly. When I
reached Howard he reluctantly told me his clients were performing at
some Lake Tahoe joint. I dialed the number.

When I did reach them, Jay Tarses told me a little about himself and
his partner. Jay was from Baltimore, Tom was from Michigan. They

worked out of Lancaster, Pennsylvania, and had never even been to Los Angeles. They'd certainly never heard of me, but they said they felt that Dick Howard wasn't much of a manager. I told them I liked their stuff and to call me when they came to town. They did. I gave them an enthusiastic spiel about how I could get their careers going, but I knew anyone could do that, so I also told them what I thought of the business: it was mostly run by a bunch of fakers and a little cynicism would not be out of place. Tom and Jay liked that. They asked me to represent them. I stuck out my hand, we shook, and I said, "My wink is binding."

The first thing I told Patchett and Tarses was to forget about being performers. "Be writers," I said. I figured that with sitcom writer-creators beginning to get more respect, power, and money, Tom and Jay were perfectly positioned to take advantage of the changes happening in TV. We talked about one production company that really stood behind their talent: MTM Productions, named after Mary Tyler Moore, and run by her then-husband, Grant Tinker. I've always thought they were the best comedy factory ever, doing classics like *Newhart, Rhoda,* and *WKRP.* I believed Patchett and Tarses belonged at MTM.

It took a while but they worked their way up to writing scripts for *The Bob Newhart Show.* Soon they had staff positions as story editors and eventually became the show's executive producers.

Jay Tarses gave Grant Tinker much of the credit when he said he could, "diplomatically, and through cajoling and acute sense of humor and craftiness, get you to kill yourself for him. He'd say, 'If this show is good it's because of the writers.' He never took credit for anything, but it was his presence and spirit that were the key to everything."

Patchett and Tarses generated such good word of mouth that if they'd gotten then what show runners get now, they'd have earned $5 million a year or more, easy.

• • • • •

During their first or second year on *Newhart,* Tom and Jay called me at the office one day and said, "Look, there's a kid from William Morris here. He has a big space between his teeth, and he's driving us crazy. He wants to represent us and we're not going to sign with him. Can you get him off our backs?"

I called the kid. His name was Mike Ovitz. I told him to come see me.

When Ovitz got to my office he started giving me the standard William Morris speech about why my writers should be with the agency. "We're better. We care."

All horseshit. What he really meant was, "We'll take them on and hope they get lucky." No one can promise you anything or guarantee delivery. And having been with William Morris myself, I knew the speech by heart. In fact, just to shut him up I said, "Stop. I *wrote* that fucking speech."

He got the message and we talked like real people. Ovitz was smart and charming. I was so impressed that I offered him a job. He didn't take it. I understood. He had a career at William Morris and I was a little manager. This was before *Saturday Night Live*, before *The Muppet Show*. I wasn't yet *Bernie Brillstein*. We decided to stay in touch.

Laura, however, hated Ovitz on sight. Every time he'd sit in my office, facing me, she'd stand in the doorway making faces behind his back. For some reason he scared her. As it turned out, she was much more intuitive and right about him than I was.

· · · · ·

One Saturday afternoon in the summer of 1972, Jim Henson and his wife, Jane, dropped by my house at 1240 Loma Vista. Soon we were pacing around the kitchen, arguing. If it was 110 degrees outside, it was definitely hotter inside.

This was the problem: I wanted Jim and Jane to make a merchandising deal for the *Sesame Street* characters. They thought it was a bad idea. The Children's Television Workshop needed the deal because the revenue would ensure continued independent support for what had become a huge public television hit. But Jim and Jane owned half the rights, and *both* sides had to approve any arrangement.

"You have to merchandise," I said.

"No," said Jim and Jane at the same time. Jim hated the idea of selling out. When we were first together, I'd get offers of fifty or sixty grand for him to do a commercial. Jim needed the money, so I'd say, "Let's do it to pay the overhead." Sometimes he'd agree, but usually he'd pass. "Not this one," he'd say, "because they want to *own* the character." Jim's rule was simple: Don't sell anything.

The Hensons were artsy-craftsy. They always wanted to do things for the right reasons, God bless them. They thought educating kids on public TV and then selling them toys based on the characters didn't mix. It wasn't even about specific items. Jim's deals always built in controls to protect his vision. Even though there would never be Oscar the Grouch cap pistols or Big Bird cocktail napkins, the whole idea of merchandising made them feel like sell-outs. As artists, they couldn't live with that perception.

I completely understood their hesitation, but as Jim's manager I was paid to have my own long-term vision. Fortunately, Jim was not the kind to act stubborn and say, "I just won't do it." If I had a counterargument, he always listened and considered it fairly.

"There are three reasons you have to do this," I said. Number one, you have every child in America watching this show, and one day it will hopefully be worldwide. You're educating kids better and more creatively than TV ever has. Shouldn't they have good dolls instead of the shit they're buying now? Shouldn't they have Kermit and Bert and Ernie? You can't *not* give it to them.

"Second, you will have full control of what's done. Yes or no. You will kill anything you want to kill. You'll approve every license. Everything will be reasonably priced and above reproach.

"Third, if what I believe will happen with this merchandising happens" — which it did, so now I sound like a genius — "you will make enough money to have artistic freedom for the rest of your life."

Artistic freedom. Those two words sold him. Jim didn't get much of a paycheck from *Sesame Street*, so for an artist to imagine being able to do as his heart desired without asking anyone for money . . .

Jim and Jane said okay.

The merchandising bonanza surprised even me. After a couple years my end of the first royalty check was nearly six hundred grand. This went on for five years. In late 1975 we sold *The Muppet Show* to television and a year later we merchandised the non–*Sesame Street* characters as well. Eventually there was so much money rolling in that I was willing to renegotiate my deal. I reduced my percentage of the *Sesame Street* merchandise to $50,000 a year in perpetuity, and took 10 percent of the other Muppet merchandising. It stayed that way until 1989, when, during negotiations with Disney to sell them his company, Jim bought out my shares in everything to make sure they didn't screw me.

In 1982, after five years of development, *Dark Crystal,* Jim's elaborate fantasy movie inspired by the artwork of British illustrator Brian Froud, and co-directed with Frank Oz, was released. By then, Lord Lew Grade, who had backed *The Muppet Show* and previous Muppet movies, had sold out to another British mogul-producer, Sir Robert Holmes A'Court. Jim didn't like the way Sir Robert was handling the film, so he called me and announced he wanted to buy back the movie.

"You're out of your mind," I said. "What are you going to do with it?"

"I'll control its destiny," he said. "I love it."

"But Sir Robert will want fifteen million."

"I don't care."

"Tell you what. I'll come to your office right now with a Gucci bag filled with fifteen million in cash. Take a look at it. Say good-bye to it."

"Bernie," he said patiently. "Remember ten years ago in your kitchen you said I'd be free to do what I want? Artistic freedom? I'm calling it in."

And that was it. Once he could afford it, and with the support and urging of David Lazer, Jim was determined to own everything he created. He wrote a check and he bought back the movie. It was costly in the short term, but eventually we made back all but a million. Jim didn't mind. He just wanted to own his stuff. End of subject.

• • • • •

ABC wanted a replacement series for the summer of 1973, so I sold them a Burns and Schreiber special with guest stars Valerie Harper and Jack Klugman. ABC loved it and ordered ten more, which became *The Burns and Schreiber Comedy Hour.* When we set up the deal I told Jack and Avery, "You don't have any money. I have a few bucks. I know we can produce the show for what the network gives us *and* make a profit. If it goes over, I'll cover the deficit. Let's be partners and I'll guarantee you you'll make your salaries and maybe more."

What did they have to lose? We made the deal, and I finally got to take my own advice and own a show.

I didn't really have *that* much money, but I'd seen how TV was produced. There was money wasted all over the city. I could do that, too, but

I figured *making* money would be more interesting. Based on my *Hee Haw* experience I thought I could pull it off.

Here's why: First, salaries still weren't that high and the unions were easier to deal with. Second, the advance fee from foreign distribution would add to our cash flow. We'd make our salaries from the license fee and put the foreign advance in our pockets. Third, by renting studio space ourselves instead of taking on a studio partner, we could save the 15 to 25 percent overhead charge a major facility like Warner Brothers would take off the top of the license fee each week if they co-produced. Yes, they'd provide office space and other services — including picking up budget overruns — but I already had an office, and I knew how to make a budget. Why did I need to be on the lot? It never seemed worth it to me. After ten shows, the overhead saved would be substantial.

The key was to pick good writer-creators and make them my financial partners — then we'd have no chance of losing money. I only wanted to work with people who were as interested in making a profit as I was. They wouldn't try to get everything up front. They'd be responsible producers, I'd help them, and one day we'd all be farting through silk. It was also about more than money. We wanted the freedom to make the show we wanted to make, without shortchanging quality and without studio politics and interference. The network would, as always, have the final say, but the middleman — the studio — was eliminated.

In these situations, my pitch was always direct: "Why don't you own this? Why are we giving it away? If you're really good and you really have talent, why don't you put up some of that talent and see if it'll pay off in a really big way?"

My gift, if you can call it that, was somehow being able to make them understand what the future could look like.

• • • • •

Some people think I started the whole business of managers producing. That makes me feel good, but whatever I did — and I'm not certain I did it first, only popularized it — wasn't some great invention, just a twist on an old one. If you know your show-business history, you'll realize I emulated what my hero Lew Wasserman did at MCA before 1962, when the government made him choose between running a talent agency (MCA) and producing TV shows (Revue) and movies (Universal).

The Justice Department didn't like the idea of MCA being both obligated to find work for their clients *and* owning the TV and movie productions those clients might work in. The government said it was a conflict of interest that might create an irresistible temptation to abuse power. Wasserman was cornered, so he gave up the talent agency and concentrated on making movies and TV shows.

Although agents couldn't produce, no law forbade managers from doing it, because the manager is not *legally* responsible for getting his client a job. Technically, he cannot be both the seller and the buyer at the same time. I know I've said that the guy who controls the talent may be king, but the truth many seem to miss is that no manager really *controls* his clients. I can't force anyone to take a job, whether it's on a show I own or not. I can't force the producer of a show I own (or don't) to hire someone he doesn't want to. It doesn't matter if the producer is also my client. I still have to call and say, "Could you see this person please?" If it works out, great, but then the producer still has to get network approval. No matter what some unhappy clients want to believe, it's not all about me and my supposed power.

If I really *controlled* my clients, then they'd be the most rational people in the world and they wouldn't need me. When a situation comes up, the manager's just the guy in the middle between the production and the star. "I don't like that line." "We love the line." "Say the line." "Don't say the line." "Try it and see if it gets a laugh." "It's out of character. I don't care if it gets a laugh." "Let's try it. Give them that. Get the laugh and then change the line." It's what we do all day long. We're Kissinger. I believe I am so moral that I can walk the middle of the road in any dispute. I actually believe that if my star wants too much money, I should be able to say to him, "You're overreaching." And I do. If something stinks and the money is good, I'll say to my star, "You want the money? Great. But this stinks." I tell the truth, and the day I stop telling the truth and begin pandering to my clients, I should get out of the business.

Lately, the media have raised concerns about potential conflicts of interest when managers produce. The topic is worth talking about, if you know what you're talking about. Unfortunately, that's not the case with some personality journalists who, as part of a larger story, try to tackle business issues and nuances that they really don't understand. At best, their attempt to air the issues and enlighten the public is noble. At worst, it's their way of sucking up to the "abused" celebrity they're profiling.

Let me cut quickly through the confusion.

There are two types of manager-producers. The first doesn't really produce, he just gets a fee and screen credit for delivering his client to a network or movie studio. He says, "You want him, you take me." Beyond that the manager performs no discernable hands-on work and is in no way financially responsible for the project. He gets the perk because he can. He can because his client is enough in demand that the studio or network doesn't put up an argument.

Does this create a conflict between manager and client? Not exactly. In fact, it can't happen *unless* the talent goes along with it. No smart manager will risk using his client's name in vain as leverage for his own benefit. What if the studio or network blows him off and it costs the client a job? The talent has to be at a high enough level and feel fairly sure that they won't risk work before they okay their manager going along for the ride. (Or the manager has to be enough of a big deal and the client not, in order for the talent to feel it's in their best interest to go along with the situation.)

Stars typically want their managers as producers because they want someone around to protect them. But that's not the only (or most important) reason. The client knows that if his manager gets a producer's fee from the studio, then he can't commission the talent's salary. Quite an advantage. In other words, if the studio is willing to shell out a couple hundred thousand dollars to the manager on top of the client's fee, then the star is home free and doesn't have to part with 10 to 15 percent of a multimillion-dollar paycheck. (As always, follow the money.)

Most studio and network executives complain about this type of arrangement because it forces them to give credit where it's not due, and pay for a producer who does nothing. Pushed into this situation, there's not a studio in the world that wouldn't like to see the star's manager dead and buried after the deal is made — until, of course, there's trouble. Then the studio goes running to the manager, and if he can fix things, the fee is suddenly more than worth it.

Brillstein-Grey doesn't work this way. We're at network meetings, run-throughs, tapings. We're behind the scenes dealing with the usual and unusual problems. We run the show. And most important, unlike the producers-in-name-only, we have a financial stake in the TV shows we make. We pay part of the overall development-and-production tab and take part of the fiscal hit if things fail. We're entitled to profit.

So where's the conflict of interest? Occasionally producing shows that employ our clients? (We also produce shows without them, like pilots for Ben Vereen, Sherman Hemsley, Brian Benben. Also *The Naked Truth* with Tea Leoni, and, before David Spade joined the cast, *Just Shoot Me.*) Like I said, we can't run the talents' lives. They do what they want, and we try to help them along. If we find a great pilot for one of our stars, we don't say, "You have to do this." We say, "What do you think?" He or she says, "Let me meet the writers. I have some ideas." If we also represent the writers, it's still up to all our clients to figure out if they can really work together. Plus, they all have lawyers, agents, and business managers who are supposed to check everything.

However, we like to work with our clients because we think they're talented. That's why we represent them in the first place. And our production company is one reason talent wants to sign with us. Everybody wants an edge. We have lots to offer. But no one puts anything over on anyone else. We don't force our clients to let us produce. We all know how the game works. Remember that next time you pick up the paper and read generalizations about how all manager-producers are screwing their poor, naive clients out of their fair share, or representing their own interests above the talents'.

With *The Burns and Schreiber Comedy Hour, Ben Vereen — Comin' at Ya, Buffalo Bill, The Days and Nights of Molly Dodd,* and *The "Slap" Maxwell Story,* I simply pushed the boundaries of what a manager could do. There was no master plan. I just wanted to make a living and I couldn't see giving away money to studios when I didn't have to. The toughest part was convincing the networks that I could pull it off. After all, I'd be spending their money and I had to give them something they could put on the air in return.

Why did they trust me? The key was my experience and the talent I represented. I'm not dumb enough to think the networks were dazzled by my charm. I had the guys they wanted — or I made them believe I did. I could have been Jack the Ripper, or represented him. The only thing that matters to a network is getting the show on the air, with the actors they like, and keeping it there.

• • • • •

Producing a network TV show always means having to go far above and beyond the call of duty. Sometimes it's better never to discover how far that really is.

The Burns and Schreiber Comedy Hour was taped at the Hollywood Palace the night before it aired. John Moffitt was the director. ABC wanted hip young acts, so I booked the Ike and Tina Turner Review. They were hot as a pistol and I thought it would be good energy to supplement the comedy.

Ike and Tina were supposed to do two numbers, but they arrived late and said they didn't have much time. Moffitt shot the first number, "Proud Mary," without rehearsal. Afterwards, Ike said, "Okay, we're leaving now," and headed for the door. I stood there dumbfounded, not only because I'd just paid him $7,500 for one number, but because not one of my colleagues, including Jack Burns, Bob Ellison, the producer, or Burns and Schreiber's agent, Sandy Wernick, tried to block his exit. I said, "Where are you going?" but Ike just ignored me, walked outside, and got in his limo.

I stormed down Vine Street after him, got to the limo and went crazy. I opened the door, leaned in, grabbed Ike's shoulder so hard I must have left fingerprints on his white suit and said, "Listen, you cocksucker, this is the first show I've ever produced. I wanted Ike and Tina Turner because I love you. You can't do this to me."

Ike stared at me. I didn't know about his reputation and that he might be carrying a gun. In those few seconds he was probably deciding whether to hurt me or just leave. If he drove off, the show would be three minutes short. If he wanted to hurt me, I might be dead now. To my surprise he said, "Girls, out of the car." Then he smiled at me and said, "Okay, Mr. Brillstein, we'll give it another pass."

Ike and Tina came back and Moffitt shot the second song in one take with a handheld camera. It was sensational — and not only because I'm still around to talk about it.

• • • • •

Seven years in Los Angeles had changed me. I'd been up, down, kicked in the ass, and had kicked back enough to thicken my skin with layers of experience. The same fears, and nerve, and need to be included and loved were still my motivation, and I remained at least in my heart the young man who had driven through Beverly Hills ogling big houses — only now *my* car was brand-new and I owned one of those houses myself.

My troubles with Laura notwithstanding, life was for the most part great. My fortunes had turned around. Some nights I'd be in the pool at my home, way up Doheny Drive, looking down on the city, and I'd think, "Frankie Laine is at the Flamingo making twenty grand a week, so that's three thousand for me. Norm Crosby is making twenty thousand at the Sahara, so that's three for me. Jim Henson is on *Sesame Street* and I'm making . . . Burns and Schreiber are making . . . and I'm swimming on a balmy night, under the stars. Could things get any better?" I really believed I'd made it. Then, before I took another stroke, I'd invariably think, "Yeah, but that's going to stop next week." Why? I'm always waiting for those two words — "how come?" — to upset everything.

Somewhere between those two sentiments lay the truth. If anything, maybe I'd dignified the management business just a little by pushing its boundaries. I would never be a coffee-getter or schlepper. I was more like the backroom guy who worked for a rich entrepreneur. I designed the overall plan, picked the investments, and hid the money. I had a percentage and was on my way to becoming a millionaire, but I had to accept that the front man made the ultimate decisions. He was the guy who got laid. Somehow, that was okay with me. I never had the balls to be out front, a performer, but apparently I had what he needed: the ability to sell his thoughts. I practiced the art of making people believe.

Because of that I was in the action and I wanted to miss nothing: Oscars, Emmys, concerts, TV tapings. Turn on a light and I'd be there. Even though I didn't consider myself part of the entertainment establishment who wore suits and ties and held office jobs, I loved the feeling that they'd begun to accept me. But not so much that I'd let myself become a faceless guy in a huge company. I liked being on the outside. I liked going against the flow. I liked having pulled it off. I liked being me. Finally, that part seemed to be working.

■ *In Transition*

One evening years ago, when TV variety was still alive and well, I was hanging around at NBC in Burbank talking to Ray Katz, the manager who had once offered me a job before I joined Marty Kummer. That night I had Norm Crosby on The Dean Martin Show. *Ray had the late Eva Gabor. Ray was almost sixty, already wealthy and accomplished. While our clients did their hair and makeup, we bullshitted in the halls and caught up. Suddenly, Eva Gabor leaned out of her dressing room door and said, "Raymond, will you be a darling and get me a bottle of wine?"*

"Of course," he said, and dutifully hurried off.

You know how certain moments stay with you forever? That was one. I love Ray; I've got nothing against Eva Gabor, and I don't mind doing something out of courtesy. But for a grown man to be sent like a schlepper for a bottle of wine? If a client is working and I see he's perspiring, I'll get a towel like I would for a best friend. But if he says, "Get me a towel," I won't. That would make me feel like the guy who used to be Bernie Brillstein. I swore I'd never end up that way or stay on past my time. This town is no place for a "once-was" or a "used to be" to hang around.

That's why I keep asking myself what I'm still doing at Brillstein-Grey. Now I'm just a working stiff, not an owner. I wake up with the sweats. People at the company used to drop by my office for a visit and a handful of sweets from the candy bowl. Now I don't even keep the bowl full anymore. I'm in a slump. At night I sit in my huge house alone and think, "What the fuck? How did I end up like this?"

• • • • •

I remember that day in Brad's office, getting ready to sign the papers. I looked around, like it was my first time in there, trying to get a sense of the moment. There were family pictures, a computer, and, along one wall, his huge horizontal Ed Ruscha painting of a white-hot shooting star against an electric blue background. The metaphor has never been lost on me. The room seemed empty compared to mine. That's not a put-down. Brad's office hasn't yet been filled by a life in show business — but he's working on it.

Neither one of us wanted a confrontation. It was already difficult, awkward, and a little unpleasant for me: one guy's career going up and the other guy's career going sideways, at best — most likely down. I was sickened by the inevitability of it all. I was old. He had become the driving force of the company and my ego couldn't take it. I knew no one could erase my accomplishments (he wasn't trying to) but you know that feeling you get when you realize you were once the center of attention and suddenly it's not about you anymore? Everything had been negotiated and laid out by intermediaries. I just wanted to get the paperwork off the desk.

Brad said, "Hey, you know I love you. You know I'd do nothing to hurt you, ever. This is just the way it is."

"I know," I said. "I believe you. I love you, too."

Then I signed, we hugged, and I got out of there before the emotions boiled over and made a mess. It took less than fifteen minutes.

I went back to my office and stared out the window. I felt used up. And you know something? I was used up, so I went home early. I don't drink or do drugs, so all that was left to me was stone cold sleep.

• • • • •

Now I've got too much time on my hands.

For thirty years I rarely slowed down. My mornings were crazy. I spent four hours before lunch just putting out fires. I handled clients and production problems, and listened to one frantic question again and again: "What should I do now?" The day was phone call after phone call, crisis after crisis, opportunity after opportunity. I was involved 110 percent. Now the phone doesn't ring that much. Instead of one hundred people a day coming to me with their problems, they go to Brad. It doesn't mean my advice is any less valuable than it used to be, but it sure leaves me with a lot of time to play golf.

Before the company changed hands, Brad, like a son, said, "You can't tell me that you still want to keep at this day to day, on the line. You've been doing it for forty-two years. Don't you want to give up some of it? Don't you want to enjoy the rewards? Don't you want to have a good time? You deserve it."

My first reaction was, "No, I don't." Later, I thought of a story Lorne Michaels told me. He said, "Bernie, I created Saturday Night Live in 1975. The whole idea was to do a television show for people who were brought up on television. Isn't that simple? Twenty years later I come to the first meeting every week and I'm surrounded by forty people much younger than me. And all I can think is that they're looking at me and wondering, 'What the fuck is he still doing here?'"

Then, I knew what he meant. Now, I get to find out how it feels. People have been treating me like a wounded veteran, stuck in a wheelchair. But I don't want anyone to feel sorry for me, particularly Brad. He can't do much about it, anyway. Brad's got no time to wait on me. He has a company to run. It's not so easy being king.

A couple months ago, when I was really acting up — being snippy and moody and of no value to anyone — he called me and he said, "Look. You're walking around with this long face. I know you're not happy and you're making it very obvious."

That's one big difference between Brad and me. I never would have confronted me. I would have let me just go into the shithouse, marked me dead, and gotten rid of me. Those are the rules I play by when someone doesn't follow my rules. But he confronted me. He said, "Bernie, I must tell you, with this deal we made, I sleep well every night because I think it's really fair. More than fair. My conscience is clear."

How can I argue with that? Once I'd made up my mind that I was willing to sell, it was all about how much I'd walk away with. I didn't think about how I'd feel afterwards, just how much I'd get for all the aggravation. After the divorce I didn't want any more big battles, and at sixty-five the last thing I wanted to worry about was money. I'm not complaining about the deal. Every sidewalk punchball player from the West Side should get what I got. Could I have scrounged a few more million? Maybe. But that's not the problem.

The problem is that I feel useless. I didn't have a stroke, I didn't go blind, I don't have cancer, I didn't turn stupid overnight. I don't even feel that Brad running things is a repudiation of me. We didn't disagree much about the business.

I always thought his ideas were great. Some of his management style he learned from me, some of it is better. He turned Brillstein-Grey into a real powerhouse. I wanted Brad to have the chance to bring his vision to life, I just never stopped to think that one day that vision might not include me.

I need to figure out what to do. Should I go to Palm Beach and play golf every day? A part of me wants to have no responsibilities; just set up the kids and take off. But what do I do with my brain? Do I take some of the money and invest it with a few other people and stay in the action? Do I start another company or take a big job somewhere else? I'd consult, except I remember what a friend once told me: "Don't do it. It never works at your own company. After a month, no one's going to ask you about anything, and if they do, they're not going to do what you tell them to." Maybe I should just make a clean break, go home, and take it easy. Why worry about anything? My obituary is already written. What I've accomplished is already on the record. No one can take away what's already been done.

Meanwhile, I've got a pain inside that I can't process. Call it seller's remorse. To expose myself to being nothing after so many years. It's weird to doubt everything I've done for forty-two years. I feel put upon by fate. I thought I could handle the transition, but giving up the company made me feel old and alone and dirty, like there's something wrong with me. And goddamn it, there is something wrong: I sold out. A real man would have fought. Now, I'm just high-priced labor. I get the salary whether I show up or not.

Why didn't I fight?

I might as well ask myself, "Why am I old?"

In my heart I still feel twenty-one, but the rest of me is sixty-five. And being sixty-five ain't so great in show business. Or any business anymore.

Making the Money

Chapter 6

Have a Good Listen

I met Lorne Michaels in 1968, at the NBC-TV studios in Burbank. I had Norm Crosby on *The Beautiful Phyllis Diller Show;* Lorne and his partner, Hart Pomerantz, wrote for her. We kept bumping into each other in the halls late at night, because there is nothing more boring than waiting backstage at a TV taping for the show to wrap. By 2 A.M. everyone is desperate for conversation. Lorne loved to talk, so we hit it off. I learned that he and Hart were a stand-up writer-comedy team from Toronto who'd worked on a Canadian Broadcasting Corporation radio show before coming to Hollywood to try their hands at TV.

Hart had a Mel Brooks–type personality, animated to say the least. Lorne was the straight man: articulate and laid-back yet not without great stamina and a carefully modulated energy. What I remember most is that Lorne was Lorne from the minute I met him, and in thirty years he hasn't changed much — except that he now has much better clothes. But Lorne always had style, was always soft-spoken and extremely bright. I think of him as Gatsby, if Gatsby was a producer. I liked him instinctively. We spoke the same language.

I wanted to sign Lorne and Hart immediately. But Hart was against it. He wanted to go back to Canada, and they did.

In Toronto, Lorne and Hart did quarterly specials that were a lot like what *Saturday Night Live* would become. The shows did well, but the partners didn't. Hart wanted to perform, Lorne wanted to produce. Finally, all they could agree on was to break up. Around that time we had one more writing position open on *The Burns and Schreiber Comedy Hour.* It paid $500 a week for ten weeks. Lorne's agent, Sandy Wernick said, "Remember that kid you loved, Lorne Michaels?" "That's great," I said. "Bring him down."

Lorne settled into a room at the Chateau Marmont, a hip hotel just off the Sunset Strip, and started work. He could write, perform, and produce, was a cut above the rest, and had interesting friends. He also asked me to manage him. I said yes.

At one of our first meetings Lorne showed me a little film he'd made called *The Great Hockey Puck Crisis.* The premise is that in Canada hockey pucks grow on trees. When a plague wipes out the crop, no one can play the game. Everyone goes nuts and into mourning. I loved it and I started to understand where Lorne's personal comic sensibilities lay: call it Woody Allen meets Monty Python, with a touch of elegance and a twist of chaos. Lorne said, "What I'd really like to do is a TV variety show with live sketches and filmed pieces." I made a mental note to keep listening.

· · · · ·

I supported Lorne's ambitions, but between *Hee Haw,* my other clients, TV shows, and growing the business in a one-man office, I just didn't have enough time to get personally involved with everyone. Laura picked up some of the slack, especially with Lorne. She did his books, and when he had a hard time with his marriage to writer Rosie Shuster — which eventually ended — Laura cared for him. She championed him, and loved him as much as she disliked Peppiatt and Aylesworth, who were starting to stiff me on some bills. It didn't take much for Laura to get pissed at anyone. Sometimes she and I would fight in public about business and not care who was watching. Years later, in typical Lorne fashion, he told me that he'd "found that interaction funny and endearing."

The Burns and Schreiber Show didn't last, but Lorne soon had two job offers to choose between. I brought him the first: a TV special with Mama Cass, Jackie Gleason, and Art Carney, for $10,000. The other was to write on Lily Tomlin's second comedy special for CBS, *Lily,* for $3,500.

I thought Lorne should take the higher-paying job, but he explained that he wanted to work with Tomlin since she was a fan of stuff he'd done in Canada and that working with her seemed more attractive because at that time conventional TV was, to his generation, "the great Satan." Movies and music had been revolutionized; TV lagged. It would be a while before the kids who'd grown up on the new medium came to dominate — and Lorne was among the first.

Even though I was from the very generation he believed had lost touch with a changing world, I understood his choice. At least I wasn't so far gone that I didn't recognize he needed to follow his own instincts, which were part of what attracted me to him in the first place. Besides, Tomlin was quite popular, even if she paid less.

At first Lorne's and Lily's working styles conflicted, but Lorne wanted that job and stayed the course. His reward was a writing Emmy. Afterwards, Lorne drifted through various projects, among them a Perry Como Christmas show and a Flip Wilson special, but none were satisfying and he was restless. Then Tomlin moved to ABC, and the next thing I knew I got a call from Frank Brill, at the network.

"You represent this kid Lorne Michaels?" he asked. "We'd like him to be a producer on the Lily Tomlin shows."

I nearly fainted. I told Lorne the news, but he seemed oddly unexcited. "Yeah, I know," he said. "Lily told me and I forgot to tell you." I was still impressed. In those days, to produce a special, especially with Lily Tomlin, one of the hottest comedienne's going, was big stuff. I got Lorne thirty grand, which was probably more than he'd made the entire previous year. He also used me in the show: in one sketch, the police arrested all the fat people in Beverly Hills and I was one of them.

Now Lorne was on my radar.

· · · · ·

In the couple years since I'd met Mike Ovitz, the gap-toothed kid from William Morris had begun to attract some attention. He was twenty-eight, ambitious, and unhappy. I don't need to repeat here the well-enough documented reasons, but even before Ovitz had a history, I knew what bothered him. It was the same old William Morris story: They favored the loyal company man. New ideas and creativity just spelled trouble. No one knew better than the agency board of directors. I remember telling my bosses, "Let's open a sports department." It was 1959, before anyone was doing it.

They said, "That's not our business."

"Hold it!" I said. "Sports are now on TV three hours a day and it's only going to get bigger. Let's represent the athletes and the leagues."

"That's not our business," they said. They didn't get it.

Like his predecessors, Ovitz knew the only way to get ahead at William Morris was to leave the company.

I'd heard about Ovitz's plans because he'd told me. He and four other William Morris agents — Ron Meyer, Bill Haber, Rowland Perkins, and Michael Rosenfield — were leaving to form their own company. They wanted to depend only on themselves. Under the circumstances it was all they could do.

Ovitz's call came at an interesting time. Lots of information filtered through The Brillstein Company and I knew something I thought might interest him. "Three guys from the International Creative Management (ICM) television department — Gary Nardino, Lee Gabler, and Sandy Wernick — are also thinking of leaving. Why don't you all meet at my office? Maybe you can get together."

That's me: always the middle man.

A few days later, nine people crammed into my little suite on South Beverly Drive. It was so crowded we had to use the window seats. The guys all knew each other from the business. Ovitz said he and his partners wanted to represent film people, and I figured the ICM guys could run the television department. Ovitz already had a bank loan, and he went over the plan about how they wanted to set up the new company — Creative Artists Agency. He spoke with conviction about what they hoped to accomplish. Everyone loved it, so the soon-to-be-former William Morris guys asked their ICM counterparts if they wanted to join up. I thought they should jump at the opportunity, but suddenly Nardino threw a monkey wrench into the works. He kept insisting the new company pick up his country club membership and pay for his leased Lincoln.

Ovitz said, "We're not taking salaries, we're not having car allowances. We're bringing card tables from home to use as desks. Our wives will be our secretaries. We're going to start this thing on a shoestring and live by our wits."

I knew what Nardino was thinking: "If I'm going into a new business, why should I take less than I had before?" There's nothing wrong with that. People used to being salaried employees want the same or better when they jump jobs. Nardino had the chance to become an owner, but he couldn't think like one. He didn't want to take risks. Ovitz and his partners wanted to wager it all, even their security. They had to believe they'd be successful, and boy did they become successful. Who knew? They bet on themselves, which as I've always said, is the only way to do it. They understood that you have to be willing to sacrifice at the beginning if you want to collect on the other end, or at least take a step up. The only way they were thinking about country clubs was maybe one day owning one.

The meeting broke up and the partnership never happened. As everyone left, I asked Sandy Wernick to stay. We already shared Lorne Michaels, Burns and Schreiber, and a few other clients, and he'd been the one to tell me the ICM guys wanted to break off. When we were alone I said, "Look, these guys aren't going to make it together. There's no marriage here. Why don't you come work with me?"

> Sandy Wernick:
> I went home to talk to my wife about Bernie's offer, and the next morning at eight, the phone rings and it's Marvin Josephson. He was head of ICM.
> "I hear you're leaving," he said.
> I said, "What are you talking about? How do you know I'm leaving?"
> "Because Bernie Brillstein called me this morning and told me that he made you an offer to join his company," he said.
> He was right. That's how Bernie operated. He took care of it in one fell swoop.

Ovitz left William Morris on Friday, January 10, 1975, and CAA opened for business the following Monday. They made smart moves, like getting heavily into movie packaging — putting together all of a film's elements and selling it to the studio. They didn't invent the practice, but they so perfected it that after a while people thought they had. Another genius move was going after the stars' lawyers to get access to talent that wouldn't normally have signed with such a new agency. Ovitz made alliances and paid attention to them. One lawyer, Barry Hirsch, represented Robert Redford, and pretty soon Ovitz represented Redford. The same with Paul Newman. The rumor was that Ovitz took them for nothing just to get big names on his roster. Ballsy kid and great idea. What actor wouldn't love a free agent? It's easier to like someone if you don't have to pay them. And when you're a big star you get sent all the good scripts anyway, which is one reason big talents think they don't really need agents. Ovitz would soon correct that impression.

. . . . .

I needed Sandy Wernick. Laura didn't really know business and I was swamped. At least now there were two of us, plus a couple secretaries.

Sandy probably knows more about how show business works than anyone not currently at a movie studio or TV network. He's the consummate inside man who can execute a deal. That lets me handle the people and the strategy. With him as my second in command, we quickly developed a working relationship that in twenty-three years has come to resemble an old married couple. You know: We bicker, we're impatient, some days we barely tolerate each other; but we know how to make the other laugh and we respect our history. Down deep, I love him, though at times I figure he must have hated me because, in 1986, I sold The Brillstein Company to Lorimar and didn't cut him in on the deal. I say "I figure" because we've never spoken about it.

On the other hand, Sandy has since been extremely well compensated and is still with the company, which says a lot about how he and I really feel. It's silly, but I think a sign of our enduring friendship is that even though I've stopped filling up the candy dishes in my office — I'm losing weight again — Sandy still pops in a couple times each day for no other reason than to shoot the breeze.

He assures me that it has nothing to do with the fact that he also likes to use my private bathroom.

Sandy and I work very differently. I'm an immediate person. I want an answer right away. Sandy always needs another conversation. "Let me wait a little," he says. Right or wrong, I never had that much patience. I like to say, "Give me an answer *now.*" But I understand what he has to go through dealing with the business-affairs people. They're notoriously cantankerous, slow, penny pinching, and sentence bending. Talking to them is probably the most thankless job in the world; because of Sandy I never had to do that. I could pay attention to our clients, and get new ones; or as he would probably say, I did the schmoozing while he did the real work. Not quite. You can't get the money unless you represent the talent, and to make The Brillstein Company work we needed both skills: someone who goes from his gut and someone who can grind the business-affairs boys for the extra seventy-five cents. It was fine with me that Sandy could do the latter. In fact, I urged him to.

We've handled many clients together; still do. But he deserves all the credit for taking Adam Sandler under his wing and helping him evolve from an appealing kid who sang perverse and funny songs on *Saturday Night Live* into a mega–million dollar movie star with an unlimited future.

• • • • •

Business was wonderful, but my private life finally fell apart. Mixing the personal and the professional had taken its toll on my marriage. I was about to tell Laura it was over when I discovered that she was sleeping with her gynecologist. It was typical Laura; a preemptive strike. Do it to them before they do it to you.

Okay, I probably forced her into it. I slept in the den a lot and hadn't touched her sexually in years. I began to realize that the reason I originally wanted her — to attain the unattainable — was fine for landing a client in business, but it couldn't be the basis of a marriage. I had stopped loving her.

Her doctor friend was a Tyrone Power–type grease ball. Dull, from New Jersey, with dyed black hair. He'd gotten a divorce himself, and, blind schmuck that I am, I had suggested they go to our house in Aspen together, where she could help take her friend's mind off his misery. A few days later I went to join them, and the minute I walked in the door, I just knew. It really shook me up. I had no right to, but I felt cheated on.

Of course, so did everyone else in the country. It was the summer of 1974, and the Watergate revelations were about to result in Nixon's resignation. But making light of the situation didn't help.

I told Laura, "I'm getting out of here. I'm leaving tomorrow morning." I started packing. I had some money, but not that much; I still wasn't *Bernie Brillstein*. I was just some schmuck whose personal life had fallen apart again. I was forty-three, loved the kids, worried about them . . . It's a terrible thing.

The next morning I left a note for Laura in the kitchen. "I'm taking the car to the Aspen airport. I'll park it there and leave the keys." Then I drove away, feeling horrible. Just my luck, the plane was late. I sat in the lounge imagining myself as Robert Redford in a big love story: Laura would read the note, come flying down the hill, beg me to stay, and maybe I would or maybe I wouldn't. That's when I looked out the big picture window and there she was, getting out of a cab . . . with the doctor. They got in our car and drove away.

As soon as I got back to Los Angeles I took $5,000 out of petty cash and went straight to the MGM Grand in Las Vegas, where I promptly lost $10,000. I started drinking crème de menthes early, and by the time I ran into Gary Pudney, a friend who worked at ABC, in the lobby of the MGM Grand Hotel, I had lost not only my money but my mind. Pudney had some people with him: Joel Briskin and Joel's sister, Debbie, and their parents, Thelma and Mort Briskin. Mort was a lawyer and a real rounder. He'd handled Abbott and Costello, run Desilu Studios, and written and produced the movies *Walking Tall*, *Ben*, and *Willard*.

They'd all just seen Burns and Schreiber and the Jackson Five in the Grand's showroom. Debbie, a petite, blonde divorcée with green eyes and a great sense of humor, said she'd danced onstage with the Jacksons at the end of their show. They were on their way to catch Elvis at the International, and Debbie asked if I wanted to tag along. I passed. I wanted to get back to my crème de menthe misery. But she pressed, so I agreed to meet them at the MGM Grand delicatessen after the Elvis show. I guess I'd already gotten a little crush on Debbie, and she on me. Not that I could do anything about it. I would be off to Canada the next day with Peppiatt and Aylesworth, for a Paul Anka special. Besides, I needed time to myself.

When I got back to Los Angeles I moved out of my house and into the Beverly Rodeo Hotel. For weeks, I waited like a fool for Laura to call and say she loved me and wanted to save our marriage. The call never came. (Actually, it did, but it was twenty years too late.) In the divorce, Laura kept our home and lots of money.

Six weeks later, I was in my office one morning fighting a terrible migraine. The phone rang and it was Debbie. She said, "You remember your friend from Las Vegas?" It was October 1974. We went out that night and got married in June of the following year.

Debbie had two sons, David and Nick. They were six and two. Like all my kids, I absolutely adore them. Laura's son, Scott — who wasn't doing so well at school — also wanted to live with us, so we needed a larger place. Debbie sold her home and gave me $50,000 for a down payment on a bigger house in Beverly Hills. With us, Scott's grades went from D's to A's and he really turned himself around. Then Laura pulled him back, saying it was time for him to live with her. I was heartbroken, but my lawyer, my father, and a group of friends took me aside and said, "Look, Bernie, you're not the natural father. You can't get him back. It's a losing battle. It will keep breaking your heart. You have to give it up." So, with great regret I did. I thought it would kill me.

It didn't, and a couple years later I had new kids of my own to think about. In 1979, when I was forty-eight, my son Michael was born. My daughter Kate came in 1983. Laura had broken me, but I've always thought that Debbie brought me luck. First, a family. And in business she was there for *Saturday Night Live, The Muppet Show*, meeting Brad, success in TV, running a movie studio, forming Brillstein-Grey. Through her I made a comeback. We had lots of good times together, we laughed and socialized. Unlike Laura, she never challenged my work or acted competitive.

Was I surprised? Not really. Debbie hated show business.

• • • • •

Lorne turned thirty on November 17, 1974, and threw himself a party in the lobby of the Chateau Marmont. He'd made it through some uncertain times. Although an early pitch to NBC for a *Saturday Night Live*–like comedy-variety show had gone nowhere, Lorne had done well with Tomlin, and it looked like he could have work whenever he wanted it. That was reason enough to celebrate.

I told Debbie, "I have to go to this kid's birthday party at the Chateau; I have to make an appearance." Me being me, going to a party is usually a drag. If the party is called for seven to nine o'clock, I arrive early, say hello to the guest of honor, get my picture taken with the host, walk out the back door and get home to my easy chair by seven-thirty. And why not? Most parties are always full of the same people saying the same things that I've already heard eight hundred times. If I sat and schmoozed for two hours I'm sure the other guys would go home to their wives and say, "I was with Bernie Brillstein and he told the same story as he did before."

Lorne probably didn't think I'd even show up. I may have guided his career, but we didn't really see each other socially. His world wasn't my world. I didn't hang out with thirty-year-old kids after hours. I never wanted to be that hip. I'd go to hockey games. Lorne's crowd started its nights at eleven o'clock. That was my bedtime.

The invitation said eight o'clock; I was there at ten to eight. Nothing was set up. I called Lorne's room. He'd just gotten out of the shower. "Where is everyone?" I asked. Reluctantly, Lorne threw on some clothes and came down, and we sat in the lobby for twenty minutes making small talk. For some reason I thought that Debbie and I were the only two people who had shown up, while Lorne, knowing better, understood no one would be prompt. Then Lorne said he had to finish dressing. Debbie and I decided to stick around, and by the time Lorne returned, people had begun to drift in. Soon the party was in full swing. I discovered that, right under my nose, Lorne Michaels was really *somebody.* In walked Richard Pryor, Lily Tomlin, George Carlin, Graham Nash, and many other creative people I would soon hear lots about. It seemed like Lorne was the king of underground comedy. It wasn't even *underground,* but my calling it that just shows how out of place I felt.

I'm still glad I stayed, because none of these young people had heard my stories about New York, the Copa, William Morris, and early television. Even though they clearly wanted to make the future their own, they were genuinely interested — not negative — about the way things used to be. I've always believed that if young people *really* listen to older people, they can learn a thing or two. That's how I'd done it — and now, for the first time in my life it hit me that *I* was the older person.

Maybe that was part of why Lorne respected me. I probably represented to him what he'd left behind in Toronto: a middle-class Jewish life, men who ate tuna sandwiches and watched football games on Sunday, men who knew something about real life. He also knew that I understood audiences, networks, and fundamental truths about show business that for all his creative energy he still needed to learn. I could make decisions on instinct while he agonized over the fine points. Plus, I was funny, and in comedy you can't trust anyone who isn't funny.

• • • • •

When Lorne told me that he "wanted to do a television show for people who were brought up on television," it sounded not only interesting but workable. With Sandy Wernick and producer Bob Finkel, we pitched Lorne's idea for a different kind of hip comedy-variety show to Larry White at NBC. White did programming and worked for then–NBC President Herb Schlosser. Lorne showed him *The Hockey Puck Crisis* and some Monty Python stuff. He told him about a completely different kind of comedy than anything else on the air. He explained how the world had changed and that TV lagged behind.

White thought it was a terrible idea. He said that no one who watched TV would get it.

What none of us knew was that things were happening at NBC that would eventually bring us face-to-face with them again, on the same topic. Johnny Carson complained that he didn't like *Tonight Show* reruns on the weekends. Herb Schlosser, a guy who always had ideas, drew up a memo for a variety show called *Saturday Night Live* to fill the Carson rerun slot. Dick Ebersol, who had just come from working with sports maven Roone Arledge at ABC, was put in charge of late-night development at NBC. Ebersol wanted to develop pilots and air them on Saturday nights as a launch pad. If any hit he'd move them to prime time.

It never happened because Ebersol's pilot plan was shot down, as well as his subsequent idea to rotate four shows a month in a Saturday late-night "wheel." Instead, he was asked to fulfill Schlosser's *Saturday Night Live* vision. When asked who he thought should produce the show, he mentioned two names. One was Lorne's.

Lorne wasn't exactly available. He'd agreed to write a movie for a guy named Ken Shapiro, at Paramount. Nonetheless, Lorne met with Ebersol again, starting out in Sandy's office and then going down to a coffee shop to talk for a couple more hours. The next time we heard from Ebersol was when Lorne got a message to meet him at the Polo Lounge in the Beverly Hills Hotel at 7:30 the next morning, to speak with Marvin Antonowsky and Dave Tebet, two top NBC guys who had to approve of Lorne if he was going to produce *Saturday Night Live.*

The rest, no matter how often it's written about, will never be precisely recalled history. Who knew how it would all turn out? No one took notes. As Angie Dickinson once said, "When you're living history, you're just living. It becomes history later."

All those meetings just seemed like meetings to me. That's what the workday was all about: meetings, phone calls, schmoozing, meals, tapings, more meetings, and dragging your tired ass back home to get some sleep so you could do it again the next day. Jobs and project ideas lined up like planes on the runway, waiting to take off. Only most didn't have the right fuel mixture and could never get off the ground. When one did, we were happy, but that was about it, because you can't prepare for a hit. The best you can do is get up to bat and hope like hell you get a pitch down the middle.

When Lorne put *Saturday Night Live* together, he wasn't thinking "hit." He was thinking "survival." But he did more than just survive. With John Belushi doing the Samurai, Aykroyd doing Bass-O-Matic, Chevy falling on his ass each week, Gilda saying, "Never mind," the show had an enormous cultural impact. A new generation of TV and movie superstars emerged. Maybe I should have kept a diary and considered writing a book. But it's never like that, is it? You don't think, "Oh shit, this may be important someday." I had never seen anything like it before so as America watched and learned, so did I. And yet, that's the greatest, most interesting thing about show business: you *never* know.

· · · · ·

In the beginning, Lorne worked on *Saturday Night Live* out of a back room in my office at 144 South Beverly Drive. Most days for lunch, he and I, and sometimes Sandy or whoever Lorne was interviewing, would eat across the street at a little place called the Breadwinner. Lorne liked to talk about his plans, and we were mesmerized. If he was Lewis Carroll's Alice, then I felt like we had tumbled down the hole into Wonderland together.

I was constantly amazed at the people he brought in. They were the kind who ate at Duke's, a loud and ramshackle breakfast place in the old Tropicana Hotel on Santa Monica Boulevard in West Hollywood. They stayed at places like the Chateau Marmont, got together late at night, and talked about changing everything. They were into music and film and kicking open the door of a TV industry still run by their parents' generation. What did I know of that? Not much. When Lorne took me to the Groundlings Theater to see Laraine Newman, a young woman he thought he might want in the show's repertory company, I loved her — but I would be lying if I said I had any idea who she was.

Lorne eventually hired Laraine. He also offered a writing job to someone named Chevy Chase. I'd never heard of him, either. Chase passed because Lorne didn't want him to be in the cast; he took the job a week later when another opportunity didn't work out.

When Lorne finally moved to New York, he interviewed hundreds of people, auditioned comedians at local comedy clubs, and finished putting together the group he wanted. I met Gilda Radner over the phone when Lorne asked me to convince her not to do a syndicated talk show with the comedian David Steinberg. Lorne wanted her to wait six months instead and take the *Saturday Night Live* job — which, incidentally, paid less. I told her that more people would see her on NBC. It was the truth. I'd already met her friend Danny Aykroyd when I was in Canada with Norm Crosby. Jane Curtin, Garrett Morris, John Belushi . . . names not known to me. It was the same with most of the production and writing staff, including Michael O'Donoghue, Anne Beatts, Alan Zweibel, Al Franken, and Tom Davis. The only exceptions were Lorne's soon-to-be-ex-wife, Rosie Shuster, and Herb Sargent, a writer-producer from my generation with vast TV experience.

For Lorne it was perfect. The cast and staff were *all* in keeping with his grand design of not wanting to hire anyone who'd worked much, or at all, in television. The idea was that if they weren't old dogs, he wouldn't have to worry about old tricks.

· · · · ·

I flew into New York the week before the show to watch it all come together. I spent most of my time with Lorne, making sure he survived until opening night. The panic backstage at studio 8H and in the show's offices on the seventeenth floor at 30 Rockefeller Center was a stark contrast to the sights and smells of the city in October: a whiff of chill in the air, the aroma of smoke and leather in a good steak house, the legs of a well-dressed woman on Fifth Avenue. To me, this was sheer happiness. It was good to be back in town.

George Carlin was the first host, Janis Ian and Billy Preston the first musical guests. Andy Kaufman was the featured comedian, and both Billy Crystal and Valri Bromfield had solo pieces. At one point, NBC wanted to tape-delay Carlin because of his infamous "Seven Dirty Words" routine, but they relented. The day before the show the set still wasn't finished and the sound system didn't work correctly. On Saturday,

Lorne blew up at Dick Ebersol for tampering with the closing credit crawl. Ebersol, who listed himself as executive producer, had moved the names of companies who'd given us free stuff to the top. Lorne quit. I knew that Lorne didn't really want to walk, but his frustration was so intense that the only way to vent it was to abandon ship.

I had to change his mind. "Don't worry," I said. "This will all work out." It was a promise I'd repeat many times in the years to come.

At *Saturday Night Live* there's always an hour between the full dress rehearsal and show time. This is when Lorne retreats to his office on the ninth floor, above the studio, to figure out which sketches to keep and which to cut, and to determine the running order. There are a million details and considerations, but he has to put the show above everything else — personalities included — which sometimes means cutting a performer's only appearance that week or trimming a sketch everyone loves that didn't go over well in dress rehearsal. In other words, Lorne tears down the show and rebuilds it on the spot. It's the moment that defines his job, when he has to summon every bit of his talent and experience. Outsiders are not allowed in during this process. I like to leave Lorne to his magic, but sometimes I've been on hand and think I've witnessed pure alchemy.

That debut night, when Lorne came out of his office with the show's running order, I stopped him in the hallway. He looked tense, but I ignored it. "Okay," I said. "It's time to get ready here. When's the band going to put on their tuxedos?"

I'm sure Lorne wasn't in the mood to laugh but he couldn't help it. "Bernie," he said, "they're going to wear jeans." I clearly recall at that moment thinking that if an older person listens to a younger person once in a while, he can learn a lot.

Then Lorne's smile faded. He said the show was too long and things had to be cut. He hurried off.

Carlin opted out of a sketch, which helped, but more had to go. Lorne told Bromfield and Crystal to cut their bits from five minutes to two. Bromfield agreed. Crystal said, "No, I can't," and wouldn't compromise. Lorne sent for me. I found him and Crystal and the comedian's manager, Buddy Morra, in the long hallway outside studio 8H. Billy not only wouldn't cut his piece but he wanted a guarantee that its full length would be placed in the first half of the show. Otherwise, Morra said, they would walk. If I'd been Crystal's manager at the time I probably would have done the same thing. And under normal circumstances Lorne would have tried to work it out. But there was too much pressure. This was Lorne's first live ninety-minute show, it was opening night, and who knew what was going to happen? No one had time for Crystal's whining. Billy went home and nursed a grudge for years.

I walked back into the studio and ran smack into a commotion. John Belushi, already dressed for the show's cold opening — that abrupt first scene before the opening roll that always ends with "Live, from New York, it's Saturday Night! — was arguing with Craig Kellem, a producer. Kellem was panic-stricken. He needed Belushi to sign his contract. "You can't go on the air unless you do," he insisted. Nothing wrong with that. It's standard operating procedure. God forbid the network let someone on the air without a contract only to have him turn around later, after they've spent a million dollars, and say, "You can't use me."

I heard Belushi say something about "favored nations" and "Mickey Rooney–Judy Garland." What he meant was that if one cast member got a raise, every cast member had to — not that at $750 a week the first year they were making much, but the whole cast had agreed to the deal. I didn't understand why Belushi was having a problem, but he ran up to me, waved the papers in my face and said, "He insists I sign this contract."

"So sign it," I said. "What's the big fucking deal?"

"What do *you* think?" he said. "Would you sign it?"

Kellem said, "Bernie, tell him why he *has* to sign."

So I explained: "Listen, kid. I helped devise this contract, so of course you should sign. It's very fair. It's really okay." It was a grand statement, yet somewhat true. I managed Lorne so I had negotiated certain things into the document, but it was *still* an *NBC* contract. Belushi cocked an eyebrow and looked at me out of the corner of his eyes, quickly sizing me up. "Sign it," I said, flatly. "Besides, you're going on in five minutes."

"Tell you what," he answered. "If you manage me, I'll sign."

"You got a deal," I said. Belushi grabbed a pen and scribbled his name, then took his place on the set. I figured I'd never see him again. And then it hit me: He was pretty smart. He knew I managed Lorne, and who better to represent you than the boss's representative? It was almost as if he'd planned the whole thing.

Two minutes to show time. I found my seat in the audience next to

Debbie and my good friends Norman Kartiganer and his wife, Pat. The red light on top of the studio camera came to life. Michael O'Donoghue, the show's head writer who was in the scene with Belushi, said, "I would like to feed my fingertips to the wolverines." Belushi repeated the line. This went on until O'Donoghue's character had a heart attack and collapsed on the floor. Belushi did likewise. A moment later, Chevy Chase walked out, smiled at the camera, took a deep breath, and said, "Live from New York, it's *Saturday Night!*"

• • • • •

In those days I could never sit still for long. After twenty minutes I turned to Debbie, excused myself, and wandered around studio 8H. I rode the elevator to the ninth floor and spotted Marvin Antonowsky and Dick Ebersol standing together, clearly agitated.

"Bernie," said Ebersol. "We've already gotten two hundred phone calls about Carlin's monologue!"

"Complaints," added Antonowsky.

"What are we going to say?" Ebersol groaned. "What are we going to do?"

"Do?" I stared at them and tried not to laugh out loud. "Two hundred calls? You schmucks, it means we have a hit!"

• • • • •

Sometimes my experience with *Saturday Night Live* reminds me of when my father used to take me to the beach and public steam baths. First I'd get sunburned and then he'd go, "Come on, kid, we'll take a steam." I'd follow him into the white-tiled room. Not only did the hot droplets of condensation sting my already raw skin, but since I was a kid I was at eye level with a hundred Jews' testicles. All I could see were hanging balls. At first it was scary, but for some reason, I loved it. And that's the point. Today, even from a loftier perspective, I still love it.

I've never made a secret of my belief that Lorne Michaels is a genius — even though that word is overused. He created *Saturday Night Live*; not me, not Dick Ebersol, not Herb Schlosser. Lorne had help, ours and that of many, many other talented writers, performers, and production people, but aside from the title, it was his baby from the beginning.

No one else can take a nickel's worth of credit. Without Lorne, who can say where anyone involved in *Saturday Night Live* might have ended up? Without Lorne, who knows where *I'd* be? More than anyone, he yanked me out of the '50s and '60s, brought me to the TV generation's big party, and helped me establish a rock-solid business where there had only been ambitious dreams before.

Lorne left the show in 1980, before the sixth season. When he returned to *Saturday Night Live* in 1985, he did it again. Many of the new comedians and comic actors he introduced to America were or became Brad's and my clients. We couldn't force him to do that, but he did, and guys like Dennis Miller, Dana Carvey, Jon Lovitz, David Spade, Phil Hartman, Norm MacDonald, Kevin Nealon, Tim Meadows, Adam Sandler, and others who became household names helped Brillstein-Grey become the success it is today. I owe Lorne a lot.

Not only has my nearly-twenty-five-year association with *Saturday Night Live* kept me current, it's also prompted the media, at times, to call me a king of comedy.

Believe me, there's no such thing. There are too many different types of humor. Some people like Gallagher, others love Rich Little. Some hated Lenny Bruce, believe it or not. Opinion is divided on everyone from George Carlin to Burns and Schreiber to Billy Crystal. Same with comedy movies and shows like *Saturday Night Live* and *MAD TV.* You can never account for people's taste. Put yourself in that exalted position, act like the protector of some throne, and you're in trouble. Comedic taste changes all the time, and quickly. If I was ever a king, it was only of my own company. Otherwise no one in town is royalty except the talent.

The credit I *can* take for the first five years of *Saturday Night Live* is only for inside and below-the-line stuff. Sandy and I negotiated and renegotiated contracts, won concessions for Lorne and the Not Ready for Prime Time Players we managed: Belushi, Aykroyd, Gilda Radner, and, for a time, Chevy Chase, as well as writer Alan Zweibel and others.

We also dealt with their neuroses. Lorne always had to put out fires and handle conflicts between cast members who believed that he liked one more than the other. Everyone was anxious about their airtime turf. Some weeks everyone hated everyone else, including me, especially when Lorne would ask me to help settle everyone down.

But mostly I just listened. That's how Lorne wanted me to take care of him. I'd been through the TV and talent wars and I could be an ear when Lorne complained about how, say, Chevy was driving him crazy by giving Danny Aykroyd notes on how to do a Scottish accent after they'd just spent eleven hours working together.

A manager's job all comes down to those moments. I'll always remember the day when Brad and Lorne and I were on our way out to lunch. Jon Lovitz passed us in the hall and said, "Have a good listen." That's exactly what I do and everyone knows it.

I wasn't yet forty-five, Sandy was younger, yet we were the old men of the operation. Lorne, and to a lesser extent NBC, counted on our expertise to guide these kids through the trouble spots, and I guided Lorne as well. That was my job. I tried to bring out the best in everyone. I wasn't some asshole interested only in making the next money move. I wanted to do the right thing. Had I not been there, *Saturday Night Live* would still have happened, but it might have been harder to do.

Beyond that I can't quantify my contribution, so I'm happy to settle for what Lorne told *Playboy* magazine about the night he accepted his Emmy after *Saturday Night Live*'s first season.

"I clutched my Emmy and thanked a lot of people. Then I thanked Bernie for being the one person who would listen to me when I complained about all the people I had just thanked."

· · · · ·

Yes, Lorne has class. He's the only guy I know who sends Sulka pajamas and bathrobes as a Christmas present. Everyone who works for him on a movie gets a photo of the stars in a silver frame after they wrap. Whenever I walk into the *Saturday Night Live* offices in New York, Lorne's attentions make me feel like God Himself is visiting. (Okay, like Mom and Dad have come to check up.) He always has diet soda in the office refrigerator. He sends flowers to my apartment. On show night, a girl always waits downstairs at NBC to bring me and my guests upstairs. That's the way it should be.

Lorne insists that I taught him much of this stuff, and if I did I'm proud of it, but I think it's mostly his own instinct. Lorne's regard for relationship, stability, and the past is unusual today. He doesn't do it just for me. When the late *New Yorker* editor William Shawn retired, Lorne gave him an office, gratis, at Broadway Video, but not so they could do business together, just out of respect.

I believe it all comes down to manners.

If more people brought their manners to business, they would do better. The workplace shouldn't have separate rules of behavior. At home you're trained to say please and thank you, to be on time, to consider the other person's feelings. It's the Golden Rule. I've been better at it some days than others, but I know the bottom line.

Say thank you. Answer or return every phone call. Not long ago, I was in the middle of putting together a movie of Alan Zweibel's play *Bunny, Bunny,* based on his book about his relationship with Gilda Radner. We needed a director and I said, "Why don't we go to Christopher Ashley, who directed the play? He's really good." I called Ashley, he said, "Great." I called Warner Brothers, they said, "Great." I called Ashley's agent, Sam Cohn, at ICM, I never heard back. Two months later he returned the call. Two months. I couldn't believe it. I said, "Tell Mr. Cohn that I have passed away," and hung up.

By the way, Sam Cohn, who for a long time was an icon in the agency business and represented people like Woody Allen, Mike Nichols, Whoopi Goldberg, Bob Fosse, Meryl Streep, Paul Newman, and Susan Sarandon, was last summer bought out of his ICM partnership and summarily removed from his position as vice chairman and head of the agency's New York office. Despite quirky personal habits like not returning phone calls, a deep antipathy for Los Angeles, and a tendency to eat paper when nervous, Cohn had a great eye for talent and developed some huge stars. And since we're speaking about manners, to further prove how screwed up our business can be, the people in ICM's L.A. headquarters had to read about Cohn's ouster in the papers! No memo was ever circulated beforehand. Shows what happens when you keep the office doors closed.

I keep mine open. I don't like to be interrupted, but if someone wants to walk in badly enough, I *want* to talk to them. You can call my style mom and pop, but I think it's just good management. I'd rather know what's going on by wandering the halls than by staying in my office and collecting information secretly.

Some people think manners have no place in business because it's one big power game. The less you care, the more you're in control. Bullshit. Why can't you be polite and still have power? Being polite stands out against the times you can't be — giving you more power. We all have to break someone's balls sometimes, but does that mean you can't write a thank-you note? What does it take? If you're too busy to put pen to paper, dictate it to a secretary.

When I go on vacation, where is it written that I can't call my clients? When I'm in Europe I'll give myself a half hour each day and check in with one client. When *they* go on vacation, I send a present — a bottle of wine or something — that's waiting for them when they arrive.

I also call people I care about to congratulate them on an opening weekend, for working hard, for finishing a project. Too often I hear, "Bernie, God bless you. Besides my wife, you're the only person I've heard from." What's with this town? If you notice something, call or write. Send a little gift. Or do it for no reason at all.

Even more important, make the call when someone is cold, when they've been fired, when their movie doesn't do well. Bill Maher floundered for three or four years before *Politically Incorrect* hit it big, yet I spoke to him every week. After I said, "How are you?" I mostly listened. Then I said, "Hey, Bill, what you do is different. You don't look like everyone else, you don't sound like everyone else. It takes longer for guys like you to make it, but when you make it, it's really going to be there." And now it is. And he's never forgotten that I cared.

If I'm remembered for anything in this life, I hope it's for caring.

Chapter 7

May All Your Deals Come True

At NBC's insistence, Lorne and I had put Jim Henson and a brand-new group of Muppets on *Saturday Night Live*, but by early 1976, only months into the first season, I had to get the Muppets off. In a moment of typical pique, head writer Michael O'Donoghue spoke for the staff when he announced that he "would no longer write for fucking felt." Good thing Scred, Ploobis, and the Mighty Favog weren't real; his caustic manner would have torn their Muppet hearts in two. His attitude didn't bother me. Without the Muppets NBC never would have put the show on the air and O'Donoghue would have had to ply his perverse talents elsewhere.

The truth is that O'Donoghue and the rest *couldn't* write for felt. Unlike Kermit the *frog* and Rowlf the *dog*, these lizard-like Muppets were abstract characters. No one knew how they were supposed to act, and it made the writers uncomfortable. Also, the Muppets needed a gentler touch than the ever-edgier *Saturday Night Live* scribes could muster. The Muppet and *Saturday Night Live* cultures just didn't mesh.

Lorne and Jim respected each other and wanted to end things without insult. The solution was to act like their exit was my idea.

I said, "Lorne, I think the Muppets should leave the show."

Without argument, he agreed to "try and get them out."

Done. I was glad our little one-act play had gone easily — but it wasn't much of a victory. Although Jim was always doing guest shots on one TV show or another, and he had *Sesame Street* — which he loved —

the *Saturday Night Live* gig had been yet another frustrating attempt at Jim's most elusive goal: reestablishing adult credentials.

We'd been trying for a long time. When *The Sonny and Cher Comedy Hour* was canceled in 1974 after the couple filed for divorce, Cher agreed to do her own variety series in early 1975 with *Laugh-In*'s creator, George Schlatter, producing. I booked Kermit on the show. When I got to the pre-taping, I watched him and Ray Charles sing "It's Not Easy Being Green." As the last note faded, Kermit put his hand on Ray's shoulder. It was only ten in the morning, much too early for such a tender moment, but the whole place got misty.

Afterwards, while Jim and I chatted with Schlatter, Perry Lafferty from CBS walked over. He'd been watching from the wings. I'd tried unsuccessfully to sell him a Muppet show for years, and suddenly I heard, "We're trying to fill the Sunday night at seven spot. I have ten thousand dollars for a presentation. Interested?"

"Of course," I said.

The next Saturday, at a little studio on La Brea, Schlatter, Jim, David Lazer (The Henson Company's new president), and I put together a twelve-minute tape compilation of the best Muppet characters and guest appearances. We loved the result and gave the tape to CBS.

We made it all the way to the finals. Then CBS had to choose between *The Muppet Show* and a program they had aired since 1968 that hadn't really taken off. We lost not only because CBS owned *60 Minutes*, but because it fit perfectly into their game plan to counterprogram the family fare on NBC and ABC with a show for grown-ups.

I was left with a great presentation and nothing to do until *Saturday Night Live* came along.

I wonder whatever happened to *60 Minutes*?

• • • • •

While Lorne's show steadily became required viewing for the TV counterculture, I tried to figure out what I could do to make Jim's vision equally as appealing to a network. The Henson Company was plenty busy: *Sesame Street* had hit its stride, the merchandise was selling like crazy, and Jim constantly churned out new ideas. But we needed to create some media momentum. I booked Kermit and Rowlf on Julie Andrews's show, and even sold a couple Muppet specials to ABC, as pilots — *The Muppet Valentine Special* starring Mia Farrow and *The Muppet Show: Sex and Violence* — but they didn't rate well and the network lost interest in doing more.

Then, a little guy named Hal Huff, working out of a back room at the local CBS station in New York, got the idea that the Muppets might make a great syndicated show in the new 7-to-8-P.M. prime-time-access hour. It was off-limits to the networks except on Sunday night — hence *60 Minutes.*

On his own, Huff called in the idea to his friend, Pierre Weiss, who worked at ITC, the American sales and syndication arm of the English entertainment conglomerate ATV, owned by the late Lord Lew Grade, a robust entrepreneur and one-time champion Charleston dancer whose family migrated from Russia to London's East End when he was six years old. Grade's real name was Winogradsky. Alone, and with his brothers Bernard (Lord Delfont) and Leslie, Grade cobbled together an empire that for a time controlled British show business. He also had a great sense of humor. Before James Cameron made *Titanic* and became King of the World, Lord Grade also spent a bundle on his movie, *Raise the Titanic.* When the cost overruns threatened to destroy his film company, he said "it would have been cheaper to lower the Atlantic."

ITC's president, Abe Mandel, heard Huff's idea and went looking for me. When he found me I flew to New York with my twelve-minute Muppet presentation. I took a car to his house in Scarsdale and walked into the middle of a bad day. Mandel wore an eye patch. His den floor was flooded. I asked myself, "What the hell am I doing here?"

"We want to do this show," he said. I was all for that.

"Great," I said. "What's next? What do I have to do?"

"I've got a hundred thousand dollars for a pilot," he said.

"You don't have to spend a hundred thousand," I said. "I have the pilot in my pocket." He had no idea what I meant. Maybe he expected me to pull a Muppet out of my pants. I handed him the tape. "Just look at this."

I explained what we wanted to do: a whimsical, satirical, funny family show that was smart enough to engage kids *and* adults; that meant the Muppets would be lovable, but not *too* lovable. Like *Saturday Night Live*, there'd be a guest host each week, and music.

Mandel was sold. He recognized then what *Time* magazine would later say about Jim Henson: "[He] is the rarest of creatures in the imitative and adaptive world of entertainment — an originator."

I went back to Los Angeles while the lawyers worked out the details. When Mandel called, he found me at the old Brown Derby restaurant on Wilshire and Rodeo, having lunch with Michael Ovitz. They brought a phone to the table. Mandel said, "Congratulations. We're ordering twenty-four Muppet shows to start." My packaging fee would be $4,000 per show, or ninety-six grand. I managed to keep the merchandising for Jim, but gave 10 percent of the net merchandising profits to Grade.

Jim was in London on business. I called him immediately and gave him the news. He said, "I love you," and hung up. Then I told Ovitz what had happened. All through lunch he kept repeating, "Ninety-six grand?" Good money at the time. After nine years of never giving up on a Muppet show, it was one of the greatest days of my life.

There was still one loose thread. Since the show was syndicated and had a less-than-network budget, there was no room for George Schlatter as a producer, even though he'd been so helpful. When I broke the news he backed out like the wonderfully sweet guy he is. He didn't ask for a penny. Schlatter could have, and considering the money we later made — and he didn't — he deserves enormous credit for never complaining once.

The Muppet Show debuted September 20, 1976, at 7:30 P.M. on the CBS owned and operated stations. Most people then didn't know the difference between a network show and a syndicated show, so it seemed like we were on CBS proper. That detail had helped me sell Jim on the syndication idea in the first place.

The story line was the same each week: the personal relationships and craziness behind the Muppets' attempt to put on a show in their Muppet Theater. Once Scooter knocked on the guest host's dressing room door to announce that it was curtain time, and the Muppet theme song played ("It's time to put on makeup / It's time to dress up right . . ."), anything could happen and it usually did. *The Muppet Show* introduced Miss Piggy, and transformed her from a member of the chorus into the star she always knew she'd be. Her imperious nature and infatuation with Kermit became a "cause célèbre." Statler and Waldorf, the curmudgeons in the box seats, were based on a guy who used to heckle Milton Berle, as part of his act. In case you're wondering, Waldorf's wife *was* named Astoria;

they were all named after famous New York hotels. Other memorable characters included Fozzie Bear, Rowlf, the Great Gonzo, Dr. Floyd Pepper, Animal, Lew Zealand, and Rizzo the Rat. Kermit ran the whole affair and desperately tried to keep it all from falling apart.

Of course, the Muppets couldn't do it on their own. They got help and inspiration from the men behind (or underneath them): Jim, Jerry Nelson (Floyd, Dr. Strangepork, and Lew Zealand — who manages a boomerang fish act); Steve Whitmire (Rizzo); Dave Goelz (Gonzo, Zoot); Richard Hunt (Scooter, the shaggy, nine-foot Sweetums); and Frank Oz (Miss Piggy, Fozzie Bear; and on *Sesame Street* Bert to Henson's Ernie, and Cookie Monster). I've always thought of Frank Oz and Jim Henson as one of the great pairings of all time, right up there with Martin and Lewis, Abbot and Costello, Laurel and Hardy.

As 1978 drew to a close, *Time* magazine said, "With *Laugh-In* long gone, [*The Muppet Show*] is, give or take *Saturday Night Live*, the funniest show on television." You know I had to love that. They also called *The Muppet Show* "the only adult show on television." Finally reading that after so many years must have felt to Jim like Kermit singing in his ear.

· · · · ·

When Jim was ready, David Lazer and I sold Lord Grade on the idea of making *The Muppet Movie.* The story was about the Muppets' journey from obscurity to stardom. The budget was $9 million. A couple studio heads I told thought Grade was a moron because Disney was making kids' movies for a million and a half. Grade, God bless him, believed in Jim — and not only because he made millions from *The Muppet Show.* Jim had proved himself. Grade, who bore a striking resemblance to the short, bald Muppet mad scientist, Dr. Bunsen Honeydew, said, "Here's the money. Go do it."

At first, no one was sure it was technically possible to make a full-length movie that paired humans and puppets without everything looking ridiculous and out of place. And even if it worked, could the pace of a thirty-minute *Muppet Show* be stretched to ninety minutes without falling flat? The director, Jim Frawley, wondered how, when the Muppets ventured outside, they'd get around without feet. Even when those problems were solved, Jim Henson wasn't sure what he had or who the audience would be.

When *The Muppet Movie* opened at the Cinerama Dome in Los Angeles I drove down Sunset Boulevard on Friday night to see what was happening at the theater. From a block away I didn't see a soul out front and I panicked. Jim was waiting for my report. I kept driving, slowly, and then I saw people lined up around the corner and down the block. It was unbelievable.

A reviewer called the film a "tour de force of puppetry," and by now it's grossed over $100 million, most of that made in 1979–80 dollars. The Henson Company went on to do other films, including *The Great Muppet Caper,* directed by Jim; *The Muppets Take Manhattan, Dark Crystal, Labyrinth, The Muppet Christmas Carol,* and *Muppet Treasure Island.* Soon the Muppets will travel to outer space, Elmo will be lost in Grouchland, and Kermit will have his own cable channel.

Recently, *Time* magazine TV critic James Collins called Jim one of the hundred most influential entertainers of our century, noting, "Jim Henson . . . had the most profound influence on children of any entertainer of his time; he adapted the ancient art of puppetry to the most modern of mediums, television, transforming both; he created a TV show that was one of the most popular on earth. But Henson's greatest achievement was broader than any of these . . . he helped sustain the qualities of fancifulness, warmth and consideration that have been so threatened by our coarse, cynical age."

In 1981, after five years on the air, Jim decided he'd rather quit the TV show on top than risk running it into the ground. He wanted to concentrate on films and emerging technologies. ITC resyndicated *The Muppet Show.* Never before had a first-run syndicated show been stripped a second time. When it was all over, the take was $100 million. Based on my percentages, $2 to 3 million trickled down to me.

The Muppet Show was a phenomenal success, reaching an estimated 250 million viewers each week in more than a hundred countries. It won three Emmys and numerous other awards. After that, as I once told *People* magazine, "Jim belonged to the world."

• • • • •

Jim was patient and rarely raised his voice. He didn't like confrontation, so he usually gave me the unpleasant jobs. I knew it was dead serious time when he told me to fire his head writer, Jack Burns, who was my good friend and client. The way Jim did it was perfectly Jim. He called from London and said, "Hi, Bernie, how ya doing?"

"Fine. How does everything look?"

"Fine," he said, and paused. "You know something, Bernie? Jack Burns gives me a stomachache."

I knew exactly what he meant. Time to make a change. "How soon?" I asked.

"Soon," he said.

Jim had his reasons. Jack is by nature tough. He'd go at the puppeteers and argue about jokes. He didn't think they knew what was funny. He knew he'd ruffled some feathers, and ultimately he went head-to-head with Jim.

I will go to my grave believing that Jack Burns really helped make *The Muppet Show* a hit. His writing gave it that show business-y edge. Some people thought it wasn't quite the Muppet style, but that's what the program was about: *putting on a show.* The genius was the weave between the musical numbers, the hundreds of characters, the writing, and the guest stars.

But that's just my opinion. I still had to give Jack the bad news. My rule is to give it directly and immediately. Being able to make the bad call separates the men from the boys. I learned to do it when my father used to say, "Go in and talk to your mother." It's tough. You don't wake up in the morning and think, "Geez, I'd like to ruin somebody's day." Lots of people avoid this. I know lots of network executives who *never* make the bad call; they hire someone to do it for them. When the networks choose their next season's shows each May, you know it's good news when the network boss is on the phone. When it's someone who works for them, it's time to follow Plan B.

The toughest times to call are when someone's died. Literally. Just while writing this book, I've had to make calls about the late and gifted Chris Farley and Phil Hartman, both our clients. Having been through similar circumstances with Belushi, Gilda Radner, and Jim Henson didn't make it any easier.

Next is when a client's career is in critical condition. When trouble is in the air, some agents will say, "Don't worry, I'll take care of it. There's another job around the corner." The manager will say, "We're working on this." The lawyer will say, "Oh, don't worry, we're fine." It's all bullshit. Someone has to find the nerve to say, "We're fucked. We'd better start at the beginning. We better get off our high horses and get working again; otherwise we'll be out of business." When you do, you hear the deep breath on the other end of the line, and then the anger. This is not what a client wants to hear, but he has to be able to depend on someone being honest, no matter how much it pisses him off. I've seen too many people disappear from entertainment because everyone they'd paid to advise them said, "It's all okay." Yeah. Zip-a-dee-doo-dah, and all of a sudden six months go by and no one's called with work.

There's a flip side to this. I have the balls to say almost anything to anyone. I have that sort of smile and manner that lets me go, "Oh, and how about fuck you?" and get away with it.

I told Jack that Jim wanted him gone and he took it well. Then I convinced Lord Grade to back another show starring the Hudson brothers, with Jack producing. It was the least I could do.

· · · · ·

In 1987, the Friends of the Los Angeles Free Clinic held a fundraising "roast." I was the guest of honor. On the dais were Jim Henson, Richard Dreyfuss, Garry Shandling, Norm Crosby, Dabney Coleman, Jay Tarses, Jackie Gayle, and Brandon Tartikoff, who emceed. When Jim's turn came, he showed a clip of Miss Piggy talking to her manager, Bernie, made a few jokes at my expense about *ALF*, another "puppet" show I produced, then gave me a token of his affection: a Bernie Muppet. It's eerie, but Jim captured me perfectly, from the white hair and beard to my open mouth and the phone at my ear. I only wish I was as thin.

When Henson did a short routine with the Bernie Muppet, his impression of me sounded more like Rowlf the dog, but he ended on a high note when "Bernie" said he was going to sleep with my wife even though he didn't exist from the waist down. "Debbie told me not to worry," he said. "That's what she's used to."

I keep the Bernie Muppet in a glass case in my office. I've only added one thing: a green ribbon from Jim's funeral. Above it on the wall is a framed and signed picture of Jim at his happiest. Kermit sits high on a bookshelf nearby. Kermit was Jim. Jim was Kermit. Since Jim died in 1990, it's just one more way for me to stay connected.

· · · · ·

Over at NBC, there was nothing more exciting than to hear, "Live, from New York, it's *Saturday Night!*" The show had become the place where the voice of the TV generation was finally heard in all its rebellious, politically incorrect glory. It, too, would become a force larger than anyone had anticipated.

Nowadays, everyone thinks the show was an *immediate* hit. Not quite. The audience grew steadily, and reviews ranged from positive to ecstatic, but it still took a couple seasons for *Saturday Night Live*'s influence to extend beyond its original fans and into the culture at large.

Visiting studio 8H and the seventeenth floor of 30 Rockefeller Center was always exciting. When I dropped by I'd arrive at 1 P.M., though sometimes Lorne didn't get there until 3, so I'd sit in the bleachers and watch the rehearsals. I saw the first time Danny and Steve Martin did "Two Wild and Crazy Guys." I watched Bill Murray do Nick the lounge singer, and as Buck Henry looked through the glass coffee table at Gilda and Laraine's underpants as Uncle Roy. The media quickly caught on and gradually stories on the show appeared in New York, Los Angeles, and other big city papers. But the heartland wasn't fully penetrated until the success of *Animal House* caused millions of new fans to invade Belushi's TV home. By then, *Saturday Night Live*'s impact was undeniable, its characters and routines talked about at water coolers Monday mornings.

When the Rolling Stones went riff-to-riff with the Blues Brothers on the fourth season's opening show, *Saturday Night Live* went supernova. In the celebrity-studded audience watching it happen were: Steve Martin, Paul Simon, Steven Spielberg, and New York mayor Ed Koch. During the show I liked to stand near Lorne, but that night I kept my eyes on NBC president Fred Silverman. I'd seen the dress rehearsal, so I knew what was coming. When Mick Jagger licked Stones guitarist Ron Wood on the lips on live TV, Silverman's mouth fell open, his face turned white. I'd never seen a look like that on a network president, though when he got a load of *Hello, Larry* and *Supertrain*'s ratings, it must have been good practice.

That night was the payoff of an instinct I had a couple years earlier when I first suspected that the show had destiny written all over it. Just before the second season Paul McCartney called me to say, "We're having a little birthday party. I'd like to hire John Belushi to do his Joe Cocker impression."

"Fine," I said. "That's great." Great? Incredible!

He said, "We'll give him six thousand dollars." Belushi was making eight hundred dollars a week. I took it.

We never looked back.

For the first couple seasons, NBC was only marginally aware of what it had in *Saturday Night Live.* The management had a big important network to run; *Saturday Night Live* was only one show, and in late-night at that, where Carson was already king. You can bet the suits didn't stay up until 11:30 on Saturday night waiting to see what outrage the writers and Not Ready for Prime Time Players would come up with next. To tell you the truth, the network guys were mostly afraid: of no one watching, of complaints from those who did, of spending too much to please Lorne, of scandalous material slipping by the censors and going out live on the airwaves.

Lorne and I were able to use the network's apprehension and tendency to bury their heads in the sand against them every year when we renegotiated his contract. NBC never wanted to pay Lorne what we thought he was worth. I'd fight for more money, they'd be difficult, and then Lorne and I would say, "Give us a piece of the show instead. What the hell difference does it make? It's not worth anything anyway." They did and we smiled and took it. Could I help it if NBC undervalued future syndication and thought that the only thing you could sell on home video was a porn film? (By the way, in those years, that *was* most of what was on video.)

For the fourth season Lorne finally got a big raise. It was almost seven times what he'd made his first year. NBC also paid Lorne extra to produce a couple *Best of Saturday Night Live* prime-time specials. Lorne used the money to start his production company, Broadway Video, which did the specials. When we renewed his contract for the fifth season, Lorne ended up sharing video and syndication rights equally with NBC.

• • • • •

Lorne once told me that *Saturday Night Live* had a rock and roll mentality and that it needed people involved who understood that. He was so insistent that I wondered why anyone would want "showbiz" Bernie Brillstein hanging around. To me, rock and roll meant energy, youth, rebellion, and thinking outside the box. It made sense for me to manage Lorne; we had a history and trusted each other. But what about

Belushi, Chevy Chase, Gilda Radner, and later, Danny Aykroyd, Alan Zweibel, Rosie Shuster, Don Novello, and others? I was an old-school guy, with roots in an earlier era. You'd have thought these kids would want someone younger looking out for them.

Apparently not. This doesn't mean I was some fat Pied Piper who charmed them into following me. As always, it was circumstance. Look at Belushi; he instinctively spotted an opportunity and played it brilliantly in two minutes flat.

My connection to Lorne also helped with my other *Saturday Night Live* clients. If someone asked about me, Lorne would say that I was honest, smart, and adaptable. He believed it. He also knew that if anyone else handled these people he'd be worse off. I'd protect him until I couldn't anymore, but I'd go to the wall trying. Better to have me around than some money-hungry fool who would give Lorne's people bad career advice — in other words, urge them to leave the show early for greener pastures. Lorne wanted everyone to stay so that the show had continuity and could grow intact. He believed the whole cast needed more time to mature as performers, not to mention become adjusted to their new high-profile circumstances. He was largely correct. Sticking around never hurt anyone. (Just ask the former supporting players on *Seinfeld*.) Even though no one could predict how crazy in-demand the *Saturday Night Live* cast would become, and how the pressures of superstardom would rip everything apart no matter how much we wished otherwise, staying loyal seemed like common sense.

Because of Lorne's tacit support and whatever God-given gifts I have that make artists comfortable around me, I became godfather to a new crop of comic talent. To my surprise, they loved the idea that I'd already been there and done that yet didn't sport open-to-the-navel shirts, gold chains, and a well-chewed cigar. I didn't wear a headband or Nehru suit or try to use them to get myself laid. I knew I was funny, but I didn't try to out-funny them. And I didn't try to *be* them. That was the last thing Belushi, Aykroyd, and Gilda wanted.

I discovered right away that these kids needed my stability. They had enough people around them who were nuts. I wasn't a crazy. I had a family, I didn't stay out until 7 A.M., I didn't drink or do dope. Belushi used to tell me, "You walk into a party backwards," meaning that I walk into a party already leaving.

They also respected what I'd done and seen. Belushi used to spend hours talking to me: "Tell me about Martin and Lewis. Tell me about Jackie Gleason." For a long time we planned a trip to Vegas because he had never been there with me. He wanted me to show him *my* Vegas, take him into the health club, get a massage, gamble, see a few shows.

These kids also loved that I came to the office in Adidas sweat suits — not to be a trendsetter, but because "corrective clothing" is more comfortable when you're fat. They loved that I didn't tell them what I thought they wanted to hear but listened instead to what they had to say. They expected me to be *hamish*, to be wise, to be a calming influence in an often dysfunctional family, and to always be there when needed. I was a surrogate dad. In the midst of insanity and users and yes-people they needed at least one person to tell them the truth.

Even though on the surface we were very different, in the most important way we were *exactly* alike: we all loved comedy. Once I saw them in action I understood what they were trying to do. You didn't have to be "rock and roll" to get it.

· · · · ·

Between the second and third seasons of *Saturday Night Live*, a script by Doug Kenney, Chris Miller, and Harold Ramis about a slobby college fraternity arrived at my office for Belushi. I read it and, genius that I am, told Sandy Wernick, "It's funny, but who cares about fraternities? They couldn't be colder."

Sandy said, "Let me go have lunch with [the director, John] Landis and [the producer, Ivan] Reitman at Universal." When he returned he said, "The movie sounds pretty funny. And they *want* Belushi."

Sandy said filming would start in October 1977, after Belushi finished a small role in Mexico in Jack Nicholson's movie *Going South*. The third season of *Saturday Night Live* was scheduled to kick off in late September, so John would have to commute between New York (where he worked Wednesday through Saturday), and the *Animal House* location in Eugene, Oregon (where he worked Monday and Tuesday). Fortunately the shoot would only take thirty-one days.

I said, "Okay. The main thing is that it will keep Belushi off the streets." With Chevy's departure from *Saturday Night Live*, John was squarely in the spotlight. The audience loved him. But the demands and disorientation of superstardom, combined with his naturally impulsive tendencies, put extra pressure on what had become an explosively unpredictable personality. More and more he swerved between a fragile sweetness and anarchistic darkness. I figured as long as Belushi was working, he would be less likely to make trouble for himself. In those days I could still trust that he'd be okay. Later, I couldn't.

Belushi had already met Landis and liked him. He wanted to do the picture. We made a deal and John got $35,000 for the role of John "Bluto" Blutarsky.

While *Animal House* filmed in the Northwest, I kept hearing that everything was more or less fine. Nothing out of the ordinary. Maybe a little trouble now and then, but nothing serious that Landis couldn't handle. Then word filtered back from Universal that the dailies were fantastic. In the spring of 1978, Universal screened the film in Denver. It went over the top. A couple days later Landis came to my office with an audiotape of the audience response during the screening. It was nonstop laughter. I couldn't believe it. I was so excited. The next thing I knew, the word of mouth began that there had never been a movie quite like *Animal House.*

Before the *Animal House* premiere in New York on July 28, 1978, Belushi and I strolled down Fifth Avenue, a couple heavy-set guys with great expectations. John was in good spirits. He believed he had a hit on his hands. Sean Daniel, the Universal Pictures production executive in charge of the movie, agreed. Company president Ned Tanen wasn't so sure. My attitude was wait and see and hope for lightning in a bottle.

The New York premiere can only be described as lunacy in an enclosed space, but the review in the next day's *New York Times* was lukewarm: "*Animal House* is by no means one long howl, but it's often funny, with gags that are effective in a dependable, all-purpose way." Belushi shook it off and told me to wait until we got to Chicago. That was home. People were less uptight and knew how to laugh. They'd go wild. He was right. Before the week was out, *Animal House* was a hit. Most film critics found the movie endearingly subversive. Kids wore togas to weekend parties. Beer keg sales must have tripled. Belushi became an overnight sensation, gracing magazine covers. Suddenly he was magic.

The day after the premiere, I picked up another client, *Saturday Night Live* writer Alan Zweibel. His good friend Gilda Radner introduced us, and one evening over dinner at the River Cafe in New York she asked me to take him on. I met Zweibel for breakfast. He said he had another manager, but he had let their contract expire and waited a few months to speak with me so that it didn't seem like he was simply jumping ship. He asked me to sign him and I said fine, on three conditions: "I get ten percent, I want first option to be executive producer of your projects, and if I find out that you've been bad-mouthing me behind my back, it's over." He said, "I wouldn't do that." I said, "Well, then, I guess we have nothing to worry about."

There was no contract, no lawyer. I just stuck my hand across the table. Alan told me later it was like making a pact with Vito Corleone.

• • • • •

Only Belushi could have made the role of Bluto work. When talking about why they wanted Belushi, *Animal House* co-writer Chris Miller once said, "The core of a great animal-house fraternity is a great animal. We all looked at each other and said, 'Belushi!'" As the box office climbed, John started getting movie offers. Among the callers: Steven Spielberg. He'd met John during the first season of *Saturday Night Live* and they'd immediately liked each other. Spielberg planned to direct a comedy; Belushi had just starred in the summer's biggest. Working together seemed like a no-brainer.

Spielberg's film was *1941*, a comedy spoof about a Japanese military strike on the California coast during World War II. He wanted Belushi to play Wild Bill Kelso. I read the script and told him to pass. Nothing against Spielberg, but I just didn't get it. It was too big, too mushy, and not funny. I figured if I knew anything, it was the meaning of funny. "It's supposed to be a huge comedy," I told him. "If it's not done right it will be a disaster."

Spielberg was an icon, the man who'd made *Jaws* and *Close Encounters.* Everyone wanted to work with him, and Belushi was no exception. He also wanted Aykroyd to play Sergeant Tree, and said he wouldn't do the film otherwise. He didn't have to posture. Spielberg recognized Dan's talent and quickly agreed. The only thing left for me to do was make the deal and see that everything went smoothly. It didn't matter that I thought the whole thing wouldn't work and that the boys had made a mistake. They'd decided. It was their lives. I could only suggest, not control. It was time to stop being a critic.

I got Belushi $350,000 — ten times his *Animal House* fee — and negotiated Aykroyd's deal as well. Neither had an agent at the time. Danny also became my client.

1941 didn't live up to anyone's expectations, including Spielberg's. He realized during filming that it wasn't funny enough. That I turned out to be right doesn't make me happy, but I think my instincts made John and Danny respect me more down the line. John used to go around telling everyone that I'd told him not to do the film, as if it were some badge of honor.

Sometimes you can predict the future. Sometimes you can't. When director Tom Shadyac came to see me about being a client, I told him not to do *The Nutty Professor.* I thought Eddie Murphy had lost the humor that used to sparkle in his eyes. To me he was never better than he was in *Trading Places.* I told Shadyac "Man, don't do it." I was wrong. Later, I called the producer, Brian Grazer, and said, "I wouldn't have done it, but you did. God bless you."

After *1941* started filming in October 1978, I got a call from Mel Sattler, the head of business affairs at Universal Pictures. Mel was a friend of my father-in-law's. He said, "*Animal House* is huge and we've got to have Belushi."

I said, "You don't have him. There are no options on his deal and I've got calls for him coming in from everywhere." I left it at that. Before long I heard from Sean Daniel, who put it on a personal level and told me he had to deliver Belushi. Thom Mount, then head of Universal Pictures, called, too. I was friendly, but noncommittal. However, down deep I figured we'd end up at Universal out of loyalty. They'd brought John to the dance with *Animal House.* I believe in giving the edge to those who demonstrate their faith early; not that I told them that.

Having that edge — in other words, all things being otherwise equal, having the potential to have events go your way — is what greases the show-business wheel. Suppose a writer or producer comes to my office with a great idea. We have a star who loves it. Where do I go? Probably to the studio who gave me the last hit, the one I have the most access to, or the guy I owe one to. Sometimes they're all the same person. There's no cheating in this, it's not dishonest, but it's not an open game. If I have a hot sitcom, I go to the networks in a certain order, appropriate to our relationships with them at the time. It's not some creative mystery. A salesman goes where he's received best, depending on the product he's selling.

When I recently got involved in HBO's *Mr. Show*, starring Bob Odenkirk and David Cross, I was flattered that they had come to me. My instinct said they were really good. I went to Chris Albrecht and Carolyn Strauss at HBO and said, "This is great, guys, take a pop. I'm behind it." When I say that, it means something. My passion helped it get sold. But I also had an edge. At the time, our company had *The Larry Sanders Show* there, and Dennis Miller's show. We do business with HBO all the time, so I knew they might say, "Let's take a chance on Bob and David. Bernie's behind it, Brad's behind it." And it paid off. In 1998, *Mr. Show* was named one of the year's top ten programs by the *New York Times; Entertainment Weekly* wrote it up as the show all the funny and hippest people watch.

That same relationship helped us sell *The Sopranos* — an hour-long series about a modern mob boss's midlife crises — to HBO, where it became a critical hit before it even aired, and a hugely popular one when it finally did. Now we really have an edge!

That's what all those business dinners and vacations together are about: edge. That little something to put you over. The equity of trust and a track record. It's what makes deals come true. Otherwise, negotiating is probably the least dramatic thing I do. In fact, I've never negotiated a great deal. I have only negotiated what people want to pay — and maybe a little more. Period. Negotiation isn't one of the great arts; that's why lawyers do it. Sometimes it gets dirty and mean, but all this talk about the "art of the deal" is usually just media-intensified story-telling. Generally, it's about finding the proper strategy to move things ahead, not about whose dick is bigger. Sometimes I think that if we lived the lives the media gave us, we couldn't call them lives at all.

Here's the truth about the art of the deal: it all comes down to who's your client and how desperately the other guy wants him. It's about a moment in time, nothing more. After *Animal House* I could get just about anything I wanted for John Belushi because he'd hit like a fucking rocket. I could have been a moron and still have made out.

No one at Universal knew *Animal House* would be a hit, but it came right out of the blocks, and John "Bluto" Blutarsky was the character everyone remembered. Overnight, Belushi became a movie star. Later on, in the fall, his new teenage fans would flock to *Saturday Night Live* and push the show's ratings into the late-night stratosphere.

Mel Sattler called back to say Universal really wanted to make a deal. I began to feel my oats. I said, "Look, Belushi made thirty-five grand on *Animal House*, and you guys are making millions. Now everyone's coming after him. But I'm a loyal guy. You took a shot with him. So how about a few retroactive points of the profits?"

Maybe I got the balls to say that because I knew John Landis had gotten a similar deal. Or maybe it was because Mel had mentioned my father-in-law a couple times in the conversation. I sensed he was trying to make friends with me. It was a different approach than Universal's usual heavy-handedness. But Mel said there was no way he could give any points. I decided not to push it.

"Okay," I said. "Here's what I'll do: Send me two hundred and fifty thousand today. Call it a bonus, a show of good faith" — this is 1978 and Belushi was making $1,000 a week on *Saturday Night Live* — "and I won't make a deal with another studio until you make me a three-picture offer. If I like it, he's yours. If I don't, we're free. Give it your best shot. I'll decide on the spot."

Next I checked in with Belushi. He asked me how things were going and if I thought he and his wife, Judy, would be able to afford $1,800 a month to buy an apartment in Greenwich Village.

Mel messengered the check to my office. It was so easy that I figure I should have asked for a million! The next day I went to Universal. I met with Sattler and Thom Mount. I got there a little early because I always believe in smelling the room before any meeting to see if the situation is right for me to do business. Believe me when I tell you that the room smelled like money. We talked for a while and then I said, "I'm going to walk outside for ten minutes. When I come back, give me your best numbers."

I found a phone and called Belushi. I told him how things were going and, before I hung up, added, "Oh, I think you'll be able to afford that apartment."

If there was any art to this deal, it was putting the onus on Universal. I left them to figure out what we wanted and that meant they had to give me more than usual. In fact, they couldn't afford to lose. After *Animal House* hit, it would have looked terrible for Universal chairman Lew Wasserman to lose Belushi. It wasn't really their fault that they didn't have an option on his services; who thinks of taking an option on a TV actor getting thirty-five grand for a part in an ensemble film? Who knew that Belushi would wind up the poster boy for a summer's worth of toga parties and a million guys who looked like him? Belushi was "Every Guy

Who Couldn't Get a Date" — the one who had something crazy in his head but rarely got laid. He had to look at the naked girls through the window. From now on, the girls would be looking in his window.

When I walked back into the meeting, Sattler and Mount laid out the numbers: three pictures. $350,000 for the first (which would be *1941*), $500,000 for the second, $750,000 for the third — and the $250,000 just for listening — plus per diems and all the usual star perks.

Done. I called Belushi. He couldn't believe it. That was great money in those days and he thought I was an atomic scientist. I wasn't. I just had my first big acting star, and the guy had pushed us both into a whole new world. Belushi had become *BELUSHI!* I could hardly believe it myself.

I'd also left the meeting as Belushi's movie producer. It was not a payoff from the movie company for having delivered the prize. Belushi himself insisted I executive produce. A couple months before, when I'd talked to Universal about making a Blues Brothers movie, the first question I asked John and Danny was, "Don't you want Lorne to produce?" After all, the whole thing had originated on *Saturday Night Live.*

"Absolutely not," they said.

"We want you," Danny said.

"I'm not going to make movies without you to protect me," John added.

It was nothing against Lorne. Lorne had always been the boss, but this was their way of symbolically leaving home. John and Danny wanted to be in control and this was their shot. Before the fourth season of *Saturday Night Live,* John was already thinking of leaving the show. Danny, too, only less so. I didn't want them to, for the same reasons I wanted Chevy to stick around, but the movie work was piling up, and the boys were feeling boxed in at *Saturday Night Live.* I could feel the space between the rock and the hard place growing smaller. It would take another year for them to quit, but this was a first step toward separation.

• • • • •

Here's when I knew I'd finally made it: September 9, 1978, the night the Blues Brothers opened for Steve Martin at the Universal Amphitheater in Los Angeles. I'd loved the Blues Brothers ever since John and Danny, backed by the *Saturday Night Live* band, occasionally warmed up the audience before shows during the third season. Soon, John wanted to play on the air, and he kept bugging Lorne, who finally gave them the go-ahead. The Blues Brothers debuted on the April 22, 1978, show. Steve Martin was the host, and from start to finish, that night has been called the best *Saturday Night Live* ever. Afterwards, I had an idea: Since the Blues Brothers *were* real, the music so great, and the show so popular, why not capitalize on all that and make a Blues Brothers album? It was too easy. I called Michael Klefner at Atlantic Records, who offered $125,000, and we had a deal. John promised to assemble a top-notch band.

Next, I arranged for the Blues Brothers to open Steve Martin's nine-night stand at the Universal Amphitheater, just after Labor Day. Martin's agent, Marty Klein, owed me. A couple years earlier he'd wanted Lorne to have Steve Martin host the show, but he couldn't get anywhere. Martin's arrow-through-the-head comedy wasn't Lorne's type of humor. Klein asked for my help. I suggested Lorne check out Martin's act again; he did and changed his mind. Not only did Steve Martin become a *Saturday Night Live* mainstay, he's long been one of Lorne's best friends.

When I made the Amphitheater deal, Klein said, "I can only pay seventeen thousand for all nine nights." That was birdseed, but I didn't care. (John and Danny used the $17,000 to pay the band.) By then, Steve Martin was the hottest comic in the country, in part due to *Saturday Night Live.* I knew we'd have a friendly crowd, perfect for recording the shows live for the album *Briefcase Full of Blues.* I thought of it as investment in the future; so did Belushi, who used $100,000 of his own money to record the gigs because the record company money was too slow to arrive. We were both right. The album came out on December 5 and right away went to number one. By the time the Amphitheater gig rolled around, an earlier investment — *Animal House* — had also paid off. That only made the crowd more enthusiastic.

The day before the sold-out shows, John and Danny asked me to come to their rehearsal stage somewhere in Hollywood to see the entire set for the first time. The boys had been working hard and wanted me to wait until they were ready. They were *ready.* I was floored. I had only one comment. I said, "John, when you come onstage at the Amphitheater, please don't saunter out like you do on TV. It's a long walk and you don't have the time."

"Don't worry," he said. "I can make the greatest entrance since Jimmy Durante."

Durante was known for his entrances. At the Copa, he used to come onstage banging the piano, throwing sheet music, yelling, and screaming. By the time he got to the microphone, there was a riot in the place. I was impressed that John knew about Durante's opening and wondered how he would top it.

As the band broke into Otis Redding's "Can't Turn You Loose," Danny Aykroyd, wearing his Elwood Blues getup — black suit, Ray-Ban shades, skinny black tie, and Fedora hat — stood patiently onstage, waiting. Then he said:

"Good evening everyone and welcome to the United States of America. And indeed we have congregated here at this time to celebrate a most treasured wellspring of contemporary music . . . Tonight, assembled exclusively for your entertainment pleasure, from the music capitals of this continent, this is the hard-working all-star show from Jake and Elwood Blues. Ladies and gentlemen, these are the Blues Brothers."

This was usually when John Belushi, as Joliet Jake Blues, walked out, casually twirling a key on a long chain. He'd unlock a briefcase handcuffed to Dan's wrist, and Danny would take out his harmonica and begin to wail.

But not tonight. This night would be different from all other nights.

Over the Otis Redding backbeat, John, hardly the most athletic figure in show business, triple-cartwheeled from the wings to center stage. The audience went nuts and so did I. It had been a long time since I'd felt such electricity surge through a crowd.

As the Blues Brothers played and bedlam broke out all around me, I found myself in a quiet place in my head as it hit me that I was no longer a little packager who'd sold a few TV shows, managed some of the people involved, and had gotten a little hot. Somehow, everything I'd worked so hard for came together and fell into place that night. *Saturday Night Live* was nearing its peak. *The Muppet Show* was among the world's most popular TV series, and their first film, *The Muppet Movie*, was in production. Patchett and Tarses had led *The Bob Newhart Show* into sitcom history. *Animal House* was not only a box-office smash but part of the culture.

Earlier that summer, when John and Danny were in Jerry Greenberg's office at Atlantic Records, wearing Blues Brothers hats and posing for pictures, Danny told me he had a story for a Blues Brothers movie. I thought, What the hell? and called Universal Pictures production vice president Sean Daniel from Greenberg's office.

I said, "Blues Brothers movie?"

Daniel said, "Deal." We'd work out the details when we had time.

Because of *Animal House*, any studio in town would have bought *The History of Air* if John agreed to star in it. A couple months later, *The Blues Brothers* would become the second film under Belushi's new three-picture Universal deal.

And I was in the center of it all.

After the concert, everyone celebrated at Victoria Station, a restaurant near the Amphitheater. The place was jammed with industry heavy-weights: actors, comedians, studio execs, record company presidents, network heads, and rock stars — and, for the first time in my life, they all kept coming over to talk to me. Sure, I knew that if I just stayed put, people had to wander over, but that night there was so much schmooze swirling around me that even my usual cynicism took a backseat to in-dulging in the temporary wonderfulness of it all. I didn't want to go home or go to sleep. I was Cinderella with a beard, at the ball, and it was way past midnight. Not even a clock striking twelve could have done a damn thing about my party attire. I wore a velvety jacket with a broad collar, a fancy shirt, Ray-Bans, a Blues Brother hat, and to top it off, a white scarf.

The party was for Steve Martin, John Belushi, Danny Aykroyd, and the band, but I felt like the one coming out. Everyone figured John and Danny were comic geniuses, so the guy who represented them must also be a comic genius. At the time, John and Danny gave very little credit to Lorne Michaels for putting them on the celebrity map, so I got much of the credit, undeserved. But I wasn't going to say, "Hey, I had nothing to do with these guys. I'm just a schlep." By keeping quiet, I assumed power. That's a great lesson: let people talk themselves into what a genius you are. People will assume just about anything.

Of course, I had contributed greatly. But after that night, and for years to come, I was "the gatekeeper," the only one who could get Danny, John, Jim Henson, Lorne, and Gilda on the phone, at any time. I had total access to people everyone wanted. If they ruled, I ruled. The three things I desired most when I started in the business — to be recognized, to get the calls, and to have the act everyone wanted — were suddenly mine.

Overnight I'd become a wheeler-dealer, and it had only taken twenty-three years. I felt like I was glowing. Most guys in my position might have taken some time to sit back and enjoy feeling like they had the keys to the kingdom. I did that — for a moment. Then I thought, "How the fuck am I going to handle *this*?"

· · · · ·

Becoming successful is the most fun of all. I'm not talking about *being* successful or *staying* successful. I mean the *getting there*, the instant you arrive, and the first time you think, "Where did I go right?"

For me, there is nothing like that moment. I'd built the client list I'd dreamt of and then realized, in the middle of a party packed with movers and shakers, that I'd done it. I'd made it.

Driving to work the next morning, the sun shined more brightly than usual. Maybe I still had a bit of a hangover, but it didn't matter. I knew one thing for sure: success had happened for me. Now anything was possible. I stopped for the red light at Sunset and Crescent, but inside I felt like the road was wide open. It took me a few years to realize that I had actually been at a treacherous intersection. Peaks are exhilarating and dangerous. Unless you have exceptional balance and stamina (read: experience and wisdom), there's nothing left to do but fall; nowhere to go but down.

Waiting for the light to change, I somehow realized that whatever had happened to me, my struggle should not be to stay on top, but to stay loyal to those who'd helped me get there. I didn't invent the idea, but it's a rule I've always tried to follow: I promised myself never to forget who brought me to the party.

Now, all I had to do was keep that promise.

Chapter 8

Everything You Think
You Want, You Don't

With *Saturday Night Live* in New York, *The Muppet Show* in London, and The Brillstein Company headquartered in Los Angeles, I was not only on top of the world, but sometimes I spent so much time traveling around it that I verged on being a basket case.

Jim Henson would say, "When are you coming to England?" I'd leave home Sunday and be in England for Monday, Tuesday, and Wednesday. Thursday morning I'd take the Concorde to New York and stay there Thursday, Friday, and Saturday for *Saturday Night Live*. Sunday I'd either go back to my office in Los Angeles — I talked on the phone to my office many times a day in any case — or rest up in New York, find time to see my father, and then do the London–New York circuit again.

If I wasn't on my way to the airport, on a plane, or in a cab to my hotel, then I was in a meeting, on a call, at a dinner or show, shooting craps at the Curzon Club in London, or trying to get a sandwich and a few hours sleep at the Carlyle Hotel in Manhattan. In Los Angeles I was at my desk earlier than anyone else, which added up to an extra workday a week. The pressure, much of it self-inflicted because I didn't want to risk missing a thing, was relentless. Meanwhile, I let my body *and* my ego swell, and too often I acted like a clichéd, pain-in-the-ass show-business character. After Belushi died, I fired a client just for saying, "You spend more time on a dead guy than me." He was right, but I didn't care.

For years I'd wanted, now I had, yet too often I'd sag into another airplane seat, dead tired, and think, "So *this* is what it's like to live your dream." I'm sure it sounds ungrateful to complain, especially within earshot of anyone who still wants the brass ring, but success wasn't quite what I'd expected. The thrill of getting to the top had vanished and all I thought about was staying there. However much I loved working with talented people — and sometimes the joy was more than I could stand — most mornings I had a stomachache from waking up afraid that everything I'd accomplished could just disappear. The fear was a guest that wouldn't leave, and I'm not sure I wanted it to: I'm not superstitious, but I began to believe that if I didn't wake up apprehensive, then I didn't have what it took to be *Bernie Brillstein.* How could anyone be calm about this business? People get unhappy that you did well. Your good fortune makes them feel inadequate about their good fortune. It's not enough for them to succeed; you also have to fail, and they'd like to help you all the way. Anyone who's made it knows that you have to be like a fox or you'll end up a dead fox.

· · · · ·

In London I usually stayed at the Hotel Dorchester, but on one trip in late 1978 my wife, Debbie, wanted to try the Berkeley. When she and I and her brother, Joel — who worked for me — checked in, I felt uncomfortable. It's a beautiful place, but I'm a creature of habit and the hotel seemed foreign. I'm not sure why; maybe it was just that everything from the bed to the bureaus to the toilet paper wasn't where I expected. Familiarity doesn't breed contempt, it breeds comfort.

When we got settled I decided to get busy. Jim Henson was at home in Hampstead, working on *The Muppet Movie.* I called to arrange a meeting. There was no answer. When I tried again, the line was busy. I called ten minutes later, again no answer. Then busy. I couldn't figure out what was going on.

Debbie and Joel wanted to go shopping, so I stayed behind. When they left, I called Jim again. Same thing: no answer or the line was busy. I kept dialing, and soon I was in the middle of a full-fledged anxiety attack, only I wasn't concerned that Jim might be in trouble, I was worried about myself.

Was Jim trying to avoid me? Maybe after eighteen years together he didn't want to work with me anymore. Did he think that by being inaccessible I'd get the message? It made me crazy. Things were going so well.

Maybe that was the trouble: What better time for disaster to strike? I'd been around enough to know that no matter who you are, when you deal with talent, you're always waiting to be fired. How many guys did I know who got that call out of the blue to tell them it was over? Too many.

I wanted to take a car to Jim's place but didn't. I figured if I showed up and he was trying to duck me, I'd look like an idiot. There'd be a confrontation. On the other hand, if I rushed over, all worked up, and nothing was wrong, I'd *feel* like an idiot.

I tried to force myself to calm down but I couldn't. I was jet-lagged and overworked. Just the day before, in New York, I'd had to iron out yet another crisis between Belushi and Lorne. John had been a bad boy and was blowing off steam. Lorne asked me to try to turn the Belushi-monster back into the sweet Chicago kid everyone loved. I guess I did — for the moment — but now I couldn't even remember what the specific problem had been.

It was like that a lot. *Saturday Night Live* was high school: a huge group forced to work together from September through May, in a pressure cooker of fame, money, success, and, increasingly, illicit substances. They had to be continually creative in spite of and because of their individual and collective neuroses. Little revolutions always flared. Lorne was the commandant, overseeing it all. I was his trusty aide, sometime fixer, and constant confidant. It was getting to me.

I couldn't relax. I grabbed my room key, wandered around the hotel and ended up at the roof swimming pool. I fell into a lounge chair, fully clothed, and tried to shake off my self-doubt. I couldn't. My brain was ice. I put my head under a towel and crashed.

I woke up a few hours later and went back to my room. Debbie and Joel were there. I pretended everything was fine, said I'd been working, and tried calling Jim again. Still busy. I told Debbie I was tired and climbed into bed for a nap.

The next thing I knew, the phone was ringing. It was morning. It was Jim. "Bernie, my phone's been out of order," he blurted. "I knew you were in town, but I couldn't find you at the Dorchester. I've been looking all over. I'm glad I found you. When do you want to get together?"

"As soon as it's convenient for you," I said, not betraying a hint of what had gone on the day before.

Later, in the shower, the whole episode reminded me of the classic "Jack Story" Danny Thomas used to tell onstage. Being Danny Thomas, he could stretch a one-minute joke into thirty-five minutes, but in a nutshell: A guy's car blows a tire in the middle of nowhere. He doesn't have a jack, so he heads down the road looking for a gas station. "What could the guy charge me to borrow his jack?" he thinks. "Five dollars? Ten?" An hour later, he's still thinking, "What could it cost? Twenty dollars? Twenty-five?" It starts raining and still no station in sight. "Forty dollars? Fifty?" It gets dark. "Seventy? Eighty?" The longer he walks, the higher the price climbs. Finally he see a gas station in the distance. He stumbles the last hundred feet, goes inside, walks up to the attendant, and screams, "Oh, yeah? Well, you can just take that jack and shove it up your ass!" For one irrational, scary day that was me, in spades.

It was my nature to employ my own fear of failing as a prod to keep me on my toes, but full-blown paranoia wasn't my style — at least not so that anyone would notice. Yet the longer I was out of touch with Jim, the more unmanageable my fear grew. I longed to be Mr. Confidence, but I realized that no matter how far I'd come from being the fat smart-ass kid with the dysfunctional family, I would never be successful enough to feel secure enough. What a depressing thought.

What shocks me is that it was such a surprise at the time.

Hadn't I built my career on not trusting show business and never depending on one client? Beneath my self-confident, wisecracking exterior, didn't a part of me always watch my back, prepare for the worst, feel relieved if nothing went wrong, and be amazed if things worked out? So why did the idea of Jim maybe moving on make me so nervous? No one wants to lose a big client, and I loved Jim, but it was more than that. Then it hit me: My self-protective cynicism was just a veneer. Underneath I still clung to the romantic notion that success equals safety. What's more, I wasn't prepared to let it go.

I've had years to think about that anxiety attack, and I've realized, from the perspective of someone with many subsequent ups and downs under his belt — maybe that explains my fluctuating pants size! — that my reaction was not atypical and had almost everything to do with being new to success.

Hiding at the Berkeley Hotel pool that afternoon, my particular dread was so basic it's embarrassing: I was petrified of going broke. I'd been broke too often and I didn't want to scramble for money again. Then, I lived most days afraid that at any moment the bogeyman would come to my house, take my cash and my firstborn, and leave me to start over. After a certain point I knew I couldn't go broke, but I still acted like I didn't believe it.

Making it is so much fun precisely because ignorance of what you can lose *is* bliss. On the way up, I couldn't know the shit I'd step into. I had no idea what was behind those corporate smiles. I didn't realize how treacherous it is. I didn't realize how high I could go, or how far I could fall. Now that I know how the business really works, I'm always amazed that I made it as far as I did. I must have really wanted it badly.

Success can arrive after years or literally overnight, and either way the transition is abrupt. There's money in the bank, you get important phone calls, people know your name, and everyone says, "You're so bright!" You have no perspective. Later, alone in your big, new house with the black-bottomed pool and sweeping city vistas, introspection and doubt invariably grab hold. What if you're not *that* smart? You could be exposed as a lucky imposter. What if you can't follow up with another hit? Suddenly the idea of making it and then blowing it is much scarier than the thought of never making it in the first place. You become your own worst enemy.

The irony is that the more you worry about staying hot, the more likely you are to get cold. The trick is to keep doing exactly what you did before success arrived instead of trying to protect your accomplishments. Sometimes you still fall on your ass, but that's an act of God. A rumor can destroy your business. A client can sue or leave — or die. A movie can bomb. A TV show can be canceled. (Remember: talent never blame *themselves* for being cold.) Or you can follow a pure hunch and be plain wrong. Big deal. That's real life. As long as you avoid mind-fucking *yourself* into the abyss, you're still ahead of the game.

· · · · ·

In early 1979, in the middle of *Saturday Night Live*'s fourth season, John Belushi told me he was ready to leave the show. He'd already explained to his brother, Jim Belushi, why he wanted to split, saying that *Saturday Night Live* is "like high school. You go four years and then you graduate." Simple enough.

The truth is more complex. Belushi was just too busy and too big to stay on. He was already a TV star. *Animal House* had made him a movie star. The Blues Brothers gave him rock star credentials. In show-business terms his hat trick was virtually unprecedented. Plus, he loved the attention, the adulation, and the power. To stay at *Saturday Night Live* restricted his ability to enjoy and use the rewards.

Belushi and Aykroyd had started shooting Spielberg's *1941* the previous October and still weren't finished. The pressure of flying back and forth from coast to coast each week wore them down — especially Belushi. He partied as if he thought he was indestructible. When John's role finally wrapped in April 1979 he was exhausted, with still a month to go until *Saturday Night Live* shut down for the summer. He'd have scarce time to rest: *The Blues Brothers* was scheduled to begin principal photography on July 1.

Caught between *Saturday Night Live* and his other commitments, Belushi fought with Lorne, who was himself caught in the unenviable position of trying to put on a show, accommodate Belushi and Aykroyd's extracurricular projects, *and* swallow their barely concealed attitude that no matter how much they'd once loved him or the show, *Saturday Night Live* had become less and less relevant to their careers. Perhaps as a response, Lorne found it tough to give John and Danny their due for pulling off the Blues Brothers miracle without his help. He admired what they'd accomplished but believed it hadn't been done in a vacuum. John and Danny's success also put more pressure on the other cast members to use the show as a stepping stone. That was yet another reason Lorne had to appear unperturbed and in control to the remaining players.

When John told Lorne he probably wouldn't come back for a fifth season, I knew I had to do my best for both clients. Fortunately, Lorne made the transition easier than it might have been. If he had a problem, he never blamed me to my face. I felt he trusted me enough to know that I wasn't pushing John out in order to pick up extra commissions. He was also smart enough to know that if I could have gotten John to stay, I would have. My interest was in keeping the show together for Lorne, the guy who was responsible for everything.

Lorne decided to focus instead on keeping Danny around. Lorne says Danny agreed to return for the fifth season as a performer only, not a writer. I figured the minute John was out the door, Danny would follow. The boys may have had different personalities and sensibilities, but they were strangely connected. Spiritually inseparable. They had bunk beds in the writers' room on the seventeenth floor at 30 Rock, for God's sake, and slept there a good deal of the time. Danny knew he had to go, but he ended up dragging out his decision and made up any excuse to avoid a discussion because he knew he'd have a hard time giving Lorne the bad news.

In early September, I called Lorne to tell him Danny wouldn't be coming back. He took it hard, almost harder than John's leaving. I believe Danny's exit was the beginning of a series of disappointments that would result a year later in Lorne himself abandoning *Saturday Night Live.*

• • • • •

Thanks to *Saturday Night Live,* I had a front-row seat at comedy's changing of the guard from the prewar variety show sensibility to the social commentary of the baby boomers. Watching Milton Berle hand Lorne an Emmy in 1976 for best Comedy-Variety series was a metaphor for the revolution. Yet I still had one foot in classic comedy with Norm Crosby, Pat Cooper, Jackie Gayle, and others making between $15,000 and $25,000 a week in Vegas. They still got me excited — but not *as excited.*

Saturday Night Live was a whole new ball game, and its immense popularity, as well as that of *The Muppet Show,* made my business grow so quickly that I couldn't pay as much attention to the older clients. Between Lorne, John, Danny, Gilda, and Jim, I was managing full-time, executive-producing movies, and indulging in the heat and power my associations brought. And why not? What's the point of being a player if you don't play?

Eventually I had to hand over direct responsibility for some of my acts to Sandy and a woman in my office named Fran Saperstein (who now handles Gregory Hines), and hired agents to do the booking. Still, I'd see their shows when I could. They knew where I was if they needed me. I made it work the best I knew how and my door was always open, but the days when Norm Crosby and I would go over his material and even his wardrobe together were gone and there wasn't much I could do about it.

It made me heartsick. I hated leaving anyone behind workwise, much less emotionally. Their talent hadn't disappeared. They still booked jobs. But their audience was older and preferred silk jackets and Vegas dinner shows to club hopping, cognac swilling, and cocaine snorting.

Their comedy was safe, not seditious. We all have to accept who we are and for some of my clients, no matter how much I loved them, that time had come.

Not everyone embraced that rationale and I can't blame them. Who wants to not be hot?

When a client doesn't understand, his resentment can come out in funny ways. He'll be at your house one day and say, "Hey, I built this room!" It really annoys and saddens me, especially if it comes from someone I've been in business with for a long time. Next thing you know, the client is telling people that you just used him to make a name for *yourself* — as if he didn't get anything out of the relationship. Makes me want to put a fist in his face. A good manager knows his business is based on the ability to make his *clients* successful. Anything he gets out of it is gravy. Thank God most of the people our company represents know what we do for a living.

If what goes around comes around, then at Brillstein-Grey I'm the old guy now. Most clients now sign on because of Brad or Marc Gurvitz or Cynthia Pett-Dante or Gerry Harrington, or any of the other fine young managers in the office. Believe me, I understand. Today's hot acts want to be with someone hip, powerful, and on their level.

· · · · ·

I've always hidden from the limelight, which is not the same as hiding from success, but occasionally, just because my clients were so big, I'd slip briefly into the public eye myself. Mostly it was unintentional. But not always.

When the Blues Brothers, *Animal House*, *Saturday Night Live*, and the Muppets hit, I had dangerous moments in which I thought, "I have the key. I am dominant. All these other people were fools." Christ! I was Mr. Hot. I couldn't get enough of myself. "Why didn't you people recognize it sooner? Here I am! I've been here all my life. You're morons! I had to struggle." Thank goodness I usually said this stuff only to my wife or Sandy, or my mirror. Then, because I calmed down, reality came back to Andy Hardy.

A more typical managerial offense is something I call "posing"; that is, having to let everyone know that you're important because you have important clients. For instance, when Norm Crosby worked at the Sahara

Hotel, I'd walk around and around the showroom, and in and out of the backstage entrance, so that everyone in the audience could see that I had special access.

When John and Danny filmed *The Blues Brothers* in Chicago, I couldn't get enough of being with the boys. God forbid I shouldn't pose in a picture with them. There was also no merchandising item we sold that I didn't wear. One day I even went with John to Chicago's city hall to meet the mayor. There was no reason for me to go, but I didn't care. We all had lunch, then John and I went to the steam bath.

When I got back to my hotel there was a note from Debbie: "I've left." I called all the airlines, then the hotels, and finally found her at the Palmer House, where I guess she was waiting for me to come and get her. "You're really getting carried away with this stuff," she scolded. "You're too old to do this." I'd fallen under Belushi's spell. Sometimes I felt like I was onstage with him.

What Debbie said didn't really sink in until about a month later, when I was in New York, staying in Lew Grade's suite at the Regency Hotel on Park Avenue. I got dressed to go to *Saturday Night Live,* and on the way to the elevator I passed a mirror in the hall. I finally saw myself: a huge, slouching, bearded forty-eight-year-old man in a Blues Brothers hat, scarf, and nylon jacket. Ray-Ban sunglasses completed the ensemble, and, so you wouldn't miss the point, I wore a Blues Brothers pin. I laughed and shook my head.

Debbie had nailed it. I was an ass. Enough already. I went back to the room and changed into a Rangers hockey shirt and sports jacket.

Seven years later I walked into the same suite at the Regency Hotel to meet with the producer Don Simpson, and there he was wearing every bit of merchandise from *Days of Thunder.* I would have laughed, but I recognized the "Look at me, Ma, I did it" display. We had put others onstage while we stayed in the background. This was our small public way of saying, "See? I was right."

I don't know if Don ever got the message.

• • • • •

When Chevy Chase left *Saturday Night Live* after the first season, the other actors were able to grab center stage. Gilda Radner emerged with dead-on characters and characterizations, from Lisa Loopner to

Roseanne Roseannadana to Baba Wawa, and quickly became America's late-night sweetheart.

Behind the scenes, Gilda used other attributes to get ahead. *Saturday Night Live* historians always go on about how tough it is for women at the show, that it's a boys' club. In many respects that's true. The writing can be sophomoric and have lots to do with female breasts — give them six good women writers and the show won't have that problem — so women have to fight harder however they can. Gilda knew the score and didn't have an attitude. Instead, she baked cookies for the writers. Did each say "Write something for me" on the back? No. Gilda just happened to show up with food at midnight. She used her head, she had talent, the writers wrote for her.

It all comes down to people using their natural qualities. I use my sense of humor to make money, to survive, to get laid, to have friends, to join clubs, to be recognized. I didn't wake up one morning and say I'd better develop a sense of humor — you can't do that. I was born with one. It's like being fat. People are not scared of me. I have a big smile and I'm funny. It gets me everywhere.

Gilda was the first person Lorne wanted for the Not Ready for Prime Time Players, and I helped him convince her to do the show. By the end of the first season, probably at Lorne's urging, she asked me to be her manager. Although Gilda could hold her own on the show, she was deluged with the intrusive demands of stardom. It got too much for her to handle alone.

Gilda was like a best friend: always willing to listen, easy to hang out with. She was accessible and giving. She loved to socialize. She was the first to arrive at a party and the last to leave. She loved to dance. Once, she took her mother and me to Studio 54. Gilda and I watched her mom gyrate on the floor, trying to attract attention, and I could see how competitive she was with her daughter. Sometimes Gilda and I would stroll around New York. She walked like a ballet dancer, on her heels and toes. I'll remember her always in jeans, a white shirt, a light linen jacket, and a Yankees baseball hat, with her ponytail stuck through the back. Wherever we went, people waved and said, "Hi, Gilda." Everyone loved her, and a little bit of that love even rubbed off on me.

After *Saturday Night Live* ended, Gilda would sometimes come to Los Angeles and stay at the Beverly Hills Hotel, across the street from my house on Crescent Drive. She'd pop over, bring her dirty laundry, and play with my kids, who loved her. After Belushi died and I'd moved to Connecticut to escape the business, it seemed like we always saw Gilda and her husband, Gene Wilder, who lived in nearby Stamford.

Because of her bulimia and then the cancer that came out of nowhere, most people remember Gilda as fragile. She was that, as well as vulnerable, insecure, and lonely. But when she wanted to, Gilda could also be tougher than any man. She was a rich kid, used to getting her way. On *Saturday Night Live*, the more she watched Belushi and Aykroyd push the stardom envelope, the more she wanted the same for herself. But it wasn't always the right situation.

In 1979, Paramount Pictures decided to make a motion-picture version of *Popeye*, starring Robin Williams. It was the era of the first *Superman* movie, and everyone thought there were riches to be mined in the comic strips. The notorious Robert Evans — production head of Paramount during the *Godfather* and *Chinatown* era — would produce, and director Robert Altman planned to shoot it on the island of Malta, in the Mediterranean Sea due south of Sicily. Altman wanted Shelley Duvall, an actress he'd worked with before, to play Popeye's love interest, Olive Oyl. Duvall certainly looked the part. Robert Evans wanted Gilda and offered her $850,000 for the role.

Gilda could have used the break, but after we talked it over we passed. The script had problems. There was no guarantee the role would get better, no matter how big her paycheck. The part might even have deteriorated. In fact, it did.

Even more important, Gilda wasn't about to spend her summer vacation six thousand miles from where I could protect her. Altman, although very creative, and Evans, who's had one hell of a life, are not easy guys to be with for any length of time, particularly in a remote, closed environment. Both were wild men. Gilda wouldn't have lasted a week. If the movie had been shot on a lot, maybe. But Malta? Everyone agreed it was possibly the worst shithole on the face of the earth; a place where after a month a woman you'd normally rate a two would suddenly start to look like an eight. No, a ten. No, a twelve.

Paramount didn't want to take no for an answer. I got calls from Evans, from Paramount Pictures chief Barry Diller, from Diller's second in command, Michael Eisner, and from production head Don Simpson. Simpson didn't think Duvall was attractive enough for the part. Simpson told me that Gilda and I were "making the mistake of our careers."

"I have to go with my gut," I said. I didn't try to explain further because Simpson didn't have the patience or the inclination to listen. You think he really gave a damn about me or my future prospects? His job was to scare me into getting Gilda to change her mind. He *had* to make the call.

The studio wanted Gilda so badly that they figured I was the problem, and tried to go around me. They called her. They romanced her. Evans sent flowers. None of it worked because, contrary to the way Hollywood usually thinks, we weren't holding out for more money or a first-class plane ticket for me, or some other stupid perk. We'd been honest and no one could understand that. She didn't do the film for her own reasons, and in the end those are the only reasons that matter.

Although for me it was never about being "right," years later Bob Evans told me in no uncertain terms I'd made the correct decision.

Paramount's offer confirmed what I'd believed all along: just like Belushi and Aykroyd, Gilda had *BIG STAR* written all over her. After being offered *Popeye* it should have been easy for her to fulfill her potential, but it wasn't. I hate to say this, but in retrospect, Gilda's career was probably very nearly at its peak when I took over in 1977. In many ways she never got any bigger than the loopy, brilliant girl everyone loved, holding her own with the rowdy boys on *Saturday Night Live.* She tried many things: movies, Broadway, a record album, TV appearances; but for nine years after the show, until her death, nothing clicked for Gilda like *Saturday Night Live.* At first it bothered her, then it didn't. Gilda's life wasn't all about stardom. She had other priorities.

• • • • •

By the time Gilda met Gene Wilder in 1982, on the set of *Hanky Panky,* her marriage to musician G. E. Smith was over in spirit, if not in fact. Gene was every Jewish girl's dream. Gilda used to tell everyone that he smelled good, which I considered a positive sign, if not something every woman should routinely expect from a man. Once that was settled and they fell in love, she decided that nothing was more important than getting him to marry her so that she could fulfill her dream of being a good wife and mother.

In September 1984 Gilda succeeded. That's when our relationship began to change — as it should have. She became part of Gene's life.

Gene was a movie star. He had his own set of friends: Mel Brooks, Carl Reiner, Alan Alda, and Dom DeLuise. Naturally, he was more comfortable with them than he was with Gilda's friends, like Lorne, writer Alan Zweibel, or me. I'm not saying Gene didn't like us — quite the opposite — but if your husband would rather hang out with *his* friends, you make new friends. Gene was very set in his ways; he wasn't going to adopt Gilda's. Gilda could be strong, but not with men.

When Gilda worked, she made movies with Gene, like *The Woman in Red* and *Haunted Honeymoon.* I didn't care for them. In fact, I thought they made her look bad. But what could I say? Gilda's relationship was more important to her than her career, and if she was willing to fail in show business in order to enjoy married life, who was I to tell her that her career should come first? In fact, I didn't believe it should. Someone's life is always more important than business. Gilda was happy and she wanted to give being "Sadie, Sadie, married lady" a first-class shot. I stepped back and didn't interfere.

In 1986 Gilda was diagnosed with ovarian cancer. She had a hysterectomy, and the doctors thought she'd beaten it. Brad and I had lunch with her. She told us she wanted to find a way to stay happily married and come back to television.

Then she got sick again. The doctors discovered the malignancy had spread. Gilda refused to lie down and die. She did everything she could to fight for her life.

I didn't give up, either. Gilda still wanted to work, and in 1988, when we all thought she was in remission, Gilda did an episode of *It's Garry Shandling's Show* and got an Emmy nomination. She also worked on her book about her life and battle with cancer, *It's Always Something.* Gilda still wanted to do TV, specifically a take-off on Jack Benny's old radio show in which *she* did an old radio show and people came to her house to rehearse, and I got her a thirteen-show commitment from Michael Fuchs at HBO for *The Gilda Radner Show.* ABC also wanted to work with her. But, in the end, she ran out of time.

Most of us, myself included, had no idea how Gilda suffered. She never complained, she would just disappear. When she was with Gene, Gilda was not really a part of our lives like she'd once been. I learned a lot about the years I'd missed just by reading her book. I cried like a baby at her pain, her resolve to live, and her acceptance of the unthinkable alternative.

One of the last times I saw Gilda was at a birthday party for one of Alan Zweibel's kids. She looked so jaundiced and thin that I feared the end was near, too near. Not long after, Gilda died. I can still picture Gene Wilder in the cemetery in Greenwich, Connecticut, standing in the rain, by the beautiful blue-gray casket, holding their dog Sparkles. Such an awful and beautiful moment. No one spoke at the ceremony, but had I been able to, I would have said that I'd lost a wonderful friend who made me happy whenever I was with her, and always made me laugh.

• • • • •

Although I briefly represented Carol Burnett, Marsha Mason, Joan Rivers, and Geena Davis in the mid-1980s, and Roseanne for about three weeks just before her sitcom went on the air, Gilda was the only woman I ever really managed.

Today Brillstein-Grey represents many women — actresses, writers, producers, comediennes — and I think that's terrific. But that's never been my style. Don't get me wrong: I love women. I've been married often enough to prove it. But the God-given attraction notwithstanding, it's obvious I've rarely been good with them in my personal life, so why should I think I'd do any better professionally? By the way, this is not an official policy. There's nothing written down. I don't even claim to be right. I'm just being honest. And I could change at any minute.

I'm more comfortable with men. My perceptions were set long ago. I come from a generation where the comedian was on the road and the wife/mother stayed home with the kids. When I got into the business, there weren't even that many comediennes, and those who had careers didn't need my inexperience to help them.

Later, other issues arose. I feel managing women takes more time because they seem to need a different type of representation than men, from extra care to an on-call escort. Chris Rock calls this "the other husband," who takes a woman places her number-one husband could care less about, like the Ice Capades. In my day we called these guys "walkers." If a female star had to go to an opening and she didn't want to go with another big star, then she went with her manager or her hairdresser or her haberdasher or a male friend. Men could show up alone.

Of course that's changed, but *servicing* has never been my style, even with male clients who can easily be just as high maintenance.

When the situation crosses that line with either sex, I get uncomfortable. The reason it's tougher for me with a woman is something you can blame on my first basket case, my mother.

There are also practical matters between myself and a woman client. The minute she gets married — assuming she isn't already — the husband doesn't want a guy like me around. He's the man; he's the protector. If my wife made a couple million a year in the movies or on TV, the first thing I'd ask her is, "What do you need this manager for?" I'd want to make the decisions and save the commission. Most any husband would, *especially* if he's also in the profession.

· · · · ·

It was one thing to fight with some network or studio exec on my clients' behalf and another when those clients fought among themselves. That left me in middle, trying to represent everyone fairly — and still have a business. Maybe I was wrong to handle so much talent at *Saturday Night Live*, or to have writers and producers I represented work with Jim Henson or with each other, but I didn't give it much thought at the time. When trouble occurred, I made decisions on the fly. My attitude was, Be honest, let fate play its hand, and hope everyone comes out a winner. It wasn't always easy, especially when a client would say, "Yeah. Honesty is great. Now get me what I want."

On June 28, 1979, the consequence of representing too many people who worked with each other almost ruined my business.

Earlier that year, in the shadow of John and Danny's enormous success with the Blues Brothers, Lorne and Gilda embarked on a project of their own: a comedy album called *Gilda Radner: Live from New York.*

John and Danny had not included Lorne in anything they did outside of studio 8H, so his working with Gilda seemed a perfect opportunity to try and make lightning strike *Saturday Night Live*'s extracurricular projects twice. Of all the Not Ready for Prime Time Players, Gilda was closest to Lorne and the easiest for him to work with.

The project was born in part because of Lorne's guilt over a failed NBC deal for Gilda to do a variety series of her own. The new network president, Fred Silverman, loved Gilda and shared my belief that she could be the next Lucille Ball. Plus he needed to boost NBC's ratings. Add all that up and his answer was Gilda's own show on Wednesday nights at

9 P.M. Silverman wanted it for fall 1979, which meant it would be concurrent with Gilda's fifth year on *Saturday Night Live*. At first Gilda wanted to do it. It was a great opportunity, Silverman was supportive, and we'd worked it out for Gilda and Lorne to own the show (always an inducement). Silverman thought he had a deal. Then Gilda and Lorne had second thoughts, or came to their senses — depends on your point of view. The pressure and responsibility of doing two shows a week would fry them both, so Lorne passed, adding that he'd still do it if Gilda wanted to. Gilda wouldn't go against Lorne, so she passed, saying she was too tired. The truth was that she didn't believe she could do it alone. Silverman didn't see the change of heart coming and he went nuts.

To make it up to Gilda, Lorne got involved in *Gilda Live*. At first it was just supposed to be an album of Gilda singing and doing characters and impressions. But everyone got so excited that plans were made to expand it into a Broadway show and, possibly, a movie.

Belushi and Aykroyd thought the project was a direct challenge. That didn't stop Gilda. She was competitive, and, as the dominant *Saturday Night Live* female, she saw no reason not to use the show as a platform to make some star moves of her own. I saw no reason not to be as supportive of Gilda and Lorne as I had been of John and Danny. There was room for everyone to succeed.

But Belushi told Blues Brother keyboard player and musical director Paul Shaffer, with whom he had put together the band (Steve Cropper, Donald "Duck" Dunn, Steve Jordan, Matt Murphy, Tom Scott, Tom Malone, Lou Marini, and Alan Rubin), not to get involved with Gilda's album because he wanted Shaffer available for an upcoming tour. He was a little late. Shaffer and Bob Tischler, who would produce Gilda's record, were already signed on.

When the *Saturday Night Live* season finished, John and Danny took off until they had to go to Chicago and start filming *The Blues Brothers* the first week of July.

June 28 was Gilda's birthday. Lorne invited her to his house in Amagansett for a little party. At Lorne's request, and as a surprise for Gilda, Shaffer showed up with a tape of the album. After spending months and piles of money on postproduction, he and Tischler were the only people who had heard the final product. Lorne invited me as well, but I declined. I'd been at the recording sessions and I had a feeling there was no way the album would work. This was comedy, not a Blues Brothers band that had

In my prime.

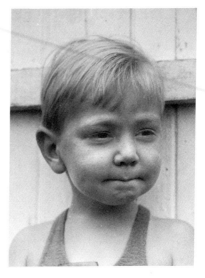

In my early thirties, at the Englewood Country Club. I actually liked the way I looked. Best picture of me ever taken — with my own camera, naturally.

What I like to think I look like today.
(Bonnie Schiffman)

The Eldorado, Ninetieth Street and Central Park West.

Moe and Tillie Brillstein.

What I aspired to be. Left to right: Uncle Jack, Bing Crosby, Jack Benny, Chico Marx.

Marilyn Boroy, where are you? At the Copa, 1953, on leave from the army.

The Stork Club, 1955: Just out of the army with Aunt Winnie and Uncle Jack.

WILLIAM MORRIS AGENCY, INC. PAY VOUCHER		
NAME	DATE	AMOUNT
BERNARD BRILLSTEIN	JUN 22 55	32.45

My first pay stub from William Morris.

At CBS' Studio 50 for Elvis Presley's first TV appearance, on *Stage Show*, 1956.
Service with a smile. Elvis admires the new sweater I'd just bought for him.
(© Alfred Wertheimer)

In my fancy publicity office at William Morris with my assistant,
Danny Bernstein.

With my first wife, Marilyn,
on our wedding day, 1957.

I was head of publicity at
William Morris, so I could get
stylish photos of my daughter
Leigh and myself for free.

With my dad, Moe,
and brother, Sam.

When I left William Morris, they wrote a memo reassigning my acts. As if they knew who they were . . .

WILLIAM MORRIS AGENCY, INC.
New York Office

April 2, 1964

TO: TV STAFF - NY, CHICAGO, COAST

Please make the necessary changes on the present list of Agents responsible for particular clients with respect to television in the East.

All of these were previously handled by Bernie Brillstein:

Ford and Hines - Sol Leon (Stan Kamen handles Coast)
Patty Duke - Larry Auerbach
The Muppets (Jim Henson) - Larry Auerbach
Johnny Gilbert - Arnold Sank
Willis Sisters - Ben Griefer
Linda Bennett - Marty Litke
Shennanigans - Larry Auerbach
Chuck McCann - Larry Auerbach
Dr. Pepper Company (John Simmons) - Lenny Rosenberg

Leonard S. Kramer

The Management Three partners, years after we broke up. Left to right: me, Marty Kummer, Jerry Weintraub. One of the few pictures of us not taken at a craps table.
(Rosemary Orlando)

With Robert Goulet, at his peak, and Norm Crosby, backstage at Basin Street East, 1965.
(Mort Shuman)

Saturday Night Live, the beginning, with President Ford. Left to right: Chevy Chase, Lorne Michaels, Chevy's then-wife, Jacqueline, John Belushi, the President.

The Muppet Show crew on the *QE2,* 1977. Clockwise from bottom left: Jim Henson, me, Joe Bailey, Jerry Juhl, Don Hinckley, Jerry Nelson, Frank Oz.
(© Southern Newspapers Ltd., Southhampton)

With my most demanding client.
(Marcia Reed)

With Sandy Wernick, who came aboard in 1975 and never abandoned ship.

Gilda Radner's birthday wish for me.

Here we go again, Bernie — this time with your eyes open! no drinks! no cigarettes! I love you
HAPPY birthday, Gilda

Backstage at the Universal Amphitheater, September 1978. The Blues Brothers opened for Steve Martin, blew everyone away, and I knew I had finally made it. Left to right: me, Leigh Brillstein, John Belushi, Judy Belushi, Smokey Wendell (John's bodyguard), Billy Belushi.

(Peter C. Borsari)

The *Fridays* gang, 1980. Top row, left to right: Gary Pudney, me, ABC's Tony Thomopoulos, my ex-brother-in-law Joel Briskin, Sandy Wernick, ABC's Lew Erlicht, Stu Bloomberg. Bottom row, left to right: Bill Lee, Jack Burns, John Moffitt.

(Courtesy of The Brokaw Company)

With Lorne in 1980. After five seasons of *Saturday Night Live* it was time to move on.

(Edie Baskin)

We made *The Muppet Show* happen. Left to right: Pierre Weiss, David Lazer, Jim Henson, me, Lord Grade, Frank Oz, and Abe Mandel at the final season's last party.

With Belushi on location for *Continental Divide.* Two fat guys rapping. He was healthy, and he looked great.

With Tom Patchett (left) and Jay Tarses. Difficult and brilliant. Maybe they're the same thing.

Belushi said, "I have the heart of a high school senior." His grave on Martha's Vineyard (since moved for privacy). The end of the road for the rock and roll star.

Ghostbusters. Left to right: Bill Murray, Dan Aykroyd, Harold Ramis. Ovitz took the credit and didn't even invite me to the party afterwards.

With Lorimar CEO Merv Adelson.
A visionary who believed in me.

With Brad Grey, my protégé, my partner,
my successor.

This is the best comedy
troupe in the world, my kids
at the Broad Beach house,
1985. Left to right: David,
Kate, Leigh, Nick, Michael.

My "Friends of the Los Angeles Free Clinic" roast, 1989. Bottom row, left to right:
Richard Dreyfuss, me, Dabney Coleman, Brandon Tartikoff. Middle row, left to right:
Jay Tarses, Garry Shandling, Jim Henson, Norm Crosby. Top row, left to right: Carl
Reiner, Jackie Gayle.

Jim Henson presents me with the Bernie Muppet at the "Free Clinic" roast.

Mike Ovitz and me, on opposite ends as usual. In between (standing, left to right): CAA's Bob Bookman, Richard Dreyfuss, Mrs. Frank Price, Judy Ovitz; (seated, left to right): Mrs. Bookman, Mrs. Dreyfuss, CAA co-founder Ron Meyer, Meyer's then-wife, Ellen, TV- and movie-production legend Frank Price.

Meeting Princess Diana at the *Dangerous Liaisons* command performance.
(Pic Photos)

Who is this masked man talking to me?

With Chris Farley on
the set of *Tommy Boy*.
Another brilliant guy
brought down by excess.
(Elliott Marks)

At New York's famous 21
restaurant. Marty Short
au naturel, at a party for
his new talk show, which I'm
producing. Seated, left to right: me,
TV syndication impresarios
Roger and Michael King,
KingWorld President of First-run
Programming and Production
Andy Friendly.

My friend and client
Rob Lowe and my
wife, Carrie.
(Courtesy of Mel Weinstein)

My wedding day, December 20, 1998, with the family. Left to right: Nick, Leigh, me, my beautiful bride, Carrie, Michael, Kate, David.
(Courtesy of Mel Weinstein)

With legendary movie producer Robert Evans at the 1999 Aspen Comedy Arts Festival. I brought him up to read from his book, and he brought the house down.
(Courtesy of Charles Evans Jr.)

The three Godfathers, left to right: Brad Grey, James Gandolfini aka Tony Soprano, star of the hit HBO drama *The Sopranos*, me.
(Lee Salem Photography Inc.)

John Register, *Nebraska,* 1987, oil on canvas.
(Courtesy of the Modernism Gallery, San Francisco)

THE BIG "C"

by

Gilda Radner

I was giong through life
As free as a lark,
In the world of acting
I was making my mark.

In Second City,
And then on T.V.,
Not thinking once
About the big "C".

I saved up my money,
An apartment I bought.
My wealth was my own,
Or so I thought.

I can't even tell you
How often you cry.
When the dreaded "C"
Starts draining you dry.

Friends try to console,
And tell you they care.
But deep down you feel
That this is unfair.

Now before I upset you,
And lead you astray.
I just want to tell you,
I'm feeling okay.

Cancer's no problem,
'Cause I'm in remission,
The "C" I refer to,
Is Bernie's commision.

so much power that if even half the energy made it onto vinyl it would still kick you in the ass and halfway across the room.

That afternoon, a call from Amagansett confirmed my worst fears. Gilda's only surprise, said Lorne, was how bad the record sounded. Gilda had locked herself in a bedroom and couldn't stop crying. Lorne was angry. The album would never see the light of day. Lorne decided to focus on preparations for the *Gilda Live* show, scheduled to open that August at the Winter Garden Theatre on Broadway, and to rerecord the album there.

That's when all hell broke loose.

Shaffer was scheduled to join Belushi and Aykroyd in Chicago to start *The Blues Brothers.* But right after the listening party, Lorne asked Shaffer to stay with Gilda and help out with her show. So there was Shaffer, with a terrible album, a guilty conscience, trapped in Amagansett, facing an impossible choice. Knowing how smart Lorne is, that was probably his intention. But Shaffer wouldn't decide on the spot.

Shaffer called Belushi when he got back to New York. Belushi told him to dump Lorne and Gilda and come to Chicago for the movie, which would start shooting any minute. Lorne asked me to pass the message to Shaffer that he'd do whatever it took to keep him around for Gilda. From what I could tell, Shaffer wanted to please Lorne, but he wanted to do the movie more. He had an acting role, he loved the music — and it didn't hurt that Belushi was number one in America.

On the other hand, Shaffer wasn't crazy about the way John acted when he was high, but he would have put up with it if he hadn't felt so bad about Gilda's album. Shaffer also remembered that Lorne, a fellow Canadian, had brought him to *Saturday Night Live,* and in the end he couldn't shake his loyalty to the man who'd brought him to the party.

Neither Lorne nor Belushi made it easy for Shaffer. Belushi told the bandleader that if he went with Gilda he would never again be a Blues Brother. Belushi said the same thing to Lorne. Lorne threatened no one — it's not his style — but he can be very persuasive when he has to be. When Belushi and Lorne got nervous waiting for Shaffer's decision, they called me, the man in the middle. If that wasn't enough pressure, Universal Pictures was also breathing down our necks to resolve the situation.

Everyone expected me to make their desires prevail. I didn't know what to do. If I tried influencing either party, I'd soon be a traitor without clients. I could only listen to everyone bitch, hope someone had an epiphany along the way, and tell the truth. I didn't want to tell one lie and have to tell seven others to cover it.

Finally, Paul Shaffer decided. But he didn't call John or Lorne, he called me. "I'm going to do the show with Gilda," he said. I didn't ask him why. I'm not sure I cared. When it's final it's final and you have to move on. Now I had to tell Belushi. I forced myself not to panic, even though no one in their right mind would have wanted to make that call. Belushi could easily have said, "Fuck Lorne, fuck Gilda, fuck Shaffer, and fuck you! What good are you if you can't deliver?" My job — what I got paid to deliver — was the bad news. Someone had to make the bad calls. I reached Belushi in Chicago and told him the complete story. He went nuts.

"The fucking movie's off!" he screamed. "Shaffer's out. He'll never be a Blues Brother!"

I let him vent and then I let him have it: "Are you John Belushi or are you not John Belushi?" I asked. "Does your life depend on *a piano player?*" Whatever John thought, I wasn't insulting Shaffer. I simply wanted to put the situation into perspective for John. He had a movie to make, duties to himself and others. I waited for an answer but there was only silence.

Then, as if none of the yelling had occurred, Belushi said, "Wait. I've got the guy. I'll call you back in ten minutes." When he did, he said Murphy Dunne could take Shaffer's place. It was easy. All John wanted to do was make the movie — and he did. All Lorne and Gilda wanted was to have Paul Shaffer do her show — and they did. *Gilda Live* had a rocky start but went on to sell out most of the time.

Sticking with Gilda didn't hurt Shaffer. He and Belushi made up and Shaffer rejoined the Blues Brothers tour the following summer when the movie came out. Later, Shaffer made friends with David Letterman and kicked off a nice career.

And me? Because I didn't lie to anyone — which is the point — I kept my clients and lived to tell the story.

• • • • •

Making *The Blues Brothers* movie also had its tough moments. The director, John Landis, was a crazy kid. He has the most annoying voice; it cuts right through you.

Through the entire picture Landis fought to control Belushi. He called Belushi to the set too early and made him wait around for hours. Other actors screw or drink in their idle time, but John sat in his trailer and did drugs. Landis acted surprised. I didn't understand why. He'd caught John with drugs on the *Animal House* set, too — and thrown them away. He knew all about John.

I didn't condone John's drug use, but I couldn't strong-arm him into stopping either. I told Landis, "Don't call him to the set so early. Let him stay home where he's not so bored. Give him one of those radios. Call him when he has to show up." Landis wouldn't do it. John's drug use continued.

Months later, at a *Blues Brothers* press conference at the Plaza Hotel in New York, Landis went on a self-promotional tear. He stood at the podium with Belushi and Aykroyd and kept talking and talking and talking. "This is a thirty-three-million-dollar movie, the best thing since *Gone with the Wind*," he said. Not only couldn't I stand his whiny voice, I had told him not to reveal how much the movie cost. I knew the press would use it against us, and they did. I sat in the audience, getting more and more upset.

Finally, the guy next to me, a reporter from some Cincinnati paper, raised his hand. "Yes?" Landis said.

"I think Mr. Belushi and Mr. Aykroyd are the stars of this movie," the guy deadpanned. "Could we hear them talk?" Landis looked at me. To this day he thinks I set that up. I swear I didn't. But I wish I had.

· · · · ·

In the fall of 1979 I went to a bachelor party for my client TV director John Moffitt. His best friend was Bill Lee, vice president of Dick Clark Productions. Bill is the guy who brought Clark out of daytime and into prime time with *The American Music Awards* and *New Year's Rockin' Eve*. Moffitt and Lee had met at some TV special and took an immediate liking to each other. Moffitt started working for Lee, but what they really wanted to do was go into business for themselves.

After the party I asked them to take a ride with me. We hit the bowling alley, then a restaurant. They talked about the future they imagined for themselves. Finally, I said, "What if I could make a deal for you guys and put you in business with ABC? Would you do it? How do you feel about it?"

Bill said, "You know, Bernie, it's something we've been wanting to do for years. We just never had the means."

I said, "Okay, that's all I wanted to hear."

I called Fred Pierce and Tony Thomopoulos at ABC and tried to sell them on Moffitt and Lee. My pitch was that while ABC had sports people and sitcom people, they had no one like these guys. Moffitt and Lee could do specials and they knew comedy. ABC agreed. I set up a meeting and walked away with a two-year development deal. ABC paid their expenses, gave them office space, a salary, and committed money to develop projects.

Thomopoulos and Pierce were also in awe of *Saturday Night Live's* success and wanted to do something just like it. I know because they called to tell me that a show had been approved and I was the guy to do it.

I couldn't believe it. For a second I was flattered. They wanted *me* to produce.

Then I understood: Who else would they go to? They couldn't get Lorne, he was signed to NBC. I represented Belushi, Gilda, Aykroyd, Zweibel, Burns, and Moffitt and Lee. They didn't come to me because I was some great genius or their friend. It was simply logical.

Talk about mixed feelings. After so many years of scrounging, to be offered backing, ownership, and creative control was immensely appealing. Managers feel chronically underacknowledged. Most never see their name on the screen, and ache to get their validation somewhere. And God knows I could have used the money. I wasn't as rich as everybody thought. Now here were a network chairman and president telling me, "We love you. Do this for us." I knew I could do the job and I asked myself, "Why not do it on your own? Why not try it?"

The whole thing was confirmation that I'd finally become *Bernie Brillstein*. But Bernie Brillstein was no fool. "What the hell are you talking about?" I asked. Did they think I'd sell out Lorne for the chance to own a network show?

It was an offer from the Devil himself. I passed.

Without missing a beat, Thomopoulos said, "Then how about Moffitt and Lee?"

Maybe at that point I should have gotten out completely. On the other hand, I'd given up owning and producing the show, which they had already named *Fridays*. My conscience was clear and it was obvious they were going to proceed with or without me. Moffitt and Lee were my clients and it was my job to get them work. I had to consider it open season. What should I have said — that they wouldn't do it? Even ABC knew that Lorne had once asked Moffitt to direct *Saturday Night Live.* Of course they wanted him.

Moffitt and Lee signed on as producers and Jack Burns joined them as well. When ABC actually ordered the show — meaning there was no turning back — I told Lorne. I waited because what if nothing ever happened? I don't remember the phone call exactly, but neither one of us is an in-your-face kind of guy. We tiptoed through the minefield. I'm sure the words "very upset" would be apropos to Lorne's feelings. I had my guilt. But I believed I'd played fair. Fortunately, Lorne not only understood the game, he knew I loved him.

None of this went over well with the *Saturday Night Live* gang. I was called an opportunist for having anything to do with *Fridays*. After the show debuted, I was on the phone with Lorne when his future wife, Susan Forristal, got on the line. She screamed at me: "How could you do that? *How could you do that?*"

I said, "Susan, I'm representing a client. I'm getting a package commission on the show. *It's not my show.*"

She was unrelenting: "How dare you be involved?"

I understood, but I said, "In no way can this hurt Lorne, and that's why I'm part of it."

I don't think she heard.

Even though Lorne was not pleased at my involvement, he would never scream at me, or even confront me directly. To this day we've rarely talked about this.

It's been reported that in fact Lorne and I didn't speak for a year over *Fridays,* but that's not true. We were into negotiations for a sixth year at *Saturday Night Live* and speaking every day.

In other less tense circumstances clearer heads might have prevailed, but things at *Saturday Night Live* had already begun to unravel. Drugs contributed to the madness — but it was more than that. They were just a symptom of the fame-money-power craziness. Lorne was at the top of his game. Whether he liked it or not, his every mood was scrutinized. His every decision was read like tea leaves. "Should we have tuna fish for lunch? Does Lorne like tuna fish? Does he want raw carrot with that?" Who can live like that?

If you put me on the stand today and asked if I did the right thing, so help me God I could only say yes — for myself.

"Do you want to produce this show, Bernie Brillstein?"

"No, I can't. I would never do a show like *Saturday Night Live* against Lorne. Never. I just wouldn't do it. It's not right. I couldn't live with myself."

"Well, who would you suggest to do it? Who would you have done it with, if you *had* done it?"

"Moffitt and Lee and Jack Burns."

Few decisions where divided obligations are concerned are perfect. I had to make my own rules for what was right and wrong. I'm not saying I was correct — that's up to a higher power to one day judge — but I did what was best for my survival, for my business, and my clients.

No one knows this, but ABC wanted to put the show on Saturday night. I told them it wouldn't be a good idea. I'm glad they listened.

Fridays aired for two seasons and was quite unfavorably compared to *Saturday Night Live.* The press called it a slavish imitation. Perhaps if it had been a better show they wouldn't have complained as much. After all, Perry Como, Carol Burnett, Dinah Shore, and other variety shows all co-existed on the air. And Lorne never claimed to have invented hip sketch comedy; he just devised a new look and a new feel for an old business. If he hadn't done *Saturday Night Live*, someone still might have thought of *Fridays.* Lorne hears from people all the time who tell him they also thought of doing *Saturday Night Live.* At first he didn't know what to say, then he figured out a simple, "Oh, what a drag! You should have done it," would suffice. He already knew how much thought and effort went into doing the show, and how many things had to go right in order for it to work. He's never felt threatened because the secret is that there is no idea *there*, it's just the doing it. It's the thousand little decisions that you make on the way. As Woody Allen says, "Eighty percent of success is showing up."

Fridays made *Saturday Night Live* look better. So did Roseanne's sketch comedy show and *MAD TV,* and everything else that's been sent to destroy *Saturday Night Live*, including Howard Stern. Lorne is accustomed to the competition; in fact, he welcomes the opportunity to fight the inevitable inertia that plagues long-running shows. The show will always be uneven by virtue of being live, and no matter what the critics wish, nothing can compare to the first five years, when *everything was still a surprise.* People judged the show on its own merits. These days everybody thinks that all you need is a group of crazy people and it's easy.

It's not. There's a reason why *Saturday Night Live* is still on the air after twenty-five years. People always watch.

• • • • •

From 1975 to 1980 *Saturday Night Live* was one of the few bright spots in NBC's otherwise dismal ratings picture, and the network wanted Lorne to return for a sixth season. But for a company that wanted to re-sign him, they didn't seem to be in any hurry to settle Lorne's affairs. Johnny Carson's and Tom Snyder's contracts were up for renewal and NBC said they wanted to take care of those matters first. Lorne began to realize he wasn't a high priority after all. In fact, NBC's attitude implied that they thought Lorne would be no trouble at all. Fred Silverman ran an empire; *Saturday Night Live* was a small province with some occasionally unruly subjects.

They were wrong. Lorne was already on the fence. *Saturday Night Live* was his baby, his life, and he didn't want to give up what he loved, yet it seemed like everything had fallen apart. Danny and John were gone. The rest of the cast — everyone but Garrett Morris — and most of the writers wanted to move on. And Lorne was worn out from doing *Gilda Live* — the album, the stage show, and the movie.

Lorne told me that to come back he'd have to do less, maybe executive-produce, and let others handle some of the workload. He also had to as-semble a new cast and wanted to delay the season debut until December 1980 or January 1981. But NBC kept saying they couldn't get to Lorne until they'd wrapped up the Carson and Snyder deals.

I wondered why we should even open contract negotiations. Every year NBC tried to bust our asses. Who needed that? And they were still pissed that Lorne and Gilda had turned down a prime-time series — and then gone on to do *Gilda Live.* Besides, everything had broken down. Putting it together again would be like trying to make Humpty-Dumpty whole, and everyone was burnt out. No one had the strength. It was time to take a deep breath, do movies; take a deep breath, do another television show; take a deep breath, see what happened.

Finally, NBC president Fred Silverman and his new programming head, Brandon Tartikoff, scheduled a meeting with us six weeks in ad-vance, for May 8, 1980.

Before we walked in I asked Lorne to tell me how committed he was to returning. He said he was 80 percent sure he didn't want to come back, but he didn't want to slam the door. I said I was *180 percent* in favor of him leaving.

Of one thing I was certain: without Lorne, NBC *would not* do the show. Lorne wasn't so sure.

The first thing we noticed was this: Fred Silverman wasn't in the room, only Tartikoff and NBC's business-affairs guy, Irwin Moss. Tartikoff explained that Silverman had just done an all-nighter setting the network's upcoming prime-time schedule. Understandable. But it would have been nice if he'd called. We could have met another time.

Things got off to a famously bad start when Irwin Moss looked at me and said, "So, are you here to gouge us again?" NBC had paid $2.5 million for the right to air *Gilda Live* before it had bombed at the box office, and Moss's little joke was meant to deflate any big expectations we'd brought to the meeting.

His attempt at humor backfired. Next Moss took Lorne's old contract from a folder, put it on the desk, and said, "What do you want this year?" I couldn't believe what I was hearing. Lorne's needs were simple. He was focused on how he could put everything back together. Even during our preliminary talks and without being certain that he even wanted to return, Lorne had tried to keep his core group of talented behind-the-scenes people from dispersing.

Then we found out that NBC wanted the sixth season to start on time because they'd already sold ads for October based on the show returning. No one had told us.

In the spirit of Silverman's earlier offer of a series for Gilda, Lorne also wanted to produce some prime-time shows for the network. But Moss offered us only a six-show commitment. We needed more. To me, the six-show commitment, which Silverman started, was a warning signal that the TV business was in trouble. A situation comedy or a variety show doesn't hit its stride until the eleventh show. It takes three months for a cast and a group of writers who have just met to get rid of the kinks, the wrong guesses, and the wrong casting, and make everything smooth. When I'd started out, it was *thirty-nine originals and thirteen repeats.* If a show failed after that, fine, but you had to give it breathing room.

I asked Moss for a seventeen-show guarantee, just like Lorne had gotten five years earlier. He said, "If you don't want to do the show, we have a lineup of producers who we're ready to do it with."

What could I say? "Then fucking do it with them," I said. "And let them produce *Saturday Night Live*, too."

The meeting degenerated quickly into acrimony. While Brandon and Lorne looked on, Moss and I got into a shouting match. It was ugly.

Lorne and I were out of there.

Lorne Michaels:

That meeting was one of the rare times when it was clear to me how emotional Bernie is. In a weird way I'm less emotional than he is. Not to the point of the icicle in the heart, but I'm more removed. I'm always so overwhelmed by what I think of as the consequences that I try and think everything through four or five steps beforehand. Because of that I wasn't as blown out by how Irwin Moss treated us. I knew that Fred Silverman had been to the affiliates meeting the night before, up until four o'clock in the morning, and that he'd just gotten the shit kicked out of him. I didn't think his failure to show up was particularly about me. Bernie took it personally. He also really hated Irwin Moss's behavior. It was an instant conflagration between the two of them because Bernie was hurt by the way I'd been treated. He was caught up in the theatricality of it in a way that, say, a lawyer never would have been. A lawyer would have talked about underlying rights. But emotion clouded us both. Bernie identified with what went on during that extraordinary five-year ride so completely that he felt like he was walking away with me. He wanted me to leave because he had been through all the battles, too. He felt my pain — and his.

After the meeting, Lorne and I went to dinner and talked about what had happened. We were both frustrated. "They won't understand you until you're not here," I said.

Lorne agreed. "Okay, let them know," he said. "That's it. I've gotta leave sometime. I'm outta here."

I left to pick up my father. We were flying back to Los Angeles and we had a plane to catch. Fred Silverman — whom I disliked then but am friends with today — caught me at the hotel before I left for the airport. He said he was sorry for not making the meeting. He wanted to reschedule for the following day, and he wanted me to be there. I said I couldn't, that my father and I were trying to make a plane.

Instead of backing off, Silverman said, "I insist you don't go to California."

I said, "I'm going with my father."

He said, "You have to be here. We can solve this whole thing."

Insisting doesn't work with me. Besides, I was still pissed. Maybe I should have stayed, not that I thought it would make any difference. I really didn't want to solve anything, but I didn't say that. But my attitude was unmistakable. "I don't work for you," I said. "You can't tell me what to do. I'm with my father and I'm leaving."

He said, "You can't leave."

I said, "Bye."

Lorne met with Silverman on Friday, May 9. Later he told me Silverman had been incredibly charming, generous, and supportive. Great. Lorne had been offered more money, more production possibilities, a relaxed work schedule — in other words, whatever he wanted. The keys to the kingdom. Silverman had even apologized. They agreed that Lorne would stick around. The next night Lorne even told a few people at the show that he'd decided to return.

Unfortunately, "Limo for Lamo," an Al Franken skit criticizing Silverman for having "door-to-door limousine service" while Franken had to take cabs to work, made it on the show that night. Silverman saw it and freaked out. He thought Lorne, who'd approved the bit and with whom he believed he'd just reached an understanding, was out to get him. Franken had to write Silverman an apology.

No matter how he felt personally, Silverman didn't want to lose *Saturday Night Live*. He asked Tartikoff to handle the negotiations and ensure the show's survival, with or without Lorne. The two met a few more times, but Lorne just couldn't make a commitment.

Tartikoff decided to find a producer elsewhere. Against Lorne's advice, he chose *Saturday Night Live*'s former talent booker, Jean Doumanian, who, when she took the job, withheld the news from Lorne. Betrayed by Doumanian and disappointed by NBC, Lorne finally understood it was time to go and quietly walked away.

Lorne took a one-year deal at NBC to produce a few specials, but it was really a face-saving move for the network and nothing much came of it. *Saturday Night Live* was over for him. Time to rest and imagine the future. Among the possibilities were movies.

Six years earlier, Lorne had abandoned writing a movie script to take on *Saturday Night Live*. Film still intrigued him, and even before he left the show, studios wanted to work with him. The idea wasn't to spin off *Saturday Night Live* characters into movies. That would come later. They wanted Lorne as a producer and writer. At one point both Paramount and Warner Brothers wanted to sign him. Paramount offered a nine-picture deal. (It could have been one with an option for eight, but they said nine.)

I turned it down. Barry Diller called me and said, "If you don't take this offer, you'll ruin Lorne's career."

Diller is one of the best executives in show business today, but at the time I liked the Warner Brothers guys' style better. John Calley, the head of production, Frank Wells, the head of business affairs, and Ted Ashley, chairman of Warner Brothers Pictures, showed up at my house unannounced one Saturday at 9 A.M. I was out back playing tennis, and I was so arrogant that I asked them to wait. They waited. When I finished I found them in the living room. They'd brought bagels and lox. As we ate they told me they'd take care of Lorne. I knew that under their regime, Warners had a reputation for supporting filmmakers. Calley was gentle and erudite. Wells was smart and efficient. All they could talk about was Lorne's career. I liked that word *career,* so I made a three-picture deal. The first movie would be a big-screen version of *Gilda Live.*

Their guarantees turned out to be lies. I'd been sold a bill of goods. They promised to protect Lorne and make good movies, but when *Gilda Live* came out, Warner Brothers didn't support it. They didn't even take out an ad on *Saturday Night Live,* as they'd promised. Of course, Lorne made a fuss and wanted out of his deal.

Eventually Frank Wells, an imposing guy who a couple years later would become Michael Eisner's number two at Disney, dropped by my office to make a settlement. I wasn't sure how I'd handle the meeting or what I could get. When he walked in, my brother-in-law, Joel Briskin, buzzed me on the intercom and whispered that Wells was perspiring — and it wasn't hot outside. That was the tip-off. I knew I was home free. Warner Brothers had made such a fuss about caring for Lorne that I think Wells was embarrassed at how it had ended up. It wasn't his idea for Lorne to leave, but it was too late. I got all the money they owed us.

In retrospect, maybe I should have taken the Paramount deal, but I was swayed by the personalities and promises. It taught me an important lesson: no one ever treats you as well the day after you sign as they do the day before — but it's what happens afterwards that counts.

• • • • •

The Blues Brothers movie came out in the summer of 1980, and Belushi and Aykroyd toured with the band to support it. The first screenings in Los Angeles didn't go over well. It seemed like there were too many car chases and crashes. I also thought that saving the Blues Brothers' concert for the end of the film was a mistake, even though it probably couldn't have been done any other way. After seeing Cab Calloway, Ray Charles, James Brown, B. B. King, Aretha Franklin, and all the rest, who gave a shit?

Some critics believe the film is overindulgent. I agree. But you know what? So what? See it today. It still works.

After *The Blues Brothers*, Belushi and I realized that he needed to break out of the funny-fat-guy straitjacket. When Spielberg slipped him the script of *Continental Divide*, he desperately wanted to play the lead character, Ernie Souchak, a tough Chicago reporter hiding out in the Colorado mountains from the mob. There, he meets an independent-minded eagle researcher (Blair Brown), and after the usual cinematic difficulties, love ensues. It was the final film of his Universal deal. Belushi totally cleaned up his act and got to work. He lost weight, looked great, and the movie tested well. The reviews covered the gamut, but when the people spoke, the box office was disappointing. Nonetheless, we both considered it a solid first step in recasting his image. But first, Belushi and Aykroyd reteamed for *Neighbors*. When it bombed we decided the two should try working apart for a while.

By then, I'd gotten the boys an agent, Mike Ovitz.

He'd worked to ingratiate himself with me by claiming that I didn't know anything about the movie business. I thought I did.

"How much did you get to produce *The Blues Brothers*?" he asked me, one day.

"One hundred and fifty thousand," I said.

He didn't seem too impressed. That was okay with me. One hundred and fifty thousand was a lot of money then, and I was happy to have it. He said he could do better.

I knew what Ovitz really wanted: my clients. Not one had an agent. I thought it through. After only five years, Ovitz and CAA were hot. I figured if my people went with him they would get great attention. I spoke to Belushi, Aykroyd, Gilda, Patchett and Tarses, and Alan Zweibel, and they agreed to give CAA a try. The move was also good for me. It didn't hurt that Ovitz told everyone that he and I were best friends.

Soon after, Ovitz called me at home to tell me about *Neighbors*, a movie based on the Thomas Berger book. It was set up with Frank Price, at Columbia.

He said, "You're not going to believe this, but I can get Belushi a million and a quarter and Aykroyd close to that for *Neighbors*."

"Great."

"What do you think I can get you?" he asked.

I played along. "I don't know. What can you get me?"

"Four hundred thousand."

I nearly plotzed. I thought Ovitz was crazy. And then it struck me: Maybe I *really* didn't know the movie business. Maybe I was at heart still a television guy.

As a gift, I decided to send him a $7,500 gold Rolex watch. Two days later, the box came back in the mail with a note: "Stop being a schmuck. I can't accept this gift." Without a second thought I sent it back with another note: "Don't be a idiot." Ovitz sent it back again: "I am telling you, I can't accept this gift." I returned it, writing, "I'll really be insulted." This went on for three weeks. I didn't know what was going on, but I wasn't about to give in. Finally he sent it back with a note that read: "This is it. On our friendship, I can't accept this." I thought, "All right, fuck you." I opened the box up and inside was a lousy Timex. Okay, so the guy had a sense of humor.

For the next few years Ovitz and I did so much business that the whole town thought *I* was signed with CAA. He'd set out to seduce me and he'd done a fine job, so fine in fact that I never stopped to think that by taking on an agent like Ovitz — a guy no one could easily control — I'd break my old friend Larry Auerbach's cardinal rule about not letting anyone else with an agenda talk to my clients.

I'd soon regret it.

Chapter 9

The Rock and Roll Star

One day in early March 1982, I flew with John Belushi from Los Angeles to Martha's Vineyard in a private jet. We had it all to ourselves. He was thirty-three. I was fifty-one. The accommodations were first class and we should have been having the time of our lives. We weren't. In fact, John Belushi no longer had a life. He was stretched out across two cramped seats in the tiny jet, wrapped up in a body bag. Our destination was his funeral.

. . . . .

Everybody loved John Belushi. The problem was that he didn't love himself enough to believe he had value in the world and that he wasn't indestructible. As John's TV, then movie, career took off, and his fame grew, so did his inability to control his appetites. After he left *Saturday Night Live,* his life lost the discipline having weekly responsibilities imposed, and his erratic behavior became more frequent. Total strangers gave him drugs just to get close, to be cool, to tell their friends they'd done it. And John consumed it all. It wasn't just an over-large lust for life; he was trying to fill a hole inside. If God hadn't created drugs, John would have found something else to abuse. Lorne and I thought Belushi craved love and acceptance. I could identify with that. I wanted the same things; we all do. But instead of using drugs I became a personal manager.

Belushi could be, and often was, a great guy. The rest of the time, as he careened toward the end, he was either crashed out or out of control. Those who cared about him would say, " You're hurting yourself and the people who love you," but he'd just try to charm his way past the warnings. When I pushed him too hard to straighten up, he'd tell me to back off.

I've asked myself over and over if that's when I should have tried even harder. The answer, I think, is no. Look at Chris Farley, who also died from a drug overdose when he was thirty-three — just like his hero John Belushi. We represented Farley. His manager, Marc Gurvitz, did everything humanly possible to help him. Farley went into rehab so many times I've lost count. In the end he made a stupid mistake and killed himself. What can you do? You can't lock them up. You can't follow them around — at least not if you have any intention of living your own life. If they don't want to help themselves, if they won't stick with the program, you're out of luck. Then one day you get that phone call . . .

. . . . .

There's nothing more painful than watching a man you love destroy himself. I don't know why it happens. I'm not a psychologist, though sometimes in my job I have to act like one. I suppose there are as many reasons as there are people who fuck up: Fear of success. Fear of failure. Fear of being a fake. Feelings of worthlessness. A need for love. Arrogance. Narcissism. They're played out with drink, infidelity, drugs, domestic violence, and other weird behaviors that are hard to imagine. Even performers who aren't screwed up sometimes act this way, so it's hard to tell what's going to happen or how serious it is — until it's sometimes too late.

I knew fear myself, but it seemed to have little to do with what pushed Belushi over the edge. I wish, before we lost him, that he'd told me what drove him. Believe me, I asked, even though it's not my nature to ask too many personal questions. I guess I didn't ask enough. Maybe if he'd been more articulate about the pain, maybe if he could have shared it, this wouldn't have happened. But he kept it all bottled up inside until the cork blew.

After John's death, Lorne Michaels told the *New York Times* that John had "difficulty controlling his appetites." He said that after leaving *Saturday Night Live* Belushi lived in an environment with fewer controls.

I agree. Here's another way of putting it: John was already an excessive personality. In his heart of hearts he wanted to be a rock star.

Instead, he just lived like one. And died like one.

In Chicago it was nearly impossible for John to go out in the street. Everyone knew him, loved him, hugged him. One night when we were just sitting around he said, "I've *got* to go out — but I'm going to put on a disguise." He wore makeup, a hat, and dark glasses. We went to a bar and mingled with the people. After half an hour he ripped off the facade and said, "I'm here!" He *had* to let them know. "Drinks for everyone!" he said. Then, "Bernie, do you have a hundred bucks?"

John would never do drugs in front of me. I think it's because I was like a dad. If someone offered me drugs when we were out together, Belushi would push them away and say, "Don't you ever insult him like that."

Of course, I knew he was doing something — many people did drugs at the time — but because I didn't tag along, I never realized the extent of it. I'd only see him after a toot, or hear stories about how he'd gone wild. I'd had my own problems with gambling, and I know that I never wanted to believe I was out of control. No one likes to hear that. I hated it when my wives told me to stop; in fact, that only made me do it more. But I got past it, and no matter how wild John sometimes got, there was no apparent reason for me to think John wouldn't get past that phase, too.

Besides, I wasn't an expert when it came to drug use. I tried cocaine, but not for long. One day Lorne said, "Bernie, you know the trouble with cocaine? People talk and they never listen." I knew then and there he was telling me to stop it. And that was it; I never did it again. I had my livelihood to consider, not to mention my health.

I thought John used mostly pot and coke. I had no idea about the heroin at the very end. I couldn't have predicted it. I absolutely know he was deathly afraid of needles, and even today I still don't understand what pushed him to try anything that involved one.

Everywhere John put his hand a packet of cocaine mysteriously appeared. After the wrap party for *Continental Divide* near the end of 1980, John and I went back to his suite with his bodyguard, Smokey. John took off his black linen sports jacket and turned it upside down. Eleven grams of coke fell out.

"That's what my good friends gave me tonight," he said, sardonically. John had gotten healthy to make *Continental Divide*. He weighed probably one-eighty-five. He had a trainer and a bodyguard. He was so pure it was unbelievable. He flushed the drugs down the toilet. I was proud of him and I thought maybe we'd gotten over the hump, but after the film Belushi slipped back into his bad habits.

Occasionally John and I would argue about his drug use when I'd tell him the word would get out. He always told me that no one would care as long as his films made money. The worst time was after more than one movie studio told me they were reluctant to work with him because he might have trouble getting insurance. No insurance, no career. I came down on John, told him he had screwed up, wasn't taking care of himself — the usual warnings, only stronger.

I said, "You've got to get help because it's gotten to the point where everyone in town knows it. Forget your career, it's going to make you sick."

He got angry: "I don't pay you to be a bodyguard, father, or friend. You take care of John Belushi from eight to six. From six to eight, John Belushi takes care of himself." For the first time I felt like an employee — which, by the way, I was. I wasn't insulted, just hurt. I'd broken one of my cardinal rules and forgotten my real place.

But his anger faded just as quickly as it flared. "Anyway," he said, with his characteristic, charming bravado, "I have the heart of a high school senior." Then he went off to a steam bath to counteract the effects of his high.

• • • • •

When Belushi and Aykroyd started principal photography on *Neighbors* in April 1981 on Staten Island, there wasn't a soul around them who wasn't nervous. John was clean for about two weeks and then started using drugs again. Soon it got too much for even him to handle. I was there the night John filmed the quicksand scene and nearly drowned because he wouldn't listen to director John Avildsen's advice about how to shoot it safely. Sometimes Belushi was so high he couldn't come out of his trailer. Other times he had parties in the trailer because Avildsen would call him to the set early. Avildsen figured he could limit John's drug use if he made him sit around and wait on location. But getting drugs on a movie set is even easier than getting them in prison. Belushi had already seen one bodyguard–personal watchdog come and go — he wore him out — so I hired another to try and keep Belushi straight. Had there been rehab centers like there are today, we'd have pushed him to go once the film was done.

John's problems were made worse by his nonrelationship with Avildsen. I thought he'd be a good director because, after all, the guy had won an Academy Award for *Rocky*. But he and John were doomed from the start. The day John, Danny, and I met Avildsen at his office and saw the NO SMOKING IN THIS OFFICE sign on his desk, we immediately lit up. We didn't want to piss him off, we wanted to see if he could laugh. He did, sort of. But he didn't mean it, and after that everything went downhill in a struggle for control. John complained about him constantly. Every day he wanted Avildsen replaced. John and Danny didn't think the guy knew anything about being funny.

After the movie wrapped, John and Danny went to Martha's Vineyard for the summer. John called me constantly to say things like, "Oh my God, we're cooking lobster!" John, his wife, Judy, and Danny seemed to be having a great time.

Just after Labor Day, I went to Amagansett for Lorne Michaels's wedding to his second wife, Susan Forristal. I arrived very early, like I always do, and watched the important people stream in, everyone from Paul Simon to Jann Wenner to Jack Nicholson — and, of course, the *Saturday Night Live* family. After a while in walked this guy in a white suit and white Panama hat. He stumbled up to me, loaded out of his mind, and said, "Do you still handle rock stars?" It was Belushi. He clearly had no idea who I was. He looked like he was about to pass out any second. After the ceremony, Michael Klefner, the record executive who'd signed the Blues Brothers, and I half carried/half walked John behind the hedges near Lorne's swimming pool. We put him on a lounge chair and he slept through the reception. It completely broke my heart.

Belushi and Aykroyd weren't happy with Avildsen's rough cuts of *Neighbors* and let him know about it. By this time work on the film had moved to Los Angeles. John arrived in late September for looping and other postproduction duties. Of course, he was high.

The bad John would walk into my office at 8:30 in the morning, after being out of touch for days. I could tell he'd been on a toot. A party animal well into the party is not nice to look at and not nice to smell. This wasn't just staying up until two o'clock in the morning. He could stay up for forty-eight hours or more. Many times I couldn't get him on the phone. I'd leave ten messages. Finally, he'd show up at the office just to let me know he was okay, then lie on the couch and fall asleep. Maybe those who saw him stretched out peacefully knew what was going on; if not, no one asked. His sleep was the privilege of stardom.

When John woke up he'd always be apologetic, though he would never actually admit to having been high. He'd say, "I was a bad guy. I got in trouble." Belushi was like a child who knows he's been naughty and doesn't want his parents to be mad. He'd do anything to avoid being scolded. He'd make up some story just to get me to laugh. "You know how I get," he'd say, sheepishly. John always had an excuse. Sometimes it was only an imploring look. Most of the time I'd just let his behavior slide. I wasn't his parent. I loved him, but he was a grown man. If he didn't take responsibility for himself he'd never get better.

I was also naive. I wanted to believe in him. I went on first instinct, something that both Lorne and Brad have taught me is not *always* a good thing. Once, Belushi told me he was moving in with a married couple while staying in Los Angeles. I thought that was great. He wouldn't be in some ratty hotel, getting into trouble at all hours. I called Lorne to give him the good news. He listened patiently, then said, "Bernie, the wife is the biggest drug dealer in California!"

I had figured "married couple" equaled stability. Lorne put it in perspective. Just because two people are married doesn't mean they're solid. In fact, it doesn't mean a damn thing.

"Bernie, let me spell something for you," Lorne said. "A-C-T-O-R. John Belushi can make you feel any way he wants to make you feel. He can make you believe what he wants you to believe. He's an actor, and a good one."

Though he could turn at any moment, John had frequent good periods. He'd drop by the office and we'd go to the Mandarin Restaurant in Beverly Hills for Chinese food, or the farmer's market, where he would talk to the old people. He loved talking to the old people! Sometimes we'd go to the Russian Baths for a steam.

The good John would walk down a London street holding hands with my kids Nicholas and David (from Debbie's first marriage) and Leigh (from mine), singing Blues Brothers songs. Tell me another star who does anything like that. The good John once visited my father in a Miami hotel and spent three hours with him, eating salami sandwiches and eventually cleaning out his refrigerator. Of course, he also hit up my old man for $100 before he left. Moe thought it was classic.

The good John was a huge Chicago Bears and Cubs fan. He was also fascinated by the roots of comedy. He may have dreamt of being a rock star, but his humor heroes were Jackie Gleason and Jimmy Durante. Even I didn't suspect that he loved them until he told me, but if you look at his work, some of it is very similar. I know why Durante and Gleason, both of whom I'd seen perform, appealed to John. He was a traditionalist. He didn't like sissy, soft comedy; he didn't like doing comedy in drag; he liked the hard edge. He asked me time and time again to tell him stories about Fifty-second Street and nights at the Copa in New York. The one thing I regret is that we never went to Vegas together. He wanted me to show him the Vegas I knew, the old Vegas that in the late '70s was taking its final curtain call. Too bad we never found the time.

• • • • •

The longer John stayed in Los Angeles in the fall of 1981, the more there were days when I'd have given anything not to be in business with him. I didn't want to be within a hundred miles of John Belushi. I still loved him, but he was like a child stuck in the terrible twos. I just wanted to put him in his room and shut the door, or give him to the nanny. I had a business to run, other clients and pressures to handle.

Sometimes when I knew John was coming to the office, I'd take a powder. Like a guy who lives with a woman who's a little nuts has to disappear every once in a while, I'd slip out a back door. I'd make Sandy Wernick or Joel Briskin sit with him. I just couldn't handle it anymore. I was depressed and started having terrible migraines. My routine was to go home, take two Fiorinal with codeine, get under the covers, and "goodbye Charlie." I needed to break open the valve and let out the pressure. This doesn't happen only to me. Even Brad, on occasion, has told me, "I just feel like going home and putting my head under the pillow and leaving it there." He was probably speaking about having to deal with Garry Shandling, but I can't be sure.

Eventually Belushi literally became a pain in the ass. Dealing with his craziness gave me an incredible case of hemorrhoids. A few months later, in New York, during the press junket for *Neighbors*, the pain was so intense that I had to sit in the bath in Belushi's suite while he was downstairs giving interviews. He kept running up to the room to check if I was all right. He took care of me. I guess he knew he caused me pain, and for a little while the good John was back.

· · · · ·

As long as Belushi was my client, my responsibility was to keep him in business. I may not have been any good at telling him how to live, but I still had to get him jobs and help him be happy with the jobs he had. I had to think about the big picture.

Even after the *Neighbors* disaster, Belushi continued to be in demand, at ever-increasing prices. We'd brought in Mike Ovitz as his (and Danny's) agent, and there were plenty of movie offers. My new idea was for John to try a smaller role. Too many aging superstars have gone out of business because their managers or agents said, "You're too big. You can't do that." Look what Arnold Rifkin accomplished with Bruce Willis, who was a little cold when he became part of the ensemble in *Pulp Fiction.* Same thing with Travolta, in the same picture. Now Travolta gets $20 million a picture and Willis is not far behind. Why? Because the audience likes them again. Look at Don Ameche and Ralph Bellamy in *Trading Places.* That was John Landis's idea. I hate to give him credit for anything, but who else could be better for those two roles?

After *Neighbors* I also advised Danny and John to do movies separately. They agreed that the team should break up for at least a little while. Unfortunately, I picked *Doctor Detroit* for Danny's next picture. On a positive note, he met his wife, Donna Dixon, during the shoot, and I'm sure neither one of them is sorry he made the movie.

I still believe Belushi would — without a doubt — have been resurrected. Danny was, even then, developing *Ghostbusters* for himself, Bill Murray, and John. If John had lived to make it, I'm sure he'd have been back in a big way.

· · · · ·

At the end of 1981 John decided to do a romantic comedy/caper called *Sweet Deception* — but only if Don Novello (*Saturday Night Live*'s Father Guido Sarducci, also a client), would help rewrite and make it funnier. Working with director Jay Sandrich, who'd helmed *The Mary Tyler*

Moore Show, Ovitz sold it to Michael Eisner at Paramount, promising a return to the funny Belushi of old. John walked away with a $1.85 million deal. He and Novello got to work. They also changed the title to the more aggressively pompous *Noble Rot*.

A few months later, on a flight to London to see Jim Henson, I read the script. It was terrible. Nothing was funny. It's okay to say that, because no manager is worth anything if he or she isn't honest. The screenplay was neither fish nor fowl. It was no good. It didn't even make sense.

Belushi knew I would give it the once-over on the plane, and as I expected, there was a message for me to call him waiting at the hotel.

First I phoned Debbie and told her the bad news. I was frantic. She told me to calm down and read it again. I did. It wasn't funny.

Then I called Ovitz. We agreed the script was a mess and talked about how to tell John. After I hung up, the phone rang. It was Belushi. I took a deep breath and told him the truth. We agreed to wait for Eisner's reaction.

A couple days later, Ovitz heard from Eisner. He hated the script. Eisner spoke with Ovitz and me and said he'd call Belushi. John disagreed with his assessment and offered to fly to Los Angeles and explain it to him.

Then John called Ovitz, who tried to lead him to the conclusion that the script was substandard.

Belushi fired him.

John called me. I repeated what I'd said before. "John, it's no good."

"Goddamn it!" he said.

"I'm sorry," I said. "It stinks. You want me to lie to you? I've never lied to you and I'm not going to start now. This is not good."

"Ovitz didn't like it either," he said, "so I . . . fired him."

"And . . . ?" I said.

"And, well . . . let's think about it," he said. I explained that it was only a first draft and there were sure to be rewrites. He should take it easy. Then we hung up. I was glad to be in London.

When I got back to Los Angeles we talked over the possibilities. Eisner and Paramount still wanted to be in business with Belushi. His $1.85 million deal was pay-or-play, but *Noble Rot* was not in the cards. Eisner suggested replacing that film with *The Joy of Sex*, based on the bestselling book. John's friend Penny Marshall wanted to direct. I didn't like the script, and I wasn't sure it was the right move for John. The only good thing about it was Penny Marshall — who, incidentally, didn't direct the film when it was finally made. It was all too confusing to be sorted out in a few phone calls. What John really needed was to get in a room with Eisner and his lieutenant, Jeffrey Katzenberg, and figure out his next move. And he had to be open-minded.

On March 4, 1982, the day before Belushi died, he came to the office to meet with Eisner. He also asked me for $1,800 to buy a special guitar that had once belonged to Les Paul.

He said, "I have to pay cash."

I didn't believe him. "What guitar costs eighteen hundred bucks? You're gonna use the money for drugs."

John didn't deny it. Or confirm it. Instead, he acted like the kid who thinks that because he's crossed the street without looking both ways many times and yet survived, he's invincible. That he was *in my office talking to me* was supposed to prove, ipso facto, that he could take care of himself. I still refused him the money.

By the way, it's not unusual for any client to come to the office asking for money. One thing about people with lots of money: they often don't carry it.

Later that day, Michael Eisner showed up for our meeting about John's pending movie. Once again, Eisner said he didn't want to make *Noble Rot*. He wanted to convince Belushi to do *The Joy of Sex* instead — and as a way to smooth things over, Eisner told him he could continue to rewrite *Noble Rot*. This time, after months of resistance, John seemed willing to consider the proposal. Eisner and I were very happy.

But then John grew restless. While Eisner sat in my office, he asked me again for the money to buy the guitar. What timing. I couldn't say "You'll use it for drugs" with Eisner there. I thought about telling John we'd talk later, but he was antsy and I didn't know if he'd pitch a fit. Plus, he'd been better in the meeting than I'd expected. He'd pleased me and he knew I instinctively wanted to please him. Also, that I wanted to believe him. So I just said okay, I'd get him the money, he should consider it "a belated birthday present." He said good-bye to Eisner, got the money from my assistant, and walked with me to the elevator. We hugged. John's movie career was hardly in great shape, but at that moment I felt more positive about John's future than I had in a long time.

· · · · ·

John was scheduled to meet again with Eisner and Katzenberg on the afternoon of March 5. It was the session I hoped would lead to a new beginning.

My office tried to reach Belushi with a wake-up call around 9 A.M. at the Chateau Marmont, his hotel on Sunset. He was living in Bungalow #3. We tried and tried but couldn't get through. It didn't seem out of the ordinary for John. Just business as usual.

About 10 A.M. I got a call from John's trainer-bodyguard, Bill Wallace. He was at the Marmont, in John's bungalow. He sounded crazy. Freaking out. John hadn't answered the door, so he'd let himself in. He said John was "having trouble breathing. I'm having trouble waking John up!"

I told Gigi, one of the secretaries, to get my brother-in-law, Joel Briskin, someone I could trust, over to the Marmont right away. She also called John's doctor, and the nurse said she'd call the paramedics. A couple minutes later Wallace called back: He said John *definitely wasn't* breathing, that something was horribly wrong. I told him Joel and help were on the way and that as soon as I hung up I'd go to the Cedars-Sinai emergency room. Whatever was happening, I wanted to make sure they took good care of John and that there would be no press.

It took less than ten minutes to get from 9200 Sunset to the hospital. I knew just where to go. Like all parents, I'd been to the emergency room before with my kids. I drove my car up in front and left it.

I ran through the sliding doors.

Inside, a handful of people in the waiting area read magazines or stared into space, clearly lost in their own hopes and anxieties. I walked up to a nurse and said, quietly, "Look, John Belushi is coming in here. I'm his manager. He's had an accident and I want to keep it quiet. The minute he arrives, can we just get him into a room?" She said, "Okay."

That's what managers are supposed to do: keep things under control; keep the press away. It was my first big emergency. I'd never been through it before; I didn't know the drill. But it was my job and I knew I'd figure it out as I went along.

Along the wall were three phone booths. I called the office for news. Nothing. I gave them my number in case they heard from the Marmont and needed to alert me.

All I could do was wait. And perspire. When I'm nervous I pace and sweat and smoke. I kept thinking, "Where the fuck is he?" I wanted to call the office again but I didn't. Anyway, they knew where to find me. Maybe the ambulance hadn't even gotten to the Marmont yet; you never knew with 9-1-1. The thought crossed my mind that the situation might be worse than I expected, but I didn't dwell on it. John had been having a bad time. This may sound terrible, but the whole incident was just another in a long string of Belushi incidents. It would work out.

I walked to the automatic doors and stood half inside and half outside. I lit a Viceroy. I kept my eyes on the driveway and my ears on the phone. I wondered what was taking so goddamn long. Maybe the doctors were still working on him. Maybe they'd gone to another hospital.

I walked back inside, past the phones.

I walked outside and watched for the ambulance.

I ground out a cigarette butt with my heel, and started another.

For the hundredth time I thought, "Where the fuck are they?"

Now the dark thought that things might be worse than I believed tried to take root, but I blocked it. The situation was just another Belushi annoyance. Soon it would be over, John would be okay, he'd smile, and everyone would feel fine until the next emergency unless John could somehow pull himself out of his self-destructive spiral.

Suddenly I felt very heavy, and my mental defenses crumbled. I realized there'd be no good news to come out of any of this.

The phone rang. I took three long steps and grabbed it. Fran Saperstein — one of the assistants — was on the line. In the second after she spoke my name I knew for certain that everything *wasn't* okay, might *never* be okay. My stomach began to hurt. Then I heard her say, "John's dead."

"Wh-a-a-at?" It came out like a little stuttered giggle. It's a strange thing when you hear about death. Sometimes you can't stop the laugh, although there's no reason for it. My hand suddenly felt wet and empty and I realized I'd dropped the receiver. I picked it up and said, "Oh my God. I'll be right back." I looked at my watch. It was just past noon. Then I slumped against the phone booth wall, consumed with the reality of what had happened. I could wait for John forever. The ambulance would never arrive.

I knew I had to keep control of the situation, and not only because it was my job. It was just like when I was a kid getting in between my parents fighting, trying to make everything okay. Taking control of things was my way of dealing with my own fear.

I also had to make the bad call.

From the hospital I phoned Danny Aykroyd at his office in Manhattan. It was afternoon on the East Coast. I said, "Danny, sit down. Now, listen to me. We have no time for overreaction. John is dead." He didn't say anything. I didn't add any niceties. "You have to leave your office *now*," I said. "Go directly to Judy's house" — Judy Belushi — "so she doesn't hear it on the radio. You have to tell her."

He said, "Yes," and left.

Years later, Danny told interviewer David Sheff of *Playboy* magazine:

> Bernie Brillstein . . . called me at the office. It was a beautiful
> March day and absolutely spectacular in New York. The weather
> was warm and clear and the streets were full of people enjoying
> the sunshine. I'll never forget that walk from 150 Fifth Avenue to
> Morton Street to Judy's house, because I was thinking, "I can't get
> in a cab, I've got to keep walking." Richard Pryor described it
> when he was burned: He just kept running to stay alive. He knew
> if he stopped he was going to die. I had that same desperation. I
> knew if I stopped, it was going to get me, so I just had to walk and
> get there before Judy heard it on the radio. I managed to get there
> and I told her. "He's dying" is all I said. And that was the most
> painful part for me.

I don't remember much about my drive from Cedars back to 9200 Sunset. When I walked in, the place was so quiet it could have been the weekend. First, I called Jeffrey Katzenberg to tell him that John wouldn't make that day's meeting. Katzenberg wanted to know why, but I couldn't say. He didn't accept that and got testy. I said I was sorry, I just couldn't discuss it. I would have liked to tell him, but I figured he'd find out soon enough.

Later, I discovered that within minutes of my conversation with Katzenberg, Ovitz had called Eisner about Belushi and said, "He's dead." Eisner thought he said, "*It's* dead."

"You mean he's not going to do *The Joy of Sex?*" said Eisner.

"No," Ovitz said. "He can't. *Belushi* is dead."

After I hung up from the Katzenberg call, the office was eerily quiet again. Then almost simultaneously every one of our phone lines lit up and rang. The news had spread and the media were on the line. One call was from Roone Arledge at ABC.

"Bernie, you have to be on *Nightline* tonight," he said.

That seemed ludicrous; nauseating.

"What am I going to do — go on and say, 'Hello, I'm a celebrity dead person's friend'?" Even though Roone was a pal (we'd been in the army together), I had to say no. That night, the only person they could get was Milton Berle. I thought that was hysterical. Berle's only connection to John was that they both were comedians and that Berle had hosted *Saturday Night Live*. (By the way, Berle's show was one of the worst *Saturday Night Live*'s ever. Berle actually planted shills in the audience to applaud him. The show was so horrible that Lorne will never let it be repeated or released on video.)

It was Friday afternoon. Everywhere it was business as usual and everyone in town was getting ready for the weekend. But not for me. All hell had broken loose. John was dead and I couldn't do a goddamn thing about it. I felt like crying — but that would come later.

Then, a godsend: Gilda called. She and Gene Wilder wanted me and Debbie to come to their house that night, so no one could get hold of me. We gladly went. She cooked dinner. I was in shitty shape. The news was all over the TV. We didn't want to watch and get more crazed, but we also didn't want to miss what was being said. The worst thing was that I couldn't stop thinking about how I had to dress John on Saturday and take him back East for the funeral.

The next day I went to Bungalow #3 at the Marmont and cleaned it out. The scene was not only depressing, it was depraved. I couldn't believe John had lived there. Cold coffee, stiff toast, wine, magazines, phone messages, scripts, dirty clothes. Nothing had been touched because it was a crime scene. I grabbed the messages, a letter on the desk, and one of John's jackets, and split.

Next I went to the Pierce Brothers mortuary. John had dirty fingernails, as usual, and I was obsessed with cleaning them. The undertaker finished dressing John with the jacket I had taken from the Marmont bungalow. I later discovered the jacket belonged to Cathy Smith, the woman John was with before he died. She had grabbed his by mistake, after injecting John with the speedball that killed him. She was indicted for her complicity in his death, then convicted. She served a few years and today speaks to groups about the evils of taking drugs.

· · · · ·

On March 7, I flew John's body back East. The Blues Brothers albums had been recorded for Atlantic Records, which was owned by Warner Brothers, so Warners loaned us a Westwind private jet. It was a seven-seater, but so small and narrow that a coffin wouldn't fit inside. The undertakers put John in a canvas body bag and the airport handlers lifted him into the plane. They laid John across two seats, I climbed in, and we took off.

Debbie decided to take an American Airlines flight instead of coming with us. Nobody wanted to ride with the body.

If it had been a scene from a movie, I'd have said something like, "You stupid kid! I loved you! How could you do this to yourself?" I would have poured out everything. I was angry, and hurt, and sad, and disgusted, and a million more emotions I can't put a name to. But it wasn't a movie moment. It was real life. I could talk all I wanted to John's body but he wasn't going to answer, apologize, or explain. It was just his body. It wasn't John.

I was exhausted, so I slept, a fitful, depressing sleep.

We landed on Martha's Vineyard late that evening. The airstrip was crowded with cars. I got off the plane, glad to see anyone. It was very cold and a bit windy. John's body was unloaded and placed on the wing. I thought, "Thank God, everyone's here." I said, "Okay, who's coming to the funeral home with me to dress him and make sure everything's all right?" I never saw cars leave so fast in my life. Judy Belushi stayed. She had a shirt and jacket that she wanted John to wear. We went to the funeral home and took care of the details.

Later, Danny held a wake at his house.

On March 9, we buried John on Martha's Vineyard, at Abel's Hill Cemetery. According to Danny, the Vineyard was the only place John ever slept well. The Samurai had wrought his devastation and now it was time to say good-bye. Lorne had arranged for private planes to get everyone up there. In the Greek Orthodox funeral ceremony the casket is open and the body faces the altar. My seat was in the second row, on the aisle. Right next to John's head. Phew. All I could think was, "When is this going to end?"

At the funeral I was the maître d', a good manager to the end. I faced the press, an enormous number of paparazzi, and the people streaming through the front door. From the corner of my eye I saw Bill Murray sneak in the back, when the press wasn't looking. I've always admired Billy for that. He was the only celebrity who didn't want his face in the papers.

The service was cold, stark, beautiful. Danny led the procession to the cemetery, on his motorcycle. James Taylor sang "That Lonesome Road" at the grave site. People cried. Snow fell.

Afterwards, I caught a plane to New York and went to the Regency Hotel. On the TV news I watched myself in the funeral procession. The next night we had another wake in my hotel suite. Everyone showed up.

About midway through, the phone rang. It was Thomas Noguchi, the Los Angeles coroner. He said, "We found that Belushi died from a speedball" — an injected mixture of cocaine and heroin. Then he said, "You have half an hour to notify the family before we release the results." I hung up and turned around, and before I knew it Noguchi was on TV, walking out to a press conference, saying it was a speedball. Some half hour. What a prick. What a bad scene. None of us could believe it. We thought John was petrified of needles. We thought he would never be stupid enough to try heroin.

• • • • •

After John's death, *Washington Post* reporter Bob Woodward wrote a book about him called *Wired.* I spoke to Woodward; so did many other people. I figured he'd write something fair and evenhanded; he'd done *All the President's Men*, for chrissakes. Debbie tried to warn me off. "Don't ever talk to him," she said. "He won't get it." She was absolutely right, but I didn't listen. I wanted to meet Bob Woodward. Everyone did.

I sat for hours with Woodward, really trying to explain Belushi. I talked about when John was good and when he was bad. I wanted to help Woodward understand the whole man, but after reading *Wired* I'm not sure he even tried. Instead, I believe Woodward came to town and looked at the situation through the eyes of a guy who knew nothing about the times or the environment or the people. He didn't want to understand how Hollywood worked. He just wanted to condemn it. I think he already had his mind made up.

What Woodward also didn't get was that even if Belushi had stayed in Wheaton, Illinois, where he (and Woodward) grew up, he might *still* have met a sad end. I'm not denying the terrible facts or consequences of his drug habit, but had Woodward drawn a complete picture of John, the sense of tragedy he was striving for could only have been made more poignant, the lesson more significant, the loss greater — because the good died, too. That was supposedly the point, wasn't it?: to communicate the towering loss of a super talent, not simply to indict the world he lived in.

Woodward blamed John's death on what he thought was a morally corrupt business that indulges its stars with reckless disregard for their well-being because so much money is at stake. That really offends me. We'd have to be scum. Inhuman. No amount of money in my pocket would have made me ignore John's health for my own gain. There's just a limit to how much you can help someone who doesn't want to help himself.

We'd talked about institutionalizing Belushi but never did. Why? The choices at the time were limited to hospital psychiatric wards and white-bread joints for alcoholics. Belushi's death, perhaps the first high-profile cocaine casualty of the '80s, certainly signaled a need for drug rehab centers. But people like Woodward think that if you're in show business, somehow you're born into the big time and know all about these things. Let me tell you: you don't know until you need to, and then it's usually too late.

· · · · ·

The sorry truth is that you just never know what's going to happen with anyone. Remember David Begelman, the former agent and studio head who got into trouble for writing checks and forging Cliff Robertson's signature? We were old friends. We both loved ice hockey. One day, years after his public troubles, he walked into my office and brought me a hockey stick signed by the new Kings coach. Then he told me he was down on his luck and asked for a loan. He was stuck with a movie company and only needed $35 million. What he asked for was $150,000. I told him I'd speak to Brad over the weekend. We decided to give him $50,000. Monday morning we called Begelman to tell him the news and discovered that he'd put a bullet in his head. He killed himself because he was no longer *David Begelman.* He thought he was nothing without being *David Begelman.* That's the sadness of this business and it had all finally caught up with him. He couldn't fake it anymore. Was I supposed to know he was going to kill himself? Did he look like a guy who was going to kill himself? I just thought he looked like a guy in trouble.

Did I know Gilda's cancer would come back to her after it went into remission and she wanted to work again?

Would I have let Jim Henson walk in the street if I had known, when he dropped by one afternoon to kiss me good-bye and he had a cough, that it was the last time I'd see him and he'd be dead in three days?

It just never occurred to me that Belushi would die. I knew he was hurting his career, his marriage, his friendships, and certainly his health. But die? Who believes a thirty-three-year-old guy, built like an ox, is going to die? Did Michael Eisner, who met with him the day before he died, tell me after Belushi left the office, "Oh my God, get this boy to a home"? No. Maybe some of his celebrity and drug-using friends knew the symptoms, but all we saw was a guy in front of us who always looked like John Belushi: sometimes good, sometimes bad, sometimes in need of a swift kick in the ass, more often in need of a hug.

He thought he was Superman. I guess we wanted to believe that, too. In hindsight, we were fools, but then hindsight is always perfect.

I suppose if Woodward wrote about the death of Chris Farley, he'd once again blame show business. That's bullshit. At our insistence Farley was always in and out of rehab. We personally escorted him there. We talked and talked to him until we could talk no more. We warned, cajoled, threatened, but it did no good. *It can't do any good* when someone doesn't care enough about themselves to live.

The press made a lot out of Farley's fascination with Belushi. He did consider John a hero, but believe me, Chris *did not want to die.* He wanted to accept himself. But he found solace and strength in a liquor bottle and coke spoon. *And there was nothing anyone could do about it.* You don't know when it's coming. You always think you can get by one more time.

Sadly, not always.

· · · · ·

I don't like to play amateur psychiatrist, especially on myself, but between Bob Woodward's inferences and writing about all this now, I think maybe there's something about me that explains why I reacted to Belushi the way I did. It all has to do with my relationship with my mother, and *her* drug dependency.

For thirty years she took pills. The doctors prescribed them: Tuinal. Seconal. Reds. Blues. Four to sleep during the day. More to sleep at night. If it rained she'd take pills. She used to bounce off the walls. And pretty soon, though no one in my family would admit it — there are few things stronger than Jewish denial — she was an addict. I don't know how she got that way, what started her off. I just remember her always in bed.

When I got home from school, it wasn't long before I'd hear the intercom buzz. Then her voice: "Berrrnniiieee. Ged me sum bwead an' buddah." I can still hear her slur, and feel the anxiety and anger that buzzer caused. I'd get her what she wanted and then I'd call my father and say, "We've got to do something about her."

He'd say, "What are you talking about?"

"She's stoned!"

"No. She just doesn't feel well. Everything's okay."

Excuses, all the time. We *both* knew it wasn't okay.

Now we know she was a depressive. But in those days, the '30s, '40s, and '50s, the medicines weren't as sophisticated as today's Prozac and Zoloft. Doctors simply gave out pills. It was "Shut up and go to sleep," and there wasn't a great deal of FDA argument to the contrary. Four of her friends were the same way. It was terrible. I once opened one of my father's suitcases. What I discovered would make you think he was the biggest drug dealer on the East Coast. Reds, blacks, yellows. I was so dumb; I didn't know what they were. I'm telling you, a *suitcase* full. Unlike the Blues Brothers' "Suitcase Full of Blues," this was a suitcase full of sleep.

Anything could happen. More than once she fell asleep with a cigarette burning. She could have torched the apartment. (During the second season of *Saturday Night Live*, Lorne bought a loft in downtown Manhattan with the first real money he had. While it was being remodeled, Belushi asked if he could stay there. Lorne could never say no to anyone. He gave him the keys. John fell asleep with a cigarette and burned it down.)

Once I got so frustrated that I went to her druggist at Ninety-first and Columbus and said, "I'm going to put you in fucking jail."

"How can you?" he said. "Your father gives me the prescriptions. What do you want me to do?"

I said, "Help me. I have an addict on my hands."

"She's sick," said the druggist.

Yes, and the pills were making it worse.

At first, her condition scared me — like it would any normal human being. I kept hoping she'd get better. She didn't. After a while it became a way of life. Her natural state. She was always out of it. I got used to it.

I stopped worrying.

It was commonplace. When you see your mother's stomach being pumped after the third or fourth suicide attempt, red Seconal flowing through the tube, not a lot in life is going to bother you after that. Constant exposure makes some depraved things become very, very ordinary. The longer they continue, the less you think about them, or of the worst happening. You become desensitized. You no longer hear alarms. It's miserable to live with but eventually you have to get on with your life and hope that what they say is true: crazy is crazy only for a little while.

It all adds up to how I handled Belushi's condition. At first I tried to help, then I just got used to it.

I still don't believe I could have stopped John from killing himself. After fifteen years the best I can come up with is that perhaps if I'd had a different family I might have remained more connected to John's bad habits near the end and not grown numb to the danger. I might have reached out just one more time . . .

· · · · ·

Now it's long past too late. Do I feel responsible for Belushi's death? No. I have no guilt about that. Do I feel bad? *I feel awful.* Do I wish I'd been smarter? Yes, I really do. Do I wish he was here? You betcha.

Belushi was responsible for a great part of my success. But he was much more than that to me. I loved him. He was fun. He was exciting. He was like a son.

During the third season of *Saturday Night Live,* Tom Schiller made a short film starring Belushi called *Don't Look Back in Anger.* Belushi plays himself as an old man wandering around in the Not Ready for Prime Time Cemetery in Brooklyn. It's winter and Belushi reminisces about his co-cast members, all of whom he's outlived. "They all thought I'd be the first to go," he says. "I was one of those 'Live fast, die young, leave a good-looking corpse' types, you know. I guess they were wrong."

I don't wish the others ill, but I wish Belushi had been right.

Now when I think of John it's always this way: The first night of the Blues Brothers shows at the Universal Amphitheater. He's in his black suit and shades, doing cartwheels onto the stage. He's the rock and roll star he always wanted to be. He's living his dream.

• • • • •

Years after his death I found some Polaroids buried in a box. I hadn't seen them for fifteen years, and for a moment I didn't even remember what they were. But when I scrutinized the fading images of Belushi in the vinyl body bag it all came back: The awful solitude of that seven-hour flight; my hands shaking as I tried to hold the camera steady. I don't know why I took the photos; I must not have been thinking straight, but who wouldn't be crazy, or worse, in that situation? I guess I wanted proof of the horror, for me and me only. I didn't know I would never need it. What happened to John has been impossible to forget.

The pictures made me sick inside all over again. I threw them back in the box and hid it.

I don't remember where.

10

Sweetheart,
Are You Happy?

When John Belushi died I thought my business was over. Not because he brought in all the income; that was hardly the case. I believed his death was not only his failure, but mine. I couldn't shake the feeling that I'd enabled it, that I didn't know or want to know his limits, that I could have been smarter. I didn't give him the drugs; I didn't tell him to shoot whatever he shot. But I felt guilty, like I should have known how serious it really was, like I should have been able to see the future. Even though I once told Lorne that losing John was out of our hands, I'm not sure I always believed that myself. I was embarrassed and ashamed and wanted to do some sort of penance. I'd always feared that the bogeyman would appear and take everything away. Instead, the bogeyman died and I was left to clean up the mess and say enough is enough.

· · · · ·

In the summer of 1982 I bought what I've always called "the Belushi House," in Connecticut, and went into semi-retirement. I even flirted with leaving the business entirely, but too many people depended on me. I also had too big an ego to be washed up at fifty-one. As sort of a compromise, I got out of town.

With my lawyer, John Irwin, and his wife, Vicki, Debbie and I drove north from New York in a black-and-gray stretch limo and looked at a few houses. In New Canaan we saw a beautiful Georgian home: twenty-four rooms on eleven acres and a three-quarter-mile driveway with Canada geese walking through the grass on either side. We strolled around the property, me in my sweatsuit and Irwin, thank goodness, in his lawyer suit. (Someone had to look like they could afford the place.) Debbie and I loved the house. I told the real estate agent, "We'll take it."

Boom. Eight hundred thousand dollars.

The agent said, "Good. Come back to my office and we'll start the paperwork." As we pulled out of the driveway and drove down the street, I saw a country club at the corner. It was so old and white-on-white-bread that the tennis court fences were wood posts with wire mesh. Just for fun I said, "Hey! There's even a country club. Where do we sign up?" The poor saleslady didn't get the joke. "Five-year waiting list!" she said. (She might as well have added, "And no Jews allowed.") I didn't care. I was happy to still have a sense of humor.

The house needed some work. We put in a swimming pool and tennis court. Around Easter 1983, we moved in.

Our relocation encouraged visitors. My in-laws were around for the whole summer. Gilda and Gene lived in Stamford, so we saw them a lot. Lorne came up some weekends. I didn't hate the idea, but I soon realized that I was too depressed for social obligations.

Meanwhile, I tried to run my company at arm's length. The routine was mind-numbing. I'd wake up late and read the newspaper. I'd eat lunch at some good local hotel. Afterwards, I'd call Sandy in Los Angeles for the news, check in with clients, then nap until dinnertime.

I was only about an hour by rail from New York City. I could have gone in, seen Lorne, Henson, network people, done business, but I hated taking the train almost as much as I hated to drive. It was a flimsy excuse. I was just burned out on managing. My biggest client had died and the next biggest wasn't working. Henson kept doing movies and I had money from *Sesame Street*, but no one burned brightly. Everything was middles. I couldn't stand it. I kept thinking, "I'm not hot anymore. My clients aren't hot anymore. I better get the fuck outta here while the getting is good."

Instead, I marked time and tried to shake off my bad memories. Like my clients, I also needed new opportunities.

Lorne stayed busy with Broadway Video. He produced a Neil Young concert film, helped with some Rolling Stones videos, did a Simon and Garfunkle show in Central Park, a Steve Martin TV special, a Randy Newman concert. He hung out, built a pond on his Amagansett property, traveled to Egypt, and dabbled in the movie business.

My TV writer and producer clients, the cream of the variety-show crop, also faced major changes in the early '80s. I kept telling them to think of new ideas because the classic variety show was dying. "Get into situation comedy," I said. Most of them didn't listen as well as I'd have liked.

Only Henson stayed hot. In 1982, he finished the movie *Dark Crystal* and started the HBO series *Fraggle Rock*. He created characters for *The Empire Strikes Back, Return of the Jedi,* and other films. He was by far the most prolific of my clients. Between his commissions and the merchandising income, The Henson Company pretty much carried The Brillstein Company for a time.

I was still available when someone needed a sympathetic ear — which was often — but my responses ran to the words I also needed to hear: "Everything will be fine; everything will be okay; don't worry." And in case I was wrong, well . . . at least we all had a few bucks put away.

I wish I could have relaxed more and enjoyed the time off, but life in Connecticut was too much like living in exile. Being away from the action gave me the cold sweats. I don't think I lasted five weeks before I went back to Los Angeles to plot my next moves. I wasn't exactly welcomed with open arms. Nothing was ever said to my face, but I knew that the attitude around town was that with Belushi dead, my most visible (but not actual) meal ticket had been punched. I had to change the perception.

Debbie and the kids stayed in the East. I commuted until they returned, when school began. We kept the house a couple more years, went there for holidays and another summer, but finally I said, "Let's sell it. I'm not enjoying it." Debbie loved the house and hated California. She wasn't happy at all.

In Los Angeles I had a surprise waiting. I had recently switched business managers. After the new guy reviewed the books he called to say, "Everything's honest and fine, but you've been deferring income for five years and you owe three million in taxes. Now."

I nearly had a breakdown.

That was everything I had, my life savings that I'd stashed away bit by bit. Just when my business was cold, the government wanted it all. Talk about being depressed. Fortunately, I had no time to indulge myself. I had to get to work.

• • • • •

I went back to basics. I took on a few new clients. One was John Belushi's brother, Jim. We put him on *Saturday Night Live*, with producer Dick Ebersol, and got him a cameo in *Trading Places* with Aykroyd and Eddie Murphy. We weren't trying to re-create John, nor was Jim riding on his brother's coattails. He's always been his own man with his own voice, and the length of his career proves it. I also started a management-consultant sideline, helping out Joan Rivers, Gabe *"Welcome Back, Kotter"* Kaplan, and whoever else would pay me $250,000 a year. I liked consulting. I made a lot of money and didn't have to do the actual management dirty work.

I also pushed further into television. For my clients John Moffitt and Bill Lee we secured the rights to an English comedy show called *Not the Nine O'clock News*. They wanted to do an American version called *Not Necessarily the News*. We couldn't do a pilot, but ABC gave us some money to send Alan Zweibel to London so he could look at all their episodes and put together a clip reel to show ABC roughly what we wanted to do. When Zweibel returned and screened his fake pilot I laughed so much that I called Lew Erlicht, the new head of programming at ABC and said, "We're coming over with it right now!" Erlicht also loved it and I thought we had a deal. Then he said, "There's only one problem with it, Bernie: it's too British."

Too British? What did that mean? The clips we'd used for the presentation were from the original English show. Erlicht knew that in advance. Was he saying he didn't get the humor because it was too British? Or that the structure was too British? I went nuts. I screamed, "Gimme the goddamn tape! Gimme the tape!" Erlicht moved so slowly that I ripped the tape out of the VCR myself, and took off down the hall.

Erlicht chased me, saying, "No, don't go, Bernie!"

I said, "No, I'm getting outta here! You're not getting this show!" I stormed off. ABC's Los Angeles headquarters is Century City, home of the famous twin towers. You see them in every show that flashes the city skyline. HBO was in one of the towers. I got off the elevator, walked across the mall and rode up to Michael Fuchs's office. I pushed the tape into his VCR and he bought it on the spot. *Not Necessarily the News* lasted eight years on HBO.

Erlicht didn't always have the best of instincts. About a year before

Entertainment Tonight debuted, I came up with a concept called *Show Business* that I thought of as the *60 Minutes* of entertainment. I got Sandy Hill and David Frost to host. In the pilot we did stories on the theory that Marilyn Monroe's alleged suicide was really murder, something on the movie *Buddy Buddy,* and a piece on the Rolfing craze among celebrities. Erlicht shrugged and said, "Come on. Nobody cares *that much* about show business." Then he passed. I think he also once said that the sitcom was dead.

How did I know HBO would come through on *Not Necessarily the News?* I didn't. I had a great relationship with Michael Fuchs, but selling TV shows is like professional sports: on any given day any team can win. I got lucky and he said yes: point in my favor. If he'd turned me down, Fuchs still knew that I'd thought of him: point in my favor. If I had to go back to Erlich at ABC, he probably would have taken the show just because I'd let him off the bonehead hook: point in my favor.

Sometimes anger and yelling is useful in business. A writer once called me a nice guy who knew how to lose his temper. The knowledge around town that you might have a short fuse — in other words, "Don't get Bernie mad" — is often more valuable than actually losing your cool. This may sound weird, but it can help if people believe you're slightly insane. I wouldn't make it a way of life, like Mike Ovitz did, but there's nothing like a little fear to stir up a transaction. In the case of *Not Necessarily the News* my anger was spontaneous and honestly felt, and being a big guy, when I get angry, I get *really* angry. That little rant was just what I needed to warm my blood. I began to feel like the old Bernie again.

• • • • •

Telepictures, a hot company that supplied off-network syndicated shows, wanted to meet with me. They'd already done wonders with *The People's Court* and some children's cartoon properties and become Wall Street darlings. Feeling their oats, and sitting on piles of money, they dreamt of expanding into owning, producing, and distributing network shows. In other words, they wanted to become a mini-studio. Because I was a TV packager with great clients, a solid reputation, and a good chance of getting something on the air, Telepictures thought I could help.

I was flattered, and I would have loved to sell them a show, but beyond that I wasn't exactly sure how I could be of service. I sent Sandy, who already knew the four Telepictures guys — David Salzman, Michael Garin, Dick Robertson, and Michael Solomon — to take the meeting.

Afterwards, Sandy explained to me that Telepictures wanted to buy The Brillstein Company and make us consultants. Buy me out? Not interested. Sandy urged me to meet with them anyway; maybe it would still result in some business. I'd dated Solomon's sister when he was still a kid, and we'd played a little basketball in the Central Park West days, so I agreed to dinner at Jimmy's in Beverly Hills. Sandy was right: How could it hurt? It turned out to be a great meal. I still didn't want to sell my company, but it looked like they were going places, and I agreed to help them expand their business.

A couple weeks later, I was in New York. David Salzman and Dick Robertson asked me to meet for breakfast downstairs at the Regency Hotel, where I always stayed. Salzman brought his young son. We talked for a bit about what we could do for each other. Then Salzman took a check out of his coat pocket and handed it to me. My first year's consulting fee.

It was a million dollars.

I had never seen a check for a million dollars before. Some people believe that money will solve everything. They think, "All I need is some money in the bank and a way to get laid once in a while, and everything's going to be okay." Yes, and not always.

Something told me that even though my big tax bill had dried up my cash reservoir, I shouldn't take the check.

I asked the Telepictures guys if they'd excuse me for a moment. I wanted to go upstairs and see my wife. One spaced-out elevator ride later, I showed Debbie the check. Everyone should see something like that at least once. Then I said, "I'm not going take it."

"What?" she said. "Why?"

"Because for a million it's more than consulting. They'll think they own me. I'll take two hundred fifty thousand dollars and still be independent. Money is nice but independence is more important."

"Fine," she said. Better than nothing, I guess. I went downstairs to see Salzman and Robertson. "I'll take two-fifty and let's see if it works," I said.

The first project I brought to Telepictures was from Eric Lieber, one of my producer clients who actually listened when I told him to get out of variety TV and think of new ways to make money. His idea, he claimed, would do *The Dating Game* one better. On that show, three men or women vied to be chosen for a dream date. On Lieber's *Love Connection*, singles would view clips of potential dating partners, choose one, go out, and then appear on the show to report on the experience.

We made a pilot and discovered that the dating partners' offhand, brutal honesty about their often inept and unsatisfactory encounters, mediated and provoked by host Chuck Woolery, was hilarious. Sandy Wernick suggested that Eric let the audience watch the introductory clips and vote on who they thought the contestant should have gone out with. Lieber agreed, and he added that to the show.

We took the pilot to Dick Robertson. He wasn't sure. He said, "It's a game show." I said, "But it's so funny." He still passed. I called Michael Solomon, the chairman of Telepictures.

"Michael, please," I said. "Look at this pilot yourself, then put it on the air. It's a huge hit."

Solomon said what I'd hoped he would: "Bernie, if you say so. we're going to do it," and overruled Robertson. We pitched it to Tartikoff at NBC, but he passed, so Telepictures decided to do what they did best: syndicate the show themselves. The original *Love Connection* was on for ten years. Lieber and Telepictures each owned half. For The Brillstein Company's small percentage of the gross, we made more than $600,000 a year.

With that success, the Telepictures arrangement quickly become a love connection for us both. Apparently my instincts were not out-of-date and my luck was improving. It just showed to me once again what I'd always believed: hot is over quickly, good is a career.

• • • • •

I gave Mike Ovitz clients like Belushi, Aykroyd, Gilda, Zweibel, and Patchett and Tarses.

He gave me Dabney Coleman.

To my surprise it was a perfect match. We were both into sports, gambling, the big life. He is a mean fuck, but he made me laugh. We fell in love.

When I say "fell in love," that's *show-business love*. It's part of the pal-this and sweetheart-that vernacular dating back to Broadway and Damon Runyon. It means I thought of Dabney as my type of person — at the moment. Nothing wrong with that. Show-business love is great because it's not the until-death-do-you-part stuff, so, unlike in real life, there's no limit on how many people or projects you can fall for passionately — at the moment. If a project falls through and you like the people, you work with them again. If not, good-bye and good luck.

Loyalty is another matter entirely.

I've tried hard to be steady in my likes and dislikes, but I'm often in love one minute and out of love the next, like some moonstruck teenager or a bad hooker. Lorne and Brad and my other friends never hesitate to give me a hard time about it. I don't mind. I love or I don't love. There are no middles. Middles are what I don't even mention.

Dabney had just come off *9 to 5*, *On Golden Pond*, and *Tootsie*. I couldn't get Brandon Tartikoff at NBC to take *Love Connection*, but I did convince him that Dabney could do a great sitcom. All Dabney wanted was something out of the ordinary. That suited me, too. I never could stand bland, basic sitcoms. If I was going to take my own advice and get out of the variety business and into half-hour comedy, then I didn't want to do something that had been done before.

Tartikoff not only wanted to work with Dabney, but he wanted to do a show about a TV personality who was lovable on camera but a prick off camera. What an inspiration. I felt like slapping my forehead. Sometimes, the wonderful thing about show business is that you just have to look around the house for great ideas. Everyone in the business knows someone like that. Plus, the character sounded a lot like Dabney. I got Tartikoff to bring in my clients Tom Patchett and Jay Tarses, among the hottest writer-producer teams in the business, to create the series. That also seemed like a good match. All three were *men*, in every testosterone-soaked sense of the word: big, opinionated, stubborn, competitive.

Tom and Jay wrote a pilot called *Buffalo Bill*, about the onstage and backstage life of "Buffalo Bill" Bittinger, the mean host of a morning talk show in Buffalo, New York. It was tough, hard-hitting, chauvinistic. Rather than pack in the laugh-track jokes, the script subverted standard sitcom conventions and went for character-based humor that never blinked. Buffalo Bill was, as Tartikoff envisioned, unlikable. The other characters were Max Wright as Karl Shub, the station manager; Joanna Cassidy as Joanna "Jo-Jo" White, the director; Geena Davis as Wendy Killian, the researcher; Charles Robinson as Newdell Spriggs Jr., the makeup man (not in the pilot); Meshach Taylor as Tony Fitipaldi, the assistant director; and John Fiedler as Woody Deschler, the stage manager. It was a great group.

Tom, Jay, Dabney, and I became partners to own and produce *Buffalo Bill.*

Tom and Jay had a reputation for wanting things their way, and Dabney was no different. He asked to have writer-producer Dennis Klein rework the pilot to make it better reflect *his* personality. (Why *act* if you can be yourself, especially if your comic persona is yourself?) Dennis did a great job and stayed on to run the show. He wrote many episodes, including two of the best: "Hit the Road, Jack" and "Jerry Lewis Week."

The show was as contentious as its creators and star. It refused to shy away from a dark and cynical (realistic?) take on the human condition. Tom and Jay and Dennis wanted to get as close to the edge as network TV in the early '80s allowed — and then some. If there was anything the entire team had in common it was an undiluted distrust of show business and the powers that be who hired creative people and then tried to tell them how to do their jobs. That's why they didn't hesitate, either directly or through clever allusion, to bite the hand that fed. It was both a matter of revenge and just plain fun.

If you think about it, *Buffalo Bill* was in many respects *The Larry Sanders Show* of the '80s. None of this is casual coincidence. Years after *Buffalo Bill* went off the air, I delivered Dennis Klein to Garry Shandling, and he brought the same dark sensibility to co-creating and writing *The Larry Sanders Show.* Putting aside the difference in the kind of language you can use on network and cable, both were about insecure, selfish, back-stabbing, narcissistic talk-show hosts unable to have a decent relationship with women. Both portrayed life in front of and behind the camera, with lengthy uninterrupted chunks of on-camera hypocrisy. Neither *Sanders* nor *Buffalo Bill* actually filmed in front of a studio audience, but the talk shows within the shows did. Bill Bittinger could have given Larry Sanders lessons in being an aggressive male, and Larry could have taught Bill a thing or two about the passive-aggressive politics of self-interest. One more thing: with both series, the press, to say nothing of people who knew the stars, always had trouble telling where — if at all — the actor left off and the character began.

· · · · ·

From the beginning, *Buffalo Bill* was an uphill climb. Even before we got on the air in June 1983, NBC worried that a show about show business wouldn't work — which surprised me because Tartikoff had suggested the whole idea. I thought they were wrong. *Buffalo Bill* wasn't really about show business. It was about how a screwed-up man affected his world. It was about the human condition. By Tartikoff's rule *Make Room for Daddy*, *The Dick Van Dyke Show*, and *The Mary Tyler Moore Show* should never have worked. Maybe George Burns and Jack Benny shouldn't have played themselves as comedians on their programs either. In each case, show business or the media was simply background. Context.

NBC also wasn't crazy about the name. They said, "People will think it's about cowboys and Indians." I suppose the show could have been relocated to Poughkeepsie, but then something like *Poughkeepsie Pat* would have sounded just a little too fey.

That summer, *Buffalo Bill* debuted to great critical response yet only adequate ratings. NBC aired thirteen shows and put it on hiatus. We fought to get picked up again and came back for another thirteen shows between December 1983 and March 1984.

During his time off between seasons, Jay decided he wanted to write a show about Bill getting Jo-Jo pregnant and how these two middle-aged people dealt with the situation. None of us were especially keen about the idea, especially when Jay said he wanted to write a three-parter. Dennis Klein suggested a single episode. They compromised at two. Originally called "Jo-Jo's Problem," the shows quickly became known as the "Abortion Episodes." It was typical Jay. He liked to push the envelope.

When you have a network show, you always have to submit scripts a couple weeks before shooting for the suits and the censors to review. *Saturday Night Live* got away with murder because it was both live and in late-night, but for prime-time shows, the Program Standards and Practices Department was tough. Even on variety shows, after the censors combed through a comedian's monologue, we'd always have to bargain for what we wanted to keep in. I remember when Gabe Kaplan had to trade two "ca-ca's" for a "doo-doo." Or maybe it was the other way around.

We held on to Jay's scripts for as long as possible before turning them in. We wanted to give NBC very little time to make changes because we were certain, even as we handed them over, that there would be big problems. There were.

I don't remember the specifics, but there were lots of "You can't say this or that's." Of course, we couldn't *approve* of abortion. We had to show both sides. We had huge fights. I yelled at everyone from Tartikoff on down, not that it helped. During filming, NBC wanted still more changes. Their attitude was "What's going on here?" — as if these episodes would cause the world to end. I don't blame NBC for being petrified of viewer and sponsor reaction to a woman actually considering family planning choices, but it's not as if they didn't know up front what they had with *Buffalo Bill*. On the other hand, it was amazing that they even let us do the topic at all.

The problem, when it comes to TV, is that the truth is tough, and tough doesn't make viewers buy soap. Fortunately it works just often enough on TV that writers are encouraged to keep chasing that elusive goal of the breakthrough "truth" show. But even in success, these series are rarely huge hits, because people come home from work and they don't want to think a lot. Smart, edgy comedy may play great to some segment of the audience, but I'll be the first to admit that it's not mass humor. And that's too bad.

Life isn't like a neatly wrapped family sitcom that solves all its problems in twenty-three minutes. Humans aren't always on their best behavior. But sitcoms that toe the lowest-common-denominator line are meant to give viewers relief from the harshness of daily life. Larry Hagman, star of *Dallas*, once likened TV to a mass sedative and predicted that if the networks went dark, people would riot in the streets. Hmmm. Sounds interesting. Maybe it's a movie for HBO.

· · · · ·

Buffalo Bill was a sanitized version of the insanity that went into making the show itself — and it's representative in an exaggerated way of what goes on behind the scenes of some TV shows today. I managed Tom, Jay, and Dabney, and when they fought among themselves, I was the peacemaker. I also had a financial interest in the show — if we went over the license fee, we were spending my money — so when we battled NBC, I had to be the sane one. Sometimes it was like negotiating between the Israelis and the Palestinians. You do it very slowly and carefully, balancing the need for territory, pride, historical prerogative, and secure borders. Each time I had to come up with something that allowed everyone to function and not have the whole thing blow up in our faces. Fortunately I'd had lots of practice with the personalities from *Saturday Night Live*. Unfortunately, I could only stall the inevitable.

Jay couldn't stand Dabney. He thought him egomaniacal and difficult to work with. He played the star game, didn't do his lines. Sometimes Jay didn't even want to show up because he didn't want to look at the guy.

To be fair, Jay was also tough to manage. He was single-minded, stubborn, and not interested in anything but making those singular TV shows that even he believed probably no one would watch. He was irascible and opinionated and would tell network guys not to come around the set, even though they paid for the show. He felt they ought to trust him but knew they didn't trust anyone, least of all themselves.

Jay and Tom also had problems. In fact, they split up as a team almost as soon as *Buffalo Bill* began, and they did their best not to speak to each other during the entire production. I'll never forget the message on Jay Tarses' answering machine: "Hello, this is Jay Tarses. If you're looking for Tom Patchett, he's not here . . . and he'll never be here." As of now they haven't spoken for almost twenty years.

In the studio the two had separate domains and routines, and rarely strayed from them. Jay spent his workdays editing; Tom stayed onstage directing. Dennis Klein held it all together. Occasionally, I did some fancy footwork as the go-between, just as I'd done with my mother and father. I'd get everyone in a room and make them tell me their problems, then force them to come up with a solution. I also had to handle Brandon Tartikoff, who really liked the show but sometimes didn't know what to make of it. During the second season NBC insisted that for *Buffalo Bill* to stay on the air, we had to make Bill more likable. They kept suggesting Tom and Jay create another character, an adversary for Bill who was even meaner; a big prick who would cast the little prick in a better light. To us that sounded like buying a pitch about a black character in the inner city and saying, "Now if you could make him white and move him to the suburbs, we'll do it." No one was interested. Perhaps we were just young and arrogant and stupid, but we didn't think NBC would have the balls to shut down *Buffalo Bill*. The critics loved us, our fans were loyal, and we even believed that the network was proud of the show. They were. Tartikoff always said that *Buffalo Bill* was the best show he ever canceled.

After *Buffalo Bill*, I talked Dabney and Jay into doing another show,

The "Slap" Maxwell Story. Apparently they didn't hate each enough to say no, but it was a big mistake and it ended badly. I also put Tom together with Paul Fusco, who created the alien puppet ALF. The creature's real name was Gordon Shumway (go figure!); ALF stood for Alien Life Form. Patchett got rich when the show went into syndication.

My relationship with Dabney didn't last either. Just before he did *Drexell's Class* for Fox in 1991, he called me and said, "I just left my accountant. I'm paying too much alimony. I can't afford to pay you anymore. We're going to have to end it." In retrospect, I believe that someone at ICM probably put him up to it. No matter. I stand by what I said to him at the time.

"Fine."

If someone wants to go, I never argue.

• • • • •

In the fall of 1983, Lorne decided to return to weekly television when Brandon Tartikoff asked him if he'd be interested in doing a new series. Why? Partly because the network was in third place. Lorne was intrigued. Despite the tumult of his first five years at NBC, Lorne felt comfortable at the network. It was convenient. He knew the system and his way around. And he was loyal.

I also wanted Lorne to go back to work. I had faith in him. *The New Show* would be the way for him to prove to everyone that *Saturday Night Live* was not a fluke, that he was still Lorne Michaels.

The New Show debuted in January 1984 and aired Friday nights at 10 P.M. Lorne's ambition was not to redo *Saturday Night Live* but to create a show that reflected how that seminal comic sensibility had matured with its audience. But everything worked against him, from critics who compared *The New Show* to *Saturday Night Live* to Lorne not finding the right mix to satisfy himself. For me it was like watching a ship go down, and since I'd stupidly let Lorne finance the show, he had to cover production deficits. Not only didn't anyone watch, but he hemorrhaged money. I felt that I'd failed Lorne. As *The New Show* careened toward its final installment, I felt responsible for if not talking him into it, then not talking him out of it.

The show was canceled after three months. Lorne could have

complained loudly, but he's always been the type who thinks grace under fire is the more admirable trait. A person, he told me, is defined by how he behaves during a flop.

With both *The New Show* and *Buffalo Bill* off the air, that sinking feeling in my stomach returned. The failure of both shows scared the shit out of me. Tom and Jay had broken up and if Lorne became history, maybe I'd be history, too. If Henson saw me failing, perhaps he'd go elsewhere. What if Aykroyd didn't make it in movies? Maybe I'd come as far as I could.

At the Golden Globe Awards in early 1984, Joanna Cassidy, who played Jo-Jo White on *Buffalo Bill,* won Best Performance by an Actress in a TV Series — Comedy or Musical. Of course, I went. Debbie and I pulled up to the Beverly Hilton in a stretch limo. We could see fans and guards and photographers lining the walkway from the front door to the grand ballroom. Their cameras were poised to snap arriving celebrities, their mouths ready to call out a name in hopes that a head would turn in their direction for a great picture. A valet opened the limo door. I got out and took Debbie's hand. We started down the red carpet. There were a few flashes and then, in a moment that distilled everything I feared about the way my career was heading into four words, someone said, "Forget it. It's nobody."

• • • • •

Danny Aykroyd is not the world's most outgoing guy. But despite his sometimes stiff and formal manner — he once studied to be a policeman — he is a lovely human being with a mind I've admired forever. He's as close to a genius comedian as you can get. Like Lorne, Danny is part businessman, part artist, part student, part rebel. Both are Canadians, which is in itself defining. Canadians walk to a different drummer, a strange, off-center drummer. Just look at SCTV's humor and you'll see what I mean. Maybe it's because Canadians have been brought up as second-class Englishmen, like poor relatives of the United States. They are pioneers pushed into being establishment citizens. That dichotomy exists in Danny, even in the name of his company: Applied Action Research, Inc.

Just after I got back from Connecticut, Danny came to my office at

9200 Sunset Boulevard and said, "Remember my idea for that movie? I've really developed it."

For a second I didn't know what movie he was talking about. Then I remembered that he had been working on an idea for John, Bill Murray, and himself. Something about ghosts. Then John died. I figured he'd forgotten all about it. Instead, he paced around the office and told me the story of three unemployed parapsychology professors/scientists who set up shop as a ghost-removal service, trapping pesky spirits, haunts, and poltergeists for money. Then they stumble on a gateway to another dimension through which incredible evil will soon burst. Their mission: to save New York City and the world.

I loved it. Danny went on to explain the look of it and the danger of it. "Bernie," he said, "you know the buildings in New York, along Central Park, with the gargoyles and all that, like the Dakota . . . ?" Danny is very technical. If he has to know something, he goes all out and becomes an expert. Then he said, "The final scene is . . . ," and he pulled out of his bag a picture of Mr. Stay-Puft, the marshmallow man, walking through the streets of New York. Today, everyone in the world takes credit for *Ghostbusters* — which was originally named *Ghostsmashers* — but it started with Danny. (Danny also taught Belushi about the blues, then let John go on as if he'd invented them. If he's neglected anything over the years, it's his writing talents. I wish he'd get back to them.)

Then he said, "Just so I don't screw it up, give me a dollar and you can control it."

I knew immediately why Danny had said that. The movie business scared him. He understood its treachery. He was easily seduced. He figured if he let me "control" the project, then he was safe. He was right. I would do my best to keep anyone from taking advantage of him. I took a dollar from my pocket, handed it over, and I became the gatekeeper.

Danny had already written about sixty pages of *Ghostbusters*. He doesn't write his screenplays in standard form; more often they're reams of dialog and notes. Of course, Mike Ovitz knew about the project, so we decided to show the material to Sean Daniel at Universal. Daniel gave it to John Landis, to whom he gave everything in those days. Landis passed.

I can't say for sure what happened next or how, except that somehow Ivan Reitman, the eventual director, got the pages. My bet is that Ovitz was the conduit, since he also represented Reitman. Then it got to

Bill Murray, also an Ovitz client — thanks to me, who had arranged that little introduction between the two at Ovitz's request. Bill also had a connection to Reitman, with whom he'd worked on *Meatballs.* Then another Ovitz client, Harold Ramis, came aboard, and he really helped Danny whip the screenplay into shape.

All of a sudden, Ovitz had a movie package, which he sold to Columbia. I signed on as executive producer to watch out for Danny. I also got paid. Otherwise Ovitz did little to keep me involved. I don't think Reitman really wanted me around, and Ovitz sold me out to cozy up to the director. *Ghostbusters* was one of Ovitz's early big packages and he tried to take credit for inventing the whole thing. One grim Hollywood reality is that being able to say "I found" or "I did" makes you seem talented, even if you just happened to be an eavesdropper. I was used to that bullshit, but part of my job is ego sublimation, and nothing demands that talent more than the movie business. The director and his line producers run the show, and executive producer is never high on the respect list. Ovitz's exclusionary tactics still bothered me, but I didn't want to make too much out of it. No one has to tell me twice that they don't want me around.

The only negotiations I was involved in were for my client, Danny. I believe both Ivan and Bill had the best deals (with *Tootsie*, Bill's star was now higher than Danny's), Danny next, Harold the lowest. It was touchy because Ovitz represented all the elements and he had to cut the pie fairly, without offending anyone. I knew how that dynamic worked.

The movie opened in the summer of 1984 and became that year's top-grossing film, beating *Beverly Hills Cop* and *Indiana Jones and the Temple of Doom,* as well as the highest-grossing comedy film of all time. For my trouble, I had 3.75 percent of the gross after it recouped its costs. The movie was so hot that it flew past break-even so fast that no one could screw me out of my share. I made between $6 and $7 million, paid half to the government in tax, and kept the remainder for myself — which left me exactly the same nest egg as before I'd had to give my savings to the IRS.

• • • • •

Ghostbusters restored not only my bank account but much of The Brillstein Company's luster. It was such a big hit that even if I did nothing else, it bought me another three to five years of credibility in town. Not that I could relax. I was already worried about where my next hit would come from, especially while watching everyone else take bows for the movie's success.

My deal with Telepictures and the success of *Love Connection* should have made me feel better. We had momentum. The company was getting hot again. Despite *The New Show* and *Buffalo Bill*, I had survived. So why wasn't I happier?

After nearly three decades I'd grown tired of the high-pressure grind. I was no longer the bright young guy, and show business was a young man's game. I wasn't sure I had the energy or the desire to pitch projects and take care of people for the rest of my life. It just wasn't that much fun anymore. I needed a new challenge.

I suppose I could have simply dissolved the company and gone looking for a job, but every time I read the trades I'd see stories about how people were selling their companies for millions. (Today all anyone wants to do is sell out, but many forget that they have to build the company first.)

David Geffen, for instance, had sold his record company, Asylum, to Warner Brothers for $7 million and gone into their movie division. I wondered if perhaps I could also cash in my marbles. The *Ghostbusters* bonanza was a start, but I still didn't have the money I needed to retire on, my "fuck you" money that would allow me to do whatever I wanted. Nor did I trust show business enough to figure it would just land in my lap.

Besides, I didn't have tangible assets. My "marbles" were connections, influence, knowledge of the business, and track record. These were, at best, people skills that would have made me a big salesman in the garment center. I didn't have a definable trade. What could I say? "I mix well with people. People trust me. I can spot talent sometimes." Plus, I had no written contracts with my clients and I didn't actually own anything except an income stream generated by commissions and pieces of various TV shows and syndication deals. Cashing in suddenly seemed like a long shot, but I decided to float the idea anyway.

My lawyers said, "You can't sell this business, there's nothing to sell."

Next, I spoke with Ovitz. I said, "Can you get someone to buy me, to use my talents and show-business brain?" I thought I could put all the knowledge I'd accumulated to work for someone else in an arena bigger than my own. My ego was clearly a part of it. I wanted to help a larger show-business company because usually guys like me don't take jobs. I'd never been the corporate type, but I'd been in the business long enough — and been through more than a few win/lose cycles — to believe I had some inside knowledge of how the other half lived. All I had to do was adjust without giving up my identity, without becoming too Establishment. I knew who I was, and I was certain that I could come up with enough good ideas to pay back any investment.

When I told him my plan, I was afraid that Ovitz might repeat that I had nothing to sell. He didn't. It was worse. "No, no," he said. "You're better off where you are. No one would buy it anyway." Better off? For whom?

Maybe it was the way he said it, but it sounded to me as if Ovitz just wanted to *keep* me where I was. That's when I realized what an unbalanced relationship we had. I'd given him my top clients. That had made Ovitz about $20 million. In return I'd gotten what? Dabney Coleman? It was clearly a one-way street. And now he wouldn't even make a few phone calls on my behalf because it might embarrass him?

Of course, Ovitz believed he *had* given me something. He liked to say he'd gotten me into the movie business. Not true. I was already in the movie business, he just raised my price. But the only reason I got that higher price was because I represented Belushi and Aykroyd. They were big stars. Would my price have been so high with less-established draws?

I wanted to confront Ovitz and say, "What are you doing for me?" I didn't. I wasn't afraid to challenge him, it just wouldn't have been kosher, because in this business I don't believe you can ask for that kind of consideration outright. Not only is it a sign of weakness, but this is a horse-trading world. When you deliver something, you expect a kindness in return. The honorable guys do it. That never happened with Ovitz. He was good at the give-and-take only as long as you gave and he took.

Forever after I felt like he'd used me. I'm not the only one; just ask David Geffen or veteran producer Ray Stark (*Annie, Funny Girl, California Suite, Steel Magnolias,* and many more).

To be fair, I'd also used Ovitz. He was smooth and he knew the language of our business. When he spoke he had a way of whispering like he knew something you didn't know. He used codes and said stuff like, "Let's not talk on the cellular phone." He made it seem like he was in touch with and in control of everything. I've been around enough to know that no one is in control of anything — at least not for long — but anyone who has the gall to try and make it look like he does, without immediately falling flat on his ass, clearly has something going for him. I give Ovitz credit for pulling it off for as long as he did, for being a smooth Sammy Glick. Ovitz had become powerful, would become even more so, and I knew it was in my best interest that he told everyone what good friends we were.

But now that friendship seemed hollow. I was glad I'd never signed up as a CAA client myself. Then I would have really had to depend on him.

There's a lesson here. Show-business best friends are not really best friends. Even though Ovitz and I used the term, I'd never been to his house and he'd never been to mine. Show-business friends are like an air kiss. Show-business best friends maybe see each other occasionally — if it's convenient. A show-business friend is someone you're making a great deal with, so you go out to dinner with him and his wife. Sometimes you even vacation "together," but that only means you've coincidentally made Christmas reservations at the same hotel in Hawaii. A real good show-business friend is someone who, if you die, will cancel his massage appointment to attend the memorial. Maybe. Am I joking? Maybe.

I'm certainly guilty of the show-business habit of impulsively saying I love someone, or hate them, but "friend" is a term I never use lightly.

I now understood Ovitz's real nature, but he was still the best shot a guy could take in town. If he wouldn't put me on the market as a potential piece of manpower, I didn't want anyone else trying. I could have put the word out myself, but that would have seemed like begging. You know what they say: desperation is the worst cologne. I wasn't going to just quit, so the only option was to keep on going. Between Sandy and me and our assistants, we had maybe thirty clients. The downside was that they were now middle-aged comics, writers, producers, and actors. Henson was also getting up there, but he remained the creative exception. I needed fresh blood, not only on the roster, but in the office. I needed a young, sharp manager who understood the business and could get along with me, and who could attract new clients. The question was, who?

· · · · ·

I met Brad Grey in February 1984, at the National Association of Television Programming Executives convention at the Fairmont Hotel in San Francisco. Brad's client, Garry Shandling, was the entertainment.

I'd run into Shandling before when he wrote for *Welcome Back, Kotter*, and although he looked to me like David Brenner in drag, I'd helped him get an agent. Brad really believed in him, though, and Garry was good that night.

Afterwards, Brad and I had a brief, friendly conversation in the lobby. He was twenty-six. He had recently moved to Los Angeles from New York with his wife, Jill. They lived in an apartment in Westwood. Besides Shandling, his clients included comics Bob Saget and Dave Coulier. I don't know why, perhaps it was the determination in his eyes or the way he carried himself, but Brad reminded me of myself twenty years earlier — only shorter, thinner, and without my personal problems. I could appreciate stability like that. We kept in touch.

Early the following year, Debbie, the kids, and I went to the new Mauna Lani hotel on the big island of Hawaii. And who do I see? Brad and Jill. Right away he and I spent hours by the pool every day, talking. Brad had stopped working out of his apartment and now shared a small office in Beverly Hills. He also had more clients, including Dana Carvey and Dennis Miller. Best of all he was a young guy who actually wanted to hear my show-business stories. We must have really overdone it, because one day Debbie said, "Okay, enough already, Bernie. We're going upstairs." She jerked her head in the direction of our room. "Come on."

By the way, I've heard the rumor that Brad wasn't at the Mauna Lani by accident, that he'd followed me there. Look — as smart as Brad is, and as inspired a move as that would have been, I've just never believed it. And Brad denies it. Some things are just meant to be. You know how it is: you just get a feeling in your stomach.

When we got back to Los Angeles, I began having Brad over to the house to play tennis with guys like Brandon Tartikoff, Frank Brill, and Jim Berkus, who today owns part of the United Talent Agency. We'd tell stories and Brad soaked it up. He instinctively knew it was a good thing to hang around and be accepted by show-business people who had more experience. He told me about his clients and plans and never hesitated to ask for advice if he needed it.

He also asked about my business. I told him the truth. My clients weren't youthful. Sandy, my former assistant Fran Saperstein, and I weren't overworked. I was in fact burnt out and had been through a lot.

One afternoon Brad called me about 5:30. He was out of breath, almost hyperventilating. He seemed very nervous. Brad said he had to see me the next morning. I said we should meet for breakfast at the Polo Lounge. I ate breakfast there almost every day because it was right down the street and Debbie didn't cook. After we hung up I turned to her and said, "I think I have a kid in trouble. I don't know what it is, but it's probably going to cost us money."

The next morning, when Brad and I sat down, I waited for him to tell me his problem. But instead of hearing that he needed to be rescued, he proposed a plan that, in effect, rescued me.

He said, "The Brillstein Company is already one of the strongest management firms in town, but I know it's not as busy as it used to be. What if we combine our companies? With your success as a manager, your experience producing, and the fact that you're so well liked and have terrific connections, plus my energy, young comics, and the ability to sign more, we could really move forward together and take the company to another place. We could do something special for each other and together. It's perfect."

I was surprised but not surprised. I'd never thought about him working for the company. Brad had his own business and I would never have been so presumptuous as to go after him. Even if it was in the back of my mind I never would have thought to ask. However my company had aged, I still had a happy life making a couple million a year. He knew that.

But I'd also been honest with Brad about what I believed my business needed for the future. We could cruise along as we were, or, with new manpower and young clients, we could take everything to the next level. I'd asked the people who worked for me, "Why aren't you bringing me the young comics? I'm too busy handling the Muppets and *Saturday Night Live* and the rest. I don't have time to go out and find new blood." But Sandy was up to his head in production work, and Fran was about to leave. So there was no one to do the job.

Brad's timing was perfect. He'd listened well and read between my lines. Combining forces would help us both. Brad was smart, tough, and already understood management. After listening to his bold suggestion, I liked the way he had handled himself even more.

I told Brad I'd have my business manager call him. It took a couple months to hammer out the deal. Rather than do a "You keep yours and I'll keep mine" thing, we threw all the clients into one pot. It was the commonsense approach. Brad also wanted a contract. Although I didn't use them, I understood his need to have a guaranteed salary and a cushion in case things didn't work out, because even though his clients would leave with him, he'd have walked away from being an owner. So Brad signed on as an employee with a salary that was a bit more than he was already making in commissions. Afterward, he never asked for a raise, although I always gave him one.

Today, I think of Brad as my best "signing." I knew almost from the beginning that for the first time I could 100 percent depend on someone. I could have him do anything, from deal with an act to deal with a network head. He also got what *I* did, and as the years passed he put his own spin on it. He could have gone other places, with other managers, but I was the comedy guy and Brad loved comedy. It was a perfect fit. He's become more and more like a son to me, and I love working together. Brad's attitude toward the business is partially my attitude, but it's also more sophisticated. He didn't come in saying, "I'm going to take you into the nineties," but he knew what to do when they got here. I'm happy to admit it. Whatever Brad thought our merged companies would become, I don't think he imagined what we have today. But I have no doubt that he saw possibilities in management, TV production, distribution, films, and other media that I didn't — not because I couldn't, I just wasn't particularly interested. I had a mom-and-pop company that got lucky. But I figured that if things went well, maybe Brad and I could also get lucky and have a great future.

Chapter 11

They Haven't
Caught Me Yet

When Dick Ebersol decided to quit as producer of *Saturday Night Live* at the end of the tenth season, NBC programming chief Brandon Tartikoff's first choice to replace him was . . . Lorne Michaels. But Lorne was in Hollywood. His friend Steve Martin had asked him to co-write and co-produce *Three Amigos*, a film directed by John Landis and co-starring Martin, Chevy Chase, and Marty Short. The idea was for Lorne to repair his self-respect and heal from the twin body blows of *The New Show*'s failure and his recent divorce from Susan Forristal by solving creative problems among friends. There was also a generous paycheck and the plan seemed to be working. When Tartikoff called, Lorne was intrigued yet iffy. The years away from *Saturday Night Live* had not been great, but Lorne felt well enough to not be easily convinced that going back would be a step forward.

I wanted Lorne to give it a try. So what if *The New Show* had failed? We all get one of those, but *Saturday Night Live* was entirely different. Besides, what else was there to do? Was Lorne really going to just write and produce movies? Each one takes a year or two, and then the director comes in to run things — and sometimes ruin them. (*Three Amigos* would have been a bigger hit if John Landis hadn't directed, but that's just my opinion.) I could see Lorne hanging out in Hollywood — I've always thought he had a bit of Mike Todd and Irving Thalberg in him, and a lot of David Selznick — but he'd have to be in charge. Nor could Lorne be happy doing nothing while his Broadway Video business supported him. Lorne was still young; he had to go back to basics and reestablish himself.

Lorne was uncertain. He asked friends for advice. One told him: "You don't do *Saturday Night Live;* somebody who wants to be you does *Saturday Night Live.*" Part of Lorne believed it was true, that he'd already done it and couldn't do it the same way again. At the same time, another part loved what he'd done and wanted to see himself back on the seventeenth floor.

While Lorne mulled it over, Tartikoff talked to other candidates, including John Moffitt and Pat Lee (the wife of Bill Lee, who had died). But they were still involved in *Not Necessarily the News,* and HBO didn't want to let them go. I don't think either wanted to move to New York anyway.

Tartikoff called Lorne again.

Lorne was still uncertain. Also wary. He sensed correctly that he'd get beaten up by critics who would (and did) compare anything he tried to do on his second watch at *Saturday Night Live* to the show's golden years. (Once, after reading yet another "Saturday Night Dead" headline, Lorne told me, "Funny, I didn't remember them as being so golden when they were happening.")

Yet *Saturday Night Live* was his baby. Lorne still believed it was an important, even valuable, show. After ten years it had become what could only be described by a word that any of the rag-tag irregulars in the founding group would have found laughable or loathsome or both: an institution. Yet that's what it was. Tartikoff told Lorne that he and NBC thought of *Saturday Night Live* as a franchise that had fallen on hard times. The idea, he explained, was to preserve the legacy. He believed Lorne was the only one who could pull it off.

It was a tough sales pitch to resist, but Lorne had a few conditions.

He still had to work on *Three Amigos,* which could take some time. Tartikoff agreed to let Lorne serve as executive producer of *Saturday Night Live* while others did the major hands-on work. Lorne insisted on rebuilding the cast and writing staff. That would delay the season's debut past September or even October. Tartikoff said they could go on in November. With NBC starting to ride high on the success of *The Cosby Show, Cheers, Miami Vice, Hill Street Blues,* and *Night Court,* he could afford to be generous.

So Lorne took over again, glad that the show we both thought could not go on without him had been kept on life support for five seasons. I still wonder what he felt like riding the elevator up to the old offices at 30 Rockefeller Center for the first time in five years. Probably creepy. And good to be home.

. . . . .

As soon as Brad joined the company I took him everywhere, just as Marty Kummer had done with me. The idea was for Brad to meet the people I did business with, get comfortable, and be accepted. Having him by my side was a vote of confidence. My reputation and connections gave Brad access and leverage with established players, and if he was as good and as fast a learner as I suspected, that leverage and access would quickly become his own. Brad sat in on meetings, never said the wrong thing, and absorbed a lot. He instinctively knew that less was more.

Because Brad and his young clients gave The Brillstein Company a shot in the arm, I started to sign new clients as well.

The first was Richard Dreyfuss. We'd met ten years earlier in the Century City Health Club steam room, where George Schlatter, Sandy Wernick, and I used to sit around and bullshit. Sometimes Dreyfuss would show up. He was a fairly famous kid, but he didn't hide. Then, in one year (1977), he did *Close Encounters of the Third Kind* with Spielberg and won a Best Actor Oscar for *The Goodbye Girl.* The next year he hosted *Saturday Night Live.* Then his career went straight to hell. Dreyfuss did half a dozen crappy movies in the middle of a drug-and-drinking run and finally smashed his car into a telephone pole.

When he got straight he came to me for representation. I'm not sure why. Maybe because I'd just done *Ghostbusters* and my name looked good. Or because my wife, Debbie, had been a year ahead of him at Beverly Hills High. It's a small town.

It certainly wasn't my reputation with actors. I'd handled *Saturday Night Live* comedians who'd become actors, but not *actor* actors, which he immediately mentioned, flashing that familiar Dreyfuss smirk. "That doesn't mean anything," I said. "I can represent anyone with talent and the same rules apply. Get them in the marketplace, find the right thing, and if they're good, boom!"

Besides, just because I didn't represent actors didn't mean I knew nothing about them. Actors are usually loners and maybe a bit lazy. I don't think they get into the profession in order to work every day. Part of their nature is, "I need a rest after this," and "I don't want to be doing the same thing all the time." If you pay them enough and let them choose their own material, some will work only every few years. Look at Bill Murray — when you can: it's a shame we don't see him more often.

I suppose it's one way of actors' dealing with the rejection that comes with the job. A comedian can find work wherever there's a brick wall, a spotlight, and a microphone. An actor can't just walk into an "acting" club and recite Shakespeare for nothing. I guess that's why there are so many waiters waiting to be actors around. Dreyfuss wasn't serving mimosas and three-egg omelettes at Joe Allen's, but he was still in pretty bad shape.

I believe Dreyfuss had come to me because he needed to be *Richard Dreyfuss* again. I'm a sucker for talent that's a little asleep. I guess I feel bad for them, and I have enough ego to think that I can help bring them back. Everyone has cycles. You're the flavor of the month, you're not the flavor of the month. People respected Richard's talent, but not everyone trusted him to stay clean — and he knew it. He said, "You're going to have to convince people that I'm okay."

A couple weeks after Dreyfuss signed on, his ICM agent, Peter Raleigh, called with an offer. Director Paul Mazursky wanted Dreyfuss for *Down and Out in Beverly Hills,* with Nick Nolte and Bette Midler. It was a Touchstone picture, from Disney. The salary was $250,000. At that price the studio was clearly manipulating his insecurities. I went berserk and called Michael Eisner.

I'd known Eisner for fifteen years. Our kids even played on the same Little League team. He'd only been at Disney for a while, so he was a bit more accessible in those days. I said, "Michael, you can't do this. Two hundred and fifty thousand for an Academy Award winner in a major studio movie is bullshit. Richard Dreyfuss isn't a piece of crap. His last price was two million. He made some mistakes in his personal life, maybe you think that's important, but I don't think it has anything to do with his talent. Don't degrade him. You want to punish him, fine, but don't insult his dignity, because instead of an actor who has faith in himself you'll get a guy who can't carry his head high. You won't get the right performance."

Eisner just wanted to get away with not spending a fortune for talent. That's why he'd approved of casting Nick Nolte, Bette Midler, and

Dreyfuss, all of whom were cold at the box office. If someone's down and out, the standard move is to make him a low offer. He may say yes. That's business smart, but it's personally insulting.

Eisner saw my point. He came back with $650,000, and Dreyfuss took it with a smile that showed up on screen. The movie was a hit, so Disney offered him *Stakeout,* with Emilio Estevez, and a raise. Another hit. Next he did *Tin Men* with Danny DeVito for Barry Levinson, then *Nuts,* with Barbra Streisand. We had to take a little less money to work with Streisand, so I told the Warner Brothers business-affairs guy, "Listen, Richard's really not getting the money he deserves, so make him happy and throw in a new Mercedes convertible." He did. Richard used to drive around the Warner's lot saying it was Bernie's car. He was quite pleased.

As his manager, I also enjoyed some perks.

Maybe a year after signing Dreyfuss I got a phone call, right before Yom Kippur. My secretary said, "It's Simon Wiesenthal."

"Sure," I said. "Who is it *really?*"

"Simon Wiesenthal, the Nazi hunter. He's calling from Israel."

I picked up the phone and for the next five minutes all I heard was Yiddish: "Live and be well. I want to wish you a Happy New Year." Meanwhile, I'm waiting, because I think he's probably going to ask for money. That's when Wiesenthal broke into English and said, "So, why doesn't Richard Dreyfuss want to play my life story?"

I live for moments like this.

• • • • •

In only a few years Telepictures had become king of the off-network suppliers and first-run syndicators. It made them a prime acquisition target, and in late 1985, Merv Adelson, CEO of Lorimar, a TV and movie production company known mostly for its successful TV dramas like *The Waltons, Dallas, Knot's Landing*, and *Falcon Crest*, suggested a merger.

The Telepictures guys thought it was a good idea. They still wanted to get into producing network comedy, and Lorimar had the TV experience to make it possible. They also had some sporadic movie hits, like *Being There, The Choirboys, S.O.B.*, and *The Postman Always Rings Twice*. In fact, Lorimar was a company on the move. The previous year they'd absorbed Karl Video, and the new Karl-Lorimar Video dominated the charts with Jane Fonda's workout tapes. Also under their umbrella: the Bozell, Jacobs, Kenyon & Eckhardt advertising agency and half of the forty-four-acre former MGM lot in Culver City.

Telepictures was also diversified. They had a stake in five small TV stations, several kids' publications, including *Muppets* magazine and other Henson-based properties, and *US Magazine*.

While Lorimar and Telepictures worked out the details of their merger, I got involved in another sitcom with Jay Tarses, who had a thirteen-show commitment at NBC.

Tarses' project was *The Days and Nights of Molly Dodd*, starring Blair Brown. Of course, she was gorgeous. I also loved her single-minded yet accessible personality. When Jay described what he wanted to do with *Molly Dodd* — that is, try and get a real woman's life on television — the only actress I ever thought of was Blair Brown.

I arranged for them to meet at the Sheraton Universal Hotel. Jay was waiting when we walked in. I said, "Blair, this is Jay. Jay, this is Blair. I thought you should meet. Sit down. Talk." Then I left. Jay later told me that if I had not put them together, the word "dramady" might never have become part of the television lexicon. My days at the Copa also helped with finding the theme music. After reading the pilot I said, "You know what I hear? Stephen Grapelli. It's uptown New York sophisticated." Jay agreed it was perfect.

Tom Patchett also had a deal for a pilot at NBC, but we had no idea what to do until CAA asked me to see a puppeteer named Paul Fusco.

I already had the world's best in Jim Henson, but I figured what the hell. Fusco walked into my office carrying a large, black plastic garbage bag. I was immediately curious and probably a little nervous; who knew what was in the sack? I found out when Fusco pulled out this weird-looking furry, brown puppet. It looked like a bear with a long pig's snout. His name was ALF. ALF came from the planet Melmac. Then Fusco insulted me in ALF's gravelly, burlesque voice. It was hysterical. It was riveting.

I called Tom Patchett. He and Fusco worked up a pitch for the series. The three of us planned to own and produce it ourselves. In their story, ALF is Gordon Shumway, the last known survivor of Melmac. He crashes on Earth and ends up living with a suburban family, the Tanners. The show would be about friendship, honesty, love, and family, all packed into as many laughs as one arrogant little alien could generate. I called Tartikoff and set up a meeting.

We arrived early. A secretary showed Fusco, Patchett, CAA agent Eric Carlson, and me to the upstairs conference room. I think it was the same one right off the janitor's closet in which, a few years later, Jay Leno would hide and listen in while the NBC brass debated whether he or Letterman should take over *The Tonight Show.*

Tartikoff waited with his second in command, Warren Littlefield, and a couple other development executives. I sat Fusco next to Tartikoff. I was at Fusco's left. We made the usual small talk designed to lull and disarm everyone into instant receptivity and nonresistance. Then Patchett started the spiel.

Right away I knew we were going into the toilet. Patchett got lost in a long-winded explanation of the puppet and the story. It looked to me as if everyone had tuned out, save for Tartikoff, and he was close.

Because of my Muppet experiences, I knew how tough it was to sell puppets. That's why Fusco and I had a contingency plan. I kicked him under the table. He took ALF out of his garbage bag, put it on his hand, did the voice, sneezed, wiped his nose and then smeared it on Tartikoff's sleeve.

"I get it," said Tartikoff, laughing. "Let's go!" Boom. Deal. We walked out with a pilot order. On the way back from NBC, Fusco couldn't contain his excitement.

"I can't believe this!" he blurted. "No wonder Henson loves you. I was with Witt-Thomas and Disney, and they couldn't . . ."

I went into shock. I said, "Hold it a second." Thanks to Jim Henson I was considered something of an expert on puppets — whatever that means. And yet CAA had sent a puppeteer to Witt-Thomas and Disney *before* me? I went nuts. I called Ovitz the minute I got back to the office.

"For chrissakes, Michael," I said. "If after twenty years of taking care of Jim Henson, you can't send me a puppeteer *first,* who the hell are you going to send me?"

He said, "What are you talking about?" as if he didn't know. I didn't want to hear any excuses and told him so. After I hung up I had this thought: *Keep your friends close and your enemies closer.*

· · · · ·

Lorimar and Telepictures merged in February 1986. Afterwards, the Telepictures partners told me they'd talked about me to Merv Adelson. I wasn't even sure that he knew my name, but soon a meeting was set.

Merv was handsome and soft-spoken, with gray hair and a habit of checking himself out in the mirror. He was married to Barbara Walters. He was wired in with Michael Milken, Revlon owner Ron Perlman, and CBS owner Larry Tisch. He loved football. We had similar, larger-than-life personalities and spoke the same language of the street. I got him, he got me. I made him laugh. I don't know what bill of goods the Telepictures guys had sold him to get us together, but it worked. Before the get-to-know-you was over with Merv, we were in love. Merv had even said that maybe I should be more than a consultant; we should be in business together. It was nothing specific, just a gesture of faith, a way of saying he liked me. But I saw an opportunity.

"You want me at Lorimar? Buy my company," I said, in the way guys hanging around on the street corner talk when they grab their crotches and toss out a challenge. I didn't expect an answer, and didn't get one, but something in the way Merv looked at me made me think that perhaps the idea Mike Ovitz had so casually dismissed a year earlier might soon become a reality.

· · · · ·

When I skimmed the trades on the morning of April 14, 1986, I saw my name in a little box on the front page of the *Hollywood Reporter.* It read: "Columbia Going After Brillstein." The article mentioned my "individualistic style" and wondered if Columbia could even "match my income."

I knew that Columbia Pictures chairman Guy McElwaine, who'd done a great job running the place when I did *Ghostbusters*, had resigned, but no one from Columbia — or any of my fine friends in the business — had told me I was being considered to replace him. Still, it was good news. I'd always wanted to run a studio, and I figured someone had finally gotten smart. I waited for a call, but the phone never rang. A couple times I wanted to call Columbia, but I realized, why bother? Maybe the item was a trial balloon, Columbia's way of floating an idea to take the town's temperature. If the reaction was good, they'd get around to getting me on the line soon enough.

That evening the phone rang, but it wasn't Columbia. Instead, a couple film executives and friends, David Kirkpatrick from Paramount and Ileen Maisel from MGM, told me that they'd had dinner at Morton's with a pal of theirs from the *Hollywood Reporter.* In the middle of the usual conversation about who they would like to see head a studio, they all agreed it should be me. So they planted a fake item. Not only did I have a good laugh, but it was great news.

Here's why: In show business, perception is often reality. So is deception. If you think someone has money, then they do; if you think an actor is gay, then he is — to you. Neither may be true, but once an idea is out of the box, it's awfully hard to put it back in. Sure enough, the next morning my lawyer, Jake Bloom, got a call from Victor Kaufmann at TriStar, Columbia's sister company. He didn't say anything about the *Hollywood Reporter* blurb, but obviously it had struck a nerve as a possibility Columbia hadn't thought of. Kaufman wanted to meet. Not long after, he offered $12 million to buy my company and have me come to Columbia. I guess when they thought about it, me making motion pictures wasn't that far-fetched.

When Merv found out, he got crazy. He'd responded to my earlier challenge and we'd casually discussed an arrangement. I thought our talks were informal; he thought they were exclusive. But he also understood that only an idiot would have ignored Columbia's inquiry, and if I was going to work for him, he'd rather not have an idiot in the house.

Columbia's offer only increased Merv's desire. He had pretensions to grandeur and wanted to be a bigger player in the entertainment world. He said he was willing to spend $26.5 million — some in cash, some in stock, some in salary — for a five-year deal during which I'd become a piece of senior manpower at Lorimar-Telepictures. I'd advise Merv on TV and movies and corporate strategy. When the next opening occurred, I'd join the Lorimar-Telepictures board of directors.

In exchange, The Brillstein Company would become, as he described it, "an autonomous management and entertainment unit of Lorimar-Telepictures, functioning independently, with no change in staff or location." In other words, he'd own my company and the Brillstein "name," and I'd continue to run it. Lorimar-Telepictures would also get my company's income stream from all sources until it equaled the $26.5 million advance, after which we would split subsequent proceeds.

And that was it. Merv knew I had no client contracts, no shows on TV. All I had was a pilot order for *ALF* and a thirteen-show commitment at NBC for Jay Tarses that would become *The Days and Nights of Molly Dodd*. My primary assets were experience, connections, and a client list Merv hoped I could influence on his behalf — even though we both knew that I couldn't tell clients to be in a Lorimar package any more than I could tell them what clothes to wear. I felt like I had sold Merv pure air, an illusion, but if that's what he wanted, I was inclined to say yes. The opportunity to sell what I'd invested years in building might not come again and I wasn't about to pass it up.

Just before we closed the deal Merv said, "Now what's to stop you from going to the beach every day? You have this guaranteed money, you can shut your company down."

Right, like I wanted to lie around and worry about my tan. The money was my peace of mind. I'd function much better if I didn't have to worry about the next dollar. Besides, I wanted to get inside a corporation and learn something new. And I'd still run The Brillstein Company, but Brad and Sandy could handle most of it.

I said, "Just bet on my track record, and the fact that I'm a nervous Jew."

We closed the deal in May 1986. Tom Pollock, the entertainment lawyer who eventually became head of Universal Pictures for a few years before Seagram bought the company, negotiated my deal. At today's prices, $26.5 million is just spit, but then it was a lot of money. I laughed at my good luck, then remembered Mike Ovitz telling me he couldn't sell me, and laughed some more.

· · · · ·

Joining Lorimar-Telepictures was a major turning point in my career. In essence I'd taken the same advice I'd given my variety-show clients about finding new ways to make a living. I couldn't live in the past, because the tighter I held on to the good old days, the quicker they seemed to slip through my fingers. I'd reached the point where what I wanted was respect for being a player.

Of course, some people thought I was making a big mistake. Two weeks after I started, Merv asked me to meet his partner in Lorimar, Lee Rich. We had lunch at The Grill in Beverly Hills. Rich's opening line was, "Bernie, it's a wasted lunch. I'm leaving these cocksuckers. They're the worst pricks in the world." Nice. After that cold shower the waiter didn't need to refill my ice water. I didn't pretend to know what Rich was talking about, but it wouldn't have mattered if I did. I wasn't ready to listen. Merv not only bought me, but he bought my act. He understood me. It was that simple.

Mike Ovitz, however, didn't understand me. Although he had nothing to do with the Lorimar-Telepictures deal, he demanded a meeting with me and Tom Pollock to talk about it. Ovitz had heard about the sale from Mark Canton, who then worked for Warner Brothers. Canton heard it from me at a Lakers game. I had floor seats; he came over to talk. (Big guys sit on the floor not necessarily because they love basketball but because they want to be seen.) After I told Canton about selling the company he walked halfway around the court to Ovitz's seats and told him. I could see Ovitz turn to stone from where I sat. Later, when he insisted on meeting, I knew it was to scare me. That was the guy's style. He knew the town ran on fear, and for years he worked it better than I've ever seen. He could do it because he was so paranoid himself. Of course, some people say Ovitz is the smartest, best-prepared guy in show business (as shown by the Livent deal). Maybe so, but he also screwed over every one of his partners — and many more people around town. I don't care how clever he is, he can't be trusted and I couldn't be in business with him.

At the time I wasn't worried, but I'd become more and more unhappy with him. Ovitz had been sending movie scripts for Danny Aykroyd that, in lieu of a more excremental description, were terrible. I'd worked with Danny on some winners and some losers, but when Ovitz sent him *The Couch Trip,* I hated it. I said, "I don't care if it's three million, I can't have Aykroyd do that." I tried to remind him that I actually cared about the movies my clients did.

Ovitz said, "You know the trouble with you? Who asked you to be a critic? It's three hundred grand for you and three hundred grand for me. Why don't you just want to make your commission?"

When I heard that, I thought, "Now I really know what this guy is about: money." I told Danny not to do the movie, but he did it anyway. He knew it wasn't a great picture, he just wanted the check. That was fine with me. No one controls the talent.

When Ovitz got settled in my office, he said quietly, "You embarrassed me by not letting me handle the deal," betraying how wound up and irritable he was inside. I'm sure he thought everyone had noticed that I hadn't used him. "How much did you get?"

"Twenty-six-point-five million."

Ovitz's head jerked back like I'd punched him. I could almost read his mind: "This fat putz got $26.5 million. He's richer than I am." Here's what I was thinking: "I guess you were wrong about not being able to sell me."

The meeting should have ended there. But Ovitz wasn't through. He looked right into my face and in that soft, sinister voice that has seduced a generation of talent, he asked me if I was going to pay him.

"Pay you for what?" Did he really believe the bullshit that he'd been spreading — that I was personally signed to CAA? I didn't think so, but maybe he thought I did, so if there was the slightest chance that he could get 10 percent of $26.5 million from me by asking, just to see what I'd say . . . it didn't hurt to try.

I said, "You had nothing to do with it."

Now the meeting was over.

Ovitz was pissed.

Later he called and said, "You fuck with me, I'll kill you." He spewed some choice epithets and said something about his "foot soldiers." Imagine my surprise a few years later when I read that he'd said the same things to screenwriter Joe Eszterhas when they fought publicly over Ovitz's attempt to keep Eszterhas at CAA. According to Eszterhas, Ovitz said, "My foot soldiers will march down Wilshire Boulevard and blow your brains out." People weren't sure whether or not to believe that — but I did. I had to.

My response: "Go fuck yourself. I'm the wrong guy to try and scare. If you try, I'm going to the mats." I had in mind that part in *The Godfather* when the mob families are at war and the men leave their wives and kids and sleep on mattresses in empty apartments so no one knows where to find them. The funny thing is that for a guy as bright as Ovitz, he had no street smarts. He didn't even know what "going to the mats" meant. He should have spent less time acting like a gangster and more time watching gangster films.

That exchange pretty much ended our great "friendship."

I wanted to write him off immediately. But all that would get me was a bitter enemy, which is just as much of a hassle. It's not good for business, and we'd certainly run into each other again. As soon as I got to Lorimar, I asked Merv to make Ovitz head of the motion-picture department. Ovitz would never agree, but he couldn't say I hadn't made the gesture.

Merv asked and Ovitz refused.

A few years later a magazine article blamed our feud on my "unhappiness" that Ovitz's star had risen faster than mine. The implication was that once the *Wall Street Journal* had called Ovitz "the king of Hollywood," my ego couldn't take it. Absurd. I'd never pretended to be king. I didn't follow his every press clipping. That's not my style. Like I recently told two young agents over lunch: "Never look to the left, never look to the right. Look at your own career. If you're doing okay, you don't have to give a shit about anyone else. Tend to your own business and you'll do fine." Ovitz and I benefited more from cooperation than from conflict. For the longest time I'd considered Ovitz an ally. He was my man at CAA, and I didn't think anything was wrong with telling a client, "I can get Mike Ovitz on the phone. I'll just call." Every once in a while, when someone was in my office, I'd do it just to impress them. If anything, my relationship with Ovitz cost me at other agencies that wouldn't give me stuff because they thought CAA had me in the bag.

I only got upset with Ovitz when it was clear he couldn't or wouldn't acknowledge my help by helping me in return. I thought I could count on him. When I found out bit by bit that I couldn't, I went to war. I was hurt. It's that simple. I felt like a schmuck for having been so loyal.

· · · · ·

NBC screened the *ALF* pilot and loved it. So did test audiences, which gave NBC the balls to place a thirteen-show order for the 1986–87 season. When Michael Eisner at Disney heard the news, he called with an offer. Based on the great word-of-mouth, Eisner wanted back in. However, Eisner didn't simply want syndication rights or the show produced on his lot. He wanted to own it all for $8 million, a lot of money for something not yet on the air. We could have used the cash, but no one could get past Eisner wanting to retitle the show *Walt Disney's ALF.*

"ALF is not a cuddly, furry puppet," I told him. "He's a mean fuck. He's got attitude." To soften *ALF* too much would have killed it, and Patchett and Fusco agreed. I told Eisner no. Maybe there was also a tiny bit of revenge involved — Eisner had passed on *The Muppet Show* when he was at ABC — but my main reason was that if the notoriously parsimonious Disney offered $8 million, that meant *ALF* was worth a lot more down the line, especially if the show hit.

With Disney out, Fox and Lorimar bid for the right to syndicate *ALF*. Lorimar won, but even though I worked there, I didn't do them any favors. They had to pay the going rate. We took the advance on foreign distribution up front and used it and the network license fee to make the program in an old C&R Clothing warehouse south of Beverly Hills.

ALF stayed on NBC for four years. After 102 episodes, Lorimar syndicated *ALF* worldwide for $1 million a show. The studio took its 25 percent fee, and Fusco, Patchett, and I split our share, with Patchett and me each kicking an extra 5 percent from our cuts to Fusco because he'd gotten only 10 percent in the original deal. According to my arrangement with Merv, Lorimar got every penny of my share.

ALF only caused me one problem: with Jim Henson. David Lazer told me that Jim was not happy that I owned part of it. (I never heard this from Jim. Like Lorne in the *Fridays* situation, he never discussed it directly with me.) The general opinion — for the second time in my career — was that I was a shithead for being involved. I understood the concern, but ALF was nothing at all like a Muppet. ALF did hard, put-down humor; Jim's humor was soft and intelligent. ALF had a wonderful voice, but couldn't compare in artistry or design to a Muppet. To me, ALF was like the human star of a TV show. I represented more than one of those, so why should it matter if I represented more than one puppet? Did I represent only one comedian because humor was humor? In truth, ALF didn't hurt Henson's market; it probably helped. When I introduced Jim to Bob Iger, who then programmed ABC, he was able to sell him *Dinosaurs* — sort of a prehistoric take on *The Honeymooners*, only with a dinosaur family — because a puppet show like *ALF* had worked in prime time.

NBC loved *ALF*, but they passed on another of our projects, *It's Garry Shandling's Show*. Garry's idea was to do something from his house, like the old George Burns show, *The Burns and Allen Show*. Garry wanted to "break the fourth wall (the camera), talk to viewers all the time, and, as he told the *Washington Post*, "Admit that we're a show . . . because everybody now knows [that what's on TV is] a show. We watch these situation comedies and we're supposed to believe this is real life? We're the TV generation. So come on, we know it's a show, we're not fooling anybody anymore. So why not do one where you just say, 'It's a show, and it's my life'?"

Garry needed help putting it together, so I delivered my client Alan Zweibel to co-write and co-produce. To me, Alan is the married version of Garry (Alan calls *me* "the good shark" because I've survived in this treacherous business but don't kill for sport), and they clicked. We took the pilot script to NBC, but Tartikoff had reservations. He didn't like Garry talking to the viewers. He worried about him playing a comedian. He wasn't sure Garry could hook the mainstream with his quirky humor. Tartikoff passed.

Next we showed it to Peter Chernin at Showtime, who had bought Garry's earlier comedy specials. Peter snapped up the new sitcom. *It's Garry Shandling's Show* ran for four years on cable. We also sold the show into syndication while it still ran on cable — the first company to pull that off. While *It's Garry Shandling's Show* won the approval of TV pundits for his quirky and singular comedy vision, it was very low-rated and not accepted by the masses.

•••••

Just after I settled in at Lorimar-Telepictures, Brandon Tartikoff called me with a problem. Lorne's first year back at *Saturday Night Live* hadn't satisfied network expectations. The season had started well, with Madonna hosting. It turned out to be the high point. Lorne's cast of (mostly) young actors — Robert Downey Jr., Anthony Michael Hall, Randy Quaid, Joan Cusack — weren't as good with sketch comedy as they were in the movies. The writing also suffered. The critics, none of whom could possibly do (or understand) Lorne's job even if they tried, still felt compelled to write story after unforgiving story declaring *Saturday Night Live* dead. It was as if they'd been somehow betrayed.

To be absolutely fair, Lorne's ratings weren't any worse than *Saturday Night Live*'s previous year, when, after Eddie Murphy left, producer Dick Ebersol had cobbled together a free-agency season that transformed *Saturday Night Live* from a sketch show into a stand-up showcase.

Unfortunately, Lorne's ratings also weren't any better.

If you had asked Lorne why things didn't work, he would have said that the situation was nuanced and complicated. For Lorne it always is. So let me cut to the bottom line: despite his best intentions, Lorne had underestimated the task of bringing the show back to life.

Adding to *Saturday Night Live*'s problem was the relentless erosion of network viewers to cable, particularly in search of something to laugh at. The comedy-club era was in full swing; cable channels like HBO (already ten years old) and Showtime featured the hottest comics in their own specials. The language was real and no topic was barred. Networks were still forced to abide by the old Standards and Practices rules of advertiser-supported "free" TV. That meant a jiggly soft-core approach: You could ogle a woman's breasts, but you could never say "tits." You could mince around onstage like a fairy, but you couldn't make fun of the tensions between straights and gays. You could say that certain words were forbidden by the FCC, but on cable George Carlin could actually say them. Just in case you need to be reminded, they were fuck, shit, piss, cunt, asshole, motherfucker, and cocksucker.

With the competition for laughs intensifying, *Saturday Night Live* had to be that much more creative and relevant. Otherwise, what HBO's Michael Fuchs had been telling everyone would be true: HBO had taken the edge off *Saturday Night Live*.

Tartikoff didn't go into any of that. His complaint was more specific. He said it all came down to one thing: Lorne wasn't passionate enough about the show.

So Tartikoff canceled *Saturday Night Live*.

I got the call instead of Lorne because in this business bad news never travels directly. When Tartikoff broke it down, my feelings were mixed. On one hand I thought, "How could he do this to Lorne? He had only one season, and a short one at that. If Lorne can't fix the show, who can?" On the other hand, the season had been abysmal, and pulling the plug felt like an overdue mercy killing. I was almost relieved to hear, "Okay, let's end it."

I also read between the lines. While there had never been any guarantee that Lorne would one day return to *Saturday Night Live*, I felt certain that if Tartikoff had canceled the show during Jean Doumanian or Dick Ebersol's reign, it would have been the same as admitting *he'd* made a mistake by letting it go on with the wrong people in charge. With Lorne back and no improvement in sight, NBC ending *Saturday Night Live* suddenly had a certain legitimacy — or deniability. Take your pick.

I didn't argue with Tartikoff. In fact, I didn't say much, except that he owed it to Lorne to tell him to his face. "You have to sit across from Lorne and me at lunch and tell him that the show's not coming back," I said. "You have to do that much." Tartikoff agreed.

I went home that night without calling Lorne. After dinner I explained the situation to Debbie. "*Saturday Night Live*'s finally over," I said. "I have really ambivalent feelings, but it's over."

She got crazy. "How can you let Brandon embarrass Lorne like this?" she said. "How can you let him bring Lorne Michaels back and then get rid of him? How can they cancel it now? They didn't cancel it all those years when it wasn't good, and now they can cancel it?"

I didn't bother to explain the nuances. Debbie already understood them. She was right. I couldn't let Tartikoff just write off the show. Lorne is always up late, so I called him. "I think it's over," I blurted, without any pleasantries. I waited until he caught his breath, then added, "but maybe not." I recounted Tartikoff's phone call and explained what I thought was behind his decision. All of it. Debbie had gotten me steamed and I hoped to do the same to Lorne. Making Lorne angry is harder than almost anything, but it worked. Then I said he had to fly out from New York and meet me and Tartikoff for lunch. If he wanted to save the show, that would be his opportunity. He had to come prepared and be passionate.

The next morning I called Tartikoff and told him he had to give Lorne another chance. At least he had to keep an open mind and listen to what Lorne had to say before signing the death certificate. Tartikoff said, "Sure."

A couple days later we met at Marino's, a little Italian restaurant on Melrose Avenue, near Paramount Pictures. I made a little speech and then I shut up. I'd done my best to set the figurative table for Brandon and Lorne. Now they were on their own. Lorne told Tartikoff that he was still in love with *Saturday Night Live*, that it was a challenge and he wanted to win. He said, "I know I can turn this thing around. I know how to do it; I know what needs to be done."

"If you can do it, fine," Tartikoff said. "But you have to be the producer. You can't be executive producer, you have to be completely hands-on."

"The reason you let me executive-produce is because you thought if I was the center of everything, I might burn out," Lorne said. "You wanted me to learn to delegate. That was our understanding last year when you asked me to come back."

"That was my mistake," Tartikoff admitted. "You need to be more involved."

He was right and Lorne knew it. Other producers might be able to phone in good product, but for Lorne there was only one way to do it right: be there.

Before lunch was over, Tartikoff agreed to thirteen more shows. It was a short leash, but at least we didn't walk out empty-handed. Face-to-face, Brandon was a nice man and — I mean this in the best way — a sucker for a good story. He was a tough competitor, but not a tough guy. Plus, he loved Lorne. Convincing Tartikoff wasn't a hard job, but I still give him enormous credit for standing by Lorne. The easy way to go would have been to cut and run.

With Tartikoff's blessing, Lorne decided to recast and restaff. Lorne needed people who could go the distance. He decided to keep Jon Lovitz and Dennis Miller and start looking around.

Brad wanted Lorne to see all of our young comedians. He wanted me to see them, too. I had a terrible cold the night Brad insisted I come with him to Igby's comedy club to see Dana Carvey do an act that included an early version of the Church Lady. On the way home I called Lorne from the car and said, "We've got the guy for you." Lorne came out to see Dana at the Comedy Store, but he passed. Brad and I kept after him and eventually he and Tartikoff and, for some reason, Cher, saw Dana a second time at Igby's, where Lorne decided to sign him.

Lorne also auditioned Phil Hartman, who was part of the Groundlings improvisational group, where Lovitz started. In fact, that summer he looked at hundreds of candidates and eventually booked Victoria Jackson, Jan Hooks, Kevin Nealon, and Nora Dunn in addition to Hartman, Lovitz, Carvey, and Miller. For a few moments I felt like we were back in 1975, casting the first season. Our hair was grayer and our bank accounts larger, but we felt just as uncertain about the future as the first time around.

It was The Brillstein Company's good fortune to manage Nealon, Carvey, Miller, Lovitz, and, eventually, Hartman, but Lorne didn't choose them just to please me or Brad. Lorne's sense of survival is too strong to do something stupid like that. He took no one's word for anything. He had to see for himself. Talent was the only consideration.

Of course, we had an advantage. I had prime access to Lorne and a history with *Saturday Night Live*. I could get him to see people. Brad brought the new guys to the party and, thinking ahead, understood that if they did a good job, it would be the big first step into the future he'd envisioned for our company. Keeping Lorne in business kept us in business. *Saturday Night Live* was both a destination and a stepping stone.

The new cast was a calmer group than the original Not Ready for Prime Time Players. To them I was still "The Guy" because of my history with Lorne, but otherwise they sought out Brad. That was fine with me. I was already in a different world.

· · · · ·

When Brad signed on he never expected me to do something like go to Lorimar. At first he was disappointed, but it was the best thing that ever happened to him. Suddenly he had the chance to prove what he was made of. I still serviced my personal clients — I didn't trust show business enough to abandon my bread and butter — but Brad and Sandy took care of most everything else. We still talked a hundred times a day. I'd drop by 9200 Sunset if there was a management problem, or when I wanted to escape, or just because it was on the way home. Was the company better off with me at Lorimar? I don't know the answer, but I had taken the money and it was too late to look back.

Not that I wanted to. I relished every minute of my new job. I concentrated on developing the TV side with the Telepictures guys. I went to meetings about company issues that I had nothing to do with, just to learn firsthand how the place worked. Merv and I talked all the time. He called me to discuss problems. I was his guy. I felt this wonderful being-needed thing; I believed I had finally found someone who understood what motivated me and what I did best.

All my life I'd been a giver. Now, Merv was giving it back in a way that made me happy to be away from the daily management psychodrama. I became a cheerleader of sorts at the company, listening to people's problems, getting them to work together. You could come to me. I was the guy who understood everything.

Okay, so I was still a manager at heart: that's what I like to do.

Not everyone approved of Merv's personal or management style, or his ambition to build a vertically integrated media company. People called him everything from a megalomanic to an old-time mogul, fifty years after his time, to a TV person on Hollywood's social B-list who wanted to be on the movie A-list. But so what? If they don't talk about you, you don't matter. Besides, working with Merv had its perks. He had two private jets, a Gulfstream and a Westwind, to which I had complete access. He had a beautiful apartment at the Hotel Pierre in Manhattan. And he was a partner in La Costa Resort/Country Club/Health Spa. One of the first gifts Merv gave me (and Debbie) was a ten-day health cure at La Costa. I lost eighteen pounds and five pant sizes and was thinner than I'd been in a long time. Debbie and I socialized with Merv and his wife. We played tennis at La Costa or at their house. We went to ball games together. I was invited to great dinner parties.

Lorimar-Telepictures was on part of the old MGM lot. At first I took a lousy little office. Merv offered better but I said no. Merv planned to buy the other half of the lot, and I was content to wait until we moved the executive offices into the Thalberg Building. Even though Thalberg had never actually been in that building (that's Hollywood!), the idea had great sentimental value. Often, I'd arrive at work at 6 or 7 A.M., walk around the lot, thinking about the old movie stars. I felt like everything I had ever done had finally paid off. I knew I'd made it and that I'd never have to worry about money again. I was the happiest I'd ever been. I was at peace.

· · · · ·

Debbie and I were in New York for the Christmas holidays and doing the town. We felt great. *Saturday Night Live* was back on its feet and full of our clients. *ALF* was getting big numbers. My client Bronson Pinchot (who had created a buzz playing Serge to Eddie Murphy's Axel Foley in *Beverly Hills Cop*) was in a new hit sitcom, *Perfect Strangers*. Tarses' *Molly Dodd* was set to be a mid-season replacement, and *The "Slap" Maxwell Story* would soon air. Bob Saget and Dave Coulier were in the hit *Full House*. Richard Dreyfuss had successful pictures again, and I had recently sold the movie *Dragnet (1987)* over the phone for Danny Aykroyd and Tom Hanks, just by humming "dum-da-dum-dum" to the producer David Permut.

The day we planned to leave for Los Angeles, Merv called me from his apartment at the Hotel Pierre. He said, "Can you stop in for a drink before you go to the airport?" We had a three-o'clock plane and it was already noon.

"I'm with Debbie," I said. I didn't have a clue what was up.

"Bring her," he said.

Merv's living room overlooked Central Park. As we settled into the plush couches, snow began to fall. The scene reminded me of *The Eddie Duchin Story*, because Duchin lived in similarly elegant pre- and postwar surroundings. It was all very uptown for a bust-out kid like me.

"You know," said Merv. "I've been thinking. Things aren't going so well in our movie division. How would you like to run it?"

Just like that.

I wanted my stomach to settle down before I answered, so Merv kept talking. "I just got a two-hundred-and-fifty-million-dollar line of credit. We set up a distribution company. You know all the people. You can do comedy, drama, whatever."

"I'd want autonomy," I said, finally forcing some words out.

"You'll have complete autonomy up to twenty-five million a picture" — in 1999 dollars that's like a hundred million — "then I have to approve. But otherwise, it's real money and you can do what you want. What do you say?"

I'm sure my forehead was a neon sign that read "ABSO-FUCKING-LUTELY!" I know I mumbled a lot of gracious stuff that I can't remember now, but I finished with, "Let me think about it on the plane and I'll call you when I get into Los Angeles."

I didn't really have to think it over. Merv wanted me to run his movie company. How many people in the world get the chance to do that? There are only seven or eight of these jobs at a time. I felt like the words "You have been accepted" had just been branded on my ass. My ego puffed up and I thought, "Now I can really make this thing work like I think it should work, and I don't have to take a backseat to any clients." I was in a dream world. I trusted Merv and believed that when a bigger-than-life guy like him gave his blessing, then he was the right guy to take me where I wanted to go, which was all the way.

In the car on the way to the airport Debbie seemed concerned about my ability to run the movies and keep a hand in everything else, but I really didn't hear her. Or want to. I felt complete. This was my reward for all the years of being the guy behind the guy. I'd been second class and now I could be first class. I'd read every book about the movie business I could get my hands on. Harry Cohn, Louis B. Mayer, and Irving Thalberg were my heroes. And now, all of a sudden, I had the chance to call the shots and be just like them. I was a god to myself, one of the chosen. When you control $250 million, people look at you different. I could just imagine walking into my favorite restaurant feeling like I was The Man. Was I full of myself? You bet. Big ego? Absolutely. Not only had I cashed in, but I was still hot.

The flight home felt like it took forever.

The minute I walked in the front door I called Merv and said yes.

I had an epiphany. After a bad morning and another bout of unhappiness, I took out a yellow legal pad and wrote:

What has happened to me?

1. I'm sixty-six years old.

2. I've been in show business for forty-two years.

3. We've got nine shows on the air and they can all continue without me. I went on a two-week vacation cruise when I should have been going to tapings and worrying about pickups. No one missed me. The whole business didn't stand up and say, "Where are you?"

4. I always believed I was in control, but it was only a belief. The clients controlled everything and I did what I did in their name.

5. For years I made rules. The good thing about my rules is that they were pretty good rules — for me. The bad thing is I insisted everyone else live by them. One big mistake and the relationship was over. I never really took the time to see the other guy's side of it. I acted like I was holy.

6. Guess what? The whole world doesn't have to play by my rules. Who says my rules are even right? This is not the mafia.

7. If people don't have to live by my rules, there's nothing to be angry about.

8. I'm not angry.

 • • • • •

Sometimes I ask myself if I would have handled the transition the same way if I were in Brad's place.

Probably not. That's the truth. At first I felt angry and hostile about it, even though I could tell Brad didn't feel that way towards me. He was just upset that I felt so bad, and unhappy that I made no secret of it. But Brad's not me. I'm public, he's private. My office door is open, his is closed. He has a long-term plan, I just try to survive every day. Who is right and who is wrong? Neither, it seems. We each have our own set of rules and do the best we can. In order to grow up and get through this I have had to understand that deeply.

Brad and Lorne have a running joke: "Who does Bernie hate today? Who does he love today?" All my life if you didn't play by my rules, if you crossed some invisible boundary, I marked you dead. I'd become ice. I'd cut off the relationship without a second thought. I didn't do this a lot or carelessly — the ground around me is hardly littered with bodies — but sometimes I just couldn't help reacting emotionally to business situations. I made enemies, burned a bridge or two, lost friends, and in the end probably hurt myself.

I'm not saying that I regret any of it. What's done is done. There's nothing wrong with having rules. It's just that with Brad running things I've relaxed. I didn't plan to, it just happened. The pressure is off. That explains why I could wake up one day and understand that everyone does not have to act like I act. What works for me doesn't necessarily work for anyone else. I cannot inflict on the world the way I think people should live.

The way I used to live doesn't even work for me anymore.

$\bullet \ \bullet \ \bullet \ \bullet \ \bullet$

Maybe I do regret some of it. I haven't always been an angel.

When I sold The Brillstein Company to Lorimar in 1985, I also had a chance to be a generous guy, but I wasn't. I didn't make Sandy Wernick very important in the sale. I've never admitted this to anyone, but I could have provided for him, given him a taste of what I got. Sandy had certainly proven himself. Without him my life and fortunes would have been very different. But I didn't because Sandy and I weren't partners. I wasn't godfather to his children. He got some stock and a couple bucks.

I felt it was my moment. I figured, Lorimar didn't come after Sandy or the new guy who'd just joined us, Brad Grey. They wanted me. If you're the driving force behind a business, I don't care if you're twenty or eighty, there comes a day when you say, "Okay, I've been loyal to the company; so far we've always split the money, but now it's time for me and my family. I'd worked hard for the money, and the chance to do something new, different, bigger; to be my own man."

They say, "What goes around comes around," and it's true. Ten years later, companies like ABC and MCA came after Brad — not me. They wanted to lure him away.

He stayed. I left.

Screwing It Up However I Like

Chapter 12

You're No One in Hollywood Unless Someone Wants You Dead

When I became CEO of Lorimar Film Entertainment in January 1987, I felt like I'd finally arrived. For thirty years I'd played the game, the game being to protect myself and keep from getting killed. Surviving for that long in show business had counted not only for something but, along with instinct, probably everything. Maybe I'd planted the seed when I said that I loved the old studio moguls' biographies. Sometimes I'd go on and on about how awe-struck I was to work on the old MGM lot. That's not enough to run a movie division, but having made the company millions and millions of dollars in television might have been. I had a reputation for bringing in projects under budget and for a profit. Since Merv treated me like a son, it seemed reasonable that he might trust my judgment and instincts in other areas.

However I got the job was fine with me. I didn't fight it. I was too surprised to find myself with a couple hundred million dollars and the freedom to spend it, especially since I'd never considered myself CEO material. For that, I'd always believed that the blander you are the better. I'd always been an outsider: *of* the Establishment but not *in* it. I had strong opinions and I didn't hesitate to speak up when others shut up. My humor was street and cutting, my hockey-jersey-and-designer-sweats dress code out of place in the boardroom. I could wear a business suit, but I'd always fought for the talent *against* the suits. Today, John Register's painting of headless dummies wearing suits in a clothing store window hangs in the Brillstein-Grey reception lobby; it's Brad's and my way of saying how we sometimes feel about the business we're in.

If I'd ever wanted anything from the Establishment it was for the powers-that-be to recognize me for having made it without becoming one of them. To have Merv accept my quirks and give me the corporate stamp of approval was a sign that they had.

Running the movie studio was like being allowed to eat all you want in a candy store that your father owns. The town reacts to the guy with the money, and everyone knew very quickly that I had deep pockets. People treated me differently and it fed my ego. I was no longer the seller, I was the buyer. Even though 90 percent of all Hollywood meetings are horse manure, I could ask for and have a get-together with anyone. I did breakfasts at the Polo Lounge, at my regular corner table. Every day I had the same waitress, the same food: orange juice, oatmeal, and coffee — unless I was angry or nervous, and then I ate anything not nailed down. Lunches were at the Lorimar commissary or an industry watering hole, like the Palm Restaurant or The Grill, where I might run into a producer, director, actor, or another studio boss. Some guys like to keep a low profile. I wanted to let everyone know I was around and in control. But I never forgot the bottom line: The business world didn't really care about Bernie Brillstein, the man. People just wanted to schmooze me because I wrote the checks. I got it, and it was fine. Maybe I'd make a real friend or two along the way; go to a couple ball games and casual dinners. But as long as everyone else treated me with respect, didn't lie to me, or talk about me behind my back, I didn't take it personally.

• • • • •

Lorimar had already made up the 1987 film release schedule. I liked a couple, but most made my heart sink. When I tried to fix things, I had arguments with directors whose attitude was, "Who's this new guy?" Whatever. I figured that soon enough I'd put my own pictures out and be happy to stand up for my own successes and failures. As for the movies I inherited, I wasn't responsible. I just thought I had to make sure they were marketed correctly. That was naive. When they bombed, I took the shots because I was in the executive suite. But who gets the credit and who takes the fall has always been an ambiguous business in Hollywood. As *Variety* editor Peter Bart, a former studio executive himself, wrote after the premiere of Harrison Ford's *Air Force One,* when musing about who should get kudos for the film, "No studio executive is around long enough to collect his just deserts. He's lucky to get an hors d'oeuvre."

Why the never-ending game of musical chairs? Movie studios today are no longer independent companies run by a guy who loves movies. That era ended in 1989 when Lew Wasserman sold MCA to Matsushita Industrial Electrical Company of Japan; but it was for all intents over long before, when the original studio moguls retired or died. Now, the major studios are subsidiaries of publicly held media conglomerates. They focus more on financial models and price-earnings ratios than on instincts and talent. If a studio head doesn't generate quick results, the corporate boss fires him and brings in another. (It happens at TV networks, too.) These days production presidents and their teams are as interchangeable as screenwriters. There's little stability. Even if someone has good creative instincts — and many do — corporate priorities and the fear of being out of work can force someone to play it safe because he's afraid his own taste might get him in trouble. Do that for a while and you lose your taste altogether.

If there's any way out of this conundrum it's to remember that a satisfying career takes instinct, passion, intelligence, luck, and a good idea. Show business is filled with oil gushers and icebergs. Sometimes you hit one or the other, and if you can keep going long enough, you hit both — or neither, which is boring. The idea is to keep moving ahead.

Do you think that if I'd sat down forty years ago and planned out what I wanted my success to look like, I would have said, "Okay, I'll take one *Love Connection,* an *ALF,* a *Hee Haw,* some variety TV specials, and throw in a *Saturday Night Live,* the Muppets, *Dangerous Liaisons,* and *Mr. Show?*" No way. But I'll take them. You may think of some as schlock and others as culturally groundbreaking — and I may agree — but in the end it doesn't really matter. They are what they are, and they have one thing in common: they were all hits.

Today's nonestablishment rebel is Miramax co-founder Harvey Weinstein. He certainly isn't a smooth customer. You don't think, "Boy, I'd like to have a fancy dinner with him and then go to the opera." You don't imagine him running a conglomerate. But so what? He's imposing and savvy and brilliant. He has passion and he loves movies. And by loving movies, he gets the writers and the stars. Who needs the exterior bullshit when it's what's inside that counts? They stay out of the mainstream, but because they're good they influence the mainstream. You can make a lot of money by not going with the flow. Just look at my career.

• • • • •

Not so long ago, almost all the business of show business went on behind the scenes. The public maybe knew who ran the studios. They could pick Walt Disney out of a lineup because he was a brand name and on TV once a week. A few had heard of William Morris's Abe Lastfogel and MCA's Lew Wasserman, and if you had a relative in the business, maybe you knew David Begelman and Freddie Fields and Sue Mengers. Now we're all in on stories not only about the stars but also about the star-making machinery.

Why does anyone care? Because these days everyone has two businesses: their own and show business. The entertainment business is treated by the media as if it were a glamorous stock market, with us as traders. It's no accident. The goal is to make readers and viewers feel more invested, because the more we participate the more we spend.

That's the hard part: getting our attention. The big promotional machine will do whatever it takes. One way is with THE LIST: Who's Hot, Who's Not, Power Winners, Power Losers, etc. Why do we need to know? They're the ruination of our business. They create competition for the wrong reasons. Lists are not even about good or bad, only about what gets attention. The whole idea is to be self-fulfilling. No wonder frantic publicists work overtime trying to ensure their clients' place for posterity — even though that "posterity" only lasts until the magazine is thrown in the garbage. Pretty soon I expect to see a list of the Top 100 People Who Get On Lists, followed by the Top 100 People Who Make Up the Lists. Let me put it this way: the fact that we rate everything is one of my top ten show-business complaints. It's gotten out of hand. Keeping score puts pressure on people not to make good entertainment but to make the list.

Another problem of expanded entertainment reporting is a love-hate relationship between show business and the press — and I don't mean only the press that still hasn't become part of some larger media company. If a guy working for the *Wall Street Journal* or *Premiere*, making seventy-five grand a year, interviews me, chances are he's thinking, "This putz makes a couple million just for putting together a deal!" And then he either wants to kill me or be written into my will — and his story reflects that. It's like when I'm negotiating for a client. I know that the business-affairs guy at the studio or the network sees the prices we get and knows he can't make that much money in the next ten years. Immediately he doesn't like me and would like to see me dead. But his boss needs me because he needs my client. So I deal with a little hostility here and there and write it off as human nature.

I think reporters also want to know the secret of how I pulled off whatever they think I pulled off, as if there's some magic formula for success that they can use when they give up journalism to write screenplays or work for a studio.

I'm not suggesting we do away with entertainment reporting. I'm just worried that the magnifying glass over our industry — all in the name of keeping us interested enough to buy movie tickets and CDs, watch TV shows, etc. — makes it seem like, as James Poniewozik wrote in *Salon*, an on-line magazine, that our lives are about "dynastic struggles on the scale of Shakespeare's histories." Occasionally. But the rest of the time it's made to seem that way just to keep everyone glued to the set like it's some afternoon soap opera. It's the same tactic used by cable news channels to justify wall-to-wall coverage of everything from O. J. Simpson to Princess Diana to Monica Lewinsky. But we're not all subplot and subterfuge, heroes and villains. I've known saints and assholes, for sure, and have been both at times, but mostly it's just regular people trying to get the job done. Negotiating a deal or selling a company is not *that* exciting. The tiny day-to-day details of being an executive/manager/agent, etc., are a pain in the ass.

Life in the show-business trenches is still life in a trench.

As a result, what I mourn most is the loss of the mystique on which the entertainment industry was built. In the old days actors used to stand for something; their lives were mostly private and their characters lived forever. Now they're asked what they *think* of their characters, as if the characters were real people and their opinions contributed to our enjoyment of the movie or TV show. Isn't art supposed to be experienced without a setup? Will studios soon hand out free copies of the screenplay and back-story notes at the cineplex door? Once, our imaginations got us into the movie theaters. Now nothing is left to the imagination.

. . . . .

Most studio heads don't just sit in their newly redecorated offices and say, "Make that movie." They have to get the script from an agent, seduce an actor into doing the role, intrigue a director, and find a producer. When I started reading scripts and making deals at Lorimar, at first I went to people I could depend on and made commitments to the big names who would take them. Richard Dreyfuss. Jim Henson. Lorne wanted to write a film called *Women, Money and Restaurants*, using *Saturday Night Live* and showbiz as a background to examine the metaphor for the ladder everyone in the business goes up and down. Garry Shandling agreed to do *It's Garry Shandling's Movie*. I made a production deal with Darryl Hannah, who seemed bright and funny. (I even gave my client Jay Tarses' daughter, Jamie, a job.) I didn't do it just because most of these were Brillstein Company people. They were good. But part of what any film executive brings to the job is his relationship with talent. In a sense, they're his "clients." I was very careful, but I had to hit the ground running and establish myself quickly. Later I'd work on getting the rhythm of the job.

My first movie was *Action Jackson*, with producer Joel Silver. People make fun of it, but it's the only time Joel (*Lethal Weapon*, etc.) ever did an action-adventure movie for ten million dollars — even though he kept calling me for more money. I loved that the hero (played by Carl Weathers, from *Rocky*) was black, and the picture seemed like a good way to push Lorimar into the mainstream. I was right. *Action Jackson* was our division's first top-ten hit and we made good money.

I bought *Interview with the Vampire* after Ileen Maisel, one of the four film executives who worked with me, set up a meeting with the author, Anne Rice, and her producer, Julia Phillips. Phillips's record as a co-producer was gold: *Close Encounters of the Third Kind, Taxi Driver,* and *The Sting*. Frankly, I didn't know from blood and fangs, but we laughed a lot and my gut instinct was that Rice's passionate reinvention of a moribund genre was so against the grain that it would work. Plus the book was a huge hit and there was already a sequel, *The Vampire Lestat*. I made up my mind to buy the project because Ileen was very smart, I believed in her enthusiasm, and her relationship with Julia had brought in what I thought would be a prestigious project. Maybe I also liked Julia Phillips's legs. I know she'd like to think so.

I also put a Bugsy Siegel movie into development. I'd read everything about him and the Hollywood of the late '30s and early '40s.

I was fascinated that a good-looking gangster could be hotter than the number one movie star in town. I asked writers Joan Didion and her husband, John Gregory Dunne, to take the project and pitched my angle. They liked it and developed a fictional story based on Siegel.

When Warren Beatty heard about the film he called.

"I wanted you to know I've been developing a Bugsy Siegel story for a long time," he said. "I hear you're doing one, too."

"Yes, we are," I said. "Didion and Dunne are writing it and I'm waiting for the script."

"Well, I'm doing this."

"That's fine," I said.

"Well, I've been working on this a long time."

"Are you telling me not to do it?"

"Well . . ."

"Would you like to do Bugsy with me?" I asked.

There was no answer. Then: "Please don't do it." And the conversation was over.

What was I supposed to do — stop everything? Beatty or not, I plunged ahead. Unfortunately, like many projects in development, the movie never got made — but the story ended up as the inspiration for Dunne's novel *Playland*, in which I got a special thanks for "planting the seed."

A big problem for me was that no one rushed to bring their best work to Lorimar. It was my first experience with movie-business snobbery and it pissed me off. To use modern TV networks as an analogy, Lorimar was like the WB or UPN of its time. Not among the first rung. Not on the top floor. As a salesman, I understood when not everyone wanted to buy from me. As a buyer, I found it hard to accept that my studio sometimes lost projects because we didn't have the proper cachet, even though our money was just as green. We could get A-list directors but only for their B-list projects; that is, movies close to their hearts that other studios wouldn't touch. It was risky, but I needed the product.

Merv and I tried to shore up our image by getting some high-caliber producers on the lot. For instance, we offered Joel Silver and Larry Gordon 1.25 million shares of stock, plus some money, to come over. They passed. I think if another studio — Columbia, Disney, Warners — had made the offer they would have taken it and bet on the company.

To complicate matters even more, Mike Ovitz decided to freeze us out, and recently admitted it publicly in the *New York Times*. He invited my staff to his agency for a meeting, but the whole thing was a charade, his way of rubbing our faces in his power to withhold. CAA refused to come to us first with a script, if at all. Fortunately, ICM was terrific. Guys like Jeff Berg and Jimmy Wiatt and Sam Cohn were happy to get their clients jobs. So were the other agencies. But not CAA. Ovitz has said that this was his way of paying me back for taking the Lorimar job without his knowledge or approval. Typically, he's not telling the whole truth; it was really about selling my company without him. But either way Ovitz knew it would hurt his reputation if word spread that one person had gotten away with being disrespectful and standing up to him. All his power was based on fear; a perception-is-reality game. He wanted to try and punish me publicly, and he did.

· · · · ·

Ovitz also tried to punish me privately. I guess I should have felt honored, because you're no one in this business unless someone wants you dead.

At first our war was just a show-business war. I was upset that he'd left me as the odd man out on *Ghostbusters*. I didn't like my clients getting questionable scripts. I was pissed he sent Paul Fusco and *ALF* to me *third*. I was hurt that he wouldn't try to sell my company or my services as a piece of corporate manpower — but then wanted a commission on the Lorimar sale. I was angriest that he didn't seem to know the meaning of quid pro quo — or, as David Geffen told the *New York Times*, "You can scratch Mike Ovitz's back but he doesn't scratch yours back." At our level this business works on give and take. Ovitz only knows how to take.

But the situation turned really ugly when Ovitz made my daughter Leigh, who'd been a CAA agent the whole time, quit just because he and I couldn't get along.

Leigh and I always had a pretty charming relationship. She was the princess who didn't live with me and one of the reasons I was so willing to move to Los Angeles (where she'd relocated after Florida). When I came out we began to get close. Now we're close as could be. After Leigh graduated from college I asked her, "What do you want to do?"

"Being an agent sounds interesting," she said.

That surprised me, but I've never told my kids not to do what I've done. I said, "Go to CAA. They're the hot new guys in town." I called someone at the agency and got her an interview. Leigh started as a secretary. By the time she was twenty-five she made full agent. I was still tight with the CAA guys, and on the holidays and Christmas we'd even vacation at the same hotel together in Hawaii: Ron Meyer, Mike Ovitz, me, and our families.

But when our relationship turned sour because I felt betrayed, I slammed the door. According to Leigh, that really pissed them off.

She was in a CAA staff meeting one Wednesday morning when someone said that Alan Zweibel was no longer a client. Ovitz said, "What happened?" Another agent said, "Well, Bernie really fucked us this time." That precipitated a forty-five-minute Bernie Brillstein–slam discussion, while Leigh listened quietly in the back of the room.

Afterwards a couple agents went to see her and said, "That must have been really tough for you."

Leigh said, "It wasn't one of my better days, but I'm a big girl." She later told me that she'd decided then and there not to say anything to me because she was paid to be a CAA agent and didn't want to mix personal with business. Boys will be boys, she figured. They're just having a fight.

But the fight went on for months. Every Tuesday night before the Wednesday motion picture–packaging meeting, Leigh got a major stomachache wondering what would happen.

The next time I pulled a client, or they wanted to package a show and I said no — I don't remember — Ovitz again felt slighted. According to Leigh, he said, "I want a list of Bernie's clients, I want to know who we have deals with, I want to know which clients we have in common." Ovitz feels everyone owes him everything, that he's responsible, that he birthed the whole of Hollywood, that everyone came out of his genius.

When I went to Lorimar, Ovitz was pissed that he didn't know. He hates reading about things. Ego-wise he likes to bear the news rather than receive it. So when I was set up as CEO of the film company, Ovitz said, "Bring Lorimar in for a meeting, but freeze them out. Don't give them any information. Our doors are shut — but don't act like they're shut."

Of course, I knew I had problems with CAA, but I never asked Leigh for information. It's not my style. I remember when she interviewed for a job at William Morris, before she went to CAA. Someone asked her, "If we hire you, how will we know that you won't give private information to your father?"

She said, "What makes you think he cares?"

The straw that broke the camel's back was when Ovitz asked Ron Meyer to call Leigh to ask what hotel we were staying at for Thanksgiving in Hawaii. Ovitz didn't want to go to the same place. She said, "Don't worry Ron, we're on another island."

Afterwards, she thought, "This man is a partner in a major company. Could he not have called the Kahala Hilton to see if Bernie Brillstein was registered? Could he not have found some other way? No, he had to call me." Ovitz had for the first time involved my daughter in our fight. He deliberately rubbed her nose in it.

Leigh told me that she walked down the hall to Meyer's office. They'd always had a good relationship and she wanted a hug and some reassurance that she'd maybe misinterpreted what had just happened. She closed the door and said, "I don't know if I can deal with this much longer. This is very difficult."

He said, "You know we'll help you find another job."

Leigh had been at CAA for eight years. She'd come looking for a hug and a "Leigh, we're so sorry," and instead, in so many words, Meyer said that her job was in jeopardy because of the situation with me. She suddenly realized it was all a game. Then Meyer said, "If my daughters were made to feel uncomfortable at work, I would never do anything to stand in the way of their careers." Clearly, Meyer wanted Leigh to talk to me and say, "Daddy, my job's in jeopardy because of your shit with CAA."

She walked out of his office, shattered, her head spinning.

The next morning Leigh went to see Ovitz. She told him about her meeting with Meyer, that it was hard for her to deal with their problems with me and how shocked she'd been when Meyer offered to help her find another job.

Ovitz said, "Leigh, come sit down." In Ovitz-speak that meant, "Come, be on my team so I can manipulate you."

Then he told her, "Ronnie's very ill. We think he may be dying. Fred [Spektor], Rick [Nicita], and I are consulting with a doctor. He's on medication and he's obviously hallucinating. I think Ronnie's fucked so many women he's got to have AIDS or something; he's got to be sick. It absolutely makes sense."

He paused, then added, "If you repeat that, I'll deny it."

What bullshit! Leigh couldn't believe that Ovitz thought she'd be stupid enough to believe such an obvious crock of shit about Ronnie. He was doing a good cop/bad cop routine. He'd set up Ronnie to be the prick — and yet still not responsible for his erratic behavior — so he could be the hero and rescue Leigh. And all this just to get Leigh to ask me to do things their way.

Leigh decided enough was enough and told me the whole sordid story. But she didn't ask me to do or fix anything. She said, "Had they called me in and said, 'We're having problems with your dad. We don't know how to handle this,' I would have said, 'Do you have a pen? I'm the wrong Brillstein. He's at 275-6135.'"

I felt bad for Leigh but I couldn't change what was going on between Ovitz and me. And Leigh, being *my* daughter, didn't expect me to.

Leigh took it hard and stayed home a couple days with a bad back — it acts up like my stomach acts up. Ovitz called her a few times to say, "You weren't in the meeting today, how are you feeling?"

One day he called to tell her that he and I had another problem. I'd called a CAA client about possibly managing him and that had sparked another big discussion at a meeting Leigh had missed. "I didn't want you to hear about it from someone else in the company," Ovitz said. "I didn't want you to hear there was a discussion going on at that length without you having been there. So you wouldn't mistake it. We don't want to hurt you."

When Leigh told me, I said, "It's something that would have hurt you if you knew about it, so they called to tell you that they didn't want to hurt you by not telling you. Makes no sense."

The next morning Leigh walked into Ovitz's office and told him she was leaving. He said, "I won't have it." She said, "Have it. I'm leaving."

Ovitz had made her choose her loyalty between the company and her father. She looked him in the face, laughed, cried, and left. What a cocksucker. I know it's bad business, but I'll never forgive him.

Leigh Brillstein:

I was twenty-eight years old. Looking back, I get a bit of a thrill at having sat across from this guy who talks out of one side of his mouth, while telling him "I'm leaving," and he can't do anything about it. He said, "You should take some time off and think about it." I said, "There's nothing to think about. I'm not doing this after the way I was treated."

Mike said, "Leigh. Things work out. People come and go and we'll work this thing out. You really shouldn't jeopardize your career."

I still left. I got a job at ICM. I didn't jeopardize my career. I'm very happy.

My dad thinks I walked out because Mike told me to choose between my father and CAA. He didn't say that directly. He just made it very difficult for me to be comfortable and I was too stupid to know what was going on. I saw the problem as Mike and Ronnie thinking of me first as Bernie's daughter and the good agent they'd made second. I was correct, but of course, so was my dad. He sees the bottom line in situations right away.

I was at CAA for eight years. I left on a Wednesday. Payday is Friday. The company took the trouble to rip up my normal pay check and make out a new one that deducted two days from my salary.

I put about twenty films into development at Lorimar and ended up making six lousy movies, two good movies, and one great movie. Not a stellar track record, but I can live with it considering that I spent my first year scrambling to fill the product pipeline to keep our new distribution company afloat. I also didn't have lots of time for well-thought-out decisions because I was also involved in the management company and the Lorimar TV side. Sometimes I worked eighteen-hour days. I tried to do too much at once. Eventually I found my footing and made better choices, like Jim Henson's *The Witches*, based on the book by Roald Dahl, starring Anjelica Huston and directed by Nicolas Roeg; and *Phantom*, a spin on *Phantom of the Opera*, directed by Wolfgang Petersen.

Perhaps I would have done better if I'd loved the movies as much as I loved the power and competitive game of making them. It's a tough confession to make — and I didn't realize until years later — but I worshiped the men who ran the studios and made the movies I grew up watching, not the art and craft of making movies themselves. I never really cared much for hanging out on movie sets. I would go as a courtesy. My passion was for the challenge of literally willing Lorimar from fringe-studio status to major standing. It was a game more suited to the immediacy of working in TV than making art for the big screen. I thought all it would take were terrific scripts, wonderful actors, and great directors. Boom. Hit movies. I believed that if my instinct for talent was any indication, then picking winners would be a snap. It's not a snap. It's the toughest damn thing I ever tried to do. But when it worked, it really worked.

· · · · ·

The movie I'm most proud of making at Lorimar is *Dangerous Liaisons.* I was involved on an emotional level that, for a change, had nothing to do with gamesmanship and everything to do with proving what good cinema is all about.

I was in New York on business and I was tired, but Ileen Maisel insisted that I see *Les Liaisons Dangereuses.* The Royal Shakespeare Company play, written by Christopher Hampton, was on Broadway after an earlier run on London's West End. There had already been movie interest. When Mike Nichols saw the London production, he offered half a million for the rights. The producers said no because they thought they could get more money after opening in New York. Although the play, with the British cast, was a hit, it didn't win any Tony Awards, so interest died out. They'd miscalculated.

I went and fell in love.

It was just like *Dallas* with French costumes, full of sex, passion, manipulation, repression, and duplicity. I could easily see it on the screen. Ileen told me that Hampton was writing a movie script based on the play. In fact, he was almost done. I told her to arrange a breakfast immediately.

We met the next morning at the Carlyle. After exchanging pleasantries I got down to business. "Here's ten dollars, cash," I said. "Consider it a down payment. I'll buy the movie script." I had faith in Hampton and he was delighted at the gesture. I left owing him $449,990.

Alan Rickman, a fine actor, played Valmont onstage. He wanted to be in the film, but when John Malkovich found out about the movie he literally chased me down to get the role. He even offered an open option on his services. Malkovich off-screen is as seductive as he is on-screen. He has a way of looking at you that makes you wonder if he knows something about you that you don't. He's no matinee idol but women love him. I called him Whispering Smith, because he spoke with a serpentine hiss and could have talked any Eve into devouring the apple. Malkovich is bizarre and wonderful. He was the tent pole around which I built the picture.

I wanted Louis Malle to direct. His agent, Sam Cohn, arranged a meeting in my suite at the Carlyle. I loved Malle. I'd watched every movie he'd made. He knew the project and had seen the show.

"Bernie, I love it and I'd love to do it," he said. "But I can't. Milos is my friend."

Malle meant director Milos Forman, an Academy Award–winning director who had done *One Flew over the Cuckoo's Nest* and *Amadeus*. Forman also wanted to film the story, but base it directly on the book by Choderlos de Laclos. He called his picture *Valmont*.

When I heard, I approached Forman through his lawyer and invited him to combine projects. I thought it was crazy to turn such wonderful material into a race. "Why doesn't he direct this?" I said. "Why doesn't he stop this competition? I have the script already." But Forman was co-writing a script with Jean-Claude Carrière, a veteran screenwriter for Luis Buñuel, and he wasn't inclined to cooperate. He believed that turning a play into a movie had less credibility than adapting the source material. As he told the *New York Times*, "I think the play is brilliant for the theater. But my approach is always to take the original source as the basic material on which to base your vision. Theatricality is the only thing that is a kiss of death for film."

Forman is an undeniably talented man, but that was arrogant. I pushed on, only to discover other directors who all balked at competing with an Oscar winner. I spoke to everyone, all the obvious top people you'd think of for this kind of a movie — American and European — and they all ran for the hills, saying they didn't want to go head to head with Milos Forman. In fact, Forman had made it clear that he wanted me to drop out, but I couldn't run my life or company based on what he wanted. I was obsessed. I loved the play. I also wanted to show that I had taste and instinct.

Forman planned to begin shooting in the summer of 1988. If I wanted our movie to come out first, I had to hurry. But I still needed a director and the rest of the cast. Hampton suggested Stephen Frears, an English director who'd directed one of Hampton's plays for television. I didn't know Frears, which doesn't help when you have to hand over $15 million and say, "How fast can you do this?"

Ileen gave me two of Frears's movies on video. The first was *My*

Beautiful Laundrette, the other was *Sammy and Rosie Get Laid*. I woke up at 6:30 in the morning to see *My Beautiful Laundrette* before our breakfast meeting. I loved it. Frears could tell a story, and from the look of his movie, he had also done it without spending too much.

Later, we met downstairs. He described his approach to the job. I was impressed that he wanted to focus on character more than costumes, be gritty rather than lush. He didn't seem overwhelmed by the material. I was sold. I said, "When can you start?"

He took out a little black book and consulted it. "On Tuesday."

Back in my suite I watched *Sammy and Rose Get Laid*, and hated it. But so what? You win some, you lose some. I had a good feeling about Frears.

With the director set, we signed up the rest of our cast. Glenn Close played the Marquise de Merteuil, a role she had intended to do on Broadway when the British cast departed and American actors took their place. She never got the chance. According to the *New York Times*, the producers didn't consider her a big enough box-office draw. Their mistake. The play closed just before *Fatal Attraction* came out and made Close a superstar. I knew this and as soon as Hampton finished the movie script I sent it to Glenn and her CAA agent, Fred Spektor. She was immediately interested.

Before Close signed on, Faye Dunaway also pursued the role of the Marquise de Merteuil. I love Faye Dunaway but I didn't think she was right for the part. Still, her agent kept calling and eventually, just to meet me, Faye threw a dinner party at some fancy nightclub in New York. I never showed up, but it was in the paper the next day as if I'd gone and was with her. My father read the item, called me, and said, "It's disgusting. You're cheating on your wife and it's in the papers!"

I said, "Pop, I never met her!"

That very afternoon I was in the elevator at the Carlyle, and guess who stepped into the car with me? Faye Dunaway. She had no idea who I was.

Michelle Pfeiffer, Keanu Reeves, Swoosie Kurtz, and Uma Thurman also landed parts. Uma was so new that I didn't know who she was, but after I saw a picture and some tape I knew she had what it took to be seduced by Malkovich, yet stand up to him at the same time. We hung out a bit during the shoot, and one night Mo Ostin, a friend and the former head of Warner Brothers Records (he now runs the DreamWorks label), invited me to a Prince concert in Paris. I took Uma. We walked in just before Prince went on and fifteen thousand Frenchmen whistled. She was eighteen. I was fifty-seven. Our relationship was purely platonic but I felt eighteen myself.

Forman's picture was scheduled for 1989. I wanted ours out by December 21, 1988, for Academy Award consideration; we'd go wide after New Year. Frears only had six weeks of preproduction before principal photography began, and he used it to vet the cast and locations.

We started filming in May. There were few if any problems. My only tough call came on the second day. Ileen had warned me of a situation between Frears and Malkovich. When Frears rang he said, "I don't think Malkovich is going to cut it." Malkovich was willful and opinionated; he could blend the hard and soft aspects of personality seamlessly, and you never knew which facet would show next. Frears also had a mind of his own. I tried to imagine the culture shock of an English director watching Malkovich, whose period accent was at best indeterminate, playing Valmont — and then the two strong personalities colliding. Frears knew I would never get rid of Malkovich because he had made the movie happen by committing early. But I also wouldn't undercut my director. I had to let Frears know. "Stephen," I asked, "what does it say on the back of your chair?"

He said, "Director."

"Then go out and tell Malkovich what you want him to do, and that's that." He did and that was the end of it.

Christopher Hampton was also on the set every minute. Not only was he a producer, but if we had to change a line or cut something to save money, he could write it on the spot.

Everything was going well until, as the ten-week shooting schedule drew to a close, we couldn't figure out how to end the picture. The play finishes with the idle rich being guillotined, but we couldn't wrap a movie that way. No one had any ideas. I packed up and went to France to help figure things out. When I arrived, Glenn Close called me at my hotel and said, "I have the ending. Meet me at the bar at the Ritz with Ileen."

Over drinks Glenn said, "Bernie, you've seen the dailies of the opening scene, where I put on my makeup? What I want to do is take off my makeup at the end." That was perfect, and that's what we did.

Six weeks after shooting ended, Frears showed me a rough cut. It was great, but at the first screening, people walked out because it seemed like Malkovich had actually fist-fucked Uma Thurman in the seduction scene. Over Malkovich's objections we later made it less graphic.

After the screening, Warner Brothers Pictures co-chairmen Bob Daly and Terry Semel also came over. Before they could say anything I said, "Just don't fuck with the fade," meaning the ending, where Glenn Close took off her makeup. Frears loved that and later told me, "This has been a very, very good job." He'd made his film quickly, and with virtually no studio interference. A few years and a few pictures later, he said about *Dangerous Liaisons,* "I didn't know that's the best it would ever get."

Dangerous Liaisons was nominated for seven Academy Awards and won three. My name wasn't on the movie; I was just head of the studio, but Christopher Hampton thanked me from the podium. After the show, other cast members called with congratulations. I've always been quick to credit my clients instead of myself for their successes — I'm the sales, customer support, and strategy department — but I'll gladly take a bow for *Dangerous Liaisons.* Without me the picture wouldn't have happened. I pressed the "go" button. I said yes. The cast and crew made it great, but I believed in it. That's why I always say I want my tombstone to read: "Bernie Brillstein: from *Hee Haw* to *Dangerous Liaisons.*"

I like to think that had time not run out for the Lorimar movie division, I might have had the chance to feel that good more often.

· · · · ·

Just as Merv had promised, I was elected to the Lorimar board of directors. It was March 1, 1988. I couldn't have been happier. Eight days later, Merv announced that he was negotiating with Warner Communications to sell the company. The newspapers called it a merger, but it seemed more like an outright sale to me. Merv had kept me in the dark. I was stunned and angry, not because I didn't know we had problems, but because Merv had given in so soon. Only a couple weeks earlier I had walked by an open office door and heard the term "golden bullet." I asked my lawyer, Jake Bloom, what that meant. "A golden bullet means that you're being shot by the creditors," he said. "In other words, no one wants to give the company any more credit. You're tapped out."

Now I knew it was true. Lorimar-Telepictures had serious financial problems.

While I worked to turn around the movie division, with some small success, the rest of the company had come apart. A year earlier Lorimar had taken a $37 million write-down on bad debt from independent TV stations that, hit by advertising losses, couldn't pay for our programming. Then Merv scuttled his diversification plans and sold off pieces of the store: our five small TV stations, the publishing division, the ad agency. Our new mandate: focus on the core businesses — TV, movies, and home video.

TV was the cash cow. Lorimar was the largest supplier of prime-time programming to the three networks (eight and a half hours), the biggest supplier of first-run syndication (eleven and a half hours), and the number-one supplier of first-run children's programming (seven and a half hours). Even the movie division was finally headed in the right direction after taking millions in write-offs for five years, including almost $85 million since the 1986 merger. But the big blow came from our home-video business. The founder, Stuart Karl, was a onetime water-bed salesman who had made a fortune with Jane Fonda's fitness tapes before selling his company to Lorimar in 1984. It was a deal similar to the one Merv had made with me, and Karl stayed on to run things. But one day, to Merv and everyone else's shock and surprise, Lorimar discovered that Karl had been accepting video returns and not reporting them. We later found warehouses full of cassettes. No one understood how it had gone undetected for so long, but the upshot was that instead of making a projected $150 million in profit, we lost $200 million. It was a negative swing of vast proportions, and after Karl was ousted, more write-offs followed. By the time I joined the board, the $250 million Merv said I had available for making movies had shrunk considerably, while our overall debt had skyrocketed.

That was enough to make any company stagger. At least Merv was honest enough to blame the movie losses on the previous management. The media wasn't so kind; even if I wasn't wholly responsible for the deficit, they still criticized me for not having made a more dramatic turnaround even though I'd only been in my job little more than a year. I still thought we could make it work.

Merv didn't.

Rumors immediately surfaced that the first victim of any sale would be my film company. Warners already had a strong movie division run by Bob Daly and Terry Semel. They didn't need me. That scared me. Having once called the shots, I couldn't go backwards and become some anonymous vice president at Warner Pictures. My only hope was that Warner Communications chairman Steve Ross would let me oversee Lorimar Film Entertainment as a "label" under the Warner Brothers umbrella.

Ross asked Bob Daly to oversee the merger process and perform due diligence. Daly had an accounting background and was vocally against the buyout. He thought it was a big hassle, but he had to do the job. If Ross wanted to test the whole idea on the merger's toughest critic, it was a smart or lucky move.

After only a month the merger stalled. Depending on whom you talk to, Warner Communications' offer wasn't big enough or Lorimar wasn't worth what Merv wanted. I'd vote for the latter. The video division's fiasco had really screwed us.

As part of the process, Merv showed Daly the first-draft scripts of the movies I had in production. I'd asked him not to because they wouldn't present an accurate picture. He did anyway, and I think Daly used them as ammunition to lower the buyout price, and suddenly the merger was back on. Merv later sent me a long handwritten letter on yellow legal paper in which he apologized. He said it was "a strange time and we were under a great deal of pressure." I accepted his word, but at the time I was terribly hurt and, let's face it, embarrassed by the first drafts. They weren't great.

Once the talks were back on track I got a call from Warner Communications chairman Steve Ross. He wanted all the Lorimar bosses to come to New York for individual meetings before the board of directors voted on the sale. I was happy to oblige. If my company was going to be sold, I definitely wanted to meet the buyer and solidify whatever position I had — or thought I could salvage.

Chapter 13

Never Trust a Man
Who Walks You to the
Elevator with His
Arm Around
Your Shoulders

I walked into Steve Ross's Rockefeller Center office in late April 1988. A tall, thin, handsome guy, impressive in a beautiful suit, stood to greet me. His hair was gray-white and well manicured. Ross smiled and shook my hand. We'd met before, briefly, at *Saturday Night Live* — he was a friend of Lorne's. When Ross died, Lorne produced the memorial service at Carnegie Hall — but I already knew all about him.

Steven J. Ross began his business life as a clothing salesman. He went to work for the Riverside Funeral Home on West Seventy-sixth Street in Manhattan when he married the owner's daughter. It was a popular place. My whole family was "undertaken" there; we used to have a private joke about being buried "down by the Riverside."

Ross showed an early talent for deal-making when he began leasing out at night the limousines used for funerals. Next he started a car-rental business. It almost went under, but Ross convinced Kinney Service Corp., the city's biggest parking-lot operator, to give his rental cars free parking in exchange for a percentage of the rental company and the use of their name. It worked, and Ross formed a new company that included the parking lots, the funeral home, and an office-cleaning business, and went public. A couple years later, after merging with National Cleaning Contractors, the company became Kinney National Service Inc. and went on a buying spree. In 1967 Kinney purchased the Ashley–Famous Talent Agency. Two years later, they snapped up the Warner–Seven Arts movie and Warner Brothers record business. In 1971, the company sold the funeral business, spun off the parking lots and real estate — while retaining half ownership — bought a couple cable companies, and changed the corporate name to Warner Communications.

From the time he took over as chairman of Warner Communications until his death at the end of 1991, Ross was the emperor who made sure each of the company's divisions were run by someone he loved and trusted. And overpaid. Heading a Warner Communications division became a pretty sweet deal. Ross gave each chief virtual autonomy and unwavering loyalty, because he knew that the one thing that doesn't come easily in this business is stability. When Bob Daly and Terry Semel became co-chairmen of Warner Pictures, they knew Ross would back them even if they had ten flops in a row. It didn't matter. Ross figured that the next one would be a *Superman* or *Batman* if they stayed in the ball game long enough. He was right. When Daly and Semel finally announced their exit from Warners in July 1999, they'd been together nineteen years. Their movie division had placed first eight times and second five times. They'd seen production heads come and go, fought intracorporate battles, vanquished powerful foes, and in the end reigned over movies, TV, and music. They were like the Borgias: smart and dangerous. They had the best racket in the business.

Ross could also be lavish. The company had hideaways in Acapulco and Aspen and apartments in New York, which he often lent out. He'd buy gifts and send people on cruises. He figured out that show-business people would do anything for a free plane trip (and then brag about it), so he doled out rides on a Warners corporate jet — there were seven; he had his own private air force — when it seemed like a good idea. Meanwhile, Ross left the hands-on work to his team and exercised his power when necessary, knowing that the best measure of power is not having to use it often.

Ross may have had a skyscraper office, but he was from Flatbush, in Brooklyn. He had a reputation as a street guy who knew how to talk to people. I thought he'd immediately understand someone like me, which was good, because it looked like I'd soon be working for him. Lorimar was almost out of cash. The officers had lots of stock, but the price was low and going down. If we swapped it for Warner Communications securities at least there'd be an upside, because Ross knew how to run a business. In fact, he'd just recovered from a few years of his own corporate financial hell. Warners had lost almost $1 billion on the Atari video game unit, and Ross had had to pare down and focus on his core businesses: the movie studio, records, and cable. Now he'd made the money back and more, and wanted to grow. Lorimar, especially our TV division, was a prime acquisition.

I was torn. I wish Merv had found a way to hang in there, because I loved my job and I believed we could have rebuilt the company. I had told him and anyone else who would listen about Brad: "You have the guy here to run your company one day." But Merv was determined to sell, and I figured I'd at least get some good stock out of the deal — and with any luck my own boutique movie studio.

My meeting with Ross was pleasant enough, and I told him I was concerned with being able to continue making movies.

"Bernie, you can have your own motion-picture division," he said. "Of course you'll have to distribute the movies through our distribution system because I'm not going to build a separate one for you. I already did that for Laddie"— the Ladd Company —"and that was a failure."

"No problem," I said.

"You can do four or five movies a year. Don't worry."

I'd made a lot of money for Lorimar and saw no reason why Ross shouldn't consider me a valuable piece of manpower. I also knew that because I was on the Lorimar board of directors, he wanted me to vote for the merger. Other people — oil-and-entertainment baron Marvin Davis among them — had already made noises about buying Lorimar, so it didn't hurt for Ross to smooth the edges and take out some insurance by calming Lorimar employee concerns in advance.

Ross gave me his home number and two office numbers, including his private line. He told me to call him anytime I needed. Then he walked me to the elevator with his arm around my shoulders, reassuring me all the way.

• • • • •

By the time I got back to Los Angeles, Ross had issued this statement in anticipation of the merger:

> With Lorimar-Telepictures, we will immediately become the top company in television programming. Lorimar's strength in television includes a library of popular situation comedies with tremendous value in the syndication market, as well as the

industry's leading operations in both network programming and first-run syndication. We will be particularly delighted to have Merv Adelson on our board as vice chairman, bringing to us an exceptional record of achievement in the entertainment industry. Equally valuable is the creative leadership of Lorimar's people, including David Salzman, Dick Robertson, Michael Solomon, and Bernie Brillstein.

The movie company wasn't mentioned, but I was, which made me breathe a little easier, and a week later I returned to New York for the final Lorimar board of directors vote on the merger. It was probably all for the best, and I tried to be upbeat, but I felt like I was going to a funeral orchestrated by a guy who used to run a funeral parlor. My mood must have shown because MCA chairman Lew Wasserman, who was also on my flight, came over and said, "I'm going to call the office. I'll get the numbers and see how much your stock is rising because of the buyout."

The guy could be a tough sonofabitch, but he'd always been gracious to me. Now and then I'd see him at Nate & Al's deli in Beverly Hills when he came in with his grandchildren on Sunday mornings. He finished the call and told me the stock was up, then we started talking. And somewhere over the Midwest he said this magic line: "Bernie, there's only two of us left."

I felt awkward, as if DiMaggio had said, "Boy, Bernie, you have a great swing." I also felt great. You live for moments like that, when your hero, the man after whom you pattern your whole approach to business, tells you that he thinks your sensibilities are alike. He wasn't comparing us in any other way; even if he was, I would never be presumptuous enough to think so. Anyway, he'd said enough. And he was right. We thought the same: control the talent, follow your instinct, bet on yourself.

The next morning I awoke feeling weird. Something wasn't right; nothing specific, just — as Obi-Wan Kenobi might say — a disturbance in the Force. I showered but couldn't stop thinking that after the board of directors vote, all the Lorimar guys would somehow be fucked. The feeling stayed with me while I dressed for the 9 A.M. meeting, so just before I walked out the door I picked up the phone and called Peter Chernin and Ileen Maisel, both of whom worked for me. It was a quarter to six in the morning L.A. time. I said, "Green-light *Dangerous Liaisons.* Send out the confirmation wires immediately — I mean right now — because I'm going to have nothing to say about anything when this merger happens. I just know it. I'm ordering you to do it. Now."

I had no reason to believe that Warners had a problem with *Dangerous Liaisons*, but I wasn't taking any chances. The wires committed Lorimar to the movie. Had Warners wanted to stop now, it would have cost them about $7 million. I don't know where I got the balls at the last minute to pull a stunt like that; all I know is that I loved the picture and wanted to see it get made.

The Lorimar board of directors voted for the sale, a deal valued at about $700 million in stock, plus Warners taking on about $600 million in Lorimar debt. And that was that. Pending the final sign-off, which could take a year, Lorimar and all its assets, including The Brillstein Company, was now virtually part of Warner Communications. Steve Ross was in control.

I took the next plane back to Los Angeles. When I got to my office I found a note on my desk. The gist was this: I wasn't allowed to spend more than a hundred grand on anything without Bob Daly's approval.

I hit the roof. I was right. Someone got fucked and it was me. What a slap in the face. How dare he? I expected changes but I believed I'd earned Ross's confidence. This was a nightmare. Forget doing four or five movies a year; I couldn't even put a script into development without asking Bob Daly. Steve Ross had lied to me and through Daly imposed an extreme limit on my discretionary spending powers. For a second I believed it might be payback for approving *Dangerous Liaisons* at the last minute, but the more I thought about it I realized he didn't even think on that level. He just wanted the deal to close and he did what he had to do. I was out before I even thought I was in.

For the first time I knew the hollow feeling of having my power instantly sucked out into a vacuum. I hadn't been fired, just neutered, and it hurt. All I cared about was continuing with the movies. I'd gotten so emotionally involved that I'd let Ross set me up and get my vote based on my all too obvious desire to be a somebody.

There was more. Because Warners owned The Brillstein Company, I also had to submit an operating budget and get approval for any expenditures there. I'd never had to pay attention to a budget under Lorimar. If I wanted to give Brad or Sandy a raise, I'd go to Merv and say so. Now, I had to ask Daly, and when I did he said, "You can't." I was humiliated. I was boxed in.

Later, Warner even tried to stick me with my expense bill in Paris on *Dangerous Liaisons*. They said no one okayed it.

I would have liked to share my feelings of betrayal with Steve Ross, but when I called the numbers he'd given me, there was no return call.

Ever since, I've never trusted a man who walks me to the elevator with his arm around my shoulders.

• • • • •

That summer Bob Daly wanted to see my films in progress. We set up screenings. I knew he'd decide how long to keep Lorimar Pictures alive based on his reaction. Sad to say, Daly was lukewarm to disappointed about the movies I believed were good, like Henson's *The Witches*, *Dangerous Liaisons*, and *See You in the Morning*.

Penn and Teller Get Killed, which I thought was hilarious, he hated.

Penn and Teller are well-known magicians and quite unique. Others may practice sleight of hand; they're best at sleight of mind. Penn is a huge guy with a ponytail, glasses, and enough wit for two people, which is a good thing, because in public Teller is always mute. Their ICM agent, Sam Cohn, sent them to me with a bizarre movie idea — about two guys who do magic — that I thought could make them into a cult phenomenon.

We got Arthur Penn to direct and made the film for under $5 million. Before the screening I told Daly, "When you show this, please don't do it for four guys alone. It's a comedy. Please have an audience. Secretaries. Office boys. Whatever."

That afternoon that audience was Bob Daly, Lisa Henson, Warner Pictures executive Mark Canton, and I. The screening was like death. Even Lisa, the daughter of my oldest client, just stared. I sat there steamed that Daly hadn't listened. If that was what working with him would be like, I didn't stand a chance.

Afterwards, Daly and I faced off in front of the Executive Office building. He said, "This movie is morally reprehensible."

"Why?"

"Because it seems like Penn and Teller actually kill themselves," he said.

"But they don't."

We'd even added a voice-over with the end credits: "We're not really dead. It's just a joke. We'll be back for the sequel." It was very bizarre. Daly was being too Catholic in his approach. Maybe the movie wasn't for everyone, but it was funny and I thought the business needed a comedy team again.

Not that I said it in those words. I got crazy. "Do you believe that when Slim Pickens rode the bomb in *Dr. Strangelove* the world *really* ended?" I spat. "Morally reprehensible? Look at the movies you make!" I think the first *Lethal Weapon* had come out and the second was in production. "You've made movies with guns and killing. That's morally reprehensible!"

For better or worse I screamed my way through an impassioned defense of the picture. I was also venting my frustration at the last six months' events. I took the whole thing personally. I can't help it, that's me. I get emotional first. Daly didn't respond well to my anger.

Canton and Lisa Henson stood to one side watching. I saw Terry Semel walk out of the Executive Office building door and spot us. He didn't want any part of the fight and he slipped back inside. Finally, I had nothing left to say. My car was right at the curb. I got in and drove away.

You can't curse the co-chairman of Warner Brothers Pictures and expect him to forget about it the next day, but for some reason he let me supervise the movies I still had in production. I did, with Peter Chernin's help, and Peter took the brunt of Daly's discontent. Peter's since done great. He's the number-two guy to Rupert Murdoch at Fox.

After the Penn and Teller incident I spent most of my time back at The Brillstein Company. I dealt with my anger not by confronting Daly directly but by being a pain in the ass for months, telling everyone I could how he'd treated me. I thought I was a wonderful person no one should fuck with.

When *Dangerous Liaisons* was a hit and got Oscar nominations, I let that smoke blow right up my ass and carry me away. Instead of backing off in success, I battled harder. I deserved to take some bows for the movie, but Warners didn't deserve me saying how stupid they were to let me go when I'd been responsible for such a fine film. I was just so embarrassed that everything had turned to shit. I didn't want to go out a loser.

Once, because I was so pissed at not being king anymore, I spoke up in the press. Daly buried me with a few words: "All I can tell you," he said, "is that when the deal with Lorimar is closed, Warner Brothers will own what Lorimar owned and that includes The Brillstein Company."

I'm sure Daly wished that Lorimar Pictures and Bernie Brillstein had never happened. To him I was just a guy who had the nerve to think he was a genius and wanted an autonomous film division — something not then possible at Warners. I wanted Daly to live by my rules because I was still years away from realizing that the world doesn't work that way.

My problem was that I didn't want to accept that the merger had really been a buyout. When Michael Eisner bought ABC, Tom Murphy was out, just like Merv was out. And, as show-business history dictates, all of Merv's people were out. I didn't want that. I loved being the buyer, the studio head, the guy with the perceived power. But it was over. That change is very tough, especially when you like your job, and your emotion gets in the way of logical, rational, pragmatic business thinking about what to do next.

I don't blame Daly anymore. He was just Ross's executioner. He represented his company. It wasn't personal until I made it personal. In fact, I'm sure I would have done exactly what he did to an employee of mine who overrated his importance. Even if my TV shows and a couple movies made the company money, it was just a speck compared to the cash they were already generating. I was wrong to go after Bob Daly. It was stupid. If I had to take anything back, that would be it.

Warner Communications slowly absorbed Lorimar like a snake digesting a mouse, and many people lost their jobs — except in the TV division. Warners inherited our good shows, our number-one syndicator ranking, our income stream, and executives like Les Moonves, who developed *Friends* and *E.R.*, among others, when he later became president of Warner Brothers Television. Now Les runs CBS. Even though Daly was originally against the acquisition, Ross made a smart move. Warner Brothers TV is incredibly strong today, a billion-dollar enterprise — and it's all based on what we had.

• • • • •

Just before the merger became official at the end of 1988, I resigned from the Lorimar board and began a torturous negotiation to end my association with Warner Communications entirely. I believed the future was with Brad. I wanted to make him a partner and change the company name to Brillstein-Grey. I wanted to do business without Warners being entitled to any income from new projects. And I wanted to do it quickly. I worried that with Daly controlling the budget, Brad might not stick around, because it was clear that he wasn't being fairly compensated for all the income he'd brought in — especially since he hadn't shared in the proceeds of Merv's buyout. Brad told me that Daly had approached him with the idea of working at Warners, but that he'd declined. That kind of loyalty when things were such a mess deserved some payback, and I didn't want to make him wait two years.

In order for me to regain the Brillstein name and my freedom, Daly wanted in perpetuity any income from *Ghostbusters, ALF,* and *Love Connection* — which was a lot. The movie continues to make money, a *Ghostbusters 3* is planned, and both TV shows still play in syndication. Daly chose the big things. He's not stupid. Everyone extracts their pound of flesh. At first I said, "Fuck them," but Daly was in no hurry. He had me under contract. He could wait until I was ready to say yes.

Because I was so pissed, it took a year and a couple lawyers to negotiate an end to the deal. I finally agreed to terms when I figured out that I'd oversold my soul to Lorimar, that it had turned out poorly — largely for reasons having nothing to do with me — and I should just get on with my life and my plans with Brad. The decision was made a little easier because I was in profit at Warners; that is, entitled to a percentage of the $8 million or so that had accrued after the initial $26 million payout was recovered. I don't like looking back and try to have few regrets, but over the years Warners has made a fortune from the stuff I traded away.

Prior to signing the settlement, around Christmas 1990, Daly and Semel and Brad and I had lunch at the elegant Warner Brothers dining room and buried the hatchet. After salads and speculation about where the business was headed, Daly even suggested we could still stay with Warners under a new deal. I know that seems strange given all the animosity, but Daly thought it would be good business to have us around as suppliers of talent and programming. (He was right, as our post-Warners track record indicates.) We listened to his proposal, but it still included budgetary restrictions and Warners owning our income stream. We said, "No, that's not for us."

In the end, I walked away from Warners with $3 to $4 million. I'd had enough frustration and unhappiness to last a lifetime. Now I just wanted it behind me. The important thing was that once again I was free to bet on myself.

• • • • •

Lorimar and Warner Brothers were far from my final foray into the movies, and many of the lessons I'd learned would come in handy. It's important to remember the past because, as my experience a few years later with *The Cable Guy* proves, those who ignore movie history are doomed to make the same film again and again.

I first heard of *The Cable Guy* when Ari Emanuel and Tom Strickler of the Endeavor Agency called and said they had a "great script" for me that "only you would understand." I didn't take that as an ego stroke. In Hollywoodese that meant they were having trouble setting up the movie and thought maybe I could help.

I read the script right away and loved it. So did our client Chris Farley. His manager, Marc Gurvitz, and I talked to the agents and decided to submit the project to Columbia Pictures, where we had a production arrangement.

Boom. Deal. Studio head Mark Canton bought the script with Farley attached. Word went out to the trades.

Everything seemed great, until for no apparent reason Columbia dragged its heels on making Farley's deal. We knew we had trouble. If the other guys don't call you right back when you're in the middle of a negotiation, then something is up that you don't know about — and *should* know about. Our instinct was that they wanted to lowball the offer to Farley.

When Columbia finally called, all they would say was that Brad and I had to come over right away.

Mark Canton's office — once my office when I was at Lorimar — was on the third floor of the Thalberg Building, on what was now the Columbia lot, because when Warners bought Lorimar they got the lot that they later traded to Columbia for the Columbia lot in Burbank that was adjacent to the Warner's lot. Anyway, it always made me uncomfortable to go back there.

Brad and I knew the meeting hadn't been called on account of good news. We weren't expecting to hear, "Hey fellas, no problems, let's do this movie." So we decided to simply shut up and listen — which is what smart people do.

With Canton were Fred Bernstein, the Columbia business-affairs guy, and Barry Josephson, their head of production. An assistant asked if we wanted anything to drink. "Perrier? Diet Coke? Coffee?" Good thing there were only five of us. A few more people and it would have seemed like we were on a airplane. Then there was some small talk about relationships, movie grosses, other projects, and Canton's golf game — he and I had played the week before. Just like a comedian warms up sitcom audiences, this was their prelude to set the mood before getting to the real reason they'd called the meeting.

Finally, Canton said, "Guys, we have a problem here. Somehow — we don't know how — the script got to Jim Carrey."

I considered that for a minute, and then a little movie popped into my head. Obviously, Canton meant that the script, while sitting on his desk, suddenly thought, "I'm right for Jim Carrey," grew legs, hopped to the floor, snuck out of the studio and onto the street in Culver City, hailed a cab, *knew* Jim Carrey's address, delivered itself to his house, picked the lock, got inside, made a stiff drink and a couple long-distance phone calls, waited on the couch until Carrey came home, and, when he walked in and flipped on the light, announced itself brightly by saying; "Hi there. Read me. I'm your next movie!"

We knew Canton had sent it over. We're not dopes! But we couldn't do anything about it now, and Canton wanted our support for the change. Then he said, possibly as a consolation prize, "We're thinking about this for the summer." Thinking? It was already a done deal.

I could imagine how things had gone down around the Columbia offices. First, high fives: "We have Jim Carrey!" The memo/word spreads. New York. Tokyo. Sony Pictures boss Alan Levine to Sony's top American guy, Mickey Schulhoff: "We have our summer movie, we have Jim Carrey." Now it's in gold. They set a release date, June 14. A memo goes out and every other studio pulls away from the date, because who wants to contend with a Jim Carrey movie? Mark Canton, who set it in motion, is a hero for a minute and a half. He feels good.

We understood. Like all beleaguered studio chiefs in this post-*Jaws*, post-*Star Wars* (and now post-*Titanic*) era, he was desperate for a hit. But not just any hit. Canton's other films hadn't done well and he was trapped between a rock and a hard place. He couldn't get by smacking singles and doubles anymore. He needed a home run. Even since the studio's parent company, Sony, had overpaid Canton's predecessors and taken a huge loss, they'd been on a losing streak. Sony's desperate need for a win and Canton wanting to keep his job collided ominously. Jim Carrey's interest was the answer to his prayers, a serendipitous moment, the cleanup hitter on a hot streak coming to the plate with the bases loaded. If I were Canton I would have done the same thing.

Brad and I shared a look. We were probably thinking the same things: We loved Chris Farley and wanted to look out for his interests. On the other hand, we might be executive producers of a Jim Carrey film that suddenly had "big summer movie" written all over it. The question was, how could we protect Farley first, and then ourselves?

In these situations, some manager whose client has just been unceremoniously dropped might say, "Fuck you, we're going to sue," and walk away. But what would that have accomplished? Nothing, except that we wouldn't be on the picture and it would hurt our position when we tried to get Farley paid off. Maybe Columbia hoped we'd walk off in anger, making it easy for them. We have a reputation as strong, volatile guys. But we stayed put and kept quiet. Our silence threw the ball back into Canton's court.

Canton said that because we'd brought him the script, we'd of course stay as executive producers of the film — along with Carrey's managers, Eric Gold and Jimmy Miller. Brad and I said we'd get back to him after we talked about it. And the meeting ended.

Did we feel we'd been sold out? That was an easy case to make. Canton had mistreated Farley and us. In fact, he could have cost us Chris Farley as a client, because Farley could have said we'd sold *him* out by not fighting successfully to keep him in the movie. Fortunately, because we'd always been honest with him, Farley knew that we'd never sell him out. Believe me, it's always the buyer who sells you out, not the manager.

We could have been out as producers as well. But Canton wouldn't have dared fuck us. It wasn't smart. We'd brought him the script. We'd bring others. A first-look deal. We had a relationship. Sometimes the small talk when a meeting begins is about the most important stuff.

Brad and I went directly to the Peninsula Hotel in Beverly Hills, where we hooked up with Gurvitz. We told him what had happened. He also had news. After *Tommy Boy*, Paramount had the right to use Farley (and David Spade) in another film. With *Tommy Boy* a hit, Paramount's head, Jonathan Dolgen, didn't want to let Farley delay or out of his option. Farley could still have said no and caused trouble, but that didn't happen because Chris had, coincidentally, second thoughts about *The Cable Guy*. This is typical. Actors often make verbal commitments and then change their minds at the last minute. It was a stroke of luck for us. Columbia didn't know about the Paramount option or Farley losing interest in *The Cable Guy*, and we didn't tell them. Instead we got them to do right by "poor Chris" and ended up getting him not *full* salary but a lot of real world, substantial money. And we were still executive producers of a script that we loved, with a star who'd had only hits.

We were relieved. We'd dodged a bullet. Then Canton told us he'd agreed to pay Carrey $20 million to do the movie.

Show-business truth: when an actor has a huge hit, studios *throw* money at him. Before *The Cable Guy*, Carrey had three hits in a row: *Ace Ventura*, *The Mask*, and *Dumb and Dumber*. But I still thought Canton was nuts to pay him $20 million, and not that smart for Carrey to take it. It's tough for any comedian to stretch dramatically (such as my uncle Jack, Woody Allen, Jerry Lewis, Robin Williams) and have audiences accept it right off the bat. The transition usually takes a few films. To attach such a high payday to the first experiment can only come back to haunt the talent if the movie bombs. It looks like the actor's greedy for money he doesn't deserve. Even if he's entitled to every penny, perception usually trumps reality. Stretching is fine, but for that kind of money and risk, you give the people what they want: A Jim Carrey movie. A big comedy. If you want to show your versatility, do Broadway! Or do it like Nick Cage in *Leaving Las Vegas*. He took $250,000. Won himself an Oscar. Doing something good never hurt anyone, even if you get no money for it.

Of course, other actors endorsed Carrey's big raise, particularly those who thought that if Carrey was worth $20 million, they were worth the same, if not more. They were correct. There was an industry-wide sucking sound and the money bags opened. Tom Cruise, Harrison Ford, Mel Gibson, Tom Hanks, Arnold Schwarzenegger, Sly Stallone, John Travolta, etc., all demanded equivalent compensation. Demi Moore even got $12 million for showing her tits in *Striptease*, and other popular actresses got big raises for more meritorious reasons.

Now, every time a headline blares some actor's new fee, all the agents in town with clients on that level think, "Oh boy!" Fear strikes because they know we all read the same papers, and somewhere an actor's wife, husband, lawyer, business manager, or a friend is saying, "How come you're not getting as much?" Then the agent gets the angry or anxious call. In other words, every time something good happens, something bad happens. And you wonder why this business is so screwed up.

Meanwhile, the actors think, "I'm getting twelve million and that cocksucker's getting fifteen million?" Or, "If he's getting fifteen million and I'm getting twenty million, then I deserve fifty million." It's rare for an actor to tell another, "Congratulations, pal."

Is there a right price? No. If it's a hit, it wasn't enough. If it was a bomb, it was way too much. The right price is whatever you can get. I ask myself, "Is the talent hot or cold? Does he need the job? What's the mortgage on the house?" There are always eight thousand reasons for whatever amount an actor takes, and, in the end, no one ever remembers until it's time to negotiate the next film.

Here's a better question: Is any actor worth that much money?

Depends on the movie as much as on the actor. Studios pay the big money and think it's worth it because they believe these actors can "open" a picture; that is, get people into the theaters those first few weekends just to see them on screen. Too bad it's not an exact science. What happens if a studio pays a lot for a hot name, but eighteen months later when their picture opens they're already a thing of the past?

A better system would be to make actors who get big money partners with the studio. Let them get a smaller salary versus a percentage of gross receipts. If the picture makes money — like *Titanic* — or any number of more reasonably budgeted pictures that really score — Adam Sandler's *The Wedding Singer* or *The Waterboy* or Cameron Diaz's *There's Something About Mary* — the actors share the profits. If the picture loses $70 million, they get their guarantee and no more.

Of course, I've been asked, "Bernie, if you'd managed Jim Carrey, wouldn't you have tried to get him the twenty million?"

It's a fine line. I want to get as much as I can for my client, but at the same time, I don't want to be so outrageous that it reaches the point of diminishing returns or stretches the fabric of reality beyond recognition. You have a responsibility to your client not to expose him or her to failure. Even if you can get, say, $10 million, you also have to think about getting $15 million the next time, or at least the same $10 million. You have to choose based on the picture and the entire working situation, not the paycheck, because you'd like that kind of money to go on for years. The same principle applies to any client at any salary. You have to protect them.

Turn the situation around. An actor gets $20 million. He has a bomb. Then another, and another. Now he's a $20 million guy whom nobody wants to pay that much money anymore. What does he do? Does he gracefully leave the business, or does he reinvent himself at $8 million — if he can get even that? Some actors can actually shorten their careers by reaching the heights too soon, especially if their ego won't let them take a job for a lousy $5 million.

The only time it's just about money is when that's what the client wants. With successful actors that usually happens in the middle of a career. Sensing the opportunity (and time running out), they go on a cash run and do as many pictures as possible for a few years just to accumulate their retirement savings. Then, it's back to carefully chosen roles with money in the bank. Look at De Niro. Or Sharon Stone. Or Dustin Hoffman. They've all made pictures for the money. Maybe that's not artistically pure, but it's still better than working only once every three years.

The first thing we did as executive producers on *The Cable Guy* was meet with Carrey's managers, Jimmy Miller and Eric Gold. (Miller is comedian Dennis Miller's little brother. We, however, manage Dennis. Go figure.)

Carrey was now the movie's thousand-pound gorilla, so Miller and Gold told us they'd decided to bring in Judd Apatow, whom they managed, for a script rewrite and Ben Stiller to direct. Both young men were good friends with Carrey. And why not? If you control the talent you have the power. If you have the power you bring in whomever you want. Our talent was off the picture. Being executive producers sounds good, means little. We were fifth wheels. We could only nod our heads and hope for the best.

When we saw the rewrite we hated it. You always expect a few changes, but for some reason a script that was somewhat dark to begin with was now much darker. Very dark. I mean *really* dark. But that's what Carrey wanted and Canton had signed off. It was out of our hands, but I didn't plan to sit on the sidelines and just collect the money. There's no rule that says we had to play dumb. We dutifully submitted our comments. I remember one in particular about a moment when Jim Carrey's character staples Matthew Broderick's character to something. Not a comedy highlight, if you ask me.

I spoke up because I'd been through a similar situation in which expectations for a highly anticipated film were subverted. I explained to

Canton that in 1981 my clients John Belushi and Dan Aykroyd had made *Neighbors*. The picture was also a bit dark for comedy stars who appealed to a more sophomoric crowd, but that might not have mattered if something else hadn't happened. Originally, Danny was going to play the regular guy and John his weird neighbor. But at the last minute, just before principal photography, I got a call from Belushi, who said, "Danny and I were talking and we decided we'll do the movie only if we can switch roles."

I thought that was wrong. I figured people wanted to see Belushi as the crazy neighbor.

I said, "Are you sure?"

Belushi insisted he was, and I dropped it. Today I'd fight harder, but then I wasn't as smart as I am now. I went along with the party line, and so did the studio, because Belushi and Aykroyd had just come off *Blues Brothers*. Frank Price, who ran Columbia at the time; myself; Mike Ovitz, who was the boys' agent; and Dick Zanuck and David Brown, the producers — I think we're all pretty smart guys. But this was Belushi and Aykroyd, and the thousand-pound gorillas were running the show. Besides, we thought — and wanted to believe — that they knew something we didn't.

As soon as shooting began, we knew it was a mistake. You kept wanting Belushi to be Belushi, and he wasn't. Surely the audience would respond the same way. But the train had left the station and no one could stop it.

Why did Belushi and Aykroyd want to switch roles in the first place? Inside the soul of every comedian is a dramatic actor. Underneath that comic bearing is a guy who wants to be taken seriously. Jim Carrey didn't want to speak through Ace Ventura's ass forever. There's nothing wrong with a desire to grow. It's just about timing and perception.

We told Canton, "Go look at *Neighbors*." I don't know if he did.

A couple months later Brad and Gurvitz and I were summoned to Columbia to see ten minutes of the film. As we took our seats, they told us, "We loved this. We went nuts over this." Of course they'd say that. You figure if they're going to show you ten minutes, they're going to pick the best stuff.

What we saw may have been the best stuff, but it was still dark and terrible. We knew it was wrong. Afterwards, we called the studio and said, "You have a disaster here. I told you, I made this movie fifteen years ago. It's called *Neighbors*."

Canton said, "Please don't rock the boat. Please don't tell anyone that you don't like the ten minutes. You'll upset Jim, Judd, and Ben."

Even if Canton agreed with us — and I don't think he did — he was in a tough position. Imagine the balls it would take to ask Carrey to please be funnier, or to cut off the money. Canton didn't want to send *another* memo that read, "We're having trouble."

So Canton did nothing. Later, he would explain, "Once you start seeing results, once you start seeing dailies, it's difficult to pull back, because you've committed so much to that project. It's hard to be in halfway once the gun goes off."

The Cable Guy had underwhelming buzz and opened to mixed word of mouth. Columbia grossed about $75 to $80 million domestically, and a little more overseas. Financially speaking it wasn't that bad; the movie only cost about $47 million to make, including Carrey's paycheck, and the average studio film costs $35 to $50 million. (What's crazy is that movie studios usually make about fifteen films a year. Tell the head of any big corporation that you have fifteen new products and that you want him to invest an average of $35 to 50 million in each, *all in one year,* and I guarantee he'll say, "Are you insane?") Still, *The Cable Guy* was perceived as a major disappointment for a picture that Canton hoped would top $100 million and rule the summer. Did it hurt Jim Carrey, the director, the writers, or producers? No. Careers went on. Only Mark Canton suffered. He lost his job, watched as other films he green-lighted (*Men in Black, Jerry Maguire, My Best Friend's Wedding,* and others) went on to make a billion dollars, and saw the new studio chief, John Calley, bask in the warm glow of good fortune's smile.

Chapter 14

The Illusion of Power

Show business is as much about the illusion of power as it is about the power of illusion. In a town of manufactured images that runs on fear and the convenient blurring of perception and reality, it may seem tough to tell who has power and who doesn't. It's simple: real power is being able to say yes, then write the check without anyone else being able to say no. Maybe twenty people in town have real power; the rest of us just want to get those guys on the phone. Our leverage, clout, grease, edge, good will, connections . . . whatever, are measured by how quickly we get a return call, if we get one at all.

Once, power was in the hands of studio moguls like Mayer, Cohn, Warner, Zanuck, and Goldwyn. They may not seem like such big shots compared to today's entertainment conglomerate CEOs and self-made guys like David Geffen, George Lucas, and Steven Spielberg, but they were in some ways even mightier. Not only could they say yes, but they controlled the talent by *owning* the talent. Their stars had iron-clad contracts. Until television and government trust-busters forced the studio system to collapse, no one, no matter how big, worked without the studio boss's say-so. They decided which pictures got made and which didn't, who worked and how often. If Jimmy Cagney at Warner Brothers wanted to make a movie for Harry Cohn at Columbia, he had to get Jack Warner's permission. Depending on his mood, Warner could say either "Okay" or "Go fuck yourself." Now someone calls the agent and they work it out.

Today, CEOs like Michael Eisner, Barry Diller, Edgar Bronfman Jr.,

Rupert Murdoch, Gerald Levin, Sumner Redstone, and whoever else turns up in the future have the real power. They can buy and sell companies, build theme parks, direct their people to green-light pictures and approve TV shows. They can say yes and hand over the money.

But there's one big difference: they no longer control the talent.

Who does? The talent.

I don't like even nibbling at the hand that feeds me, but the whole business has paid a price for this shift in power. Just as in sports, where the rising cost of talent has caused family-owned teams like the Dodgers to be sold to guys like Rupert Murdoch as well as player lockouts, the supersized paydays of our top actors and actresses, and the lesser-but-still-large paychecks of second-tier talent, is one of many reasons why studios and networks let themselves be absorbed by conglomerates. They couldn't afford to stay in business. It was their only way to survive.

Here's the irony: it's our own fault. In order to get the talent bigger salaries, better parts, and more control over their professional lives, we trained them to be little businessmen — just like us. We taught them not to be loyal, because, after all, loyalty doesn't bring anyone the most money or the best opportunities in an actor-eat-actor world. Today loyalty means being perfectly loyal until a better offer comes along, and then it's "Thanks for everything. I was loyal until now. Good-bye." We traded in loyalty *and* stability for the short-term advantage.

Even though no one can turn back the clock and reestablish the old studio contract system — although even someone as powerful as Disney's movie chairman Joe Roth told the *Los Angeles Times* he would like to, not only for actors but for directors and producers — I think our business as a whole must regain some connection to and control over the process, and particularly the talent. If I put up $100 million for a movie, do I want some agent or manager dictating what I do? No. I want a relationship with the natural resource — the talent. So my instincts as a manager force me to ask this question: What does the talent want? The answer: To not feel afraid. They want security without sacrificing self-determination. They want to be able to bomb and not disappear from view. They want loyalty and stability, too. To get what you want you have to give what you want.

If I ran a studio (or network) I'd reopen the talent departments and start at the beginning. Think of it like baseball: The guy most valuable to the team is the talent scout out in the field. I'd get to the kids early, find the brightest prospects, and give them a try-out. If they make the team they get stability and loyalty, without having to sign up for seven years of servitude. The worst that can happen before some become big stars is that I get two or three projects out of them. Then when I have to pay more, I will, but it will be based on a relationship, not highway robbery. I figure that if I treat someone right they'll stick around and give me the next hit picture. Why should they go somewhere else? We're family. Why do you think Lorne Michaels stays at NBC? He knows his way around. He's comfortable. It feels like home.

Things used to work this way. Now everyone sits back and waits for agents or managers to bring them packages. I recently asked Time-Warner chairman Gerald Levin why he didn't just reopen the talent departments. He said he thought it was a good idea, but the look on his face said that he didn't know how to accomplish it. No wonder access to the talent has been replaced by access to managers, agents, and lawyers. No wonder we have problems.

Maybe it's wishful thinking, but however it's done, it's time to try *something* new. Agents and managers might have to take a cut in power, but it won't kill us if our talent is happy. Otherwise the inmates will continue to control the asylum and everything will spin hopelessly and expensively out of control.

• • • • •

For years the press called Mike Ovitz the most powerful man in show business. But, as author Frank Rose suggested in *Fortune* magazine, they didn't get it quite right. "It wasn't power Mike had, it was influence. The difference is between command and persuasion. [Ovitz] seemed to be in command because the top money-earners he represented [Tom Cruise, Tom Hanks, Kevin Costner, Sean Connery, Sylvester Stallone] enabled him to leverage his persuasiveness with threats."

The best we can do is influence talent, depending on their goals and our relationship. But that said, being in a position to influence them, or just being the conduit to the talent, counts for a lot to someone on the outside looking in. It creates the illusion that you have contact with everyone.

Ovitz took that illusion and ran with it because he understood that the town ran on ambition and fear. You were either a friend of CAA or you were the enemy.

Ovitz certainly had talent and drive. He built the Creative Artists Agency from scratch into the top star-broker in town, representing the biggest of the big. He criticized how huge corporations were run and then set himself up as advisor and go-between on deals that led to Sony buying Columbia and TriStar pictures, and to Matsushita buying MCA. He got into the executive job market, helped people get powerful positions, and then counted on their loyalty. He'd give one movie studio special attention and leave the others to vie over who would be next. He made alliances in Silicon Valley, hung out with investment bankers, and even got into the advertising business, for chrissakes. The man seemed like he was everywhere and nowhere. That's exactly the profile he wanted, and with the help of three publicists, this guy who never spoke to the press landed on magazine covers and on top of power lists. He'd played the image-manipulation game perfectly. He created himself for the press and let them create him in return.

But what did it add up to in the end? Ovitz still couldn't say yes to anything. Even when he worked at Disney, he couldn't green-light a movie or a TV show. Writer Rich Turner, in a *New York Magazine* piece on how the business is really full of shit, said it best: until he saw "A Mike Ovitz Production" on the big or little screen, he wouldn't think much of the guy because he'd never put himself on the line. Turner knew the emperor had no clothes. It's a great insight, if you ask me.

· · · · ·

For twenty years Ovitz ran CAA and then he abandoned ship. Why? He was tired of being the Mike Ovitz who had to take calls from whining clients asking about a script, a deal, whatever. I understand the feeling. It's part of why I sold The Brillstein Company to Lorimar. You reach a point where, because everything you have depends on your clients, you think if you get one more urgent phone call about some mundane thing you'll commit suicide. You feel too used up by the job. You want to be more creative. You want a different kind of power.

When Ovitz joined Disney many people wondered why he'd settle for being number two after being number one. I thought it was pretty clear: he was waiting for Eisner to have another heart attack, so he could take over. People even made jokes about it. One scenario had Ovitz hiding in the dark, ready to jump out and scare his new boss into cardiac arrest. Another had Ovitz tampering with Eisner's food. A former CAA colleague warned that Eisner should hire someone to taste all his meals. Anyone who knew Ovitz knew that he'd never be content as *a* player. He wanted to be *the* player. All he had to do was learn the business and bide his time.

For a guy who demanded complete loyalty, Ovitz fucked over everyone at CAA by leaving the company in May 1995 to negotiate a deal to run MCA. Companies had for years tried to hire Ovitz, but MCA seemed, finally, like the obvious move. Their empire was far flung and the stakes were big enough to satisfy Ovitz's ego. He had just helped MCA's owner, Matsushita, sell the studio to Seagram. His reward was an offer from Seagram CEO Edgar Bronfman Jr. to take the reins.

The news that Ovitz was in negotiations sent his shock troops into, well . . . shock. For years the guys at CAA had been like Hitler Youth, with Ovitz as their leader. They would go to the front for him. They'd kill for him. They'd die for him. If you fucked with anyone at CAA and they told him about it, he'd be on the phone with you in two seconds: "By insulting him, you're insulting my dignity and the dignity of my company. Don't fuck with him!" Boy, they were like an army.

Ovitz's CAA partners had a different point of view. He'd promised to take them all to MCA, give them great jobs and large sums of money — something agents never really get if they stay agents. The move to MCA would be their way to cash out. They were all counting on him.

It looked like a sure thing. Then Ovitz made a mistake.

He blew the deal.

He blew his own deal! Ovitz was too greedy and Seagram walked away. Edgar Bronfman Sr. (the father) probably called outgoing MCA chairman Lew Wasserman (the industry's elder statesman) at a crucial point in the negotiations, and said, "What do you think of this putz Ovitz?" Not being a big Ovitz supporter, Wasserman, I'm sure, said "pass." In other words, it came down to these two company patriarchs going, "Fuck him."

Wasserman didn't like Ovitz anyway. He and MCA president Sid Sheinberg were still upset that the sale of MCA to Matsushita a few years earlier — engineered by Ovitz — had turned out so badly. Yes, they'd both gotten richer when Matsushita bought their stock, and part of the deal kept Wasserman and Sheinberg on the job for five years. But the Japanese wouldn't invest in helping MCA grow — which was why they'd been convinced to sell out in the first place. MCA had opportunities to buy a network, a record company, and a cable franchise, but the Japanese just said no.

If Sony, who'd paid millions to buy Warner Brothers production executives Peter Guber and Jon Peters to head their studios, didn't have a clue and had let them run wild, then Matsushita didn't even know how to spell "clue."

Also, Matsushita never treated Wasserman and Sheinberg with the respect they were accustomed to. After more than twenty-five years at the helm, they were the most stable studio-management team in the industry. Matsushita couldn't have cared less. They insulted Wasserman and Sheinberg's dignity. Near the end, when the two flew to Osaka for a meeting to explain why they were so unhappy, Matsushita let them cool their heels for two hours, waiting on uncomfortable folding chairs. I'd have left after fifteen minutes. Unless there's a damn good excuse, anyone who keeps you waiting doesn't really care about the meeting. Wasserman and Sheinberg were hurt and outraged. The story even made the papers.

To add insult to injury, Ovitz liked to think of himself as the second coming of Lew Wasserman, an inappropriate delusion to say the least, especially since the original was very much alive.

When Matsushita finally decided to cut their MCA losses, they asked Ovitz to help them look for a buyer. Seagram demanded secrecy, and Ovitz couldn't figure out a way to tell Wasserman or Sheinberg; that is, if he even wanted to. Ovitz was in an unenviable position, with no good choices. Wasserman and Sheinberg eventually supported the Seagram sale, but they always felt that Ovitz had betrayed them by keeping mum. Sheinberg had even said publicly that if something was going on, Ovitz would let him know. Ovitz didn't, and Sheinberg looked naive. It read like Ovitz's loyalty was simply to the new owners. He abandoned his remaining equity with the old regime for an alliance with those who were now in a position to do something for him. But he miscalculated. Wasserman, who would have only honorary power in the new company, as chairman emeritus, threatened to walk away if Ovitz got the top job. To see that agent running his company was too much for the old man to swallow. As he said to the press, "Mike Ovitz is no friend of MCA's."

No matter what Ovitz says or how he spins his non-publicity, he *didn't* want to blow that deal. But he pressed too hard. After all, he was the most powerful man in Hollywood, right? He really thought he *was* Mike Ovitz. He'd bought his own myth.

Afterward, I never saw so much vitriolic behavior from the CAA partners, who had, until then, never said a bad word about Ovitz. He'd blown it for them as well. David Geffen, a longtime Ovitz foe, managed to get some payback by recommending CAA's number-two guy, Ron Meyer, for the MCA job. Edgar Bronfman Jr. was smart. He listened and hired him. Unfortunately, many of the CAA teammates Meyer hired have since left MCA — now renamed Universal Studios. Meyer had Viacom's former president, Frank Biondi, brought in over him as CEO, but after two years Biondi was canned — and who knows if Meyer is next? With few exceptions — Guy McElwaine being one — the agents are just not cut out to run a studio or network. Agents know all about deal-making but not what to do once the deal is made, except make another.

No MCA job left Ovitz still at CAA, but his super-agenting days were over. His guys were on the verge of revolt. They'd finally experienced what everyone on the outside knew: that Ovitz didn't care about anyone but Ovitz. Everyone was his best friend when he needed them. What that means is that he has no real best friend. You can't function as he functions and have a best friend. When you study so hard to become Michael Ovitz, there's no room to be anything else.

CAA clients began to leave. Young agents struggled for power, then settled in. The original partners tried to figure out their next moves. Bill Haber, one of the five founders, eventually gave up the greedy life and now heads the Save the Children charity. Good for him.

With MCA out of the picture, Ovitz was between a rock and a hard place. He was desperate, floating, insubstantial. The personal paranoia must have been overwhelming. Then along came Michael Eisner and the Walt Disney Company with a plum: be second in command. Disney had just purchased Cap Cities/ABC, and Eisner needed him. For a moment it looked like a brilliantly orchestrated move on both men's part.

After Disney swallowed ABC, Eisner had to reassure the financial community that his leadership team was in place. But he was all alone at the top of the heap, not a particularly confidence-inspiring scenario for a guy who'd had bypass surgery. Hiring Ovitz seemed like the perfect solution. And why not? For years, Eisner and Ovitz had been, well . . . best friends.

Next thing you know, Ovitz is at Disney and the town is in an uproar, trying to figure it out.

We now have some of the answers.

What did Ovitz actually do at Disney? What did Eisner let him do? Anyone who has been at a big company knows that when your boss wants to make you work, you work. When I hired Brad Grey, I thought he was very smart and took him everywhere. I anointed him with whatever power I possessed and made it clear that I stood behind him 100 percent. When I left for Lorimar he was able to run The Brillstein Company with Sandy Wernick, and when I came back I made Brad president.

(Why didn't I give the job to Sandy Wernick, who had been with me longer? Why do you marry one woman and not another? Instinct. I don't think it's an insult to say that being boss is not Sandy's style. We all have our strengths, and Sandy is the perfect inside man. Brad and I had this great Vito and Michael Corleone thing going. Marc Gurvitz came up with that in jest, but it worked. Visualization is one of my strengths, and I absolutely believe that if it came down to it — metaphorically — just like in *Godfather II*, Brad would shoot two cops for me.)

Even though Ovitz came in on top, he'd still made quite a leap, from a $250-million-a-year company to a $21-billion-a-year company. He had a lot to learn. Eisner could have helped by calling his division heads together and saying, "Listen: He's my successor. You better like him now or you won't be around later. End of subject."

But Eisner didn't. I can't imagine him telling Ovitz, "Here's what we're going to do . . ." or them going everywhere together. Instead of being designated the heir apparent, or even given a vote of confidence, Ovitz was left on his own.

When a bully is left on his own, he gets stupid.

I know quite a few guys who told Ovitz to take it easy. Spend a year quietly forming alliances, they said. Learn how Disney works. But instead of developing relationships with the division heads, who had every reason to resent this *mythical agent*'s ascension after all *their* hard work, Ovitz ignored the advice. How could he not, when he'd been called "the most powerful man in show business"? Ovitz believed a little too much that he had some sort of magic. But the magic that worked at CAA doesn't work at Disney, because you have fifteen division heads who already function quite well on their own. Each of these men and women basically runs his or her own business: theme parks, merchandising, movies, TV, animation, cruise ships, financial, sports, resorts, publishing, cable, etc. And here comes Ovitz, reputation in hand, and he says, "Okay, I'm Michael Ovitz and I already know about cruising and theme parks and sports and movies and TV."

It's all right to bullshit stars who want to be bullshitted, but you take a guy who spends years building his area, and now he's got to deal with a new guy telling him what to do? No way.

Steven Bollenbach, Disney's former financial head, resigned and left to run Hilton Hotel Corporation. I think it was a clue to what was in the cards for the Ovitz-Disney relationship, especially since Bollenbach actually criticized Ovitz publicly. That's amazing for a corporate guy. Whatever Ovitz did must have been enough for him to go, "Fuck this."

Meanwhile, Eisner, a smart man who could never be accused of overestimating anyone, just sat back and said, "Fine."

Later, he said in his book that Ovitz never understood that the company was about making products, not deals. As if he was surprised.

My theory about why the Eisner/Ovitz relationship didn't work is probably the weirdest one you'll ever read. Instead of the job being a brilliant collaboration between Eisner and Ovitz, I think it was a brilliantly diabolical plot conceived by Eisner either before Ovitz came on board or shortly after.

For years the only other guy always at or near the top of the "most powerful men in Hollywood" list was . . . Michael Eisner. Of course, Eisner had the real power. He could say yes. He also had lots more money. (Everyone always thought it drove Ovitz nuts that if he was such a powerful man, then why didn't he have Eisner's money?) When Eisner was forced to bring in help at Disney, he knew that Wall Street would be pacified if he hired "the most powerful man in show business." But he also knew, "If Ovitz works *here*, then there's only *one* most powerful man — and it's me!" Even if Eisner's ego is generally a quiet one, it still can't be discounted. After all, *power is the game.*

I think Eisner saw the opportunity to use Ovitz and then neuter him. I don't believe he made a mistake and misjudged his friend's capabilities and ambitions. I don't imagine Eisner said, two months after Ovitz was in, "Oh fuck, what did I do?" I don't believe Eisner ever had any intention of moving over for Ovitz unless he absolutely had to. In other words, he'd have to die first. Every snake has only one head. Disney has only one head. Michael Eisner. Even if Eisner had suddenly died, do you think that anyone at Disney would have put up with having Ovitz in charge? It just doesn't make sense.

I base my theory about what happened to Ovitz on having spent years watching the people involved. I see the patterns, the cycles. I understand the lessons of show-business history. I hear about everything. When I saw Eisner and Ovitz on Larry King's show, both men told King that their relationship was fine. Their body language said it was bullshit.

In a way, my scenario defends Ovitz's not so privately whispered complaint that Eisner screwed him. That's not my intention. Had Ovitz been willing — no, able — to adapt his nature to new circumstances, he'd probably still be at Disney. It's only his fault that he couldn't.

This marriage of Hollywood royalty not only fell apart, but it happened faster than most people realize. Ovitz's exit was supposedly a done deal *less* than a year after he arrived. He got to stick around an extra four or five months just so he could save face while he looked for another job. He couldn't find one. For a year he lay low and considered his options. I figured they all boiled down to self-employment.

And that's just what he did. In early 1998, Ovitz invested $20 million in Livent, a Toronto-based theatrical production company that produced *Ragtime* for Broadway, only to discover it had major financial trouble. According to Frank Rich, in the *New York Times*, Ovitz "was duped by another showbiz hype artist: Garth Drabinsky, the cofounder of Livent." The company eventually declared bankruptcy, Drabinsky and a partner were charged with conspiracy and fraud, and Ovitz lost his investment.

Ovitz's next move shocked me almost as much as the financial irregularities of Livent must have shocked him: he announced he wanted to get back into show business with "a new type of company." And what was this incredible innovation? Talent management and TV/movie producing. Early reports had Sydney Pollack, Martin Scorsese, Robert De Niro, and Kevin Costner among the first clients; in other words, mostly guys over fifty. Maybe he'll even manage them for free, like he did when he started CAA.

It's a sweet irony made tastier because Ovitz asked Brad to be his partner in his Artists Management Group. He wanted to combine Livent and the NFL franchise he hoped to bring to Los Angeles, and all the management and production interests, into one company over which they'd both rule — as if Ovitz could really share power.

Brad was too smart. He declined and wished Ovitz well. It was some time before the media even knew they'd spoken. Brad told me later that life was just too short.

Even so, Ovitz told friends he wanted to model his company on Brillstein-Grey. He also tried to convince the town that his humiliating experiences at Disney and Livent had mellowed him, that he had become a *new* Mike Ovitz. Yeah, just like the old Ovitz, only new.

Ovitz next went after Rick Yorn and his sister-in-law Julie Yorn, two hot, young managers at Industry Entertainment who, between them, represent Cameron Diaz, Leonardo DiCaprio, Samuel L. Jackson, Matt Dillon, Steve Buscemi, Claire Danes, Ed Burns, Marisa Tomei, James Spader, Anna Paquin, and Minnie Driver. This time news of the talks leaked, and the media, for some unfathomable reason still unable to see Ovitz for who he really is and willing to buy up even the tattered remains of his former reputation, pounced on the buzz like the guy had made the most genius move in the annals of show business.

Not true. It's just history repeating itself. Having never been a manager — and not having a nurturing bone in his body — Ovitz couldn't just start a management company by himself; he had to use what others had accomplished to satisfy his own craven needs. Going after the Yorns was Ovitz's way of reinventing himself with young blood, like Dustin Hoffman pairing himself with Tom Cruise. It was akin to what I did by going into business with Brad. But unlike the Yorns, when I hired Brad he had no entanglements. The Yorns were under contract as co-presidents of Industry Entertainment — a subsidiary of Interpublic Group — run by veteran manager-producers Nick Wechsler and Keith Addis.

Though some say it was Addis and Wechsler's fault for not giving the Yorns a piece of the pie when they sold to Interpublic, Ovitz seduced the Yorns into joining him before their deals were finished, just like, when he was still at Disney, Ovitz convinced ABC's Jamie Tarses to ditch her job at NBC before her contract expired. It seems that part of the plan to hire Tarses as an entertainment-division president included floating rumors that she had been sexually harassed at NBC. No wonder then–network West Coast president Don Ohlmeyer called Ovitz the "anti-Christ." I really like Jamie Tarses; she's one of my best friends' daughters. When Jamie was at NBC she developed *Friends, Newsradio,* and other hot shows. She's also one of the few TV executives I've ever seen *not* panic in a situation that would drive most network suits crazy. I remember the first table read of Paul Simms's new sitcom *Newsradio.* It was dreadful and everyone knew it. But Jamie kept her cool. "That's really not good, Paul," she said. "You know you can write better." Simms waited for the axe to fall, but Jamie just said, "Go home and get to work. We'll be here tomorrow for another table read." Simms took his cue from her calm. He wrote a new script overnight and came back the next day with the goods. *Newsradio*'s now been on five years.

But, as happens with all of us, especially when we're young, we have moments when we act like we think we invented show business. Once, Jamie told someone at NBC, "Since I cast *Friends*" — which CBS president Les Moonves will argue about since he put together the show when he ran Warner Brothers Television — "I can recast *Saturday Night Live.*" Right. Sitcoms and variety shows are not the same thing. And the *Saturday Night Live* cast is doing quite well, thank you. The lesson is that in this business delusion is an occupational hazard — and it can happen to anyone. It's happened to me. That was Jamie's turn, and she's since matured, settled in at ABC, and become a very good executive.

 • • • • •

Even knowing that Ovitz was willing to decimate a company to get them, the Yorns signed up, thinking it was a smart move. I'm not so sure. There's a real downside these days to being associated with Ovitz. Where the town once feared him, now it also doesn't trust him. That's why I told *Time* magazine that maybe the Yorns weren't that smart after all.

And guess what? Less than a month after AMG opened, Ovitz tried to lure Janklow and Nesbit, the New York literary agency that's long had a primary arrangement with CAA, to come to AMG. They declined. Then Ovitz surprised everyone by stealing longtime CAA client Robin Williams and some others to AMG by hiring the CAA agent who represented them. Rumor has it that Ovitz worked on seducing Williams's wife, who wanted to continue producing movies.

The odd thing is that Williams would still retain his manager, David Steinberg (of Morra, Brezner and Steinberg). So what does all this make Ovitz — an agent masquerading as a manager? According to a story in the *New York Times,* when Williams bolted, the new CAA heads were outraged. They couldn't believe that their onetime "boss and *mentor* was seeking to raid his own former agency."

The next day, CAA laid down the law and announced that they would no longer represent any clients who choose Ovitz as their manager. "He is a competitor, not a collaborator. His word cannot be trusted," CAA president Richard Lovett said. "We are not going to be sharing any clients." Among those artists caught in the crossfire: Martin Scorsese, Sydney Pollack, Claire Danes, Mimi Rogers, Marisa Tomei, Lauren Holly, and Minnie Driver. Within days, Scorsese, Rogers, and Tomei declared their allegiance to AMG.

"What Michael is building looks like an agency, though he calls it a management company," Lovett told *Variety*, echoing my suspicions. "He is aggressively raiding the agencies. . . . We know Ovitz. He has proven himself untrustworthy. He has betrayed the people closest to him."

It was the first skirmish of what promises to be a long war — and in true Hollywood tradition, none of the other talent agencies joined in or announced their support for CAA by promising not to sign Ovitz's clients who'd left CAA. Instead, everyone looked out for their own ass. Who ever said it took balls to be in show business?

Did any of this surprise me? Hardly. Ovitz's reputation exceeds him. I never expected the guy to change his nature, and I feel bad for those who bought his latest song and dance. Just try to tell a scorpion not to sting or a pit bull not to bite. Good luck.

I don't trust Ovitz to look out for anyone but himself, and I believe his being that way is a huge character flaw for someone in the management business, where empathy is king and clients have to believe you really care about them personally. And you should, for better or for worse. Managing is not just about finding the deal. If, as Bernard Weinraub wrote in the *New York Times*, Ovitz "loathed the hand-holding, late-night calls and temper tantrums of movie star clients," then Ovitz won't be up to the job. On the other hand, he has employees to do the real work for him, and some talent may want the Ovitz association so badly that they're willing to deal with the Devil, karma be damned. Stranger things have happened.

What I'm most concerned about is that far too many people who should know better are somehow still caught up in Ovitz's bullshit — it's as if John Foster Kane's last word wasn't "rosebud," but "Ovitz" — and that this will encourage him to be so aggressive, manipulative, and monomaniacal that he will force legislatures to consider regulating the management business. That would be fine if it stops agents pretending to be managers, like Ovitz, or in-name-only manager-producers from taking a free ride on their clients, but it will hurt those of us who have legitimate financial responsibility for their shows, actually do the work, and have productive established relationships with the talent agencies.

Because of what happened between me and Ovitz I've often asked myself if I'm happy at how far Ovitz fell before starting AMG. Not really. I feel sorry for him. I know what it's like to want a new kind of power, like he tried to have at Disney. I know what it's like to get it and then lose it — though not what it's like to walk away with $100 million–plus. I also know that his methods and mind-set are not that unusual for show business. Frankly, I'm afraid more than a few players — young and old — would wish to be Ovitz if they could.

Meanwhile, on a recent edition of CNN's *Entertainment Weekly Newstand* TV show about Ovitz's return to Hollywood as a manager, anchor Willow Bay ended the report with these words: "And now it seems that Mike Ovitz wants to be Bernie Brillstein." How's that for knowing the truth when you see it?

Still, none of it changes the fact that I intensely dislike the man for personal reasons, for crossing an ethical line with my daughter — and for how that same character deficiency is reflected in his work. But on the business front, before AMG, I figured, enough already. All that Japanese-art-of-war, get-in-the-face-of-your-enemy stuff had become so much bullshit — and old hat. I hate to kick a guy when he's down.

That's why I'm glad Mike is back in the game, particularly my game. I'd much rather kick him when he's standing up.

About a month ago a well-known Los Angeles lawyer, a music expert, asked me to lunch. Did he need to talk about publishing? Did he want me to run a record company? I didn't know, but he was a great guy, so I went. The lunch was wonderful, though nothing in particular was said. Then, right before the check came, he asked, "By the way, could you introduce me to Brad?"

Now I knew what was up. I said, "Just call him. He knows you. He'll speak to you."

He certainly didn't mean any harm. Coming to me was nice, perhaps a sign of respect or courtesy. It was also another reminder that I was no longer the guy. But it didn't hurt, not even for a moment. I had gotten better.

Later that afternoon I walked into Brad's office. Rob Lowe, one of my clients, had written a script. Brad's guy Christian Slater had read it and was interested.

Brad sat quietly at his desk. He looked like he was in pain. He explained that he'd just gotten off the phone with his longtime client Garry Shandling, who had lately given him nothing but grief. It was too bad. For years, Brad had done the most amazing job for Garry I'd ever seen. He'd helped transform him from a tentative newcomer who worried about his hair into a comedian's comedian who worried about his hair. And yet their relationship had fallen on such hard times that Brad didn't even want to speak to him on the phone.

Brad clearly needed someone sane to talk to. Suddenly, it felt like old times. I said, "You've got a stomachache."

He said, "How do you know that?"

"I had one with my last wife for ten years," I joked. "Seriously, you just know. I've been there myself. The minute the phone rings and your assistant says it's so-and-so, you get that feeling in your gut. Your stomach never lies."

Brad said, "Jesus, that's true."

I said, "Look. You're going to be forty in January, you have a great wife, three great kids, money in the bank, a wonderful company. Your life is perfect. Why do you need anyone to give you a stomachache? I don't care who it is. Release him. Stop working for him. Who needs it?"

I could tell from the look on Brad's face that he had been thinking the same thing. Brad's responsibilities at the company were enormous. He was in charge and he no longer had time to be as personally available as before. It's very difficult to be part of everything when you have nine television shows, represent 150 people, and are making deals to ensure your company's survival. Brad's clients understood that he would always be there for the important stuff — except Garry. He was needier. He'd always had his hand held and didn't want to let go. He'd call Brad at all hours, unhappy about the people he worked with, unhappy about his career, just plain unhappy.

Brad couldn't take it. He tried to work things out but finally had to let Garry go. Then the press jumped all over the breakup, lawsuits and counter-lawsuits were filed. If you ask me, none of it was necessary.

I know both guys hurt terribly. Now they hurt worse.

Pretty soon Brad and I were talking about all sorts of things, from the practical to the philosophical. We got rid of a year's dirty laundry in less than two hours. It was the Brad and Bernie I knew and loved, two guys from different generations, with shared experiences, who each kept part of the whole picture in his head. That evening I went home and felt better than I had in a long time.

Brad should run the company. It's just his time. My first instinct was right — well, half right. It was my time, as well. I mean, how can you blame someone else for yourself getting older?

I've changed and Brad has responded. I've shed my long face, he's more at ease around me. I know what I'm doing again, thank God. I don't carry the burden of the company on my shoulders anymore. If I did, I don't think I ever could have given my heart and brain to the great relationship I have with my wife, Carrie. If I was on the firing line and out five nights a week, I'd be too tired. Instead, she and I have a good time together. We can actually plan to go to a movie.

Life's not so bad.

Where Did I Go Right?

Chapter 15

It Was Fun While
It Lasted

After trying to do three jobs at once at Lorimar — movies, TV, management — being back at The Brillstein Company felt like a vacation. Brad and Sandy and the rest seemed happy to see me. So did my clients, most of whom had stayed loyal. I was amazed they had, considering how out of touch I'd been and how my perceived power had taken a big body blow.

Maybe I shouldn't have been so worried. About a year earlier, at the Friends of the Los Angeles Free Clinic roast in the Beverly Wilshire Grand Ballroom, I was the guest of honor. The roasters sat on the dais against a backdrop of movie screen–sized pictures of me, from babyhood to mogulhood. Each lampooned my exploits as a manager, studio head, teacher, friend, and human being. Everyone who was anyone in show business was there, except Mr. Charity himself, Mike Ovitz. He didn't have to show up, but he was too small time to even buy a table. It's not like the money was going into my pocket.

We made light of his absence. Richard Dreyfuss said that one reason I'd lost so much weight — I'd recently dropped seventy-five pounds — was because I'd had "one of my Ovitzes removed." Brandon Tartikoff said, "Anyone who thinks they're at the Friends of CAA Christmas party, boy are you in the wrong place." Tartikoff was such a good master of ceremonies that Garry Shandling couldn't resist asking the audience, "When did Brandon Tartikoff become so fucking funny?" Later, Jackie Gayle asked when Shandling had become so funny. Tartikoff said he'd only taken the hosting job because after I'd told him that doing *Hollywood Squares* would lead to big things, he hadn't "worked" in six months.

Sandy Wernick and Brad Grey made a little video of themselves trying to sell Brandon Tartikoff a series based on my life as a middle aged divorced man with a grown-up daughter who meets a young woman with two children, marries her, and has two more children. Okay, so that was my real life, but NBC didn't want my character to be in show business.

"How about making him a fireman?" Tartikoff suggested, as the camera pulled back to reveal a fireman's hat on his desk. "I always wanted to be a fireman."

"Me, too," said Sandy. "Me, too. Works for us." I had never seen Sandy so agreeable in a negotiation.

Henson made jokes about booking Miss Piggy and Kermit on *ALF.* I loved that he could have a sense of humor about it.

ALF made an appearance "live" via satellite. Dana Carvey, Lorne Michaels, Kevin Nealon, and my dad, Moe, all sent videotaped comments. I took a lot of ribbing for the price of Lorimar stock, which had been slowly drifting lower.

We taped the evening, and shortly after I returned to The Brillstein Company I watched it again and realized that whatever I'd been through, I still had friends. Not everyone on the dais would remain close, but it wasn't the individuals as much as the feeling in the room. No matter how much we all tried to outdo each other during the day, we were still at moments a big club. Our business was the game we chose to play, and we played it fiercely, but we could also check our work at the door to celebrate each other, as well as what we had and could accomplish.

Those who don't get it, who never show an ounce of genuine caring, are kicked out of the club sooner or later. Others, unfortunately, leave long before their time: Who knew that within two years both Jim Henson and Gilda Radner would be gone, and that both movie executive Dawn Steel and Brandon Tartikoff would not last another ten?

Today, that night reminds me of how much I miss them. Then, it reminded me of how much I missed being in the thick of the game, working with the talent, and how glad I was to be back.

Fortunately the business had done well, and we'd brought in new managers to help handle our growth. *Saturday Night Live*'s ratings were up and the show's cast consisted largely of our clients, most of whom had already become a new generation of stars: Dana Carvey, Dennis Miller,

Phil Hartman, Jon Lovitz, Kevin Nealon, and Mike Myers. The following year, Chris Farley and Chris Rock would sign on with the show, and in 1991 David Spade and Adam Sandler. Not only did *Saturday Night Live* have a new audience — as well as its traditional fans, but Hollywood again seemed interested in transforming the most popular characters into movie stars. *Wayne's World* led the pack, grossing nearly $130 million and, according to *Entertainment Weekly*, setting the stage for the "dumb comedy wave" that followed.

It's Garry Shandling's Show was in its fourth and final year on Showtime. Garry had earned increasing respect as a small-screen innovator, and I like to think that the positive reaction to his show had more than a little to do with NBC rethinking its earlier position that a sitcom about a neurotic, self-absorbed comedian and his annoying friends wouldn't work. That year they ordered a pilot called *The Seinfeld Chronicles*, and the rest is history.

I even represented Roseanne for a minute and a half, just as she was about to do the pilot for her long-running sitcom. She came to me after she had the deal. The only advice I gave her in the three weeks we were together was to resist ABC's efforts to change the name of the show. It looked like we'd be good together until during the pilot shoot, Roseanne's sister heard someone say, "Can you imagine that fat sonofabitch having her own show?" The sister said it was someone from my office. It wasn't. But what are you going to do? We were gone. We had no contract but she agreed to give $12,500 to the Museum of Radio and Television and $12,500 to the Free Clinic as our settlement.

Vanity Fair magazine called to ask if I'd be interested in being profiled. I was flattered. For years people had urged me to do a book, and while I wasn't yet ready for that, I believed the magazine story was a great opportunity to say publicly what I'd been saying privately for years about how the old spirit of show business and reliance on instinct was dying. I wanted readers to know what it was like, how it really worked. Also, in the aftermath of the Warner Brothers mess, I figured I could take a shot or two at the people I believed had treated me badly. I wanted to stick it to Bob Daly.

My plan was to control the story not by keeping the writer out but by letting her in. Way in. I allowed her to follow me around almost day and night. I took her to my house, invited her to meetings and explained the subtext of what went on point by point. I wanted her to experience being in the trenches so she'd truly understand what we all did for a living day in and day out.

The piece ran soon after I returned to the management company full-time. Some people liked it, most didn't — including me. Instead of really "getting" the business, it was a mean-spirited story that made fun of me. On the other hand, maybe I shouldn't have let the magazine photograph me wearing a sweatsuit, like a putz.

On a positive note, Jimmy Wiatt, head of ICM, called to say that his client Ed O'Neill, the star of *Married . . . with Children*, had read the *Vanity Fair* piece and wanted to drop by the office.

When Ed walked into my office he said, "I've been dying to meet you." Apparently the *Vanity Fair* story had impressed him just when he happened to be looking for a manager.

His instincts were great. Within a year we had to renegotiate his *Married . . . with Children* contract. Ed had started out at $7,500 a week. But the show had become a huge hit and Ed deserved a significant raise. When Brad and I told him the figure we had in mind, he looked incredulous and then uncertain, but he said to go ahead. For five weeks we wrangled with Gary Lieberthal, chairman of Columbia Pictures TV, trying to close the deal, but made no progress. Finally, we faced each other across Lieberthal's desk. Every time we made a suggestion, Lieberthal would punch in the number on his desk calculator, then he and his lawyer would go into another room to figure out what they could give us. At first it was cute. The second time was annoying. The third time was too much. I said some nasty things. Names were called. When Lieberthal — who is a good friend — got up to go into the other room, I grabbed his calculator, and Brad and I left the building.

Ed O'Neill got his raise. He also has the calculator, which I framed, hanging over his mantel. We call it "The Ten Million Dollar Calculator."

• • • • •

When director Paul Mazursky offered Richard Dreyfuss the movie, *Moon over Parador*, neither of us particularly liked the story. But Mazursky had given Richard his comeback break in *Down and Out in Beverly Hills*, and we felt he owed him. By the time he was finished shooting, Richard had three more movie offers on the table at about $3 million each. The first was for *Let It Ride*, the horse race picture directed by Joe Pytka, at Paramount.

Richard asked me to meet him at Hymie's Fish Market on Pico Boulevard, for lunch.

He said, "You know, I've been thinking . . ."

When an actor says, "You know, I've been thinking . . . ," you've got big trouble coming. When they say, "How come . . . ," it's time to head for the hills.

He said, "I get these scripts myself now. I, uh . . . I don't really need a manager anymore. It's a lot of money."

I knew what was coming. He wanted to leave. I was so shocked that my stomach went right out of my ass. Of all the people who have left me, Dreyfuss surprised me the most. It's not because I thought he owed me for resurrecting his career; I helped, but he had to have the talent to back it up. I'd just really been there for him. I thought we were friends.

Then he said, "But I'll let you produce those pictures if I can." In other words, if there wasn't a producer already connected to the movie, he would try and sidle me in. I felt like he was giving me a tip. It was disgusting.

My shrimp cocktail hadn't even arrived and all I wanted to do was get out of there. I looked across the table at a guy who, with his prematurely white hair and beard, looked like a diminutive version of me and thought, "What am I going to tell Sandy? What am I going to tell Brad?" I felt dirty and embarrassed. I would have given my soul for Richard, but someone had probably gotten in his ear and said, "Hey, you're Richard Dreyfuss again. What are you paying that money for?" If he'd taken the three pictures — which he hadn't yet said yes to — my portion of "that money" would have come to a million dollars. Ten percent.

I said, "Richard, I can't do that. Let's just forget it. I'm gone. I'm history."

Now he looked shocked. "But I can't lose you," he said, backtracking. "Look, we'll just keep it the way everything is, okay?"

He meant it. Then.

Three days later, I got a letter: "I don't find the need for this anymore. I want to handle my own life." All that bullshit. He said good-bye in the letter. He couldn't do it in person.

I understood. There's a defining moment in every crumbling relationship — with a woman, an actor, a studio — where the damage that's done will never be repaired. You can't take it back. After lunch at Hymie's Fish Market, Dreyfuss was, for me, a dead man. He did the right thing by leaving me, because it never would have been the same. I turned cold. He was another piece of shit to me. I felt like I'd been on the receiving end of that classic call all guys get: A girl says, "I love you, but I'm not in love with you. Let's just be friends." At that moment, your desire goes south.

Later, I came to believe that we broke up not because he didn't want to pay commission or that he'd been influenced by his lawyer. We just disagreed about the merits of the pictures on his plate. He wanted to do them all and, with the memory of his hungry years still in his head, pick up an easy $10 to $12 million. I was cool with that. Lots of actors do it. But did he also have to try to convince me that the movies were good? I didn't think he was paying me to lie to him.

Now, when I see Richard, it's like seeing an old girlfriend. I bear no grudge. I say hello. But inside I wonder, "How did I ever sleep with her?"

• • • • •

I still don't know why, but one day Ovitz called and wanted to make up. He said "Let's have a meeting and straighten this all out. We'll go to Jimmy's restaurant."

"Fine," I said. I figured, enough already. I'd never love him, but at least we could talk.

When I got there I discovered that Ovitz had rented out the entire party room. It was empty, except that in the middle was a table for two. There was no one else around. I remember thinking that the guy was some kind of drama queen who lived in a weird and self-important world. Yet there we were, two Jews who made our living selling people in show business, sitting down to make peace like it was a Mafia dinner. As we talked about renewing our friendship it struck me that one had never really existed, and I didn't believe one could. I knew who Ovitz was and he knew me. We were too different. Sometimes you can be friends again with someone who fucks you over, but this wasn't it.

I wonder if Ovitz even had an honest desire to stop a painful feud. After all, he was still Michael Ovitz then, and what could I do to hurt him? Maybe he was afraid I'd poison Brad against him — as if I could. Some lessons Brad would have to learn for himself. In truth, he'd been playing up to Brad. I wasn't too thrilled about their relationship, but Brad had never hidden it, and I understood his purpose. We'd have to do business with Ovitz and there was no point in letting my personal feelings stand in the way.

Throughout dinner nothing much was said except, "Let's acknowledge each other. Let's not be enemies." But afterwards it's not like we embraced. We couldn't go back to being the friends we never really were. I guess I was disappointed by what it all meant beyond Ovitz: if you've come to show business looking for friendship, with few exceptions, you've come to the wrong place.

By the way, in 1996, after he'd gone to work with Disney, Ovitz tried a similar peace-making dinner with David Geffen. Same result. Nothing. Less than nothing. Geffen still hates Ovitz. The only difference between us is that the Geffen dinner got mentioned in the paper.

• • • • •

During the summer of 1989 Jim Henson asked me to come to his beautiful house on Broad Beach, north of Malibu. I arrived in the afternoon. The air was fresh and clear from an offshore breeze. I could see the Channel Islands in the distance. It was the perfect setting for a gentle genius like Jim. I thought he wanted to talk about *The Ghost of Fafnir Hall*, a series I'd just sold for him to HBO, or *The Jim Henson Hour*, which I'd just gotten Brandon Tartikoff to take for NBC's 1989 season. (Although Jim won an Emmy for directing on the NBC show, it was canceled after ten weeks.) Instead, as we sat on the deck looking out at the ocean, Jim said, "Disney wants to buy me and this time it's real."

In the early '80s, knowing Disney was vulnerable, Jim wanted to make a run at taking over the company, which was still under its old management team of Ron Miller and Roy Disney. It was just idle talk that never went anywhere, and then Michael Eisner, Frank Wells, and Jeff Katzenberg took over. But a seed was planted about how perfect a Disney/Henson pairing might be, and I called Eisner and pitched him on the idea.

He was interested. A couple weeks later, David Lazer, Katzenberg, Eisner, and I met in the private dining room at Chasen's restaurant. The Disney team had done their homework and told us what we already knew but hoped didn't matter: the Muppets weren't exactly hot. *The Muppet Show* was over and except for the movies, not much was happening. Even the Muppets merchandise wasn't selling well. *Sesame Street* merchandise did, but *Sesame Street* was untouchable, part of a fifty-fifty arrangement with the Children's Television Workshop in which either side could kill any deal involving the other. Of course, we could never put anything related to *Sesame Street* on the table, but knowing Eisner, in the back of his mind he probably had dreams of one day putting mouse ears on Bert and Ernie, Big Bird, and Oscar the Grouch.

The Muppets' world renown wasn't enough to carry the deal, so Disney passed and Jim went back to work and for a while just managed to break even. The company had grown and Jim had 108 employees on two continents to support, not to mention his love of spending money on production and playing with the newest technology. I probably could have made Jim a studio deal somewhere, but it wasn't Disney and he valued his independence.

By 1989 The Henson Company was in better shape. They had more cash and exploitable material, so Eisner's interest didn't surprise me as much as his having called Jim directly. I found out that talks had gone on for almost a week without me. It was the standard Eisner/Katzenberg way of doing business with others (and later with *each* other): secret, secret, secret, secret. I started to get a stomachache.

Jim asked me what I thought of a possible deal in the $100 to $150 million range just for his company, and more for his personal services. I knew his overhead was enormous and it was tough on him. Even though he had expert assistance from guys like David Lazer, Jim needed to get out from under the organizational albatross that drained his creative energy. You can have the top people in the world, but the buck stops at the boss. People would go to Jim directly about everything and he hardly had the time. He was an artist first and foremost, and he needed to concentrate on his work and come up with magnificent ideas like he always had. With Disney's money and machinery, Jim could be fully creative.

I said, "If you can pick up some good money and do the things you want to do, then I think it's the best thing for you now. The business is changing. You want to do a 3-D movie. The cost is out of this world. If this will let you keep the Muppets going forever and help you go into the future free of worry, great."

The deal moved forward quickly. Jim and I spoke whenever he needed a question answered, but everything else was handled by his team of lawyers in New York.

Then one day he called and said, "I want to come to your house Saturday. I need to talk to you." Later that evening we sat in my den, and Jim said, "You know Disney. Katzenberg's not going to let you sell the television shows anymore because Disney will want to."

I did know Disney. I'd prepared myself to be less involved. Everyone who knows the Disney Company knows that they think they're smarter than anyone who was ever born. They like to control their own business. Jim was trying to tell me that I was out.

Jim knew what I was thinking. "I need you in my life," he said, with a sincerity that only two people who'd been together a long time can believe. "I want to make sure you're taken care of. So, I'll give you ten million right now, and five hundred thousand a year in perpetuity to be my advisor. What do you think?"

I took a dead Jew's name in vain and said, "Jesus Christ!"

It wasn't the money, or the amount, it was the offer itself. I felt like maybe I'd done something right. That would have been enough for one day, but Jim handed me a check for $7 million and said I'd get the other $3 million when the deal closed. Now I was speechless.

The money was income to The Brillstein Company, meaning I had to give it to Warner Brothers, per our still-unresolved deal. Should I have asked him to make out the check to Bernie Brillstein? Maybe. But I'm an ethical schmuck.

The $500,000 a year, however, was between Jim and me. Screw Warners.

The money bought out my shares of everything, and Jim was free and clear to make his deal.

· · · · ·

If you could pick the most illogical pairing in the world, it would have been Jim Henson and me. We were straight from the pages of *Of Mice and Men*. I don't think we ever completely understood, in our guts, what the other did. But here's the wonderful thing: Our relationship was never based on understanding. It was all about trust.

I'm not talking about the trust-you-with-my-life-money-and-deepest-feelings trust, though at times that was part of it. Our bond was the unspoken certainty that we belonged together. We were who we were and it just worked. We didn't have to discuss it or try to figure out why. We got each other instinctively. If you've ever had a relationship like that, you know it's scary, exciting, and above all, seamless.

I called Jim Henson and his band of puppeteers "the arts and crafts set." They wanted as little as possible to do with the money-first, deal-making, soul-killing aspects of show business that I confronted every day. Jim didn't want to ignore reality, he just didn't want any contact with the parts that were pollutants and alien to his company's creativity. It was better, Jim believed, to live in a fantastic world of creatures and characters that tried to speak to the humanity in us all through magical performances. He was a hippie. That's why he'd had me. I was as Broadway-Hollywood show business as The Henson Company got. Me, they could tolerate and even understand because *my* show business was about passion and respect for the talent. Jim always counted on me for that connection.

I gave Jim a solid presence in the Hollywood community; it was as if he had a branch office on the West Coast. No one could take advantage of him, and the more successful I became, because of *Saturday Night Live* and everything else, the more clout I had for Jim.

Jim, in turn, gave me legitimacy in the family and children's market, the equivalent of the Good Housekeeping Seal of Approval. Whatever else I was involved in, I could always go to studios, HBO, and other outlets and distributors with this badge of honor. Jim was wholesome, and I'd represented him, so I was wholesome. A very nice exchange.

The Henson organization started work at 8:30 in the morning, sometimes earlier. His offices were stunning. One hundred eight artsy-craftsy people worked there, and you could hear a pin drop — until I came in, the crass, commercial guy. I'm sure some of Jim's people thought of me as the anti-Christ, but they never let on.

At staff meetings, Jim sat at the head of the table. I took a seat nearby. Everyone always wanted to talk and promote their ideas, so I ran interference. Sometimes I'd posture a bit, interrupt, make everyone laugh. I played my role as the flamboyant showbiz guy who breezed into town wearing an XXXL Ranger's hockey jersey and enjoyed it.

When it came to Jim's vision I would never interrupt when he talked about a project. If Jim had an idea that I thought was a little nuts, I'd never put it down. Jim's only difficulty was that he sometimes had trouble explaining his concepts because he was such a visual person. Part of the trust we had was based on my believing that, even though he might be at a loss for words, the magic would happen when Jim actually did what he talked about.

When I made a suggestion, if Jim liked it, I knew right away. Otherwise, he'd give me one of two reactions. "Hmmmm" meant "not good, not bad." Silence meant he was thinking it through, and we all knew to say nothing. The longer he thought, the more the tension built. If Jim took too long to answer, I knew it was because he didn't want to say no to me in front of everyone. Then I'd say, ". . . or not!" and start laughing. The room would relax and you could see the relief in Jim's eyes. It was hard for Jim to say no to anybody. I'd console myself by popping an entire danish into my mouth.

My ideas weren't always winners. Once I suggested a situation comedy about a puppeteer who did a sweet show, yet off camera was a prick. Another time I wanted Jim to play the Mel Ferrar role in a remake of *Gigi* — be the puppeteer, fall in love with a young girl. I thought Jim could act. I thought it would make a helluva movie. He looked at me like I was from another planet. On the other hand, I convinced him to okay the animated series *Muppet Babies*. For a puppet company to do a cartoon was a serious undertaking. Not everyone on his informal council — Frank Oz, Jerry Nelson, Jerry Juhl, Diana Bergenfield, David Lazer, Jim's wife, Jane, and I — wanted to, but The Henson Company had nothing on the air. I believed *Muppet Babies* would give Jim a presence and merchandising income while he pursued other interests. I was right. *Muppet Babies* turned out to be a monstrous hit and is still syndicated today.

My one regret is that I never got him to do *An Evening with the Muppets* on Broadway. I believe if he had, it would still be running today.

Jim Henson was a genius who'd taken me into uncharted territory. His right brain brimmed with fantastic ideas, most of them before their time. His left brain wanted to be a commercial hit. I listened, pushed, prodded, gave in, loved, and nurtured him. I didn't use him for my purposes, I used him for his. My challenge was to walk the center line and find profitable avenues for his brilliance that still let him concentrate fully on his creations.

I like to think that I also led Jim into uncharted territory: nightclubs, gambling, Vegas. He loved it. Our personal relationship was separate from our work. At dinner we were social, friendly, and warm. We exchanged confidences like friends do. We laughed and scratched and told stories. It was a sophomoric, fraternal thing. During the third season of *The Muppet Show*, Jim and I went to the Curzon Club in London. He was into his black suits and ugly Missoni ties period, but being tall and thin he looked pretty good in any clothes. I was at the craps table, as usual, when he came out of another room, his face beaming. "Bernie, I won ten thousand dollars," he said. Ten grand meant nothing to Jim, but it still seemed special. He acted like I'd given him a gift.

For our twenty-fifth year together, he rented a yacht in the Mediterranean, to cruise the French Riviera. He said, "Invite whomever you want." I asked Peggy and Tom Pollock and Vicki and John Irwin. Both were my lawyers. Jim asked Terry Jones from Monty Python. Because he was a great guy, Jim gave Debbie and me the huge master bedroom.

The next year I rented a 174-foot yacht and took him to the Italian Riviera.

Jim grew to love the good life. He had a wonderful apartment at the Sherry Netherland Hotel. The Henson Company offices were in a gorgeous townhouse. I think it was once a library. Jim also wanted to buy the building at Seventy-second and Madison Avenue in New York that now houses Polo but lost out to Ralph Lauren.

Jim had come a long way from his office above Chuck's Composite, at Fifty-second Street and Second Avenue. And he'd taken me with him.

Not only did I have a special relationship with Jim, so did Debbie. Sometimes they'd have long conversations about the occult and otherworldly phenomena and visions. I've always called it ooga-booga but Debbie loved all that stuff and Jim did, too. He and I never discussed it at length because he knew I'd have no patience with it.

But sometimes I wonder: Six months before Jim died, he called me and said, "Let's you, Jay Tarses, and I have dinner." Jim was not the out-and-about type. His time was limited. Occasionally we'd have some laughs, but this sounded different. When I asked him why, he said, "I'd just like to see Jay," who had written two of the Muppet movies. We went to Morton's and spent the whole meal talking about our philosophies of life. I kept waiting for the other shoe to drop, but it never did. There seemed to be no point to the dinner but social.

A couple months later, Jim was back in Los Angeles and he called again. "Bernie, why don't you arrange a poker game? I'd like Jack Burns there, Jay, Paul Fusco, and Cliff Perry [a friend of mine]." Remember, Jim had me fire Jack Burns from *The Muppet Show,* and Paul Fusco created *ALF,* yet he insisted they be there. Also, though Jim liked to gamble, I'd never seen him at a poker table. We played that night in my screening room. Jim got there late, typically, because he had some kind of meeting. He also won all the money.

Even his handing me a check for $7 million wasn't exactly his style.

On reflection, those moments seem to be part of a pattern. It's as if Jim somehow knew he had less time left with us than anyone dared suspect.

By the way, I never got the advisor's fee or the remaining $3 million because Jim died not long afterwards — and believe me, I'd have gladly given up the money to have him back. Nine months later the Disney deal fell through when Eisner tried to lower the buyout value based on Jim no longer being available to render his *personal services.* Although Disney and The Henson Company did eventually end up working together, it was only on a deal-by-deal basis. Disney never got to own Jim's company and probably never will.

· · · · ·

My father broke his hip when he was eighty-eight. Hip fractures can be the beginning of the end for the elderly, but Moe Brillstein was not the type to give up easily. He loved life as much as he hated his walker, and he did without it whenever possible. It took reinjuring his hip just before we celebrated his ninetieth birthday at the Carlyle Hotel to make him accept his limitations, and then the whole night he used the walker, going from table to table, while my brother and I sang old songs.

A year later my father got ill and landed in the intensive-care unit at Roosevelt Hospital. Debbie and I went to see him, like we had a few times before, and it was sad. He lay in his bed with a Levine tube down his throat. He couldn't talk. I came as often as I could and felt relieved when, within days, he started to get stronger.

One night I sat by the bed and did all the talking. I tried to say all the right things. I didn't mind if the guy next to him, an AIDS patient, overheard. I just wanted my father to know that I loved him — he knew — and that I knew he loved me. When I was done rambling, he motioned for a paper and pencil, scribbled a note, and handed it to me.

"Sing 'Where or When,'" it read. I knew the old Richard Rodgers standard by heart, so I did.

My father smiled and patted my hand, but when I looked into his eyes I saw the resignation. He wanted to die. I told him I'd see him in the morning and kissed him good night.

The next day, May 5, 1990, I called the ICU to ask how my father was doing. "Fine," the nurse said. "Stronger." I took my time dressing, had some breakfast, and went to the hospital. As I walked toward my father's bed I saw an empty space. My first thought was, "Too bad, the guy with AIDS died." But my father wasn't in the room and the AIDS patient was. I found the nurse and asked what was going on. She told me that my father had passed away.

• • • • •

I held Moe's funeral at the Riverside Chapel. Instead of the usual somber music, I put on an album featuring Jackie Gleason and his orchestra. I heard a few of the old Jews mutter that it was crazy, but I didn't give a damn. My father would have loved it.

• • • • •

I learned a lot about life from my father.

He taught me about show business, how to love it, and how important it was to him by *letting me experience it for myself.* He also had a knack for saying the things I needed to hear at the times I needed to hear them, like when he told me to move to California if I wanted to live my own life.

My father was known for his integrity. He was a tough guy with a code of honor. When I was a kid, merchants used to sell stuff from street stands outside their stores, just like they sometimes do today. Once, on my way to the subway, I stole a carton of balloons — maybe a thousand — from a store on Broadway near Forty-second Street. I must have been fourteen. For some reason I left them on my dresser, and when my old man saw them he said, "Where'd you get those balloons?"

"Well, I was walking by this store, the man took a liking to me, and he gave me all these balloons," I explained.

"What kind of store was it?" he asked. I told him. "And the balloons are outside, right?"

"Right."

"Okay. Go and give the balloons back now. They cost the guy money. You're stealing from him, give it back." I did. And he did all this without ever hitting me. Years later, Lorne gave me a giant Langdon Clay photograph of that block where the store had been. It still hangs in my office and reminds me that honesty is the best policy.

My dad also had a great sense of humor right up to the end. When the Friends of the Los Angeles Free Clinic roasted me, this is what my dad said:

"Bernie," he said, in a gravelly voice like mine, "it makes me very happy to see you at an occasion such as this. You come to this work by way of your family, because we always joined in doing charity for people less fortunate than we are. Now, all that I can tell you is the best of luck to you and just keep up your good work." Whoever was operating the video camera said, "That's great." But my father wasn't finished. He looked at the camera, and said, "Do you think I can get the part?" And then he laughed.

• • • • •

I buried my dad, went to the Carlyle Hotel, and spent the weekend eating tuna fish sandwiches and french fries — my favorite comfort foods. On Monday I was back in Los Angeles. Two days later, Jim Henson dropped by my office on his way to the airport — he was always on his way to an airport — to give me a hug and tell me how sorry he was that he hadn't been able to come with Jane to the funeral.

"I love you," he said. "I'll see you when I come back." Jim was on his way to New York. Then, with his daughter Cheryl, he went to visit his father and stepmother in North Carolina, for Mother's Day. His next stop would be Orlando, Florida, to continue work on the new Muppet attraction at Disneyworld.

A week later, about five in the morning on Tuesday, May 15, the phone rang at my home. David Lazer was on the line. "Bernie," he began,

"I just want to tell you something. I'm here at New York Hospital. Jim just came in, I just came here. He may not make it."

My heart nearly stopped. I couldn't grasp it, didn't want to. All I could say was, "You're kidding,"

David said, "His systems are shutting down." Then he told me what had happened. Jim became unusually tired in North Carolina, had taken an earlier flight back to New York with Cheryl, and had gone to his apartment at the Sherry Netherland Hotel to rest. The next morning he canceled a Muppet's recording session — something he never did. Jim spent Monday in bed, and Jane came by that evening. He got soup and care but he didn't get better. His family wanted to call a doctor but Jim didn't. He was a Christian Scientist, but that had less to do with it than his just not wanting to bother anyone. He believed he could handle the illness on his own. But he couldn't. Just before dawn, hardly able to breathe, he agreed to go to the hospital. Jane called a cab.

By mistake, the driver dropped Jim and Jane at the main door. When he realized, he offered to take them the quarter mile to the Emergency entrance, but Jim said, "No, no, I'll walk." That's Jim Henson: don't make a fuss. We were together for thirty years without a contract and he walked on this earth like no one else I knew. Jim was my biggest account, the backbone of my office. But if he wanted a meeting with me, it was always, "Do you mind? Do you have time?"

David said that the doctors thought Jim had pneumonia brought on by a virulent Group A strep bacteria that is often mistaken for the flu. The problem was that it could overwhelm its victims before they knew to get help. The bacteria had ravaged Jim's heart, lungs, kidneys, liver, and more. He was anesthetized and on a ventilator. His family was with him. Everyone was praying. David said he'd keep me informed.

After I hung up I just lay in bed and stared at the ceiling. Then I turned to Debbie and said, "Jim's sick. Very sick."

David called a few more times that day to keep me posted, and finally, that night, about eleven, he called for the last time. "Jim's gone." He was only fifty-three.

• • • • •

I got on the first plane to New York, went to the Carlyle, and took the same suite I'd been in two weeks earlier when my dad died. I got under the bed covers and ordered tuna fish and french fries from room service, but when they arrived I could hardly eat. I was overwhelmed with the finality of it all. It was like burying my children. Belushi, Gilda, and now Jim. I thought he was indestructible. He did, too, and it was almost true. David told me that the doctors had said if Jim had come to the hospital even three hours earlier, they could have saved him.

· · · · ·

Jim's funeral was held at the Cathedral of St. John the Divine, on Riverside Drive in Manhattan — the same place we had gone for the Belushi memorial. The whole ceremony was produced by the Henson organization and the spectacle was incredible, almost incomprehensible, really. Jim had as much as planned it himself. Four years earlier, while on vacation on the Côte d'Azur, he'd written a letter to his children that he asked not be opened unless he died. In it he wrote about how he thought our mission on Earth should be to have a good life. "Have a good time, it's a good life." He also wrote, "I'm not at all afraid of the thought of death and look forward to it. I suggest you first have a friendly little service of some kind. It would be lovely if there was a song or two . . . and someone said some nice, happy words about me . . . This all may sound silly to you guys, but what the hell, I'm gone — so who can argue with me?" He also asked for a Dixieland band to play "When the Saints Go Marching In," made suggestions about who could perform, and requested certain speakers. David Lazer read part of Jim's letter at the service.

When I arrived the church was already filled with pictures of Jim and the people who loved him. Over five thousand mourners — or should I say celebrants — showed up: everyone Jim had ever worked with, celebrities, and the public. Children held Bert and Ernie dolls, Kermits — all the characters — and hand-painted butterflies. I kept thinking, "Look at what this man brought to the world."

Jim's son, Brian, who now runs the company, put it well when he said his dad "was one of the world's greatest positive thinkers. . . . My father had the (rare) ability to make the good guy the more interesting, crazy, eccentric character." Others went so far as to proclaim Kermit the Mickey Mouse of the '70s, and Jim the Walt Disney of his time. Even after his death, his influence continues to grow.

The service began with a procession while "When the Saints Go

Marching In" played. We walked around the church and then down the center aisle to our seats. Once settled, Jim's friends offered remembrances and testimonials. Frank Oz, Jerry Juhl, Duncan Kenworthy, everyone. The Muppets and Harry Belafonte performed. Carol Spinney, as Big Bird, sang "It's Not Easy Being Green," because Jim, who was Kermit, couldn't.

Then it was my turn. The night before, I'd been in my hotel suite trying to write anything I could to express my love and how important Jim was to me. But I'd hit a wall, so I'd decided simply to let inspiration strike when I was on the podium. Just then a few sheets of paper slid under the door. It was like God's hand at work. Buzz Kohan, a well-known writer I represented, who often wrote all the intros for the Emmys and the Oscars, had sent me a fax.

It read, "Dear Bernie, I know how you must be feeling and I know that you're being called upon to talk tomorrow. I know how you felt about Jim and I jotted this down in case it would help you." He'd written a speech for me. It was beautiful.

The next day, I stood at the bottom of the pulpit stairs, waiting for Big Bird to finish singing. When he did, the whole place was in tears. I slowly climbed the steps, thinking, "God, if you want to help me, then make me stop blubbering now and give me something to say." I got to the top, laid my speech on the podium, took a deep breath — and it came to me. I said, "Jim told me never to follow the Bird." The place went nuts, clapped, and reset emotionally.

Then I read my remarks:

I'm Bernie Brillstein and I've been Jim's friend and manager for thirty years. In a business where the one who shouts the loudest usually gets the most attention, Jim Henson rarely spoke above a whisper. You had to lean in to hear him most of the time, but it was always worth the effort. David Lazer and I knew how loud his whisper was. He was a man with a vision, and though his greatest appeal was to the simplest of human emotions, and the purest of ideas, he was not above using the most advanced technological means to achieve his goal. My friend Jim was, by most definitions, a genius, but not like Edison suggested. Edison said genius was one percent inspiration and ninety-nine percent perspiration. With Jim I think it was about fifty-fifty. His ability to create whole worlds of people and things is well documented and they will have their legacy forever, but after coming up with the concept he worked tirelessly on every phase of the process to see that it was the best it could possibly be. As a rule perfectionists are a real pain. They drive the people around them crazy in their single-minded search for excellence, but Jim inspired people to be better than they thought they could be, and more creative, more daring, more outrageous, and ultimately more successful. And he did it all without raising his voice. That whisper will stay with us for a long time and now we'll just have to listen a little harder to hear it . . .

I stopped. There was more on the page, but I was crying and I couldn't go on. So I decided to just shut up and let everyone hear the roar of Jim's whisper for themselves.

· · · · ·

Jim Henson's death was the low point of an emotional roller-coaster ride that began when I sold my company to Lorimar. It was also a wake-up call. Like Jim's, my life had been virtually indistinguishable from my work. I used to do a hundred things at once and not realize that when you do a hundred things you can't do one correctly. I'd done it that way for thirty-five years and made a lot of money, but I was always nagged by the thought, "Gee, if I had been around just a little more, it could have been better." Although I loved what I did in good times and bad, I now realized that I didn't want my last words to be, "I should have spent more time with my family." Maybe it was time to make a change.

At sixty years old, my obituary was pretty much already written. So far, it was a damn good read. Unpredictable at the outset, inevitable in retrospect. No matter what the future would bring — more good times and great talent, or nothing — what I'd accomplished so far couldn't be erased. The overconfident kid who, in 1955, looked around the William Morris mail room and thought that getting ahead would be no problem could not have imagined how his dream of a show-business life would turn out.

I'd done a lot. The question was, did I want to do more? Did I need the hassle of struggling with people who cared more about watching their backs and their annual bonus checks than the talent they needed to advise and respect in order to do a good job? Better to take a long cruise and play lots of golf, and let the latest crop of temporary guys make what they dreamt were permanent decisions. They'd learn soon enough.

But late one night I remembered how my friend Jay Tarses had once described me to a writer: "Bernie is the whale who's never been beached. He keeps swimming. He comes up for air and that blowhole blows and he dives again. Even if some of it is bullshit and bravura, he's very shrewd, has a heart, and is massively concerned about his clients. That's why he's still around."

Jay was right. It just wasn't my nature to fade away. The problems I saw in the business only convinced me that the care and feeding of talent was a more valuable skill than ever. So was my production experience. I saw the patterns, understood the nuances, and knew how to get things done. The habits and lessons of a lifetime — instinct, passion, honesty, stability, manners, listening, humor, cynicism, wariness, ego, and my deep need for love and acceptance — had evolved in me a complex second nature that Brad could draw upon, as I drew on his youth and energy. I knew the rules of the game, Brad made new ones. I saw the big picture, he was focused. I was the stake in the ground, Brad roamed the perimeter. We needed each other. I decided that I could still make a difference.

Chapter 16

I've Got to Stop Doing
This Before I Go Blind

On January 20, 1992, I gave Brad 50 percent of my business and together we started Brillstein-Grey Entertainment. He deserved it. Brad's vision had exceeded my expectations. The company was thriving. We had nearly thirty employees and almost ninety clients, including Nick Cage, Brad Pitt, Bill Maher, Courtney Cox, Dana Delany, Garry Shandling, Norm Crosby, Bronson Pinchot, and the usual writers and producers. Dana Carvey, Adam Sandler, David Spade, Chris Farley, Jon Lovitz, Phil Hartman, Dennis Miller, Kevin Nealon, Mike Myers, and Chris Rock had made *Saturday Night Live* a hit (again) as well as a springboard for their movie and sitcom careers. Brad's scheme of bringing in the young talent while I taught him about production and introduced him to the people I knew had totally worked.

Even before we made it official, I'd thought of Brad as my partner. He'd walked through nightclub kitchens. He knew what it took to get on-stage. He understood the uncertainty, insecurities, and indulgences of stardom. Brad is also one of the few people in show business who really gets the joke — the joke being that there is no precise art to this bullshit we do for a living. There is no secret formula for success. No guarantee. He understands why I go on and on about instinct: it's my way of working from the heart, of testing myself, of trusting myself. When it succeeds, the thrill feels a lot like falling in love.

If I lack one quality, it's an interest in the fine details of business. I've been smart enough to make the most of opportunities for my clients and myself, but I've always been a broad-strokes guy who just wants to survive. Whatever innovations I've made in mixing management and production, or signing writers and producers when there were no stars to be had, I just did to help myself keep control of my world.

Hiring Brad in 1985 had the same immediate purpose. He also liked the business part. He could talk to CEOs and the acts, and feel equally at home with both. He understood power and its uses.

Brad helped me reinvent myself. Instead of being an old manager with old clients, waiting for my senior citizens' discount to kick in, I was hot again. I knew that for however much longer I stayed in the business, my relationship — and then partnership — with Brad would be a great way to finish my career.

· · · · ·

Brad and I immediately wanted to expand decisively into television. Like I'd been doing for nearly twenty years, the idea was to produce sitcoms that we could be proud of. If we came up with hits, the benefits would be substantial, especially in syndication.

Here's what I mean: When *Seinfeld* started reruns in 1995 — three years before original production stopped — the show sold for an incredible $4 million an episode. A second round of syndication sales after the series finale fetched $5.5 million a show. The total syndication gross is now more than $1.5 billion and will probably pass $2 billion. *M*A*S*H*, at its peak, only sold for $1.1 million an episode, and the previous record holder, *The Cosby Show*, took ten years to make a billion. *Seinfeld*'s syndication jackpot is a little like Mark McGwire's home-run record — it won't be equaled soon — but you get the picture. Syndication is nice money if you can get it, and it looks like there's something for everyone.

It's also the toughest of all TV gambles. Only 1.5 percent of all series survive from the time someone says, "How about a show with this star or writer?" to rerun heaven. Or, to turn it around, there's a 98.5 percent chance *against success*. At those odds producers would be smarter to take their money to Las Vegas and put it on the red or black. Yet, if a show makes it into syndication, the rewards are so outrageous that it's obvious why TV has lately become a ghetto of sitcoms. They're cheaper to produce and everyone's hoping to cash in. TV has turned into a volume business and that's the absolute wrong thing. We see the result today.

Brad and I thought we could do better, but we had a problem: not enough money to actually make the shows. The days when I could do a series for the network license fee or less were over. Writers, producers, and stars cost more than the network license fee. That meant production deficits. Even if the overrun was as small as $100,000 per episode, that's $2.2 million a season. We couldn't afford that.

We knew, because a couple years earlier I'd gotten a call from Ryan O'Neal's agent, ICM president Jim Wiatt. He said, "Ryan wants to do a series with you. He wants you to come to his house for a meeting." I couldn't believe it. I had always been a huge Ryan O'Neal fan. We'd met in 1967 at the Beverly Hills Health Club. I thought he was a great light comedian. I believed I could do a helluva comedy with Ryan. He'd be big business. I knew we could get a thirteen-show commitment or, at worst, six shows and a pilot. A series seemed like a slam dunk.

O'Neal lived in Bel Air. His house reminded me of classic Hollywood: big, beautiful, lush, and all white — with a racquetball court. He met ICM agent Alan Berger and me at the door. He asked if we wanted a drink. All I could do was stare at his huge, high-ceilinged atrium living room. When we were all comfortable, he got right to the point. "I'd like you to meet the person I want to do the show with," he said.

That's when Farrah Fawcett walked in. They'd lived together for ten years, had a son, and now they wanted to work together. It was one of those great moments in show business when — as they say in *Bonfire of the Vanities* — you think you're a master of the universe. I felt that without even trying I'd pulled off a miracle.

Ryan approved of my reaction. "What do you think, Bernie?" he asked. "Do you want to do the show?"

Whatever the show was, of course I would. I loved Farrah, too. I'd helped her get a role in *See You in the Morning* at Lorimar. I'd really pressed the director, Alan Pakula, probably because guys like me always have a crush on the unattainable woman and want to help her in any way.

All I could say was, "Great," but now I was thinking, "Forget six or thirteen shows. I can get a *twenty-two-show commitment!*" I couldn't wait to get out of the house to call Howard Stringer, head of CBS. I loved Stringer. He'd ordered four or five shows from us and had always been very nice. Stringer also wanted Lorne to come to CBS. He'd even offered to build the Lorne Michaels Theater in New York. Obviously Stringer liked that kind of gesture; he eventually built the theater for David Letterman.

I asked Ryan why he wanted me to produce. He explained that he and Farrah wanted to do something as hip and edgy as *Buffalo Bill*. Also, *Saturday Night Live* had made a comeback, and I was known for my connections to good comedy. When the meeting ended I said, "Since we don't have a concept yet, I have to find a writer. Are you sure you're in? I'm going to make calls now. You can't change your mind."

"We're in," Ryan said.

I felt like bursting into song. "Zip-a-dee-doo-dah" would have sounded great right about them. I was suddenly a genius again. In my head I was taking bows before I even left the house. Like a major asshole, I couldn't wait to tell everyone so that the whole town would say, "Hey, Bernie did it again." Besides, because of my Warner Brothers battle, I needed to renew my faith in myself, to know I was okay again.

As soon as I got in my car I phoned Stringer, in New York.

"I'm calling you first," I said.

"Okay," he said. "What do you want?"

"Twenty-two."

"For what?"

"Farrah and Ryan."

Stringer agreed on the spot. We'd set the price later. I called Wiatt and then Ryan to tell them it was firm. Wiatt advised me that although Farrah was with CAA she was definitely in. Farrah and Ryan got $150,000 a week, together, which at the time was a lot of money for two stars.

Now I had everything but a show. I needed a show runner and a concept. Jay Tarses was busy with *Molly Dodd* and didn't want to leave. I called Alan Zweibel, who had co-written and co-produced *It's Garry Shandling's Show*. He said, "Let me think about it." I didn't like it that he wasn't as sure as I was, so I pushed him. "You want to establish yourself as a big-time writer-producer? This will do it."

A couple days later Alan called and said he was in. Within a week he was even more excited. "I think I have a great idea," he said. When he finally turned in the script, we loved it.

The show, *Good Sports*, was about the relationship between Gayle Roberts (Farrah), a former supermodel now a sports journalism anchor, and Bobby Tannen (Ryan), a retired bad-boy football star who so desperately needs a job that he takes one at an ESPN-like station where he's paired on the anchor desk with Roberts. The conflict starts when she reminds him of their steamy one-night stand during his playing days and how the tables have turned. Now she's the star.

Each episode would also feature a guest segment with Ryan interviewing a real sports figure. Kareem Abdul-Jabbar was the first; he and Bobby Tannen get into a fight. Other guests would include George Steinbrenner, George Foreman, Jim Brown, and Washington Redskins quarterback Doug Williams — all playing themselves. This was ten years before Robert Wuhl used the same idea on *Arli$$*, which, when you think about it, he took from *The Larry Sanders Show*, which probably took it from George Burns and Jack Benny.

Zweibel needed extra time to write the script, so I arranged with CBS to put the series on the air without a pilot. We taped a great first show, but it took forever, and when we were finished we were already $100,000 in the hole.

By the third show nothing was working. After every scene Farrah needed hair and makeup again. I remember all of us sitting on the stage, waiting, when her hairdresser, Angelo, came out and said, "She needs another twenty minutes." My heart sank. The audience started leaving. The way most TV shows shoot, you take at most fifteen minutes between scenes, usually three. The poor warm-up guy should have gotten a bonus. We taped the last shows without an audience.

And that was the least of it. As producer-owners, Farrah helped design the sets, and the couple got involved in editing each show, resulting in what Ryan told a reporter were "three versions" of each episode, "the director's, the producer's, and the owner's. It's fun for us. In movies, you don't get to edit your own pictures; you just walk away."

Ryan disliked the director. Ryan and Farrah fought with the writers. Ryan and Farrah fought with each other. They had the most volatile relationship I've ever seen. One day Farrah turned up with a black eye. Usually Ryan was the sweetest guy, but when he was unhappy he'd just leave the lot. Every time he did, it cost me money. Then she would leave the lot. I started smoking again. I had not smoked for five years.

We also had a problem with CBS. Barbara Corday, who'd run programming, was replaced by Jeff Sagansky. He hadn't given us an air date or time slot and didn't seem in a hurry to do so. We kept shooting shows in limbo, spending my money.

We finally went on at 9:30 P.M. Thursday, against NBC's powerhouse lineup. Our ads used to say, "Tune us in right after *Cheers*. On another network."

Then Farrah started getting nervous about the ratings. As a bonafide TV star, she'd never done less than a 32 share with *Charlie's Angels*. I said, "Farrah, no show gets a 32 share anymore." I think the first show did a 24 or 22, really pretty respectable. Meanwhile we fell behind with scripts, Farrah took longer and longer to get ready, CBS switched our time slot, and the deficit ballooned.

One morning at three o'clock, Brad, Zweibel, and I walked around the Warner Hollywood lot wondering what in the world we had done. It felt like we were stuck in the middle of the Atlantic, in a rowboat without oars. I needed rest, but every phone call was about the show. I went to La Costa for a week to chill out but still couldn't stop thinking about what I'd gotten myself into. Finally, I called Brad and asked, "How much will it cost us to buy ourselves out?"

The answer was $3.4 million. And being a complete lunatic, I said, "Let's just get out, kid. We've gotta get out. This is crazy. What are we doing here? What do we need this for? Go do it."

Brad said, "No, I don't think we're going to get out. First of all, we made a commitment to the network and we've got to live up to the commitment. We have to try to make this better. Besides that, and this should have been the first thing I said, it would cost us millions. We're not writing a check for three million dollars. Go take a steam."

Brad wasn't exactly calm, but who could expect him to be? I backed off, and after we shot sixteen shows CBS eventually canceled the series. In all deference to Farrah and Ryan, despite their problems, we started in an impossible time period and moved all over. Maybe Sagansky didn't like the show or believe in it, or maybe he had no loyalty because it wasn't his idea.

Because CBS had made a twenty-two-show commitment they paid off everyone and we covered the rest with the distribution advances we kept on shows that actually aired. In any other situation we could have blown a bundle. We were lucky. Very lucky.

I'd messed up because I believed I could predict a hit. I learned, once again, that no matter who the stars are, it doesn't guarantee a damn thing. You can get financing for a show by having great elements, but all you can take to the bank is that money. You still have to make the series and do it well. You still need a good time period. You always hope for a hit when you start off, but it's stupid to say, "Oh boy, this is going to make a hundred million dollars in syndication!" Of course, you don't go out negative either. You always try to hit a home run, but it's okay to get on base and eventually score. For instance, we believed in Bill Maher. Selling *Politically Incorrect* to Comedy Central was a good thing. Selling it to ABC was like stealing a few bases.

What I thought with *Good Sports* was the greatest package of the year was only that: a package — like Ted Danson and Mary Steenburgen in the ill-fated CBS series *Ink*. But people don't watch packages, they watch good shows.

Afterward, Brad and I made a rule: never invest your own money in show business. The idea was to spread the risk by using other people's capital. It's a more common practice today with everyone, even studios, taking production partners, but at the time it was the only way Brad and I could do it. So, during a vacation at the Mauna Lani in Hawaii, Brad got Alan Levine, the president and CEO of Sony's Columbia Pictures Entertainment's Filmed Entertainment group, to be our bank. Perhaps over drinks with little umbrellas in them, Brad convinced Levine that our production experience, comedy and writing roster, and single-minded ambition were worth taking the gamble that we could consistently create shows that would stay on the air long enough to qualify for syndication. In exchange for distribution rights (that is, a 20 to 35 percent fee for selling the shows) for five years, Levine advanced us $20 million dollars. For some more money we gave Columbia and TriStar Pictures first look at our movie projects (a couple years later, one of our projects was *The Cable Guy*). Not only would the money cover deficits, but it would jump-start our new business.

It was Brad's first big deal, and he was very smart about it, because we didn't have to sell any part of our company, give away our income stream, or share ownership of our shows.

"We're like a studio now, except that there's almost no overhead," Brad told the *Los Angeles Times*. I finished the thought: "Since there are no rules for this kind of company, we make the rules."

Rule number one was already in place.

(By the way, we have both since broken our rule and put our own money on the table for select projects. I guess we can't resist that direct connection to the action.)

• • • • •

When I talk to people about show business, they always have questions. Usually there are two answers, and only one of them is the truth. What I say depends on the situation.

For instance, I'll hear, "What is this or that celebrity really like?" I always say, "Wonderful. A creative person." Most of the time the true answer is, "An egotistical, major pain in the ass. You don't know what neurotic is. And probably gay. p.s.: And cheap. I should get a fucking medal for representing that cocksucker." Well, some days you feel that way even about people you love.

Then there's, "How do I get a job in show business?" There are many bullshit answers, but the truth is that if you're young enough — although you need a college degree—you can start in any company's mail room. That hasn't changed in fifty years. You'll learn everything.

Finally, I'm asked, "I have a great idea for a TV show. How do I get it made?"

I want to be nice, so I say, "Why don't you get me the script, I'll look at it, and if it's any good . . ." Usually it's not and I'll send it back. If it is, it can be even more problematic. The networks have a list of acceptable writers and producers. If you're not on the list, you can't sell an idea, or, if you do, you can't get any further unless someone on the list is attached to run the show. There are exceptions, like if you've written some hot film scripts and want to slum on the small screen; but even then, the powers that be want to bend you to their rules.

It takes a couple years to make the list. You start by writing some great sample scripts, getting an agent, and being lucky enough to have him or her find you a job on some show as a story editor. The idea is to work your way up the title ladder — story editor, co-producer, producer, supervising producer, executive producer — either on one hit series (the best situation) or by jumping around. If you get billing — even "co-produced by" — you're on the list. It's like being granted tenure.

Once certified, particularly if you've worked on a hit, the money can roll out like a big night at the silver-dollar slots. These days, with so many channels hunting for fresh blood and new ideas, it's not uncommon for a studio or network to pick off a third-year writer and give him or her a multimillion-dollar deal to sit around the house for a few years and, the network prays, maybe create the next *Seinfeld*. The bet is that almost anyone associated with a hit can create them and then run the show.

Nice job if you can get it; given the never-ending need to fill air time, many people do. That's why there are so many nouveau-riche writers living by the beach, driving the kids to private school, spending mornings at Starbucks, taking meetings and playing golf while they're supposed to be inventing the next big thing. I guess it's *all* part of the creative process. A couple years ago I ran into a writer named Chris Thompson on the driving range. He came up with *The Naked Truth,* and he also has the best golf swing I've ever seen outside of a pro. I said, "Hey, Chris, where'd you get that great swing?"

He said, "Viacom."

Of course: the company had just made him a $9 million, three-year deal.

These big-money deals — and Brillstein-Grey has been guilty of overspending in order to get our business started and compete with cash-rich networks and studios that themselves are just trying to survive — have changed the TV business.

When I got into TV, most sitcom writers didn't go to college, but even if they had, they'd get into the TV business by first writing jokes for a comedian. David Panich wrote eight pages of single-spaced jokes for Norm Crosby. We paid him $1,000. Not a flaw in the material. David worked his way up, wrote on variety shows, and ended up as head writer on *Laugh-In* for $6,000 a week — which in the '60s and '70s was a fortune. The same story can be told about Lorne Michaels, Larry Gelbart, Carl Reiner, Mel Brooks, Peppiatt and Aylesworth, Patchett and Tarses, and plenty others of the three-network generation. The goal was to work on a sitcom or variety show that had twenty-six weeks of originals, and twenty-six of repeats. You'd stay with it until you were seasoned, then try to sell a show of your own. No big cash advances necessary.

Today, kids from the *Harvard Lampoon* or other hip college publications go to work for Letterman, Conan, and *Saturday Night Live* right out of school and make $1,200 a week. If they're good, one of the hot young agents, like Ari Emanuel at Endeavor, notices and maybe gets them on a sitcom for $6,000 a week. Co-producers make $15,000 a week. A couple years later they're co-executive producers because their boss left to take *his* big studio deal. Then it's the kid's turn to make $1 to $3 million a year. Why live in the East Village and write off-Broadway plays, or struggle over books that don't sell, or write movies that ten other people will rewrite? Good question.

Here's the answer: too much money too soon gives young writers a sense of entitlement they haven't earned — and yet all the industry seems to want are the young and unseasoned writers, as if writers of a certain age (forty and older) don't know what it's like to be young. If they place a premium on youth because they figure it makes the shows more technically authentic to have someone who knows the current lingo, fine. But what about having someone who actually knows how to write a tight script? Here's how bad it gets: Two years ago there was a kid on *Saturday Night Live* who went to the *Seinfeld* show. When his agent called and said, "I can get you two million a year for three years," the kid said, "Boy, you insulted me with that offer."

Is that insane or incredible?

The salaries also result in questionable shows getting on the air just because the network has to justify having made a huge deal in the first place with what turns out to be a third-string guy.

I've heard the counterargument: "Look, I'm down in the trenches. I'm writing the scripts. I'm there *every* day. I go through the politics. I'm learning. Why do I have to write for nothing? Besides, who knows how long my career will last?" So he tells his agent, "Get me the fucking money now!"

But just because someone's spent a few years on a hit show is no guarantee that he is a show runner instead of a show ruiner. It's hard to know if he can even write a decent script on his own. No matter how the credits read, typically the whole staff contributes to the shooting script. If you want to find out what a writer can really do, take a look at his or her sample scripts. In the old days, show runners had to know how to do everything. Patchett and Tarses could edit, cast, direct, play politics. It takes time. Seasoning. They knew about life because they'd lived it. Today, too many of the writers know about life from . . . television.

• • • • •

In 1970, the FCC placed significant restrictions on the ability of the established networks (ABC, CBS, NBC) to engage in the active syndication of their programming. The commission imposed these constraints to limit network control and encourage the development of a diversity of programs from a variety of sources. (However, a loophole allowed a network to passively syndicate the show by "suggesting" that if you wanted it on the air, it should be distributed by a company they happened to own. In the old days CBS did this all the time with their syndicator, Viacom.)

In 1991 and 1993 the rules were relaxed in order to let the networks compete more fairly with the syndication and ancillary businesses that had now grown strong because of the original ruling. By 1995 all restrictions were gone and the networks decided it was time to get a piece of the back-end action. They figured it made perfect sense. They paid for the shows, risked their air time, and only made money from selling advertising. Why shouldn't they own?

Why not, indeed? Faced with shrinking viewership — the audience is now down to about 57 percent from almost 75 percent just a dozen years ago; in fact, some pundits argue that there's no such thing as an "audience" anymore — the networks make less selling ads than they used to. Combined with the enormous expense of keeping their few hit shows on the schedule, it's clear why the networks are desperate for the extra money.

That gives hit shows leverage. With *Seinfeld* gone, NBC had no choice but to pay $13 million *per episode* (or nearly a quarter billion per season) for *E.R.*, or see it defect perhaps to CBS, whose boss, Les Moonves, originally developed the show when he was at Warner Brothers Television. Without *E.R.*, "Must-See Thursday" could become "Must-Flee Thursday." Had NBC owned a piece of the show, allowing them to tap into the syndication dollars on the back end, they might not have had to eat into their huge profits for the first time.

This didn't happen in a vacuum. As soon as NBC gave the six *Friends* a well-deserved raise — now small change by comparison — the cat was out of the bag. Next, they handed over $600,000 per show to the *Seinfeld* supporting players — and even more to Jerry. I take nothing away from that fine program, but can you imagine how *Frasier*'s Kelsey Grammer felt for a while, having to work three weeks to make what Jason Alexander made in one? Of course, now that he's spent a season in the top ten I'm sure he's also counting his money.

Prices have gone up all over. Tim Allen made $1.25 million a show during the eighth season of *Home Improvement*. Helen Hunt got $1 million and Paul Reiser $1.25 million a show their final year on *Mad About You*. I can only imagine what Cosby got to come to CBS, or what Ted Danson and Mary Steenburgen got for their failed show, *Ink*.

Where does the money come from? Only NBC made a profit in 1997, so how about job cuts? Nineteen ninety-eight was not a banner year for employment security at the major broadcasters. They also save by making newsmagazines instead of hour dramas; did you wonder why *Dateline* is on NBC almost every night, why *20/20* is on four times a week, and *60 Minutes* twice? The third source is merchandising and syndication — but only if you're an owner. The networks needed to solve that equation.

One concern about growing network ownership is whether in a close ratings call it will influence what a broadcaster keeps on the air. Will the program they own win out? Probably. That will give good shows a chance to find an audience, and bad shows a year of borrowed time. But in the end, no one will leave a stinker on the air for long.

• • • • •

If networks really want to save money there's an easy way: eliminate TV pilots.

Each year, after months of schmoozing actors, writers, producers, agents, and managers, network executives listen to pitches for new shows. Sometimes it's a writer-producer with an original concept; other times a star wants to do a sitcom and develops an idea with a show runner he or she likes. If the network is interested, they order a script. Interested means that they like the concept, or that it's positioned as a companion piece to something they already have on the air, or that it targets the eighteen- to forty-nine-year-old demographic advertisers are dying to reach. Just having a funny show isn't good enough anymore.

If the read is good, a pilot is ordered: that is, a single sample show based on the script. Creative meetings are held, script and casting notes submitted and argued over, expensive sets built. Then the race is on to hire the same actors, directors, show runners, and crew everyone else is trying to hire for their pilots.

The average half-hour pilot costs $1.2 million, often more. The four major networks each spend about $30 million on twenty-five pilots a year. That's $120 million. If you also include pilots made for the WB and UPN networks, HBO, Showtime, Lifetime, USA networks, other cable outlets, game shows, talk shows, first-run syndication, and midseason replacements, it's even more. Lots more.

The pilot has to be finished in the spring, in time for the network to spend a couple weeks evaluating it along with all the other pilots they ordered. In May, the networks tell the advertisers and the public which shows made their fall schedules. The winners are rarely surprising. Most are safely formulaic, some slightly adventurous. Throw in a couple clones of last year's big hits and a dark horse or two and you once again have the annual preview issue of *TV Guide*.

To make and choose pilots is costly enough, but the networks have just gotten started. Now they'll spend additional millions to audience-test the shows on focus groups. In other words, they recruit suburban-mall shoppers and people with too much time on their hands who can't say no to free screening tickets. They're gathered in a nondescript room, shown a sitcom, asked often leading questions, and asked to fill out little comment cards. Their reactions are then complied into a dizzying array of statistics from which supposed general viewership preferences are extrapolated. Then networks use the data to second-guess every aspect of the pilots they only recently found so compelling. Development executives push, prod, and eventually insist — if they can — that the creators bring their bright new programs directly in line with the networks' comfort zones. It's amazing to me that twelve people in Podunk can make a network once hot on a sitcom suddenly rethink their position. Who are these people and why are they allowed to speak for everyone and against a professional's instinct? Here's why: Once there's big money involved, most creative bets are off, and the development teams lunge for the middle of the road by obliterating any interesting or artistic curves. Even though it's almost always the unconventional show that becomes a breakout hit, it's still very tough to get original on TV because research (hallowed be thy name) suggests that audiences are notoriously uncomfortable with the unfamiliar. No wonder networks think it's better to potchky a show to death with old tricks than to let loose a new dog.

This doesn't make much sense to me. The longer I've been in TV the more I've realized not to put my faith in the tests. They can be helpful, but they can never stand alone. There must be a human instinct involved, or audiences (who may like the familiar but complain that there's nothing to watch and vote that belief by tuning out most new shows) will totally cease to care. I know it makes the number crunchers uncomfortable because it's impossible to factor intuition into their equations, but that's still at the core of what we're all trying to do: make shows that people want to see, not just series that advertisers want to buy.

I remember the Muppet research: "The frog can't be the host of a show." Belushi? "Get rid of him on *Saturday Night Live*." Didn't it take three years and a couple date and time changes for *Seinfeld*, a show about narcissistic singles in New York, to find its feet?

In a *New Yorker* behind-the-scenes piece on the making of ABC's 1998 sitcom *Sports Night* — a quirky show set at an ESPN-like network, very much like *Good Sports* — Tad Friend wrote, "There are three rules for creating a hit network television show. Unfortunately, no one knows what they are."

That sums it up. Buying a new series based on a tampered-with pilot is like believing that the appetizer will tell you how good the whole meal will be. That's crazy. Still, the networks and advertisers believe in the magic, like Ponce de Leon believed in the fountain of youth. I hear he recently died without ever getting to take a drink.

The best networks can do is hedge their bets — and they do, every step of the way. They make pilots because they're afraid to trust their instincts at the outset; they do research because they're afraid to trust their instincts when they see the show with their own eyes; they cancel series when the audience doesn't confirm the instincts they didn't believe in the first place.

How about believing in great writing, wonderful casts, and talented producers? Do we shoot movie pilots before we shoot a movie? (No, we just hire six writers per script.) Networks have only to look at their dismal track records to know that whatever they're doing doesn't work. According to an AP story last year by writer Frazier Moore, of the forty-nine hour drama pilots ordered in 1997, only two got on the air and survived to return for a second year: *The Practice* and *Ally McBeal*. A 4 percent success rate. It's a little better for sitcoms, but not much, especially this year (1999), when about half the usual crop was ordered and dramas were bought instead. Yet this is the most creative way networks have come up with to pick contenders to plug the many schedule holes where last season's failures used to be.

No wonder the system doesn't work.

As Jeff MacGregor wrote in the *New York Times*, "Start with a bad idea. Add self-fulfilling research and cynical assumptions; ignore history. The result: Magic Johnson, talk show host." I'm talking about the sitcoms, but the principle is the same.

In TV you want to be the guy who takes the chances, because you score biggest by being first with something new the audience wants to see. The rest is desperation and imitation. Why would someone watch a *Friends* clone when the original is still around? Why is an imitation even on? Because on TV imitation is the sincerest form of flatulence. There's too much "air" to fill, and too few creative writers and producers to fill it well. If you're going to be derivative, at least wait for the cycle to come around again and then tweak it in some interesting way. What is *The Muppet Show* if not simply *Laugh-In* with puppets? And *Laugh-In* was once the old Broadway show *Hellzapoppin!*

Try something new. Use your instinct. Celebrate uncertainty.

Look at Conan O'Brien. When Lorne, who controls the *Late Night* slot, chose Conan to succeed Letterman, NBC had so little faith that they only gave O'Brien a thirteen-week contract. They applied the same thinking to him as they did to a new series: "If it doesn't work immediately, we can pull it." The show was rough and awkward at first, and with so many overhyped talk shows already come and gone, the press did its usual best to add Conan to the list. But Lorne believed in Conan, and he helped NBC believe long enough to let Conan find his way. Adversity must build character, because Conan just celebrated his sixth anniversary on the air.

If I ran a network I'd choose my scripts and stars and go directly to air. Forget pilots. I'm not saying that my way would produce more top-twenty hits, longer-running series, or even higher-quality shows, though it may. It just wouldn't produce less. And the networks could save millions in the process.

For the $30 million each network spends trying to decide what to put on, I could buy six sitcoms instead, at an average license fee of $400,000 per episode, give them thirteen-show commitments, and see what happens. I'd have to spend that same money *anyway* on license fees down the line, so why spend it twice?

What TV needs are human beings willing to risk making mistakes and not hide the result in a development process designed to obscure network cluelessness by promoting nonaccountability.

Networks defend the pilot system, saying, "How else do we know what we're buying?" What they really mean is how do the *advertisers* know what *they're* buying? According to CBS CEO Les Moonves, during a question-and-answer session at the Museum of Television and Radio in Los Angeles, the advertisers' desire to target what they consider the all-important eighteen-to-forty-nine and eighteen-to-thirty-four age groups results in shows being developed to capture those ad dollars. He doesn't like it because that stranglehold tends to ignore older viewers, who, common sense dictates, have *more* disposable income. I don't care what anyone says: I have more money than my sons and daughters combined and therefore I should be a more desirable target audience. I go on cruises each year with hundreds of people over fifty who spend money like it's going out of style. So what's the catch? Advertisers think that the older you are, the *less likely* you are to switch brands. So they try to establish brand loyalty in the young. But just because I'm sixty-eight doesn't mean I won't change my toothpaste, shampoo, or deodorant in a second if something else I like comes along. Old people like to be clean, too. Instead of wasting "new and improved" on household products, how about trying it with TV shows? (Any network is free to use that as their ad campaign, my treat.)

I think that the minute you have someone outside the system paying for it, the mediocre sets in. Allowing the advertisers' demographic lust to rule programming choices — because TV is essentially a selling medium, and entertainment is just the bait — is how viewers get those "prefabricated, predigested" bits.

If I ran TV, I'd commit to my shows, start shooting, give the ad guys some cassettes, and let them pick their spots. Maybe it's not as simple as it sounds, but I guarantee you that Madison Avenue will eventually find something to like for their money. They'll have no other choice — especially with the over-fifty age group growing so fast. Where else can they go for that kind of mass exposure? Someone's always got something to sell, and if there's a space available it will be filled. The networks have more power than they realize if they all stand together. Make it a commercial-time seller's market, not a buyer's.

Best of all, no pilots means reduced overhead, so if ad rates suffer for a while during the adjustment period, it's not that bad.

Limiting advertiser influence has another benefit. Networks can take more programming risks and compete with cable. They'll have to if they want to survive. They'll have to change FCC rules if they want to prosper.

· · · · ·

Cable has broken new ground by capitalizing on old ground abandoned by the demographic-seeking networks. Special movie events, like *Wallace* or *Truman,* used to be made as theatrical films or networks specials. Now you see them on HBO or Showtime or TNT. Compare the Roy Cohn bio movie on HBO with the usual woman-in-jeopardy flick and it's no contest. How do you put *Attica* on network television the way John Frankenheimer made it? You can't and be real. Cable now makes the movies Hollywood won't make anymore and the networks can't do.

HBO — specifically its former head, Michael Fuchs — also killed network comedy and variety specials. He built his business on being the alternative. Just about every major comedian for the last twenty years, starting with George Carlin, has had their own cable special. With no advertisers to worry about they could be true to the language and content of material they performed in concert. Jay Leno can joke about the president's definition of sexual intercourse on *The Tonight Show*, but only on cable can Chris Rock explain the difference between black people and niggers. Robin Williams can grab his crotch. Carlin can use his seven dirty words. Dennis Miller can brilliantly skewer the culture. *Taxi Cab Confessions* can peep into people's lives. On *Sex and the City*, four actresses can ruminate about toxic men and blow jobs. The Emmy-winning, cutting edge *Mr. Show* on HBO has the freedom to evolve sketch comedy to the next plateau, and, incidentally, I get to feel young again working with them. On *The Sopranos* even a Godfather can see a shrink and find humor in macabre introspection.

Think what Lenny Bruce would have given for HBO.

Let me turn this around for a moment. When critics compare cable and network shows, networks always come up short, because it stands to reason that if they weren't putting safe junk on the air, then their numbers wouldn't fall as fast (with all this choice they would have shrunk anyway). Then critics blame the problem on the *people* who program broadcast TV, as if they just aren't smart enough to realize what people really like; as if they just won't give in to what the public really wants.

That's not true.

Don Ohlmeyer would have put *The Larry Sanders Show* on NBC as is in two seconds if he could have. Most network executives watched it and loved it. I think Les Moonves at CBS, Scott Sassa at NBC, Stu Bloomberg, Jamie Tarses, and Bob Iger at ABC, and Doug Herzog at Fox are as hip and au courant as Jeff Bewkes and Chris Albrecht at HBO, Jerry Offsay at Showtime, and Ted Turner. If anything, Ted Turner's probably squarer than all of them, down deep. Network people are not idiots who don't know what's going on. They're just handcuffed by the old rules: advertisers, the FCC, protest groups, license renewal, special-interest lobbies. They have to be careful not to transgress against the "will of the people," which is not *really* the will of the people but an antiquated system of idiocracy.

Until recently, the most networks could get away with was soft dirty stuff like Johnny Carson used to do. You can show soft-core Victoria's Se-

cret ads, but you can't say "tits." You can talk about condoms —
finally — on network TV, but you still can't sell them. Violence, of
course, has always been thoughtless and over the top.

Thanks to warning labels, TV ratings, and the handwriting on the
wall, the situation has somewhat improved. Adult themes and occa
sional salty language are now allowed after ten o'clock. I wish I could say
it was because the broadcasters had a philosophical or cultural epiphany.
They didn't. Advertisers just realized that mature viewers also buy toothpaste, so they were willing to sponsor shows like *N.Y.P.D. Blue,* no matter
how much the right-wing Christians protested. The FCC didn't complain
and that was that.

We still have a long way to go. I think it's criminal that on network
TV, homosexual characters have to be "obvious" and portrayed as very
flamboyant, very prissy. I know many homosexuals who are as mascu-
line or feminine as the next guy, and who walk through life without anyone knowing they're gay. They don't make pronouncements, they just
happen to live with another man or woman because they choose to.

On the other hand, as much as I support Ellen DeGeneres doing her
thing on TV, the show got canned because it just lost sight of the humor.
It's one thing to spread an important message of tolerance, but what
good does it do to kill the messenger by pushing an agenda over
comedy — or by just finding laughs in the straight versus gay vein? Bottom line, but *Ellen* was a *sitcom* — not a *sit on my face*-com. As much as
the people wanted to support her, they weren't laughing.

For the networks to survive and compete, the playing field must be
leveled. Maybe that means replacing nervous advertisers with sub-
scribers. How "free" is free TV when most of it comes in over the cable
anyway? Wouldn't we pay a little more for better network shows? Once,
everyone in TV said it couldn't exist without cigarette advertising. They
were wrong. Now we need to fix the rest of it before it all goes up in
smoke.

Eliminate pilots and other network "creative" interference. Develop
talent. Let writers season so they know more about life. Encourage new
ideas. Reduce advertiser control. Level the playing field between network
and cable. Listen to the audience.

· · · · ·

As soon as Brillstein-Grey had the Columbia distribution deal, we hired writers and developed shows. We did a pilot with Sherman Hemsley (*The Jeffersons*) that didn't sell, and *Newsradio*, which did. Then *Newsradio* became a network and critical hit. We also sold two shows to Michael Fuchs at HBO — *Larry Sanders*, a critical hit, and *Def Jam*, a ratings hit — before he got dumped by Bob Daly and Terry Semel in a power struggle at Time-Warner. Fuchs is one of the most talented executives I know. To this day he is thanked from award podiums everywhere by the talent whose careers he supported, and in some cases gave their first big break. He's driven and bright and has earned a lot of loyalty.

I met Fuchs in the mid-'70s when, after working as a lawyer at William Morris, he was trying to set up HBO. He walked into my office and asked me to give him the comedian David Steinberg for a half-hour comedy special from the Playboy Club in New York. "Please," he said. "I need the favor." So I did, without telling him that I'd been having big trouble getting Steinberg a job and that he really needed the twenty grand. Even if he hadn't, I would have done the deal. Fuchs seduced me with his passion. He painted a compelling picture of HBO's potential at a time when most people in show business just thought of cable as a way to get uncut movies and TV reception in the sticks. Fuchs wanted to attract attention and be on the leading edge. Uncensored comedy would be a major part of the equation.

Fuchs never forgot the favor and has been influential in Brad and my careers, buying shows ranging from Henson's *Fraggle Rock* and *The Ghost of Fafnir Hall* to *The Dennis Miller Show* to a Norm Crosby special — hardly risqué comedy — from Hilton Head, South Carolina.

I loved that Fuchs understood in two seconds how *Def Jam* and *Sanders* would work. He seemed to know that *Def Jam*'s raw cultural and sexual humor would draw not only the obvious and significant black audience but a white one as well. White people also loved the humor but were afraid to go to black comedy clubs. The show was a way to be hip in the safety of their living rooms.

The Larry Sanders Show was a classic from the moment it was launched in the wake of Johnny Carson's retirement, during the networks' late-night talk-show wars. Fuchs realized that Shandling, a former *Tonight Show* guest host who had been offered millions to take Letterman's spot at *Late Night* as well as the post-Letterman spot on CBS that eventually went to Tom Snyder, not only knew the nuts and bolts and precise height of the host's chair, but had a comedic take on the talk-show format that revealed twisted insight deep into the cracks of the human condition. The combination was timely and irresistible, and it was a story that could only be told on cable. It was Garry's good luck that Fuchs had a similar notion that he'd been trying to get HBO to develop. When they talked they finished each others' sentences, and Fuchs picked up the show for thirteen episodes.

I was at the first HBO meeting with Fuchs and Chris Albrecht (now HBO's president for original programming), at the Beverly Hills Hotel. We didn't have to do a big presentation because Fuchs was ready to buy the concept, so we just bullshitted for a while. Afterwards, in typical, non-confrontational Larry Sanders fashion, Garry told me that he "didn't like" Albrecht, and could I call Fuchs and ask to keep him out of meetings? I had to — he was our client — so I did.

A few months later, after Garry and Dennis Klein had written the pilot script, I was in the front seat of Brad's car on the way to the first *Larry Sanders* reading, when Brad turned to me and said, "I've got to tell you something. Garry will let this be a Brillstein-Grey presentation, but you can't have billing as executive producer." Now *I* was out — at least on the credit crawl.

I was hurt, but not surprised. It was just like Garry. He probably loved the ironic twist of using his manager against his manager's partner to try and break us up. Although I thought he was quick and funny, I'd never really liked Garry personally, from the day we met. He was passive-aggressive and provocative and always tried to make me say things differently than Brad had. Devious people do that; good partners don't give in to it. I remember once when Brad and I had an intense two-hour meeting with him, he ordered lunch for himself and never even asked us if we wanted any. Then he ate while we watched. The guy acts like Mr. Nobility, but he's got as many personalities as Roseanne — and none as interesting.

He still gives me the creeps.

The more I thought about being excluded as a producer — which was hardly fair since we *owned* half the show and worked hard on it — the more I realized that at heart Garry was envious of my relationship with Brad. He wanted Brad all to himself, like some jealous lover. What Garry never understood is that there was never any competition. Even in the toughest of times, my relationship with Brad has always been secure.

I kept my distance from *The Larry Sanders Show.* I was still financially responsible along with Garry and Brad for getting everything in on time and on budget — the exact same responsibilities we had had on *It's Garry Shandling's Show* — but I figured life was too short to give it another thought. Besides, Brad was there constantly, taking care of business.

I admit I never would have believed it could happen, but Garry eventually turned on Brad. After eighteen years of close friendship, Garry acted like a spurned wife. Not exactly regular behavior. Nor was the $100 million lawsuit Garry filed — not a number one can quietly settle for less; Garry wants a public spectacle — claiming that Brad traded on their relationship to become, well . . . *Brad Grey.* In fact, Garry relied on Brad to become *Garry Shandling.* As of this writing, Garry wants 50 percent of the money Brillstein-Grey made from TV deals. He said Brad callously built our "management/production empire" on his talent and connections without compensating him. What bullshit. I was producing TV when Garry was still hanging around his mother's pet shop in Arizona. I didn't need his help. (Though he needed mine to get an agent in 1972. I wonder if he remembers.) I taught Brad the ropes. Never during any of our negotiation with companies like Columbia, ABC, or Universal did they ever say, "If you bring Garry Shandling along you have a deal." If you believe Shandling's claims, then it's genuinely amazing that our company could do *The Sopranos* without him.

Garry also charged Brad with systematically diverting *Larry Sanders* writers and producers from the show to other Brillstein-Grey sitcoms, from which Brad but not Garry profited. It's true that as a first-rate comedian, Garry knew almost every good writer in the business. They would line up and say, "Please let me work for him." We'd send them over for his consideration. Of those he hired, most left because he's nearly impossible to work with. In my opinion he's both anal and lazy, pushing every deadline until the final second, and then blaming someone else for his problems. Or they were fired. The list includes Paul Simms, who created *Newsradio;* Steve Levitan, who created *Just Shoot Me;* Fred Barron, who created *Caroline in the City,* and even *The Larry Sanders Show* co-creator, Dennis Klein.

Garry's most ridiculous claim is that Brad didn't look out for his interests. Garry now portrays himself as an innocent comedian who's been taken advantage of by an unscrupulous manager. Come on. Does Garry truly expect anyone to believe that he of all people could be so easily taken in? As Brad told the papers, "This notion of a poor guy who was out there on his own is crazy. And the notion that the guy who creates the most intelligent half-hour on the inner workings of television doesn't get it, well, you just can't have it both ways."

You can't. Bullies always blink. A few days before the trial was set to begin, and in the midst of courtroom delays and ominous news reports about the landmark impact the case would have on managers who produce, Shandling suddenly decided to drop his $100 million suit and settle. Just like that. When the deal was done, and before the story hit the press, Brad called me. I was on a yacht off the coast of Monte Carlo, admiring the royal palace and the sunset. The view was enough to reassure me that there is a God, but the joy in Brad's voice confirmed it. I didn't get every detail, and I didn't want to know — it's Brad's business now — but let's just say that the outcome of this (in reality) alienation of affections lawsuit made Brad very happy, as if he'd ended up with the house, the money, and the kids.

Here's the clincher: After Shandling filed his lawsuit and barred Brad and me from the *Larry Sanders* set, he also tossed out the directors chairs with our names across the back. I asked our company's director of TV production, Tony Carey, to rescue the chairs and hold on to them. Then I made a plan. I told Tony that on the day we settled with Shandling, he was to send my chair to my house and to put Brad's chair in his office with a bottle of champagne and a note from me that read, "Congratulations. The good guys always win." I was in the south of France when it happened, but Brad assures me the moment was golden.

Garry is a special talent, but a sad case. I can't help it that he's almost fifty and pretty much alone. He has very few *real* friends, almost no family, and is an unhappy person. That's not my doing. Whatever I did for Garry Shandling's career, I did with Brad and for Brad. Brad didn't really need me. He did a great job with his former friend all on his own. He did the same kind of deeply personal job I did for Henson and Lorne and Gilda. If the people I loved had treated me like Garry treated Brad, I would have been heartbroken. Brad is. Out of everything, that upsets me the most.

• • • • •

In December 1993, Brad approached then–ABC Entertainment president Ted Harbert at the Mauna Lani hotel in Hawaii with an idea.

(Always the Mauna Lani. They should take a commission.) In the wake of the first stage of allowing networks to own shows and share in syndication money, he was looking for a way that ABC could step through the door in a big way. Harbert had an intriguing suggestion: ABC would buy half of our television business for five years — the management company was not part of the deal — in exchange for first look at everything we developed. They'd pick up our overhead and deficits, and if they didn't like the pilots, we were free to sell them elsewhere. We could also focus on other media, such as videocassette, cable, radio, TV films, and even late-night if it became an option. Columbia would remain the syndicator. The *New York Times* later put a price tag of about $125 million on the deal, which they reported was based on our "track record nurturing talent — especially comedians — coupled with demand for programming in the expanding television marketplace." This was a way for ABC to fill its pipeline, and a way for us to grow.

After Brad and Harbert spoke, Ted ran the discussion by his boss, ABC Network Group president Bob Iger. I sat with Brad and in less than ten minutes sketched out what we wanted. Iger had by then spoken to Cap Cities/ABC chairman Tom Murphy. They called and we all met for drinks at the Peninsula Hotel in Beverly Hills. (At one point, Brad went out of the room, and I said, "Guys, whatever you're doing here, what you're getting in Brad is worth more than you know. He's going to be the next big guy in the business." I really believed it and I was right.) When the meeting was over, we let the lawyers get involved — Brad had also asked Ovitz and CAA to take part — and we agreed to meet again on January 10, 1994, to settle the deal. We did, and at a price within 10 percent of Brad's and my ideal figure.

When the joint venture was announced we were suddenly hot geniuses at the zenith of our popularity. The story made the papers along with pictures of Brad and me posing elegantly in suits and ties, with big smiles. It felt good, because we both knew that at heart we were still a couple guys who'd had the good fortune to walk through a kitchen to get backstage at a club, and had a feel for talent. We also understood that we'd broken new ground and were poised to make it in a big way.

What we didn't know was it was the last big deal we would make together.

· · · · ·

The company was on its way, and once again I considered slowing down. I was sixty-three and the idea of talking every day to ABC — nothing personal, I was just tired — was not appealing. I'd been there and done that. Nothing had really changed, except that the stakes were much bigger.

Another reason I wanted less responsibility at work was that my marriage to Debbie had fallen apart. We'd been together twenty years. That's not bad, but sometimes I'm amazed it lasted that long, since I was usually so buried in business that I didn't give my private life a fair shake.

Debbie also had personal demons that complicated matters. The year before we split up I'd brought a computer home to get my e-mail. I hardly touched the machine, but Debbie got hooked and started meeting other men online. In the end, she fell in love and flew off to meet the guy. Then they moved into our house in Sun Valley, Idaho. That was really weird, and very sad, but in the end it was God doing a nice thing for us both. There was too much water under the bridge and problems we couldn't return to and resolve.

Leigh Brillstein:
My father and Debbie had planned a 20th-anniversary trip to Africa in June 1995, with all the kids. Three days before we were set to leave, Debbie announced that she wasn't going. My father hates to disappoint anyone, so we all went without her. At one of our first lodges, in Kenya, on the actual anniversary night, we went up to the roof for a barbecue. Everyone had cocktails and some African singers shuffled out in their costumes to sing "Caribou," a welcome song. Behind them the sun set in a blue and purple sky. It was so beautiful. That's when, without warning, the waiters brought out an anniversary cake my father had called ahead to order — and had forgotten to cancel. I looked at him and saw him cry for only the second time in my life. There he was on his 20th wedding anniversary, with everyone but his wife. He knew he was all alone.

Not that I had to be. After the divorce, my friend Marcy Klein, a producer at *Saturday Night Live* and the daughter of Calvin Klein, said, "Bernie, I have a girlfriend, she's just gorgeous, and I'm wondering if you'd like to go out with . . . her mother."

Her mother? I thought she meant the girlfriend. I also must have thought I was still forty-five.

Eventually I did go out on a blind date with a woman named Carrie Winston. We met at the Ivy. She was gorgeous. But almost immediately she said, "I'm almost fifty and I'm tired of dating and telling my story. I just can't do this anymore." I said, "I'm not nuts about it either. I just came out of a twenty-year marriage." She said, "I could use a drink. Then let's order dinner and you can tell me about yourself." Three hours later we were still going at it. Two years later we got married and it's the happiest I've ever been.

· · · · ·

The summer of 1995 was a crazy time for the entertainment industry. Seagram took over MCA. Ovitz left CAA. Disney purchased Cap Cities/ABC. Needless to say, Disney buying ABC complicated our production deal. Eisner already had a vast TV division and didn't need us. When he looked at the contract I don't think he liked what he saw. Meanwhile, Ovitz tried to get Eisner to hire Brad out from under our company, saying, "We're paying for one hundred percent of Brillstein-Grey's shows; if we bring in Brad we'll really be getting our money's worth."

Eisner didn't think it made sense. He said, "I already paid for this, why should I pay twice?"

When two of our ABC series, *The Jeff Foxworthy Show* and *The Naked Truth*, had trouble and were about to be canceled, we made an unusual move and got them picked up by NBC. The idea that ABC paid for shows that had been on his network and then gone elsewhere drove Eisner nuts. Disney decided to get tough. Before the merger ABC had picked up deficits beyond the contractual limit. Eisner stopped that, meaning we had to pay the remainder out of our own pockets. With six shows on the air we could quickly go broke.

While all this swirled around us, major companies began to aggressively court Brad. Naturally, I wanted him to stay, but these things happen. My problem was less that others wanted Brad — I'd always touted him as the next big thing — and more that not one of my "friends" who were offering these jobs had the courtesy to call and let me know, even if it wasn't strictly required. That hurt. The only person who told me about every solicitation was Brad. Some were clearly not worth it, and I told Brad I didn't think he'd be comfortable in those environments. Others were far more tempting, and Brad faced tough decisions — which I also told him. He had to follow his heart.

Brad stayed with Brillstein-Grey. Even though I'd been twenty years older and at a different stage of my career at the time, maybe Brad had learned a thing or two from watching what had happened to me at Lorimar. He knew that his power came from the talent he controlled, not from working for someone who would try to control him. Brad has always liked to be in control of himself.

And that's why I didn't need a crystal ball to see that with the ABC deal Brad had come into his own. He'd fulfilled the promise I'd seen ten years earlier, over breakfast, when he'd suggested that we get into business together. Even in the '80s he'd brought '90s thinking to the company and most of what we imagined and more had come true. In a way, my era had ended when we'd moved from 9200 Sunset to two floors of spacious offices on Wilshire Boulevard in Beverly Hills. It was time to let Brad steer the ship.

In October 1995 I wrote a memo to the company. I wasn't retiring, but I said that "no company should be run by two people." From then on I'd be the founding partner and Brad could make the decisions — with a lot of input from me. It didn't take long for the rumor mill to explode with speculation that my stepping back was the only way I could keep Brad around. It sounded plausible — I probably would have jumped to that conclusion myself — but it just wasn't true. Brad was better off at Brillstein-Grey and we both knew it.

Then it was back to business. The ABC deal was in trouble — we'd end it by mutual agreement in early 1998 — so Brad covered us by selling half of our remaining half of the TV production business to Universal Studios in exchange for deficit financing and development support. Universal also hoped to distribute our shows after the Columbia deal expired. More I don't know because I wasn't asked to be part of it.

With the Universal deal in the works, Brad offered to buy out my shares of everything Brillstein-Grey. He knew I needed money to settle the financial end of my divorce, and although I wish the timing had been better emotionally, I realize that this was his way of helping me *and* himself. As always I did what I had to do. Besides, Brad gave me a fortune. I'd already sold my company once; how many guys get to do it twice?

On April 1, 1996 (the irony of the date was not lost on me), I signed the papers giving Brad everything. I took my money, Brad's assurances that he loved me, and a very nice employment contract, and walked away, back to my office, where no matter how much I believed it was legitimately Brad's time and that his love was true, the reality of no longer being king hit me all at once, and my world came crashing down.

But you already know that story, and how I made it through the emotional turbulence to the other side. That's the story of my life. So far. That's show business.

I'm king again, king of myself.

In the beginning, not being king wasn't a wonderful place to be. When I was the boss, I was the guy who did it all. Lots of people looked up to me. Then suddenly it was over. I became cynical, angry, and sad. I was scared that without my power and position no one would care about me, that I'd lose my identity. Part of being king is being afraid that if you're not around someone else will take your bows. Someone else might say, "Hey, I did that." My fear made me forget that I was more than a name on a credit roll or the office door.

The three and a half years since Brad took over have been a catharsis. I lived through something I never thought I could survive — until I remembered that what I'd always done is survive. This time I had to redefine myself. I had to learn to let other people do what I used to do, I had to be content watching and participate only when I felt the need. As a result I take more pride in this company than I ever did. After all, I started it. What everyone, especially Brad, has done with it makes me very happy.

Lorne explained his take on my transformation one night over dinner. He said I was happy again because I'd traded the responsibility of directing a company for what I always did best: management pure and simple. Dealing with people. "You took all that control freakishness and put it into your clients," he said, "and we're all doing better than ever." He's right.

・ ・ ・ ・ ・

The best thing is that I'm full of new energy and using it. For years I'd wanted to represent Marty Short. Now I've signed him. Marty's had a wonderful, steady career, from SCTV to Saturday Night Live to the movies; yet he

*never made the big leap. That's the kind of challenge I love. We talked about all
the options, including Broadway. So I got busy. In late 1998 he opened to rave
reviews in a revivial of* Little Me, *playing nine different characters, and recently
won a Tony Award as best lead actor in a musical for that performance. I also
told the King brothers (Roger and Michael, co-chairmen of TV syndication giant KingWorld — they handle* Oprah *and* Roseanne*) that Marty wanted to
try a talk show. They jumped at the chance. It debuted in September. I executive-
produce.*

*A couple years ago, my good friend and client John Larroquette was of-
fered a guest-starring role on David Kelley's show* The Practice. *They said he
would play a brilliant, psychotic, gay city councilman who blatantly commits
murder and tries to get away with it. Great Kelley script. Wonderful dramatic
part. John, who is so articulate and so bright, nonetheless had a difficult time
making a decision. It got down to the last day. We had a 5 P.M. deadline. At
4:20 we were still talking. I said, "John, we've really got to make up our
minds." I had already wrapped up a pilot deal for a new CBS sitcom called*
Payne, *an American version of John Cleese's* Fawlty Towers. The Practice
was a one-shot, not a lot of money.

John said, "Jesus, Bernie, I can't step up to the plate."

*"John," I said, "I swear, I know you can kill in this role — no pun in-
tended."*

I must have sounded sure of myself. "Let's do it then," he said.

*It was my instinct and his decision. He made the right one. In 1998 John
walked away with an Emmy for the part and has since reprised it more than
once — including an eerie cameo in last season's cliffhanger finale.*

Since then, Larroquette starred in Payne, *and then did ten hours of the
miniseries* The Tenth Kingdom *for Robert Halmi and NBC. He also turned
down two Broadway shows. I understand. Sometimes a guy has to stay at
home.*

Lorne is now celebrating his twenty-fifth season in charge of Saturday
Night Live, *having last year easily blown off a threat from Howard Stern's
Saturday-night show. Lorne was also elected to the Television Hall of Fame like
my client Jim Henson before him. It makes me more than proud.*

Bronson Pinchot jumped from his canceled sitcom, Meego, *to the movies,
playing Stan Laurel in* Laurel and Hardy. *He also went onstage in New York
and Los Angeles, in* An Evening with Stephen Sondheim.

Troy Miller, the director who put together the wonderful opening reel at the 1998 Oscars that inserted Billy Crystal into each of the five Best Picture–nominated films, produced HBO's Mr. Show, *in which my client Bob Odenkirk stars with his partner, David Cross. Miller also directed the film* Jack Frost *for Warner Brothers, starring Michael Keaton and Kelly Preston. I don't know how he did it, but he made the star, Michael Keaton, look as good as he is.*

Alan Zweibel is selling movie scripts like crazy, including Rob Reiner's latest, The Story of Us, *starring Bruce Willis and Michelle Pfeiffer.*

Alan Tudyk, whom I discovered when he played multiple roles in the off-Broadway version of Zweibel's paean to Gilda Radner, Bunny, Bunny *(which I co-produced), is on Broadway in a Paul Rudnick play. He's also headed for the movies — as is* Bunny Bunny.

Rob Lowe is always busy. He's done three independent films and a TV movie called Atomic Train *that NBC really scored with in last season's May sweeps. Rob also writes scripts, is directing, and had a great cameo in the second Austin Powers film,* The Spy Who Shagged Me, *starring Mike Myers. He played the younger version of Robert Wagner's Number 2. (Tell me: Why doesn't someone make a movie with Robert Wagner and Rob Lowe as father and son?) Also, Rob's hour drama,* West Wing *(as in White House), from John Wells, the producer of* E.R., *made the NBC night schedule and is on Wednesdays at 9* P.M. *Rob Lowe is Rob Lowe again — plus. Oh, and he has a new agent, my daughter Leigh. Brillstein and Brillstein. Imagine that.*

As for Brillstein-Grey, we're doing just great. Our new HBO series, The Sopranos, *a popular and critical hit since its debut in early 1999 — talk about its Emmy prospects began immediately — was quickly renewed, and the second season will begin in January 2000. Last summer, just as this book went to press, the show received sixteen Emmy nominations and was the first cable drama to make it into the prestigious Best Drama Series category. By the time you read this, maybe some of* The Sopranos' *Emmy nods will have turned into golden statuettes. I hope all.*

Our other series also did well, with Bill Maher's Politically Incorrect, Mr. Show, *and* Just Shoot Me *nabbing multiple nominations, including a Best Supporting Actor/Actress in a Comedy Series for David Spade and Wendie Malick in the latter. Our client Dennis Miller also got three nominations, and there were others, bringing the total for our office to thirty-three. In fact, among all studios, Brillstein-Grey Entertainment tied for second place with*

Paramount in the nominations count — beating out Warners, Disney, Columbia, and Studios USA. Not bad at all.

Also in the news: Brad ended our deal with Universal and struck a huge new one with Columbia TriStar Television to create BGTV, a TV production-studio co-venture that ensures we can keep making the best in original programming. He also signed a first-look film deal with Miramax.

Perhaps the most fun for me, besides all my clients working and new opportunities every day, has been getting to know the legendary movie producer Robert Evans.

I'd met Bob Evans a few times over the years, but he'd always been my hero. Bob and his brother, Charles, and I came from virtually the same neighborhood, and growing up they were everything I wanted to be: great looking, rich, and having more fun than anyone else — like sleeping with chorus girls whose pictures I could only stare at in the papers. Later, when we both got into show business, I followed Bob's career, especially when he ran Paramount Pictures in the '60s and '70s and put together an unparalleled slate of hits that saved the studio. Among them were Love Story, The Godfather, *and* Chinatown. *I even liked him as an actor, like when he played Pedro, the young bullfighter, in* The Sun Also Rises.

A few years ago I read Bob's book, The Kid Stays in the Picture. *We've had very different careers, but I couldn't help feeling that we'd been through lots of the same experiences. His life read like my life, only he'd done it earlier, and usually with more style. When the audio version came out, Brad made me listen, even though I'd already read the book. I went nuts. Hearing Bob's unflinching, street-smart voice and blunt insights, I realized why his tape had become a cult object to all the young people in Hollywood; they'd literally pull over and park and be late for meetings so they could keep listening to his unbelievable adventures.*

That gave me an idea. I wanted Rob Lowe to star in a picture about Bob's life. I called Bob. He got right on the phone and right to the point. "It's a good idea but I have a better one. Come up to the house."

When I arrived Bob showed me fifteen minutes of a documentary in which he'd set his audio-book narration to pictures from his life. I loved it. We also loved each other and quickly became best friends — and not just in the Hollywood sense. That afternoon Bob also showed me a couple videos that floored me. One was of his 1971 speech to the Paramount board of directors.

It wasn't simply that he'd filmed his presentation; he'd had it directed by Mike Nichols. Another was of seven chorus girls on The David Susskind Show, *all of whom had slept with Bob but didn't know about the others until it came out during the panel discussion. Then Bob gave me a tour of his home, not forgetting to point out his signed collection of Helmut Newton photos.*

Bob's final presentation was a masterpiece. I knew he'd recently had a stroke, and we talked about it, but then he decided to act it out for me. It was so convincing I thought it was real. That's when it hit me: even though Bob was still in daily therapy, I had to get him to attend the Aspen Comedy Arts Festival in March 1999 and read from his book.

Bob's appearance was the highlight of the week, more unforgettable even than the comedy. He made the front page of the Los Angeles Times *Calendar section, and the attention improved him both physically and mentally. Even his handwriting got better during two days of signing books. He's been on a high ever since. As for me, I'm producing the full documentary about his life. I love him so dearly that I feel we've been friends for fifty years — and in a way we have.*

· · · · ·

At the beginning of any career it's all about getting work. Acknowledgment comes next. If you get lucky you have some power. Enjoy the hell out of it because that's all there is to balance the enormous responsibilities. If after a time you discover you'd rather not have the power and the responsibility, it's okay. The difficulty for me was not only in the letting go but in not being ashamed of wanting to.

I don't miss running the company. I couldn't do it anymore. Now if there's a problem, it's not my problem. I tell Brad and it's up to him. That's what he wanted and he's got years to enjoy it.

What I'm good for now is stability. People come to me if they can't reach somebody or can't get a return phone call. I'm very accessible. I'm still a great closer at a meeting. I'm a problem solver. That's what age brings. I'm a consultant to my own company.

That's the great part: Brad is now my client — and through him the whole company. I'm probably more deeply involved in the spirit and survival of the whole place than I was when I owned it. Brad comes to me all the time. He's not just being kind. He asks for my input. I give him my two cents. Like any client, he will not do everything I say, but he does listen. We get along like old times. He makes me feel useful.

And best of all, in real life I've found true love with my wife, Carrie.

· · · · ·

Can there really be love in show business? I remember getting the phone call that Brandon Tartikoff had died. We all knew it was coming, but you're never prepared for the moment it happens. I felt terrible. We'd worked together so often. He was a great guy. As I suspected, the turnout for his service mirrored that. Everyone was there, even Mike Ovitz, and I once again felt like part of a big club. We can have best friends and best enemies, wars and alliances, hits and bombs, and know thousands of people, but it's times like these — and more recently for me, the first script reading on the Newsradio set the season after Phil Hartman died — that remind me we're not just ships in the night. We're all connected. That's why everyone came to give their respects to Brandon even though he hadn't been a major factor in the business for almost five years. NBC even aired a special tribute to Brandon because he did more than pick TV shows: he picked people and believed in them. The gathering reaffirmed my faith that people do remember when you actually affect their lives, and that they're happy to say thanks even when you can no longer hear it.

· · · · ·

All I want now is something to do every day, the ability to do it right, and then something different to do the next day. That keeps me going.

The other day someone asked me why, after all I'd been through, I even bother to come to work. Easy. I don't know where else I could have more fun. That's the truth. I've been up and down and up. I've made money, I've lost it. I've made friends and enemies. And for nearly forty-five years I've laughed more than most people I know. Isn't that what it's all about — or at least supposed to be? I think so.

The last time I looked at the John Register painting on my office wall, the road looked wide open to me.

These days it's good not to be king.

Acknowledgments

BERNIE BRILLSTEIN

To everyone who's touched my life these past sixty-eight years. Thank you.

To Tillie and Mo Brillstein, John Belushi, Jim Henson, Gilda Radner, Bill Lee, Chris Farley, and Phil Hartman, who didn't live to hear the rest of the laughter. Thank you.

To Pat and Norman, Joanie and Norm, Ann and Cliff, Alice and Lorne, Sheryl and Rob, and Jill and Brad. You've heard these stories over and over and yet you still make believe you've never heard them before. Thank you.

To all the friends, business associates, and clients who are far too numerous to list: you know who you are. Also to Dr. Joe Natterson, Joe DeCordoba, Tony Palladino, Francis Webb, Gigi Del Maestro, Jim Smotherman, Mike Wagner, and Kaye Coleman. Thank you. To Mel Brooks for making my favorite picture, *The Producers*, and inspiring me to steal my title from the script. To Roddy McDowell for insisting that my stories be told. To Dr. David Tannenbaum for introducing me to my wife, Carrie. Also, to Linda and Bob Weinstein, Dorothy Weinstein, Abe Hoch, Evan Galen, Steve Novick, and especially Christina Yaden. Only David and I know how much she helped to make this book a reality. Thank you.

Special thanks to David Rensin. He helped me sort through an emotional time, never once yawned in my face, and is such a good writer that he somehow kept me interested in my own life even though I already knew the story. It doesn't get any better than that.

DAVID RENSIN

As always, this is for my wife, Suzie Peterson and son, Emmett Rensin. Your love, wisdom, patience, understanding, and joy in life make me and all that I do possible. I adore you both more than words can say.

I'm grateful to those whose moral support, thoughtful encouragement, and steadfast cheer meant so much as I wrote, especially Cynthia Price, who knew a great voice when she heard it and was with me every step of the way. Also, Bill Zehme, Carrie Brillstein, Christina Yaden, Laurie Abkemeier, Pamela Marshall, Judy Clain, Sandy Bontemps, Dan Strone, Dennis Klein, Chris Rock, Tim Allen, David Spade, Hilary DeVries, Cameron Crowe, Judd Klinger, Neal Preston, John Rezek, Steve Randall, Linda Thompson, Joshua Marquis, John Davies, Paul Peterson, Apryl Prose, Richard Dean Anderson, Jen Laurie, Marc Eliot, Joe Rensin, and — always — Mom. I miss you, Pop.

I'm also indebted to everyone who generously filled in the story, and often more: Brad Grey, Sandy Wernick, Lorne Michaels, Norm Crosby, Brandon Tartikoff, Leigh Brillstein, Jay Tarses, George Schlatter, David Lazer, John Moffitt, Jack Burns, George Shapiro, Lou Weiss, Larry Auerbach, Bob Odenkirk, David Cross, Michael Fuchs, Cynthia Pett-Dante, Bill Maher, Alan Zweibel, David Salzman, Tony Carey, and Gerry Harrington. And a big tip of the hat to Marc Gurvitz for being the first to say, "You should do this."

Of course, my enduring regard and affection are for Bernie, for having the instinct to believe in me, the passion to believe in himself, and the courage to tell me everything.

Index